Date Due

JUL 1 1993			
JUL 27 1993			
NOV 9 1993			
JAN 03 1996			
JUN 03 1996			
JUN 01 1999			
6/4/01			
APR 15 2004			
OCT 28 2008			
SEP 30 2009			
VOY 11-7-09			
VOY 12/2/13			

THE **BEATLES** FOREVER

The Beatles in Liverpool after Epstein cleaned up their act, early 1962 (Keystone Press)

THE BEATLES
FOREVER

NICHOLAS SCHAFFNER

The McGraw-Hill Book Company

New York   St. Louis   San Francisco   Auckland
Bogotá   Düsseldorf   Johannesburg   London
Madrid   Mexico   Montreal   New Delhi   Panama
Paris   São Paulo   Singapore   Sydney   Tokyo
Toronto

Copyright © 1977, 1978 by Nicholas Schaffner

Reprinted by arrangement with Cameron House, an imprint of Stackpole Books

First McGraw-Hill Paperback edition, 1978

Design by Doug Wolfe, Krone Art Service, Lemoyne, Pa.

234567890 DODO 832

Library of Congress Cataloging in Publication Data

Schaffner, Nicholas
  The Beatles forever.

  Reprint of the ed. published by Cameron House, Harrisburg, Pa.
   Bibliography: p.
   Discography: p.
   Includes index.
   1. The Beatles. I. Title.
[ML421.B4S28 1978]   784'.092'2   78-6665
ISBN 0-07-055087-5

CONTENTS

THANK-YOU'S

THE MEMORABILIA WAS PHOTOGRAPHED BY JOHN JACOBSON

Special thanks to Sue, Linda, Victor Chapin, Robin Cruikshank, Danny Fields and 16 Magazine, Ron Furmanek and SOK Productions, Michele Garval, Joel Glazier, Joe Pope, Strat Sherman, and J.B.H. Stevens; to Neil McAleer of Stackpole Books, for his dedication and patience; and to Mummy, Daddy, Valentine, Elizabeth, and Timothy.

The records and memorabilia are from the collections of some of the above individuals; the author; and *Strawberry Fields Forever,* 310 Franklin Street, Box 117, Boston, Mass. 02110.

To Linda Patrick and Sue Weiner,
who saw this through

CREDITS

Photographs of record sleeves by courtesy of EMI Records Limited.

Photograph on page 163 by courtesy of Twentieth Century-Fox, copyright © 1972 by ABKCO Films, Inc. All rights reserved.

"A Piece For Orchestra" copyright © 1964, 1970 by Yoko Ono. Reprinted by permission of Simon and Schuster, a division of Gulf & Western Corporation.

"Portland Coliseum" copyright © 1968 by Allen Ginsberg. Excerpt reprinted by permission of City Lights Books.

"Alec Speaking" from *In His Own Write* copyright © 1964 by John Lennon. Excerpt reprinted by permission of Jonathan Cape Ltd., London.

"Our Dad" from *A Spaniard In the Works* copyright © 1965 by John Lennon. Excerpt reprinted by permission of Jonathan Cape Ltd., London.

"I'm a Loser" by John Lennon and Paul McCartney, copyright © 1964 by Northern Songs Ltd.

"Help," "Norwegian Wood (This Bird Has Flown)," "Drive my Car," "Nowhere Man" by John Lennon and Paul McCartney, copyright © 1965 by Northern Songs Ltd.

"The Word" by John Lennon and Paul McCartney, copyright © 1965, 1967 by Northern Songs Ltd.

"Paperback Writer," "Rain," "Yellow Submarine," "Eleanor Rigby," "And Your Bird Can Sing," "She Said She Said," "Tomorrow Never Knows" by John Lennon and Paul McCartney, copyright © 1966 by Northern Songs Ltd.

"Dr. Robert" by John Lennon and Paul McCartney, copyright © 1966, 1967 by Northern Songs Ltd.

"Penny Lane," "Strawberry Fields Forever," "Sgt. Pepper's Lonely Hearts Club Band," "Lucy In The Sky With Diamonds," "When I'm 64," "A Day In The Life," "Baby You're a Rich Man" by John Lennon and Paul McCartney, copyright © 1967 by Northern Songs Ltd.

"I Am the Walrus"* by John Lennon and Paul McCartney, copyright © 1967 by Northern Songs Ltd.

"Within You Without You" by George Harrison, copyright © 1967 by Northern Songs Ltd.

"Across the Universe," "Lady Madonna," "Hey Jude," "Revolution," "Back In The U.S.S.R.," "Glass Onion," "Happiness Is A Warm Gun," "Blackbird," "Julia," "Sexy Sadie" by John Lennon and Paul McCartney, copyright © 1968 by Northern Songs Ltd.

"You Never Give Me Your Money," "The End" by John Lennon and Paul McCartney, copyright © 1969 by Northern Songs Ltd.

"Cold Turkey" by John Lennon, copyright © 1969 by Northern Songs Ltd.

"Mother" by John Lennon, copyright © 1970 by Northern Songs Ltd.

"Working Class Hero" by John Lennon, copyright © 1971 by Northern Songs Ltd.

"Another Day" by Paul McCartney, copyright © 1971 by Northern Songs Ltd.

"Imagine," "How Do You Sleep?" by John Lennon, copyright © 1971 by Northern Songs Ltd.

"Whatever Gets You Thru the Night," "Bless You," "Steel and Glass," "Number Nine Dream" by John Lennon, copyright © 1974 by Lennon Music/A.T.V. Music Corp. Used by permission. All rights reserved.

"Back In The U.S.A." by Chuck Berry, copyright © 1959 by Arc Music Corp. Used by permission. All rights reserved.

All rights for the U.S.A., Canada, Mexico, and the Philippines controlled by Maclen Music, Inc., except* controlled by Comet Music Corp. Used by permission.

INTRODUCTION

The Beatles will be remembered not only for their considerable contribution as songwriters and recording artists, but also as the most remarkable cultural and sociological phenomenon of their time. During the 1960's they seemed to transform, however unwittingly, the look, sound, and style of at least one generation. They had, of course, a lot of help from a great many friends—but it was more than anyone else, John, Paul, George, and Ringo who set in motion the forces that made a whole era what it was, and, by extension, what it is today.

The impact the Beatles made is incalculable, not only in popular music and in every other facet of the music business—be it album cover design, the quality of recorded sound, or the size of the crowds—but also in innumerable other areas. They were among the first major public figures of our time to break down the barriers dividing the sexes, with their long hair and vivid attire; champion the use of "mind-expanding" drugs and the innovations in sound, design, language, and attitudes these substances inspired; and, in general, show the way to a life style that defied so many of the conventions taken for granted in 1963. There were others in their wake more daring and iconoclastic, but it is unlikely that the Rolling Stones, or David Bowie, or even Bob Dylan, could have accomplished what they did without the Beatles' example.

Imagine what our world might be like today, were it not for the Beatles. Rock 'n' roll as a critically acclaimed and relatively sophisticated popular art form, with words that say something and music that draws from an almost limitless variety of sources; long hair and expressive clothing on men; marijuana and "Eastern mysticism"—all this and more might well still be practically unheard of in the mainstream of society were it not thanks (or no thanks!) to the Beatles.

Of course it might be argued that they merely picked up on trends from less celebrated sources, that they reflected the times rather than made them; one may file that riddle in the chicken-or-the-egg department. But it can safely be said that the Beatles were the medium that first brought many of the present trappings of our culture (a few years back that might have read "counterculture") to the attention of ordinary folks, quite a few of whom emulated what they saw and heard.

The Beatles were great natural talents; that they lacked any formal training yet were so gifted and imaginative enabled them to do things that more conventional entertainers, composers, or musicians simply could never have dreamed of. From the moment that captivated eighty million American T.V. viewers in February 1964 with their catchy ditties and funny haircuts, through the final crescendos of *Abbey Road,* the Beatles never stopped exploring and evolving as songwriters and musicians —and as personalities.

One of their attributes was an ability to live their colorful lives in a virtual fishbowl and yet never for a moment bore or disappoint their millions of riveted voyeurs and eavesdroppers. We might imagine we knew them better than we knew our own mothers, thanks to all the columns of Beatle copy that were cranked out every day; then their careers would take yet another bizarre or unexpected twist. Despite the formidable pressures of that kind of fame, the Beatles (at least until their break-up) never stopped learning and growing, and we kept learning from them and growing with them—as the words and music improved beyond anyone's wildest expectations.

In short, the Beatles were admitted into our consciousness in the guise of a low-brow fad; like the Trojan horse, there proved to be a lot more there than initially met the eye (and ear). Once snared by the cherubic looks and the tasty bubblegum, an unsuspecting world was swept off on a magical mystery tour out of which many emerged quite different people from those they might otherwise have been.

A lot of the "changes" I personally went through as a teenager were attributable to the Beatles. The ritual of getting told not to return to school before trimming my "Beatle haircut" began in 1964; Swinging London orange bellbottoms and paisley shirts soon started to attract a comparable amount of flak from both teachers and peers, which didn't entirely fizzle out until my escape from high school. I mutilated the Lennon-McCartney songbook with a 20-dollar guitar at an early age and shared my first joint with *Sgt. Pepper's Lonely Hearts Club Band.* At seventeen I was lugging a sitar on the D-train to sit at the feet of an Indian music teacher whose services were in sudden demand, and learning to get high on life with a mantra.

These may initially have been symptoms of my Beatlemania, but I believe, because many of them turned me in directions other than those normally prescribed at the time by my environment, that the Beatles ultimately helped me "find myself" as an individual. For if they ever "stood for" any one thing, that was individuality. Throughout their career they remained nonconformists, uncompromisingly different from one another and from everyone else.

The text of this book will, I imagine, reflect some of my own peculiar views, whether I want them there or not. But I hope I have not intruded overly, and have tried to limit personal appearances to episodes common to the experience of other Beatlemaniacs.

Over 50 volumes of Beatle lore have already been published in Britain, the United States, Germany, Argentina, and many other lands. Ex-associates and discarded groupies have said their piece, as have older bystanders—professional biographers, trained musicologists, jaded critics. *This* book is an attempt to chronicle, in words and pictures, the phenomenon of which the Beatles were the focal point; to record and explore the accomplishments (both direct and indirect) of Lennon, McCartney, Harrison, and Starr; and to recapture the experience of growing up with the Fab Four. It also offers a collection of memorabilia drawn from every stage of the Beatles' career. Though the group itself may be, in George Harrison's words, "for the history books, like the year 1492," their artifacts have become the object of a growing cult of collectors, whose fanaticism is yet another tribute to the Beatles' enduring stature.

Putting together a book such as this one poses a dilemma: how much should the author assume the reader already knows? Or wants to know? Should one cater to those in the beginning, the intermediate, or the advanced stages of Beatlemania?

I have tried to include something for all of them, and can only keep my fingers crossed that I don't lose everybody in the process. Hard-core Beatlephiles may prefer to skim past certain quotes, anecdotes, photographs, and album covers that they've already seen countless times, but which I felt were essential to give a relatively complete picture for those less thoroughly versed in Beatleology. I hope die-hards will find enough obscure record sleeves, arcane facts, and previously unpublished photos to keep them happy—and that these in turn don't cause "the general reader" to bog down.

The story, as told here, begins with the Beatles' first arrival in New York, partly because that's where I live, but mainly because their conquest of the Big Apple marked the first initiation of countless Americans, who have remained the most numerous and most devoted of all the world's Beatle people.

This book has been put together in the hope of stirring some fond memories in a few of those Beatlemaniacs who in their own way are as much a part of this story as the four stars themselves —and of filling some gaps in the memories of those others who, for whatever reasons, were not quite all there at the time but would like to have been. Above all, I hope it adds something to their enjoyment of the music, to which all the other trappings of the Beatles phenomenon were, and remain, subordinate.

Beatlemania was first brought into American households by Ed Sullivan, February 9, 1964 (Wide World Photos)

THE WORLD IS AT YOUR COMMAND

They came to bring us back to life! Out of the old nightmare. Dallas, Oswald, Ruby, cops, reporters, thruways, lies, crises, missiles, heroes, cameras, fear—all that mishmash, and all of it dead. Look at *you*. They've brought you back to life. I couldn't—not after November. Nothing could.
—Robert Hemenway (from the short story *"The Girl Who Sang With the Beatles"*)

They came from Liverpool, England, but when the Beatles landed in New York on February 7, 1964, they could scarcely have stirred more hysteria and fascination had they just arrived from another planet.

On New Year's Day the names John Lennon, Paul McCartney, George Harrison, and Ringo Starr had meant nothing to Americans, but within the month millions were already dancing and swooning in the throes of a joyous epidemic of mass insanity. By the morning of the pop group's arrival (they didn't say "rock" back then), the word "Beatle," well on the way toward a place in the dictionary between "beatitude" and "beatnik," was blaring from front-page headlines. Most folks didn't need to read on about "England's singing sensation"—they had only to glance at the photographs to get the message: a freak show was coming to town. For a civilization in which long-haired men still came as rare as bearded ladies, the Beatles' appearance was in itself a phenomenon—as much so as their sound, which an Associated Press dispatch had defined as "a weird new kind of music that makes rock 'n' roll seem tame by comparison."

Flick a transistor dial in any direction and there was no missing those unmistakable trans-Atlantic accents, often wailing cheerfully off-key, accompanied by the most irresistible beat the catatonic American hit parade had featured in years. If it wasn't "I Want To Hold Your Hand," an almost instantaneous Number One across the fifty states, it was "She Loves You" or "Please Please Me," already securely in the second and third positions on New York playlists—or tracks from *Meet the Beatles,* the fastest selling album since wax was first slowed down to 33⅓ rpm.

The pundits' explanation for America's sudden Beatlemania had the country's youth reaching *en masse* for a hero figure to fill the void left by the assassination of President Kennedy. An exaggeration, perhaps, but it can be safely said that in the world of pop music the Beatles more than filled the energy gap left in the late Fifties by Buddy Holly's plane crash, Elvis Presley's conversion to mush, and the exodus of all their contemporaries to either obscurity or Las Vegas. For those of us too young to remember the Golden Age of Rock 'n' Roll, the injection of the Beatle beat into the vacuous airwaves hit the spot like a shot of Methedrine.

Come break of "Beatle Day," the quartet had taken over even the disk-jockey patter that punctuated their hit songs. From WMCA and WINS through W-A-Beatle-C, it was "thirty Beatle degrees," "eight-thirty Beatle time." All stations enlivened the countdown—"four hours and fifty minutes to go!"—with animated conversations with the airborne musicians. (Later the spoilsports would reveal that the announcers had merely been reciting lines from a script and playing back the pre-recorded Beatle responses with which Capitol Records had thoughtfully supplied them.)

Hours before the Beatles were due, hordes of giddy teenagers had skipped class to pack Kennedy International's observation deck, where 110 of New York's Finest kept them in line. "We've never seen anything like this before," said an airport official. "Not even for Presidents and kings."

When the Beatles finally alighted from a Pan-Am jet, a winter wind tussling their controversial hair, they were greeted by the same noise that had accompanied them all over England and much of Europe for the past six months. Only now the piercing shrieks were multiplied a record-and-ear-shattering 4,000 times. As the Beatles were whisked through customs, hundreds more enthusiasts clawed at the plate glass windows separating them from their new heartthrobs.

The reporters who herded into a nearby room to await the Beatles' first U.S. press conference were considerably more blasé. Most knew only that the Beatles were the latest in a long line of teen-age idols, a species that, many could tell from experience, was not noted for sparkling repartée. But after the stars had made their entrance, and the hubbub of shoving photographers had been quelled, much of the press was disarmed. Whatever the question, at least one of the quartet was always ready with a sharp answer, and, reported a *New York Times* correspondent: "the Beatle wit became contagious. Everyone guffawed. The show was on—and the Beatle boys loved it."

"Will you sing for us?" someone asked.

"We need money first," John Lennon shot back.

"What's your message for American teenagers?"

"Our message is . . . buy some more Beatle records," returned Paul McCartney.

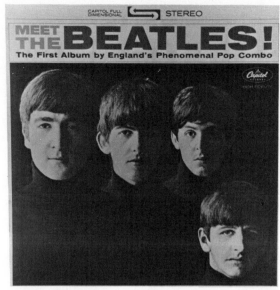

CAPITOL FULL DIMENSIONAL / STEREO

MEET THE BEATLES!
The First Album by England's Phenomenal Pop Combo

Capitol Records

L.P., USA, 1964 (Capitol)

HELP STAMP OUT "BEETLES"

"What about the movement in Detroit to stamp out the Beatles?"

"We're starting a movement to stamp out Detroit."

"Do you hope to take anything home with you?"

"Rockefeller Center."

"What do you think of Beethoven?"

"I love him," said Ringo Starr. "Especially his poems."

"Don't you guys ever get a haircut?"

"I just had one yesterday," retorted George Harrison. Added Ringo: "You should have seen him the day before."

Vintage 1964 Beatles: silly but never stupid; bright, but not for a moment serious. While they had indulged Britons with similar press conferences for months, it was to Americans the first indication that pop stars needn't necessarily be morons, or phonies, or a combination thereof.

Still, the greater part of the adult population remained, at best, condescending:

Like a good little news organization, we sent three cameramen out to Kennedy airport today to cover the arrival of a group from England known as the Beatles. However, after surveying the film our men returned with, and the subject of that film, I feel there is absolutely no need to show any of that film.
—Chet Huntley, N.B.C. evening news,
February 7, 1964

Having got rich off "teen-age lunacy" in their home stompings, these fantastic characters now have come to tap the jackpot—New York, Washington, Miami, American television. Their shrewdness in assaying a market is evidenced by the 4000 screaming, hookey-playing school-age adulators who swooned all over the airport when the Beatles arrived in New York.
These lads cultivate a vague allusion to being musicians, in a gurgling sort of way. They tote instruments, but blandly assure their fans they know not a note. (All their notes are in the bank.) Their production seems to be a haunting combination of rock 'n' roll, the shimmy, a hungry cat riot, and Fidel Castro on a harangue.
—New York World Telegram editorial,
February 8, 1964

It's a relief from Cyprus and Malaysia and Viet Nam and racial demonstrations and Khrushchev. Beset by troubles all around the globe, America has turned to the four young men with the ridiculous hair-cuts for a bit of light entertainment.
The Beatles know it. They know it's a lot of nonsense and refuse to take themselves with the seriousness of those all around them. . . . [In another month] America will have had its giggle and once more will be worrying about Castro and Khrushchev.
—Anthony Burton, New York Daily News,
February 11, 1964

Visually they are a nightmare: tight, dandified Edwardian beatnik suits and great pudding-bowls of hair. Musically they are a near disaster: guitars and drums slamming out a merciless beat that does away with secondary rhythms, harmony and melody. Their lyrics (punctuated by nutty shouts of yeah, yeah, yeah!) are a catastrophe, a preposterous farrago of valentine-card romantic sentiments.
—Newsweek, opening paragraph for
February 24, 1964 cover story

Compared to previous teen idols, however, the Beatles were a very different breed.

These were no marionettes going through the dumb motions while some behind-the-scenes sharpie manipulated the strings. They looked strange, almost like toys, but they acted like real people. They spoke their minds—up to a point; they smoked, they drank, even swore—all the while reassuring many potential adversaries with charm and wit and an eternal smile. To the Beatles—or so it appeared in 1964—the world was a stage fit only for comedy, in which their own starring role was the richest jest of all. (John: "We're kidding you, we're kidding ourselves, we're kidding everybody." Paul: "We can't sing, we can't do anything, we're just having a good time.") If they were in fact far more depraved and complicated than they initially let on, they nonetheless came across as refreshingly real where other entertainers had seemed so plastic, at the same time appearing fabulously unusual because they refused to conform to all the stale conventions.

The Beatles—John and Paul, to be precise—even dreamed up most of their music, an undertaking traditionally considered far beyond the ken of most pop stars. Aside from incorporating an average of six chords instead of three, their songs were noteworthy for speaking to kids in their own language: "You know what I mean," "Oh yeah, like I please you." If the lyrics, like the singers themselves, still catered to the romantic fantasies of fifteen-year-old girls, the message at least rang far more true than the usual unconvincing clichés of Tin Pan Alley.

Another odd feature of Beatle songs, which would persist until they stopped recording together, was that almost every one was a hit. Even those that weren't issued as singles were good enough, and commercial enough, to find their way onto tight Top Forty play lists. The Beatles practically invented the L.P. as a credible pop medium; previous rock 'n' roll albums had generally consisted of one or two smasheroos diluted with nine or so throwaways; and anyone interested in a listenable album was obliged to wait for the Greatest Hits. The Beatles changed all that; similarly, they turned single B-sides, normally a dumping ground for drek of an even worse order, into the showcases for many of their finest songs, and almost every Beatle 45 would become a double-sided hit.

Not only did every song have something going for it—so did each member of the band. Pop groups used to consist of one star plus an anonymous set of satellites basking in his or her reflected glory. But the Beatles were all stars, four distinct personalities and talents. Each brought a special contribution to the group, and their "chemistry" created a force far more powerful than the sum of its parts. (As Bea-

10

tlemania entered the mystic a few years later, these came to be viewed in terms of the elements: Fire [Lennon], Air [McCartney], Water [Harrison], and Earth [Starr]—each complementing and enhancing one another—each indispensable to the Beatles' alchemy.)

Beatle people had their pick of four different heroes, each of whom acquired a huge individual following. As would eventually be the case with their music, the Beatles' range of personalities offered something for everybody. But from the start people sensed that some Beatles might be ever-so-slightly more equal than others, and the members of the group were almost invariably billed John, Paul, George, and Ringo.

Ringo Starr (né Richard Starkey) has been called one of history's most charming bit-part players. Content to let the other three cope with the composing, singing, talking and notoriety, Ringo would remain happily in the shadows for most of the Beatles' career. But in early 1964, the diminutive drummer with the five rings, prominent nose, and unforget-

table pseudonym tended to give the impression that he was the star of the show, especially to non-afficionados who found it more difficult to distinguish the three five-foot-eleven guitarists with the common British names. Nobody would ever accuse Ringo of being brilliant or exquisite, but his self-effacing manner and goofy features seemed to stir a protective instinct in many female admirers. One somehow felt sorry for the one Beatle who seldom smiled, whose melancholy expression gave him the aura of the saddest clown in the circus.

George Harrison, while faring better than Ringo in the beauty sweepstakes, also seemed to play a supporting role. Though the best and most dedicated instrumentalist of the group, he commanded little of the assurance or presence of Lennon or McCartney. As they hammed it up onstage, George would hunch over his guitar, directing his concentration toward squeezing out the most perfect licks he could manage. Despite his virtuosity, George was the last to emerge as an individual; after all, he would not turn 21 until

Paul McCartney: The Beatles' suave diplomat (*16* Magazine)

Murray the "K" of WINS, New York was America's first self-proclaimed Fifth Beatle

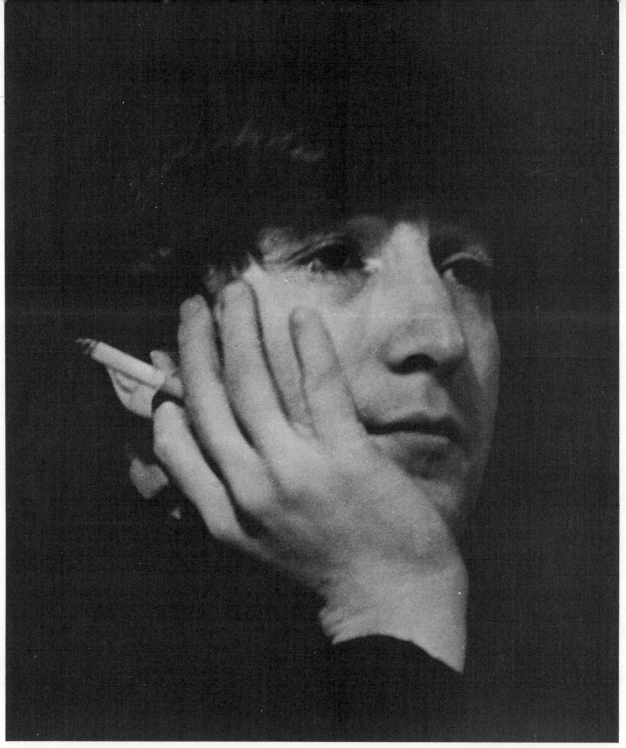

John Lennon in a pensive moment (Transworld Feature Syndicate)

just after the Beatles' first American visit. Still, many girls were snared by his relatively shy, gawky manner, which permeated his occasional vocal solos, such as "Do You Want To Know a Secret?"

Paul McCartney gave the impression of being rather more worldly; instead of whispering awkward secrets in little girls' ears, he told them to hold him tight. Paul inspired much the same reaction as some stunning, all-round-great-guy president of a senior class; all the younger girls had a crush on him, but their mothers also approved. McCartney was the most articulate, suave, and diplomatic of the Beatles; Tony Barrow, their publicity man, said: "he could have carved himself a fine career in public relations. He is a professional charmer, a prolific ideas man, the most commercially aware." On stage, where Paul liked to play Mr. Showbiz,

John Lennon delighted in mocking his smooth gestures and announcements. Paul was also the most versatile vocalist and musician—though the bass was his specialty, he was adept on a half dozen other instruments; and he was the first to develop a knack for composing timeless melodies readily adaptable to any style of music.

John Lennon was the Beatle whom the others, when pressed, would nominate as their "leader." Though a less facile instrumentalist than McCartney or Harrison, John was rumored to have the highest I.Q. He pulled fewer squeals than the others at first, only partly because he was the "married Beatle." Young girls often found him less cherubic than Paul, George, and Ringo, even vaguely menacing. Lennon, never one to suffer fools gladly, was notorious for turning his razor-sharp wit to a cutting edge when provoked. Even his early lyrics were often a lot tougher than Paul's: if John caught you talking to that boy again, he'd really give it to you. But the world would soon discover that the aggressive and cynical exterior masked an uncommon sensitivity; through all the changes, however, Lennon would continue to keep intact his integrity, unpretentiousness and almost brutal unsentimentality. While he made little attempt to sweeten his medicine for the sort of starry-eyed young romantics who fell for Paul, in the eyes of many fans with precocious, rebellious, or intellectual inclinations, John Lennon was *the* Beatle.

America's first attack of Beatlemania was an experience few of its countless victims would easily forget. Most found the fever exhilarating, but many parents, cops, and unindulgent commentators were Not Amused. The management and clientele of the Plaza, one of Manhattan's most expensive, exclusive, and conservative hotels, were in for a particularly rude shock. (It was reported that when the Beatles' entourage arrived from the airport, a dowager sipping her afternoon tea in the Palm Court inquired what all the screaming was about. Senator Goldwater, perhaps? When her waiter replied, no, ma'am, it's the Beatles, she angrily brought his "insolence" to the management's attention.)

When the Beatles' suites had been reserved a month before, the Hotel Plaza was still as unfamiliar as anyone else this side of the Atlantic with the names of Messrs. Lennon, McCartney, Harrison, and Starr. Envisaging a respectable group of tweedy British businessmen, the management was mortified when truth finally dawned. But attempts to arrange accommodations elsewhere proved unsuccessful, and for the week beginning February 7, 1964 the staid establishment would be under a state of siege, fortified by barricades, guarded by platoons of beefy cops.

As New York's schools closed for the day, the crowd outside the Plaza swelled to a surging mob. Many of the new recruits, such as this writer, were basically curiosity seekers. From a Fifth Avenue bus coming home from school, a friend and I saw the wildest scene of all our 11 years. Naturally we hopped off at the next stop.

The lights were beginning to go on in the hotel's windows, and the appearance of a shape in any one of them was enough to send the fans waving and screaming. These outbursts were punctuated with choruses of "She Loves You" and "I Want To Hold Your Hand," which tended to peter out in fits of giggles. From a precarious vantage point on the statue atop the Plaza fountain, someone dangled a banner reading "Beatles 4-Ever." Dozens of other fans held up similar signs.

Their Beatlemania was contagious. That afternoon I traipsed off to Woolworth's to invest in a Beatle album and a Beatle wig.

I bought the wig, but $2.77 seemed a high price to pay for *Meet the Beatles.* I thought I could remember spotting the same album in the window of the local 69¢ Shop a few days earlier, when the Beatles were still nothing more to me than a strange noise on the radio. With a mind to save $2.08—most of which I later unloaded for a pile of Beatle magazines—I picked up my L.P. at the famous bargain bin, and headed home to listen. But, though the record did feature "I Want To Hold Your Hand," and the four mop-topped, half-lit faces on the cover did, to the uninitiated, resemble those on *Meet the Beatles,* on closer inspection the name of the group was spelled with two "e"'s , and the music was but a dismal impersonation. (Fortunately for me, my English mother, unusually receptive to the sound of those voices from home, was willing to shell out the price of a return visit to Woolworth's.)

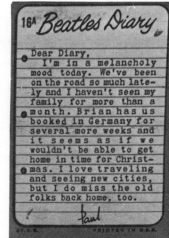

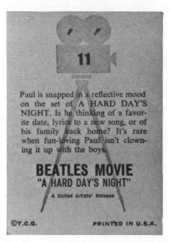

Trading cards: clockwise from top left: The Beatles Bubble Gum, series 1; The Beatles Diary; The Beatles Bubble Gum, series 2; Beatles Movie. Gum wrappers are shown on following page.

I was just one of many thousands who were similarly burned. In February, 1964, the American marketplace was deluged with Beatle-related products, and quite a few entrepreneurs didn't let their inability or unwillingness to climb on the bandwagon legitimately stop them from cashing in on a brand-new multi-million-dollar racket. Over 60 were hauled into court during the first flush of American Beatlemania on charges of misleading or unauthorized exploitation of the word "Beatle."

Only a fraction of the boom Beatle industry actually had anything to do with music. The real action was Beatle merchandise, which by the end of the year would gross over fifty million dollars. Even those hucksters who dutifully forfeited to Seltaeb (the Beatles' American licensing agency) its 10-to-15 per cent royalty before stamping the Beatles' name, likeness, and mystique on beetle and guitar-shaped brooches, shocking pink plastic ukeleles, or Beatle nut crunch popsicles, neither knew nor cared that John, Paul, George, and Ringo would soon rank among the most influential figures in the history of popular culture. All that mattered was that the Beatles were the most lucrative fad since hoola-hoops and Davy Crockett, and that America's spoiled brats be milked of every possible dollar before they found some other way to waste their allowances.

Seltaeb was the American subsidiary of a company called Stamsact, through which Beatle manager Brian Epstein's NEMS Enterprises had licensed approximately one hundred products after Beatlemania first enveloped Britain toward the end of 1963. The number of Beatle novelties authorized by Seltaeb in America has not been computed, but must have reached several hundred, easily. The only prerequisites for the Beatle endorsement were payment of Seltaeb's royalty and a modicum of "good taste"; among the few re-

Much of the boom Beatle industry had little to do with music

L.P., Germany, 1964 (Odeon)

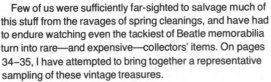

The Beatles were a revelation to many heartland viewers, even if 99 per cent of them tuned in out of idle curiosity. The ragged edges in their performance—George Harrison had come down with an untimely flu—went unnoticed by most Americans, who after all had never seen anything remotely like the Beatles before; in any case, the 800 Beatlemaniacs in the studio audience more than covered for their idols. Aware that their names had been plucked from 60,000 ticket requests (even Elvis Presley's 1958 appearance on the Sullivan show had inspired only 7,000), the lucky ticket-holders set a high standard of audience participation for fans at Beatle concerts to emulate over the next 30 months. By the time the show ended, Beatlemania had swept into the most remote crannies of North America.

Two days later, the Beatles switched cities to play their American concert premiere from a revolving stage at the Washington Coliseum, encircled by 8,000 hysterical teenagers. After the performance, the Beatles appeared as honored guests at a British Embassy charity ball sponsored by Ambassador and Lady David Ormsby-Gore. The cream of capital society gawked at and mauled the Beatles, in some cases going at them with scissors, intent at snipping off locks of that famous hair, and John stormed out in a huff.

The following afternoon, the Beatles returned to New York by train, as snow had grounded all air traffic. Two separate mobs, each several thousand strong, turned out to greet them at Pennsylvania Station and the Hotel Plaza. "In the shrieking pandemonium," the *Daily News* reported, "one girl was knocked down and trampled, another fainted and a police sergeant was kicked by a horse. At times the cops could not control the mobs and the Beatle-lovers broke through barricades in wild assaults in the station and the hotel."

The fans at the Plaza were at least rewarded with a glimpse of their idols, unlike their counterparts at the station, who, according to the *News,* "surged forward towards Track Four in the belief that the singers were arriving there. Some of the 30 patrolmen, who had to be reinforced by 20 more, went down to the ground and were trampled. Screams of 'Beatles Forever . . .' and 'I love Ringo . . .' rang through the station.

"But the British idols were spirited away from the lower level into a taxi at the Seventh Avenue entrance. Discovering they had been cheated, the fans ran out of the station shouting 'On to the Plaza. . . .' "

The quartet were back in town to star in a pair of concerts at Carnegie Hall. Like their counterparts at the Plaza, the Carnegie's management, who had previously barred Chubby Checker and Elvis Presley, had little idea of what the stately hall was in for when the shows were booked at the end of 1963. Sid Bernstein, the clairvoyant promoter who arranged the match, says he persuaded the Carnegie Board that "the Beatles' appearance would further international understanding."

Twenty-nine hundred ecstatic Beatlemaniacs gave a concert early last evening at Carnegie Hall, accompanied by the thumping, twanging rhythms of the Beatles, an English rock 'n' roll quartet.

The Beatle enthusiasts, who paid from $3 to $5.50 for the privilege of outshrieking their idols, might have been 99 percent female if one judged by the level of voices that they raised. Physical evidence, however, showed that there were a considerable number of males present, many of whom bounced in their seats but were less vocal. . . .

The audience participating lasted for 34 minutes, from the moment the first Beatle mop head could be discerned at 7:45 o'clock moving through the 150 listeners who were seated onstage until all four Beatles fled amid a hail of jelly beans at 8:19 o'clock. During this time the Beatles appeared to be sing-

jected proposals were Beatle sanitary napkins and live jeweled beetles. (In those days, much was made of the pun in the group's name. Nowadays a mention of the creepy-crawly things often brings to mind an image of John, Paul, George, and Ringo, but back then it was very much the other way around.)

There were Beatle brands of just about every sort of junk food, knick-knack, stationery, toy, clothing, and jewelry; one could put a touch of Beatles into almost every conceivable aspect of one's life. Fans might be awakened by a Beatle alarm clock, shake off their Beatle nighties to soak themselves in Beatle bubblebath, slip on their Beatle sneakers and sweatshirts, eat breakfast off Beatle plates, stumble off to school clutching Beatle lunchboxes and Beatle loose-leaf binders, and so on until the time came to rest their heads on their Beatle pillows—and pay for it all out of Beatle purses and wallets.

Few of us were sufficiently far-sighted to salvage much of this stuff from the ravages of spring cleanings, and have had to endure watching even the tackiest of Beatle memorabilia turn into rare—and expensive—collectors' items. On pages 34–35, I have attempted to bring together a representative sampling of these vintage treasures.

The Beatle bounce erupted in Manhattan yesterday as the young men with heads like unmade beds made their first public appearance here at the CBS studio at 53rd St. and Broadway.

The bounce was introduced by 800 frenzied fans on the edge of hysteria and their seats who shrieked out their love for the bundles from Britain.

From the moment the Beatles began by blasting out "All My Loving" the kids bounced like dervishes in their seats to the driving beat.

With the Beatle Bounce, performed best by wild-eyed girls aged between 10 and 15, but likely to infect adults, goes a wild screaming as if Dracula had just appeared on stage. The screams reached a pitch dangerous to the eardrums at times when the Beatles shook their shaggy locks.

—*The New York Daily News,* February 10, 1964

Most Americans got their first glimpse of the Beatles in action on the February 9 Ed Sullivan Show. Thanks to all the controversy fanned by the media over the previous two days, seventy million people—by far the largest audience ever drawn to an entertainment program—switched on their T.V.'s.

Beatles map of Liverpool, from the Beatles Souvenir Pack published and available from, the City Public Relations Office, Liverpool

ing and playing 12 songs, each of which was covered almost totally by the enraptured ululations of their devotees.
—*The New York Times,* February 13, 1964

The next day, to the immense relief of the New York Police Department and the Hotel Plaza, the Beatles flew south to pass the remainder of their U.S. visit cavorting in the Miami sunshine, chaperoned all the while by mobs of reporters and cameramen. During their "holiday," they put in another appearance on the Ed Sullivan Show, and taped a third to be aired the following Sunday (the day after their February 22 return to Britain).

When we got here you were all walkin' around in fuckin' Bermuda shorts with Boston crewcuts and stuff on your teeth. . . . The chicks looked like 1940's horses. There was no conception of dress or any of that jazz. We just thought what an ugly race, what an ugly race.
—John Lennon, from the December 1970 *Rolling Stone* interviews

February 1964:
Songs performed by the Beatles at the
Washington Coliseum and Carnegie Hall, New York
Roll Over Beethoven (George, lead vocal)
From Me To You (John and Paul)†
I Saw Her Standing There (Paul) †
This Boy (John)*
All My Loving (Paul)*
I Wanna Be Your Man (Ringo)
Please Please Me (John and Paul)†
Till There Was You (Paul)*
She Loves You (John and Paul)*†
I Want To Hold Your Hand (John and Paul) †
Twist and Shout (John) †
Long Tall Sally (Paul)
*performed on the Ed Sullivan Show, February 9, 1964
†performed on the Ed Sullivan Show, February 16, 1964

Beatle wigs became the hottest novelty since yoyos, and anyone who donned one was sure to be the life of the party (UPI)

Back in 1964, a good majority of Beatlemaniacs were female. In the United States, teen-age girls seemed to be particularly turned on by an alternative to the all-American male, whose notions of "masculinity" evidently ruled out appearance as a means of self-expression. The implications of the Beatles' relatively androgynous appearance may well have had a far more profound effect on sexual and women's liberation than anyone could have guessed at the time.

The Beatles' extraordinary looks and music triggered a form of adulation that transcended rationality, particularly in girls of an emotionally volatile age. Though acute symptoms of Beatlemania frequently manifested themselves at airports, outside hotels, in front of T.V. sets—wherever John, Paul, George, and Ringo, or even their flickering image, happened to be within screaming range—the ultimate pilgrimage was to a live Beatle concert.

Almost every note the Beatles ever performed in America was all but obliterated by their admirers' sheer lung power; each show featured a running battle between the policemen manning the barricades and the mobs attempting to break through them with the vague intention of touching a real live Beatle, or, better yet, securing a clawful of hair or a shred of collarless suit; and some concerts had to be abruptly terminated when the cops sensed they were losing the struggle. By the end of a 30-minute set, the stage would be littered almost ankle-deep with the candy and toys with which fans had bombarded the Beatles throughout the show.

Dissertations on Beatle-induced hysteria appeared in nearly every major newspaper and family magazine in America. According to Dr. Joyce Brothers:

Their Oliver haircuts and too short jackets are part of the Beatles' fanciful and original mystique. Oliver Twist, you will recall, was an orphan. By embracing a quartet of orphans as heroes, our teenagers achieve two unconscious goals:

They symbolically "kill off" the adult generation.

They show how neglected and misunderstood they believe themselves to be.

Also, the Beatles display a few mannerisms which almost seem a shade on the feminine side, such as the tossing of their long manes of hair. . . . Very young "women" are still a little frightened of the idea of sex. Therefore they feel safer worshipping idols who don't seem too masculine, or too much the "he-man."

But other experts testified that Beatle concerts provoked simulated sexual experiences that brought many fans to the point of orgasm. One Professor Joost Meerloo took a still darker view of the Beatles, saying they were "psychic germ carriers" whose loud rhythms made listeners regress all the way to the womb and the sound of Mother's heartbeat. Even *Variety,* normally more at home with boxoffice receipts than with sociology, speculated that Beatlemania might be "a phenomenon closely linked to the current wave of racial rioting."

Aldous Huxley once wrote that "no man, however highly civilized, can listen for very long to African drumming or Welsh hymn singing and retain intact his critical and self-conscious personality." If teen-age girls have a knack, even in the most ordinary circumstances, for giving one another a case of the sillies, it follows that thousands of them packed into one auditorium were quite capable of running totally amok, especially when assaulted with rhythmic music electrically amplified far louder than any Mr. Huxley had had in mind. And when the pubescent girls in the darkened theatre also happened to nurture wild crushes on the performers in the spotlight, they weren't about to pass up a chance to give vent to emotions for which most had as yet no outlet in their day-to-day lives.

Twentieth-century mass communications had made it increasingly possible for people to immerse themselves in the lives of other human beings, whom they might never actually meet, yet would still feel they knew as well as their own families. The Beatles provided millions with instant heroes, best friends, even lovers. Like other living legends to emerge larger than life through the media, John, Paul, George, and Ringo held a distinct advantage over their "real" counterparts: their followers could, in their fantasies, mold them into almost anything they wished them to be, and turn them on and off at will.

There they were in America, all getting housetrained for adulthood with their indisputable principle of life: short hair equals men; long hair equals women. Well, we got rid of that small convention for them. And a few others too.
　—Paul McCartney

As the girls swooned, the boys—who by the end of the mystery tour would compose at least half the Beatlemaniac population—began to emulate. Thanks largely to the Beatles, rock stardom eclipsed running for President as the ultimate glamorous ambition of much of American youth. It was no mere coincidence that nearly twice as many guitars were sold in 1965 as in 1963.

Many boys who lacked musical aspirations at least rinsed away the grease, or started letting the stubble on their heads grow out as far as possible. The domination over the U.S. male of regimentation crewcuts (and drab colorless uniforms) was in for its toughest challenge in decades. Nowadays people stare at early Beatle pictures and find it difficult to imagine people even calling that hair long. After all, the President of the United States is just as hairy now as the Beatles were then.* But in those stark times, for a civilized Western male to conceal the tops of his ears, forehead, and neck with his own hair seemed almost inconceivable. The Beatles' hair generated far more attention and controversy even than their noise, and everyone instantly had an opinion of it, one way or another.

To millions of us, it came as a revelation, and we wondered why we hadn't thought of it ourselves. But most Americans considered the Beatles' hairstyle an extremely bizarre gimmick, at worst scandalous, at best richly ridiculous. Beatle wigs became the best-selling novelty since yo-yo's, and anyone who donned one was sure to be the life of

the party. He would, of course, then pass the wig around, giving each of the other male guests in turn a chance to add to the merriment by modelling it for all the ladies.

Some celebrities, such as J. Paul Getty, were game enough to mug for photographers in their Beatle wigs. Others became fodder for cartoonists and retouch artists, who delighted newspaper and magazine readers with Beatlebrowed likenesses of such world luminaries as President Johnson (who had told the British Prime Minister that the Beatles needed haircuts), former Vice President Nixon, and Premier Khrushchev. (When these gags wore thin, people began superimposing crewcuts on Beatle pictures.) Some folks even refused to believe that the Beatles' own hair was real, and for the next few months a number of commentators would continue to refer in all seriousness to the Beatles' "wigs."

We male fans knew better. Thousands of us attempted to copy our new heroes in the face of stiff opposition from scandalized adults and ridicule from classmates, all of whom considered unassailable the logic that the difference between the sexes could be measured in hair. Even boys with permissive parents were certain to inspire ultimatums from teachers if they let their hair down to anything remotely resembling Beatle proportions. Until around the turn of the decade, long hair would remain a virtual invitation for taunts from strangers: "What are ya, a boy or a girl?" . . . "Get a haircut!" . . . "Faggot!"

For many of us, it was the first burning issue of a rapidly intensifying struggle with the grownup establishment. As Jimmy Carter's hairstyle seems to attest, we at least won that battle, whether or not we lost the war.*

Rare Old Beatle Albums, Mark One

In the halcyon days of Beatlemania, over a dozen fly-by-night Beatle L.P.'s were issued in the United States by almost as many labels. Nearly all were blatantly exploitative, so it is ironic that they have become coveted collectors' items, commanding outlandish prices. For the most part, these albums rehashed, ad nauseam, material recorded by the Beatles prior to their late-1963 exclusive contract with Capitol Records.

The Hamburg Sessions: In May 1961, the original five Beatles—Lennon, McCartney, Harrison, drummer Pete Best, and the late Stuart Sutcliffe—were hired to provide the instrumental accompaniment for six numbers featuring Tony Sheridan. Of these "My Bonnie" was selected for a single release in Germany, and, eventually, Britain and the U.S., credited to "Tony Sheridan and the Beat Brothers."

At those Hamburg sessions, the Beatles also recorded two numbers without Sheridan: a Lennon interpretation of "Ain't She Sweet" and a Lennon-Harrison instrumental entitled "Cry For a Shadow."

Most of this material lingered forgotten in the can for over two years. But when Beatlemania struck, it returned to haunt the Fab Four. In the U.S., M.G.M. and Atco each snapped up rights to four of the eight songs, all of which were released on singles in 1964. In February of that year, M.G.M. cooked up an L.P. titled *Beatles with Tony Sheridan and Their Guests,* containing the label's four Beatle acquisitions, plus material by artists that nobody, including the Beatle "hosts," had ever heard of. In October 1964, Atco pulled a similar stunt with its *Ain't She Sweet* album.

In 1966, both collections resurfaced on budget-priced labels, under new names. M.G.M.'s Metro subsidiary offered *This Is Where It Started,* while an Atco affiliate called Clarion Records released *The Amazing Beatles and Other Great English Group Sounds.*

In the meantime, an obscure outfit called Savage Records issued, with questionable legal credentials, four of the Hamburg recordings (along with four others falsely purporting

Nine rare
U.S. Beatle
albums

to feature the Beatles) on *The Savage Young Beatles.* This was followed by a *Best Of the Beatles* L. P. that contained, not the Fab Four's greatest hits, but some rather pathetic performances by their former drummer Pete Best. (In 1970 Polydor would reunite the Beatles' eight 1961 recordings on an L. P. entitled *Circa 1960—In the Beginning.* They'd get the year wrong, but never mind.)

The V-J Albums: V-J was the first label contracted to issue John, Paul, George, and Ringo's work in the United States. In July 1963 it released *Introducing the Beatles,* which like the two V-J singles that had preceded it, went nowhere . . . until Capitol's *Meet the Beatles* zoomed to Number One the following February. Capitol did not relish the competition, and because it controlled publishing rights to "Love Me Do" and "P.S. I Love You," was able to harass V-J by forcing the latter to remove them from later editions of the album ("Please Please Me" and "Ask Me Why" were hastily substituted).

When the tangle of further lawsuits finally made it clear that V-J wasn't going to get the Beatles back, *Introducing* was repackaged twice—as *Songs, Pictures, and Stories Of the Fabulous Beatles,* and as half of a double album called *The Beatles Vs. the Four Seasons.* (In March 1965, Capitol would release its version of this much recycled L.P., as *The Early Beatles.*)

Meanwhile, V-J had also issued an album titled *Jolly What! The Beatles and Frank Ifield On Stage* containing four of its Beatles cuts (no, they weren't live versions). In addition, V-J slapped together an interview album, *Hear the Beatles Tell All.* (Because the laws were so vague about this kind of record, another label, Radio Pulse Beat, also got away with releasing three L.P.'s worth of Beatle chatter and patter, presided over by commentator Ed Rudy. Capitol eventually decided to pre-empt this area too, with November 1964's "official" double-disk *The Beatles Story* documentary. In 1965, Recar records issued *All About the Beatles,* consisting of interviews with George's sister, Louise Harrison Caldwell.)

Had music business had a powerful consumers' board, most of the above-mentioned albums might never have gotten within striking range of a record shop. Which is precisely why none of them managed to stick around for very long—which in turn, perversely, is why they are now valuable collectors' items.

This book does not purport to be an authoritative life story of the four Beatles, and such biographical details as turn up are mostly concerned with the period after their lives had become interwoven with so many of ours. But to fill out the picture for the handful of readers who might be unfamiliar with the Beatles' rise to fame, a brief account follows.*

Richard Starkey of Dingle (the oldest Beatle, born July 7, 1940) was the only one to actually emerge from the crumbling Merseyside slums of Beatle legend though much of his childhood was actually spent in Liverpool hospitals. A sickly child, Ringo received almost no formal education.

All the other Beatles were products of middle-to-lower-middle class Liverpool backgrounds. John Winston Lennon (born October 9, 1940) was brought up by his no-nonsense Aunt Mimi after his mother divorced his straying merchant seaman father on grounds of desertion when John was five. A rebel from the word go, Lennon flaunted what he has called "a case of I-couldn't-care-less" throughout his school career. Always the class trouble-maker, the only subject he excelled at was art. Most of his masters confidently predicted that Lennon would come to a rotten end, with the exception of one who recognized his talents and got him into art college. By then John had heard "Rock Around the Clock" and all he felt like studying was his newly acquired guitar. In 1956, Lennon formed his first group, the Quarrymen.

James Paul McCartney (born June 18, 1942) was the only

*The most detailed account of the Beatles' early years appears in Hunter Davies' authorized biography; for the real dirt one can consult Allan Williams' less comprehensive yet less expurgated memoir. (See The Complete Beatles Bibliography.)

Beatle with a musical parent. His father had played piano in a ragtime band, until the demands of selling cotton and raising two boys (Mrs. McCartney died when Paul was 14) preempted his time. But Paul didn't reveal much interest in music until the advent of Elvis. Then he bought a guitar, making scant progress before realizing that, being left-handed, he might do better once he changed the strings around. As a result of this switch, Paul's would be one of the very few groups whose guitars wouldn't all point in the same direction, giving an unusual symmetry to the Beatles' presentations. (Ringo was also a leftie, but it's harder to spot such tendencies in a drummer.)

McCartney was also the one Beatle to shine in the classroom—he won a prize for literature, and thought he might grow up to be an English teacher—until John Lennon arrived to lead him astray. Even though baby-faced McCartney was two years younger, Lennon found him useful, as the kid had picked up more chords than he had, and Paul became a Quarryman. Soon the pair were turning out Lennon-McCartney originals like "Love Me Do" and "One After 909."

Before long, Paul brought into the group an even more junior partner, who knew more chords than either of them: George Harrison (born February 25, 1943), the son of a friendly local bus conductor. All three subsequently abandoned a safe and secure future by dropping out of school, George at the age of only 16, to sell their souls to rock 'n' roll. They couldn't have been better situated than the port of Liverpool, where sailors brought a constant infusion of recent American country, blues, and rock, giving the three guitarists a rare opportunity to cop a few licks from imported 45's by Chuck Berry and Carl Perkins.

The fledgling group wore out a succession of drummers before settling on Pete Best, whose mother ran a club called the Casbah, at which the boys often gigged. By this time they had also acquired a bass guitarist, Stuart Sutcliffe, a talented painter John had befriended at art school—and a new name. Like the music they played, this last was largely inspired by Buddy Holly and the Crickets. "I was looking for a name like the Crickets that meant two things," John said in a 1964 interview. "From Crickets I went to Beatles. . . . When you said it people thought of crawly things, when you read it it was beat music."

The quick-witted, witheringly cynical Lennon was by all accounts the driving spirit behind the Beatles in those days. With the exception of the moody and withdrawn Best, they all emulated John's unconventional attitudes and behavior, especially his absurd sense of humor. Even in 1960, people were struck by the Beatles' "us against the world" stance; their first manager, Allan Williams, says that they blew their chances for some prestigious gigs by refusing to sack Stuart Sutcliffe, who could hardly play a note.

The five leather-outfitted ragamuffins barely managed to eke out a sustenance serenading Mean Mr. Mustards in raincoats at Williams' Merseyside strip joint and playing at dilapidated ballrooms, where they were often caught in the cross-fire of Liverpool's considerably meaner teen-age gangs. They first tasted adulation when Williams brought them to Germany to play at the grimy clubs of Hamburg's Reeperbahn, whose motley population of prostitutes, transvestites, and gangsters was transfixed by the Beatles' vital, almost savage music and appearance. The boys were obliged to perform at the Kaiserkeller Club as long as eight hours at a stretch, which they managed to do with a lot of help from pills; but the hard work did wonders for the music.

Their act also grew much livelier. The Beatles were encouraged to "Mak Schau" at all costs; so the sweating, leather-clad musicians learned to writhe, vamp, and mug for

hours on end, punctuating their repertoire with obscene insults, food, and beer tossed at each other and at the audience. Lennon would often taunt the Germans with his impressions of Hitler, and was wont to appear on stage wearing nothing but a toilet seat and a pair of shorts. (These stories, of course, did not come to light until long after the Beatles' later incarnation as cherubic moptops had won the hearts of millions.)

Some of their antics did not endear them to the authorities. After the Beatles succeeded in destroying the Kaiserkeller's rickety stage—with a little help from fellow Liverpudlians Rory Storme and the Hurricanes, whose drummer Ringo Starr had become a close friend—and, putting a match to an inflated condom, set the club on fire, a Hamburg prison extended an evening's hospitality to McCartney and Harrison (who was also discovered to be under age). The pair were placed on a homeward-bound plane the next morning.

When the new improved Beatles regrouped in Liverpool, they began to duplicate their Hamburg success in their own

This is the.....
The Savage Young
BEATLES

JOHN LENNON   GEORGE HARRISON   PAUL McCARTNEY   PETER BEST

Recorded by THE BEATLES Hamburg 1961

CRY FOR A SHADOW   LETS DANCE   IF YOU LOVE ME   BABY WHAT I SAY   WHY   SWEET GEORGIA BROWN
RUBY BABY   YA-YA   and T. SHERIDAN

L.P., USA, 1964 (Savage)

The Beatles first US release ("My Bonnie," April 1962) didn't even bear their name; the second ("Please Please Me," February 1963) misspelled it with two "t" 's.

town, building a loyal local following at a dive called The Cavern. Eventually Allan Williams pulled the right Germanic strings and the boys were allowed to make a series of return visits to the Reeperbahn, where they played at the Kaiserkeller's rival Top Ten Club. There they were commissioned by Polydor Records' Bert Kaempfert (also composer of "Strangers In the Night") to back up Tony Sheridan, a British crooner in the Presley mold, on six recordings, one of which, "My Bonnie," was issued locally on a single. During these sessions, the Beatles also preserved two numbers of their own: a Lennon-sung version of the 1920's perennial "Ain't She Sweet," and an original instrumental by John and George, called "Cry For a Shadow."

On these visits the Beatles attracted an artier, more intellectual following than they had been accustomed to: bohemian types from the local universities. Two of their most ardent supporters were a photographer named Jurgen Vollmer and a painter named Klaus Voormann. (A picture Vollmer took at the time adorns John's *Rock 'n' Roll* L.P.; Voormann designed the cover for the Beatles' *Revolver,* and, taking up the bass, joined Manfred Mann and later played on nearly all of the Lennon, Harrison, and Starr solo records.) Stuart Sutcliffe became engaged to Voormann's former girlfriend, Astrid Kichener, and eventually decided to leave the Beatles and stay on in Germany, letting Paul take over on bass. By that time the other Beatles had followed Stu in adopting the longish hair style of Hamburg's existentialist students, thereby acquiring their most striking trademark.

Upon their return to Liverpool, record dealers began to receive insistent requests for "My Bonnie." One dealer, Brian Epstein of the N.E.M.S. department store, indulged a whim by actually going to listen to the Beatles at The Cavern. Though the dapper and refined ex-actor did not exactly fit in among the tough youths, grimy atmosphere, and ear-splitting rock 'n' roll, Epstein was instantly mesmerized by the raw, magnetic energy of the scruffy quartet. He felt Oscar Wilde's compulsion "to tame the panther"; and, after many return visits, mortified his friends and relatives by announcing that he had signed on as the Beatles' manager.

Epstein brought his new clients to London to record a demo of rock 'n' roll standards, with which he tirelessly made the rounds of the city's record companies. Each was

as unimpressed as the last, both by the tape which included such early Lennon-McCartney numbers as "Hello Little Girl," plus competent but derivative renditions of "Memphis Tennessee" and "Take Good Care of My Baby," and by Epstein's insistence that "these lads will be as big as Elvis one day." (Indeed, in songs like "September in the Rain," Paul sounds all too much like Presley, though he would find his own voice soon enough.) At long last Brian caught the sympathetic ear of George Martin, producer and A and R man for Parlophone Records. A weak sister of E.M.I. that faced the prospect of going out of business, Parlophone was willing to take desperate gambles.

As Epstein inked their Parlophone contract, the Beatles, back in Hamburg for a fourth visit, played at the newly opened Star Club. This engagement was less happy than earlier ones, as the night before their arrival Stu Sutcliffe, once thought to be the most brilliant of the lot, had died of a brain hemorrhage.

As soon as the Beatles got back from Hamburg, they returned to London to go over their material with George Martin. Their new producer tried in vain to decide which of the boys should be made the focal attraction of the act, as at that time a group without a single "star" was unheard of. But though he couldn't figure out who was the strongest talent, he had a definite candidate for the weakest: Pete Best. Apparently the other Beatles weren't too happy with him either—some say McCartney was jealous of his good looks—and Epstein was given the unenviable assignment of firing him from the band.

For a replacement, the boys tapped their old friend Ringo Starr. Though Epstein complained that Ringo wasn't as pretty as Pete, he went along with their choice. Hostile riots accompanied the new lineup's first date at The Cavern, at which irate Best fans succeeded in giving George Harrison a black eye.

When the Beatles recorded their first George Martin-produced single for Parlophone in September, they found a session-man in the drummer's seat; Ringo, much to his dismay, was handed a tambourine. Yet as it turned out, the take they finally used for the A-side was one of the few on which Ringo was allowed to play drums. (The version on the L.P. and all U.S. releases, however, features the drumwork of Andy White.)

In selecting a pair of Lennon-McCartney originals, "Love

OFF THE BEATLE TRACK

instrumental versions of THE BEATLES big hits by their brilliant recording director GEORGE MARTIN & his orchestra

ALL MY LOVING ♥ SHE LOVED YOU ♥ DON'T BOTHER ME ♥ CAN'T BUY ME LOVE ♥ ALL I'VE GOT TO DO
♥ ♥ RINGO'S THEME (THIS BOY) ♥ I SAW HER STANDING THERE ♥ LITTLE CHILD ♥
♥ I WANT TO HOLD YOUR HAND ♥ PLEASE PLEASE ME ♥ THERE'S A PLACE ♥ FROM ME TO YOU ♥

high fidelity

L.P., USA, 1964 (United Artists) George Martin would become a recording star in his own right—with surprisingly bland interpretations of his clients' music

L.P., USA, 1965 (Savage) A deceptively titled offering from Ringo's predecessor. Note vintage Hamburg photo on jacket

L.P., Germany, 1962 (Polydor) The first album to contain Beatles music, though their name only appeared in fine print on the back

A special edition for DJ's

Me Do" and "P.S. I Love You," the Beatles broke with another tradition: pop stars were never considered competent to write their own material. But Martin couldn't find anything better.

"Love Me Do," released on October 5, 1962, attracted some attention on account of John's unusually prominent harmonica. The fact that it reached number seventeen seemed an encouraging omen, as the Beatles were still virtually unknown throughout most of Britain. Most of the sales, predictably, came from Liverpool, where Best's dismissal had apparently not dampened the ardour of most of their fanatical following.

Meanwhile, Epstein was exercising his considerable flair for theatrical presentation, and the Beatles' image began to take on a more all-round appeal. Brian, with the eager cooperation of Paul McCartney, persuaded the boys to clean up their act, to wash their mops more regularly, stop eating and swearing onstage, and retire the leather outfits to the closet. These last were replaced with well-tailored matching dress suits, until Epstein hit upon the grey collarless Pierre Cardin jackets that would become one of the Beatles' most striking visual gimmicks.

Lennon has said that he felt a few qualms about "selling out" when the Beatles began to launder their once-raunchy image, but McCartney was always there to make sure his tie was straight. Rapidly changing into the cheery, cheeky, and relatively clean-cut moptops who would soon conquer the world, the Beatles consistently stole the show from the long-since-forgotten acts that headlined their non-stop British tours. Girls began to squeal, and the squeals turned to shrieks that by the end of 1963 would drown out every note their heroes might attempt to play. The Beatles' second single, "Please Please Me"—far more energetic and distinctive than the first—reached Number One on many of the British charts, and no lower than Number Two on the others. (Though George Martin did persuade the Beatles to record veteran hit-writer Mitch Murray's "How Do You Do It?" as well, their rendition was so lackluster that he gave in and let them release their own "Please Please Me." Fellow Liverpudlians Gerry and the Pacemakers subsequently did a far more creditable job with the Murray tune, earning their first Number One. The Beatles' version still festers in the E.M.I. vaults.)

Pleasantly surprised by the surge of interest in his clients,

Martin decided the world was ready for a Beatle album. But the record company was still taking no chances: all the songs had to be recorded and ready in a single day, February 11, 1963.

With Martin at the controls of the two-track tape machine, the Beatles—two of them suffering from mid-winter colds—were obliged to tear through an assortment of Lennon-McCartney originals and six recent American favorites, all of which they had been showcasing in concert. The "covers" included a pair of Shirelles hits, "Baby It's You," and "Boys," on which their new drummer got his moment in the vocal spotlight. George handled Carole King's "Chains," and the first taste of McCartney schmaltz surfaced in "A Taste Of Honey," from the musical of the same name.

One of John's selections, the Isley Brothers' recent U.S. hit "Twist and Shout," was added at the last moment when the Beatles discovered they still had some studio time to use up. It turned out to be one of the most popular songs on the *Please Please Me* album, along with Lennon-McCartney's own "I Saw Her Standing There" and "Do You Want To Know a Secret?" The latter was itself covered by fellow Liverpudlian and Epstein protégé Billy J. Kramer, whose version took over Britain's Number One position as soon as the Beatles' third single "From Me To You" had completed a long run at the top. The reaction to Kramer's "Secret" suggested two things: One, that other Liverpool rock 'n' rollers could follow the Beatles into the limelight; and two, that Beatle songs could sound good—and sell big—even when sung by other artists.

The Beatles' first album swiftly hit Number One on the L.P. charts, where it remained for thirty weeks, until a sequel arrived to take its place. Despite the rough edges, husky voices, and somewhat derivative nature of the music—the background harmonies were still the same lugubrious moans that marked most recent American pop, as the Beatles hadn't yet arrived at the blend of falsetto and scatting that would distinguish their later arrangements—*Please Please Me* proved to be just the shot of adrenalin the wimpy British music scene wanted.

With "From Me To You," which they knocked off in the back of their van on the way to work, John and Paul for the most part played it a bit safe, returning to the innocuous sing-along style of "Love Me Do." The single did, however, introduce yet another Beatle trademark: the falsetto

"whoooooo" 's linking the chorus and the verse. In performance the three front-line Beatles would, when they reached this part, lean toward the mikes, vigorously shaking their mop heads in unison to drive shivers up all the little girls' spines and insure that the next few bars be drowned in orgasmic shrieks. The Beatles were fast learning how to be cute.

The "whoooooo" 's were such a show-stopper that their fourth single was liberally sprinkled with them. But "She Loves You" also introduced that still more captivating hook: "yeah, yeah, yeah," chanted repeatedly and emphatically enough to drive any listener out of his mind, one way or the other. The phrase instantly became synonymous with Beatles, and with pop music in general. (Twelve years later, South-east Asian Peoples' Republics were still issuing decrees banning Beatle haircuts and "yeah, yeah, yeah music.")

"She Loves You" presented, for the first time, all the ingredients of the unique Beatle sound churning in the mix: Ringo's triumphant drum fills; the boosted level of the electric instruments—especially the bass—that made it difficult for listeners to resist giving the volume controls a healthy nudge; and the music that was still rock 'n' roll yet now distinctly British.

By the time of the disc's September 1963 publication, even big American stars such as Roy Orbison had to settle for second-billing on the Beatles' British tours. Teen-agers would wait in line on the street with their sleeping bags and umbrellas for forty-eight hours to get tickets, then storm the box-office like revolutionaries at the Bastille when tickets finally went on sale. The Beatles no longer dared venture out in public without bodyguards or policemen, for fear of getting torn to pieces by their maniacal following. When they appeared on stage they were pelted by jelly babies—once their favorite candy, but not for long—as well as gifts and articles of female clothing.

For months the Beatles had been front-page fodder for British music papers such as *Melody Maker* and *New Musical Express,* and dozens of unauthorized fan-magazines had begun glutting the market in competition with the "official" *Beatles Monthly Book,* which was founded in April, 1963, and whose circulation would pass 300,000 by December. Membership rolls in the Liverpool fan club, which would soon boast chapters in 50 nations, were ap-

L.P., Britain, 1963 (Parlophone)

Beatles L.P., Japan, 1964 (Odeon)

proaching 100,000. But it wasn't until October 13—when the pandemonium erupted right under Fleet Street's nose with a televised performance at the London Palladium accompanied by hysteria in the theatre and riots on the street—that the word "Beatlemania" arrived on page one of all the national dailies. But once it got there, it stuck.

The whole of the United Kingdom went bats over the Beatles. All other priorities seemed to come in a poor second as priests, politicians, psychiatrists, headmasters, and newspaper editors fell over one another endorsing, condemning, analyzing, or dismissing the phenomenon. The Beatles became the first rock 'n' rollers whose appeal seemed to transcend the barriers of class and even age.

They accepted an invitation to appear on the Royal Variety Show before the Queen Mother and Princess Margaret, and after a triumphant whirlwind tour of Sweden, took the stage at London's Prince of Wales theatre to charm the cream of Britain's aristocracy. The most celebrated moment proved to be John's introduction to "Twist and Shout": "For our last number, I'd like to ask your help. Would the people in the cheaper seats clap your hands? And the rest of you, if you'd just rattle your jewelry . . ." Said the Queen Mother: "They are so fresh and vital. I simply adore them!"

Britain's most popular newspaper, *The Daily Mirror,* ran this editorial the following day:

YEAH! YEAH! YEAH!
You have to be a real sour square not to love the nutty, noisy, happy, handsome Beatles.

If they don't sweep your blues away, *brother you're a lost cause.* If they don't put a beat in your feet, *sister, you're not living.*

How refreshing to see these rambunctious young Beatles take a middle-aged Royal Variety Performance by the scruff of their necks and have them beatling like teenagers. . . .

The Beatles are whacky. They wear their hair like a mop, but it's WASHED, it's super clean. So is their fresh young act. They don't have to rely on off-colour jokes about homos for their fun. . . .

GOOD LUCK, BEATLES!
"She Loves You" soon became the best-selling disc ever issued in Britain (a distinction it retained until Paul McCartney's "Mull of Kintyre" finally outsold it in 1977), and "I Want To Hold Your Hand" and *With the Beatles* arrived to record-breaking advance orders. They did not disappoint.

L.P., Canada 1964 (Capitol)

New Year with concerts in France, the only country ever to give the Beatles an equivocal reception, they turned to the next item on their agenda: the U.S.A.

While Beatlemania swept Britain and Europe in 1963, the United States obstinately resisted the epidemic. This came as no shock to the Beatles or anyone else; even after Epstein had booked them into Carnegie Hall and the Ed Sullivan Show, the boys remained skeptical about their Stateside reception. After all, none of England's previous home-grown superstars had ever managed to make it across the ocean. Americans had always been notoriously chauvinistic about their pop, and especially their rock 'n' roll, which was, to be sure, a local invention.

"We didn't think there was a chance . . . ," said John Lennon. "We just didn't imagine it at all, we didn't even bother. Even when we came over to America the first time, we were only coming over to buy L.P.'s."

On their first trans-Atlantic flight, Paul asked Phil Spector: "Since America has always had everything, why should we be over there making money? They've got their own groups. What are we going to give them that they don't already have?" Spector, who would one day produce the Beatles' last gasp of an L.P., assured McCartney that the boys would grab America by the scruff of its clean-cut neck; he had been among the first in the U.S. music industry to recognize their potential.

Capitol Records had not, initially, been so clairvoyant. As E.M.I.'s American subsidiary, Capitol had first refusal on Beatle product—and refuse it did. Epstein turned instead to a financially shaky outfit called V-J Records, whose main claim to fame was having once launched the Four Seasons, then America's hottest group.

In early 1963, V-J released the "Please Please Me" and "From Me To You" singles and an L.P. titled *Introducing the Beatles.* The most successful was "From Me To You," which briefly bubbled under *Billboard's* Hot Hundred. But it never bubbled any higher than number 116. So the Beatles' next single was handed to an even more moribund label called Swan, whose only claim to fame would one day be its having issued "She Loves You." But at the time—nothing.

Then the first faint cracks in America's stone wall began to appear. Hungry for some light diversion from the aftermath of the Kennedy assassination, the evening news and

Like "She Loves You," these new songs defined the Beatles' own sound. The aggressive mid-Fifties beat, the Everly Brothers' rich harmonies, the fey Buddy Holly mannerisms, and the Brill Building's inventive melodic twists—all were still hidden somewhere in the mix. ("We were influenced by whatever was going," Lennon has admitted.) But the Beatles' unusual knack for synthesis (equally apparent in all subsequent recordings) made *With the Beatles* or *Meet the Beatles* sound fresh and new, and far less derivative than their earliest efforts. Paul's "All My Loving," the first Beatle melody to become a "standard," was honored by dozens of interpretations from recording artists of all stripes.

At the end of the year, William Mann of the august London *Times* offered the first indication that a high-brow critic could take the Beatles' music seriously. His appraisal read in part:

The outstanding English composers of 1963 must seem to have been John Lennon and Paul McCartney, the talented young musicians from Liverpool whose songs have been sweeping the country since last Christmas, whether performed by their own group, the Beatles, or by numerous other teams of English troubadours that they also supply with songs. . . .

For several decades, in fact since the decline of the music-hall, England has taken her popular songs from the United States, either directly or by mimickry. But the songs of Lennon and McCartney are distinctly indigenous in character, the most imaginative and inventive examples of a style that has been developing on Merseyside during the past few years. . . .

The slow, sad song about "That Boy," which figures prominently in Beatle programmes, is expressively unusual for its lugubrious music, but harmonically it is one of their most intriguing, with its chains of pandiatonic clusters, and the sentiment is acceptable because voiced cleanly and crisply. But harmonic interest is typical of their quicker songs too, and one gets the impression that they think simultaneously of harmony and melody, so firmly are the major tonic sevenths and ninths built into their tunes, and the flat submediant key switches, so natural in the Aeolian cadence at the end of "Not a Second Time" (the chord progression that ends Mahler's *Song Of the Earth*). . . . They have brought a distinctive and exhilarating flavour into a genre of music that was in danger of ceasing to be music at all.

The Beatles got a good giggle out of this article, as they always would when intellectuals attempted to analyze their work, and admitted that they had never heard of pendiatonic clusters and Aeolian cadences before. After kicking off the

L.P., USA, 1964 (Capitol)

The Beatles with their wax effigies at Madam Tussaud's museum (Wide World Photos)

magazines like *Time, Life, Newsweek,* and *The New Yorker* started to pick up on the droll phenomenon that seemed to have been unhinging the mother country. Still, nobody suggested for a moment that it could happen here.

Until somebody at Capitol Records thought: Why not? The label not only decided to give the Beatles a chance, but, throwing caution to the winds, lavished over $50,000—an unprecedented amount at that point in the history of music-biz hype—on a "crash publicity program." It would prove the best investment since European colonizers exchanged a handful of glass beads for Manhattan Island.

As balding Capitol execs began parading about in Beatle wigs, and encouraging all their employees to submit to free Beatle hairdos, five million stickers reading "The Beatles Are Coming" appeared on seemingly every available wall, lamp-post, and phone booth across the fifty states, while a million Beatle newsletters and a like number of Beatle buttons tumbled off the presses. The most ingenious gimmick of all was that promotional record of "open-ended" interviews with which any two-bit D.J. might conduct an intimate Beatle rap-session at his leisure without even paying Ma

Bell her trans-Atlantic rates.

America got its first glimpse of the Beatles in action on January 3, 1964, when Jack Paar aired a film-clip of the boys performing "She Loves You." Most commentators, such as Jack Gould of *The New York Times,* failed to discern anything historical in the event. The Beatles, he reported, "offered a number apparently entitled 'With a Love Like That, You Know You Should Be Bad.' Also appended were 'yeah, yeah, yeah' in steady beat and then a 'whoooooo,' the standard international cue to which all young women in a studio audience mechanically respond with ecstatic approval."

Mr. Gould went on to predict that, while the Beatles' sound might "find favor among indigenous teen-agers, it would not seem quite so likely that the accompanying fever known as Beatlemania will also be successfully exported. On this side of the Atlantic it is dated stuff. Hysterical squeals emanating from developing femininity really went out coincidental with the payola scandal and Presley's military service."

Within three weeks of this prediction, America's resistance had totally crumbled. Capitol's crash P.R. campaign may have had a lot to do with it, but so did the fact that its first Beatle release was the boys' strongest record yet. "I Want To Hold Your Hand" took "She Loves You" a step further, playing sly games with time signatures. That exhilarating octave jump on the word "hand" clinched the song's grip on millions of unsuspecting Americans. "I Want To Hold Your Hand" bulleted to the top of the Hot Hundred more speedily than any record in years, and *Meet the Beatles* promptly followed suit on the album charts. When the Beatles arrived in America—to hysterical squeals that made those Presley fans sound positively demure by comparison—the Capitol brass was prepared to greet them with a pair of gold records.

One week after the appearance of "I Want To Hold Your Hand," "She Loves You" began chasing it to the top of *Billboard's* best-seller lists, followed next issue by V-J's resuscitated "Please Please Me." Now that the dam had broken, America was suddenly deluged with every record the Beatles had ever made. To U.S. Beatlemaniacs, a seemingly endless catalog of hit tunes appeared to have emerged full-blown from the head of Ed Sullivan.

Almost every week, as many as three more Beatle singles would surface on the *Billboard* listings and on the play lists of every Top Forty station in America, as Capitol, Swan, V-J and its twin label Tollie, plus Atco and M.G.M. (which had acquired those early Hamburg tapes of the Beatles backing Tony Sheridan) feverishly piled more 7-inch discs onto the Beatle sweepstakes. It was a game in which jackpots were guaranteed for all.

Dealers even began importing Canadian singles of "All My Loving" and "Roll Over Beethoven," and these, too, nuzzled their way into the American best-seller lists. Capitol responded by making plans to issue "Beethoven" as a single in the U.S., where it had been excised from *Meet the Beatles;* but this project was squashed by Epstein, who instructed the company to focus its energies on the Beatles' brand-new "Can't Buy Me Love." When Capitol announced a March 16 release date for "Can't Buy Me Love," it was swamped with over two million advance orders. Another record broken.

Capitol's patchwork *Second Album,* containing "She Loves You," a handful of B-sides, and the versions of recent U.S. Motown and rock 'n' roll hits that had been left off *Meet the Beatles* for fear they might sound old hat to American audiences, was received as ecstatically as the second coming. It became the first L.P. to top the charts within two weeks of release—an accomplishment the boys would repeat with four subsequent albums.

Such was the Beatles' monopoly on American record sales throughout the first half of 1964 that on April 4 the top five entries in the *Billboard* Hot Hundred read like this:
1. "Can't Buy Me Love." The Beatles (Capitol).
2. "Twist and Shout." The Beatles (Tollie).
3. "She Loves You." The Beatles (Swan).
4. "I Want To Hold Your Hand." The Beatles (Capitol).
5. "Please Please Me." The Beatles (V-J).

That same week, the Beatles were Numbers One and Two on the L.P. best-sellers. You can still read all about it in the *Guinness Book of World Records.* One week later, fourteen of the Hot Hundred singles were Beatle tunes. Nobody has ever come close to matching that feat either—before or since.

With the Beatles' conquest of the States, Britain and everything British became instantly fashionable. As American fan magazines like *16* printed up crash courses in hip English slang, and teen-agers all over the colonies adopted on cue such young Liverpudlian expressions as

Copies of this first Beatles bootleg L.P. flooded the US market in early 1964

One of hundreds of Beatle fan magazines (Reprinted through courtesy of Charlton Publications Inc.)

L.P., Italy, 1964 (Parlophone)

"fab" and "gear" (both synonyms for "terrific"; the Beatles themselves were christened the Fab Four), the mother country, no longer disparaged as stuffy and out-of-date, found itself in the unaccustomed position of setting American trends instead of following them. Especially in the interrelated areas of fashion and pop music.

Record companies that had missed the Beatle boat scrambled for a substitute, snapping up anything that had long hair and made noise with a British, or, best of all, Liverpudlian, accent. The 1964 English invasion was on. (And, though most of the original warriors have long since been put out to pasture, it continues to this day; *Rolling Stone's* American readers awarded British acts four out of the top five positions in both "Band" and "Male Singer" categories in a 1977 poll.)

The first groups to follow the Beatles into the American hit parade tended to be even more wholesome than the Fab Four then seemed. Combos like Gerry and the Pacemakers (who once gave the Beatles their fiercest Liverpool competition and went on to become their stablemates at Epstein's N.E.M.S. Enterprises), Freddie and the Dreamers, Herman's Hermits, etc., kept their appearance relatively conventional, and churned out harmlessly insipid sounds to match their stuffed-teddy-bear image.

The group purporting to pose the biggest threat to the Beatles was the Dave Clark Five, which, in keeping with the fascination for drummers Ringo had recently generated, took its name from the member in charge of the band's drill-sergeant rhythm. The Dave Clark Five had the good fortune of releasing the single "Glad All Over" that replaced "I Want To Hold Your Hand" at the top of the British charts. Though "Hand" should hardly have been expected to hold on forever—after all, a quarter of the phonograph-owning households in England already had a copy—its ouster made page one of all the British dailies. The Dave Clark Five's *popularity,* it was proclaimed, had eclipsed the Beatles'. (Actually, as soon as the Fab Four issued a *new* record, it went straight to Number One, as would all their releases through 1967.)

In America, however, the first non-Beatle British record to hit the top, "World Without Love" by Peter and Gordon, kept things more or less in the family. Peter Asher was the brother of Paul McCartney's steady, Jane; and the song was written for him by Paul, as were most of Peter and Gordon's

John Lennon reads a fan letter (*16* Magazine)

L.P., France, 1964 (Odeon)

subsequent hits ("Nobody I Know," "I Don't Want To See You Again," and "Woman"). Once the duo's heart-throb appeal fizzled, Peter Asher would join the Beatles' Apple Records as an A and R man.

But, ultimately, the real competition came from groups that tried to take the Beatles' accomplishments a few steps further to produce a considerably louder and blacker sound, to wear longer hair and more casual and/or flamboyant outfits, and to flaunt more blatantly anti-Establishment attitudes. Pre-eminent in this category were Manfred Mann (who played cute on singles, but the blues on their L.P.'s), the Animals (who painted their blues as gritty and dirty as their hometown of Newcastle), the Yardbirds (who spawned the first of a long series of British rock guitar virtuosos: Eric Clapton, Jeff Beck, and Jimmy Page), the Kinks (a quartet of tone-deaf teen-age punks whose Ray Davies soon mellowed into the most sensitive, witty, and British of all rock songwriters), and The Who (the first rock 'n' rollers to enliven their act with smoke bombs, film strips, and the ritual destruction of their instruments). The Rolling Stones—the only band ever to actually approach the Beatles in terms of influence, popularity, and sales—were the most uncompromising of the lot.

Most of these musicians—like millions of other European teen-agers of the late Fifties and early Sixties—grew up in the shadow of America, and invested a great mystique in its real and fancied trappings: gangster films, Coca-Cola, big fast cars, blue jeans, and the like—and above all rock 'n' roll. This obsession led them to plug in their guitars in the first place, and in much of their early music they explore an America that thrived in their fantasies long before fame and fortune gave them a chance to see what the place was really like.

Yet the British filter through which this imaginary America was presented brought (inadvertently at first, later more deliberately) an unaccustomed measure of Old World style and class to rock 'n' roll. In the process, the British groups nudged a brand of American kitsch closer to a self-con-

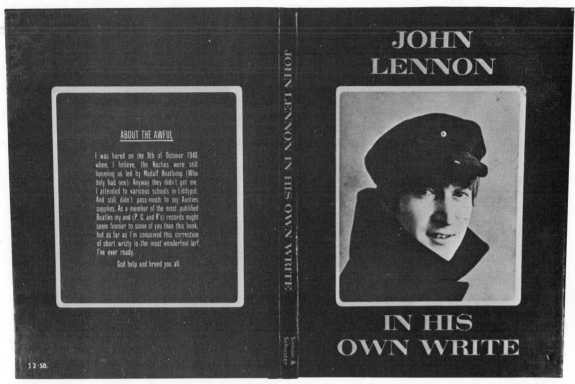

Lennon's first book, published in March 1964 (Jonathan Cape Ltd., London)

Single, Sweden, 1964 (Parlophone)

scious art form—creating in their turn a model for the next generation of U.S. musicians to emulate.

In March 1964, John Lennon offered, with his book *In His Own Write,* the first tangible proof that at least one Beatle's creative talents extended beyond writing and playing bouncy two-minute songs of puppy love.

John's writing and drawing often recalled the doodlings of a clever, bored, and unmistakably deranged lad scribbling in his textbook during math class. Yet at its best his doggerel was akin to, and compared favorably with, the work of Edward Lear. Lennon's sharp wit and sense of the absurd, already made notorious by the Beatles' press conferences, lent themselves well to the coining of outrageous puns such as "dancing with wild abdomen," "stabbed undressed envelope," and snippets of verse like "I wandered hairy as a dog/to get a goobites sleep." Or:

Amo amat amass;
Amonk amink a minibus.
Amarmyladie Moon,
Amikky mendip multiplus
Amighty midgey spoon . . .

and the illustrations were suitably grotesque.

In His Own Write came as a surprise to book reviewers whose only previous taste of John's literary talent had been such couplets as "you've been good to me, you made glad when I was blue/and eternal-lee, I'll always be in love with you"; and they responded with lavish praise for the "Joycean and Carrollian wordplay."

In a review that dubbed Lennon "unlikely heir to the English tradition of literary nonsense," *Newsweek* concluded quite insightfully that the book "suggests that when John Lennon sings 'I Want To Hold Your Hand' he is wishing he could bite it." England's Prince Philip announced that the book had given him a great deal of pleasure, and it rose high in the best-seller list on both sides of the Atlantic. All over

the world, professional translators attempted to render John's puns into their native tongues; in Finland, the job was given to the man who had translated James Joyce.

All of which may not have had much immediate impact on those of us who were still accustomed to pelting the author with jelly beans, aside from confirming the rumor that John had a high I.Q. But *In His Own Write* was a harbinger of the time when Lennon's fertile imagination and absurdist humor would be unleashed in the Beatles' lyrics—and the first clue (apart from the hyperbole of the odd William Mann) that a Beatle could win the admiration of the "intelligentsia" who within a few years would praise those lyrics so extravagantly.

On the occasion of Shakespeare's 400th birthday, John Lennon was feted at the prestigious Foyle's literary lunch. But the assembled literati found the guest of honor's speech—in its entirety: "thank you very much, you have a lucky face"—disappointingly brief. The author of *In His Own Write* was roundly booed, and Brian Epstein attempted to make a longer speech on his client's behalf.

No one thing ever opened so many eyes and ears to the Beatles, and to rock 'n' roll in general, as did their first feature film—with the possible exception of *Sgt. Pepper* three years later. *A Hard Day's Night* was launched in best Beatlemaniacal style on July 6, 1964. For the occasion, mobs of fans out for a glimpse of their heroes were given the run of Piccadilly Circus, their zeal contained only by barricades and scores of bobbies. No traffic was permitted in the area, aside from the succession of limousines dislodging the Fab Four and their glamorous guests at the London Pavilion entrance. The following morning the stampede began—not of ordinary fans scrambling for tickets (though there was that too), but of respectable critics joining the ranks of the Beatlemaniacs.

"The legitimacy of the Beatles phenomenon is finally inescapable," proclaimed *Newsweek* when the film crossed

Taiwanese bamboo tray depicting scene from a *Hard Day's Night*

Ringo with Patti Boyd on the set of *A Hard Day's Night.* The starlet/model would become Mrs. George Harrison on January 21, 1966 (Transworld Feature Syndicate)

the Atlantic a month later. "With all the ill will in the world, one sits there, watching and listening—and feels one's intelligence dissolving in a pool of approbation. Even Ringo's rings become tokens of something which is somehow important and delightful."

"So help me, I resisted the Beatles as long as I could . . ." confessed *Village Voice* film critic Andrew Sarris. "My critical theories and preconceptions are all shook up, and I am profoundly grateful to the Beatles for such a pleasurable softening of hardening arteries."

Even Arthur Schlesinger, Jr., who a year before had written speeches for the President, found himself writing about the Beatles: "The astonishment of the month is *A Hard Day's Night.* One approached the Beatles with apprehension, knowing only the idiotic hairdo and the melancholy wail. . . . But the Beatles . . . are the timeless essence of the adolescent effort to deal with the absurdities of an adult world."

Teen-age fans, less astonished at their enjoyment of *A Hard Day's Night,* often found themselves making a tenth or even a twentieth return trip, and would sometimes remain glued to their seats all day. Many older converts complained at the difficulty of catching all the Beatle witticisms, because of girls squealing in chorus at every batting of a McCartney eyelash. The girls didn't care; most of them had already memorized the script. *A Hard Day's Night* also convinced a good number of aspiring young classical and folk musicians, such as future components of Jefferson Airplane and the Byrds, that rock 'n' roll was the place to be. The movie entranced on so many levels because it not only captured the spirit and essence of the Fab Four (at least as we all imagined them at the time) but was also a stylish and inventive film in its own right, as exhilarating, fast-paced, and up-to-date as the latest Beatle chart-topper.

Drawing from both an established tradition of British comedy and the arty trappings of the New Wave of European film—helicopter shots, hand-held cameras, frenzied and often surreal cutting, and so forth—*A Hard Day's Night* recreates, in best cinema verité style, what purports to be a typical Day In the Life Of the Beatles. They travel by train from London to the provinces, dodging hordes of screaming girls at both ends; do their stuff for reporters, photographers, and producers; and finally perform a concert that brings the film—and the paid extras in the studio audience—to a resounding, ecstatic climax.

However exciting these activities may seem to a non-Beatle, to the Fab Four they are merely the daily routine, to be escaped from at every opportunity. Just like any red-blooded teen-age fan, a Beatle delights in shirking his responsibilities, to flirt with the opposite sex or cavort in the green fields. And woe to any intruder from the phony, uptight grownup world. To a Colonel Blimp character who invades the Beatles' compartment, snaps off their radio ("I travel on this train regularly, *twice a week*"), then glares at them over the top of the *Financial Times,* Lennon turns the other cheek and simpers "give us a kiss." A slick entrepreneur demanding an endorsement of some trendy shirts ("You'll like these. You'll really *dig* them. They're *fab*. . . .") is prodded in the direction of apoplexy by Harrison's laconic wit:

George: "I wouldn't be seen anywhere in them. They're dead grotty."
"Grotty?"
George: "Yeah, grotesque."
(To secretary:) "Make a note of that word and give it to Susan to use on the show. . . . It's rather touching, really. Here's this kid trying to give me his utterly valueless opinion, and I know for a fact that within four weeks he'll be suffering from a violent inferiority complex and loss of status if he isn't wearing one of these nasty shirts." (To George:) "Of course they're grotty, you wretched nitwit. That's the way they were designed, and that's what you'll want. . . . Anyway, you won't meet our Susan if you don't co-operate."
George: "And who's this Susan when she's home?"
"Only Susan Campey, our resident teen-ager. You'll have to love her. She's your symbol."
George: "You mean that posh bird who gets everything wrong? She's a drag, a well-known drag. We just turn the sound down on her and say rude things."

From such confrontations, the cheeky lads always emerge victorious, their high spirits intact for the next round. Even the more elderly movie-goer was likely to find himself rooting for them, for the Beatles (unlike, say, the Rolling Stones) never came across as nasty or unwholesome. They projected a certain innocence, and with it a sense that it was the rest of the world, not they themselves, that was depraved.

Because *A Hard Day's Night* was originally conceived in the autumn of 1963, before the Beatles had become an international household word, United Artists limited their investment to a meagre $600,000. Yet the boys and their manager were adamant that it not fall into the corny, exploitative pattern of previous jukebox musicals. As Lennon remembered in his 1970 *Rolling Stone* marathon: "It was precisely because we were what we were, and realistic, we didn't want to make a fuckin' shitty pop movie. . . . We insisted on having a real writer to write it."

That writer was Liverpool's Alun Owen, who, like director Richard Lester, was recruited on the strength of a T.V. show the Beatles admired. To take notes, Owen accompanied his subjects on a two-day trip to Dublin, during which some scenes pretty much wrote themselves, such as the press conference:

"How do you find America?"
"Turn left at Greenland."

Summer 1964: Songs performed on the Beatles' North American Tour

Twist and Shout (John, lead vocal)*
You Can't Do That (John)
All My Loving (Paul)
She Loves You (John and Paul)
Things We Said Today (Paul)
Roll Over Beethoven (George)
Can't Buy Me Love (Paul)
If I Fell (John)
I Want To Hold Your Hand (John and Paul)
Boys (Ringo)
A Hard Day's Night (John and Paul)
Long Tall Sally (Paul)

*In some shows the Beatles opened with "I Saw Her Standing There" (Paul), dropped "She Loves You," and closed with "Twist and Shout."

Polish *Hard Day's Night* poster

George and Paul miming their music in *A Hard Day's Night*—note the absence of guitar cords (Transworld Feature Syndicate)

"Are you a mod or a rocker?"
"A mocker."
"What do you call your hairstyle?"
"Arthur."

Owen successfully recreates that sort of razor-sharp repartée in the more fictitious segments, even if the boys themselves felt they were being overly tied to their stereotypes ("Me witty, Ringo dumb and cute," complained John. "We were a bit infuriated by the glibness of it.").

Yet, aside from being vastly superior as a film to, say, any of Elvis Presley's showcases, *A Hard Day's Night* was also a far more effective vehicle for the music itself. Owen managed to dispense with the sort of shamelessly contrived dialogue that almost always introduces songs in musicals (jukebox or otherwise); instead, the Beatle numbers are all neatly integrated into the totality of the film. Lester, for his part, enhanced the tunes themselves by cutting shifts of angle and distance in time to the music.

All this ingenuity might have been to little avail, however, had not the stars themselves proven their charisma fully transferable to the silver screen. ("Not bad for someone who can't act," cackled Lennon.) Enough critics were sufficiently impressed with the Beatles' natural talent for slapstick to turn the phrase "the Marx Brothers of the 1960's" into almost a cliché. Ringo was singled out for special praise, largely on the merits of his melancholy riverside stroll with an errant schoolboy (who, like Paul's grand-dad, seemed to

Camping up a scene from Shakespeare's *Midsummer Night's Dream* on the May 1964 TV film "Around the Beatles" (Keystone Press Agency)

suggest that one didn't have to be the Beatles' own age to share their spirit); later, Starr admitted that it took a few stiff drinks to bring out the pathos.

Though the Beatles' recordings would continue to improve dramatically almost to the end of their career, they would never top that first movie. *A Hard Day's Night* was also, relative to the initial investment, the most profitable film in celluloid history. A record 15,000 prints were distributed around the globe; another was buried deep in the Californian soil along with other relics of contemporary civilization, in order to give the 2960's a picture of what the 1960's were all about.

The *Hard Day's Night* L.P. was the first to rely exclusively on Lennon-McCartney originals. All were composed under intense pressure during the Beatles' French and American visits so as to be ready when the film commenced shooting in March.

Some of the tunes, such as "Tell Me Why," rehashed the familiar formula with a bigger beat than ever. But there were surprises as well, most notably "And I Love Her," the first flower of McCartney as romantic balladeer. A haunting melody, positively dripping with universal appeal, it rapidly eclipsed "All My Loving" and "Can't Buy Me Love" in Paul's ever-expanding catalog of "standards." Similar confections such as "Yesterday," "Michelle," and "Here There and Everywhere" would soon establish the Beatles' Prince Charming as the most widely interpreted songwriter of the Sixties.

Like the songs themselves, the Beatles' recordings were displaying more polish. No longer obliged to crank out a finished product within the hour, the boys were able to make the flat voices ("Hold Me Tight") and aborted licks ("I Call Your Name") a thing of the past, in the process ironing out for good the nagging whine that had driven so many seasoned music lovers up the wall the previous winter. Lennon and McCartney were each cultivating distinctive vocal styles, neatly juxtaposed in the song "A Hard Day's Night," where Paul belts out the bridge and John wails on the verse. For numbers like John's "If I Fell" they blend their voices to patent those rich and inventive "Beatlesque" harmonies, soon to be so widely imitated.

Of the 13 tunes John and Paul wrote for the film, only seven were actually used. The *Hard Day's Night* album that appeared in Britain and most other countries featured the songs from the picture on Side One and the remainder on the flip. But in America, true to form, these selections were sprinkled over a wide assortment of "product"; many were issued three times in rapid succession.

United Artists Records got to distribute a soundtrack L. P. containing, in addition to some Martin muzak, the seven Beatle songs from the score, plus "I'll Cry Instead," which had been dropped at the last moment. Capitol retaliated by dishing out all but one of these as singles, most of which were subsequently recycled on the deceptively titled *Something New*.

Between June 4 and November 10, the Beatles played over 50 cities on four continents. Though Ringo collapsed with throat trouble on the eve of their initial departure for Denmark, the show had to go on; the Fab Three rocked Copenhagen, Amsterdam, Hong Kong, and Adelaide with Jimmy Nicol in the drummer's seat. When the quartet were reunited in Melbourne, 250,000—the largest collection of Australians ever seen in one place—lined the street to greet them. At every turn the Beatles had to be shielded from rioting mobs; even cripples were regularly wheeled in their direction, as if their magical powers extended to faith-healing.

Beatlemania blanketed the North American continent for the first time in August and September, a media event that rivaled the Johnson-Goldwater campaign. (Beatlemaniacs in fact staged a mock convention of their own in New York, after which "Ringo For President" bumper stickers blossomed on the freeways.) The 26 U.S. concerts included the Beatles' first appearances at the huge outdoor arenas that would become fixtures of subsequent tours.

A pair of enterprising employees of Chicago's radio WBKB staged a classic display of Beatlemania American style when they persuaded two hotels, the Whittier in Detroit and the Muehlback in Kansas City, to part with (for $1,150) the sheets that the Beatles had slept in during their visit. Reported *Variety:*

After the purchases, the hotel rooms were plugged until the ceremony of stripping down the beds could be attended by a lawyer and witnesses. Along with the high priced bed linen came sworn affidavits by the hotel managers testifying to their authenticity and to the factualness of each having come from the specific bed of John, George, Paul, or Ringo.

Now the sheets are one-inch swatches (they yielded 6,000 squares apiece, or about 150,000 in all), mounted on parchment over the drawing of a fourposter and labeled "suitable for framing."

Each is carefully identified as to the Beattle [sic] who used it and is sealed with a copy of the affidavit. . . . They're now in the hands of a merchandiser, retailing at $1 apiece.

The pillowcases, still unwashed, are in a bank vault. . . .

Ringo rates a new record on Britain's "Jukebox Jury" TV show (*16* Magazine)

Following the American dates, the Beatles paused for two weeks to concoct a new L.P. and single, then hit the road in their own land. Come December Ringo finally got a chance to have his troublesome tonsils removed; American radio stations aired up-to-the-minute bulletins on his condition, but Starr turned down many lucrative offers for the entrails themselves, insisting that they be destroyed.

By the holiday season he had recovered sufficiently to croak "Honey Don't" for the Beatles' second annual three-week "Christmas Show" run at London's Hammersmith Odeon.

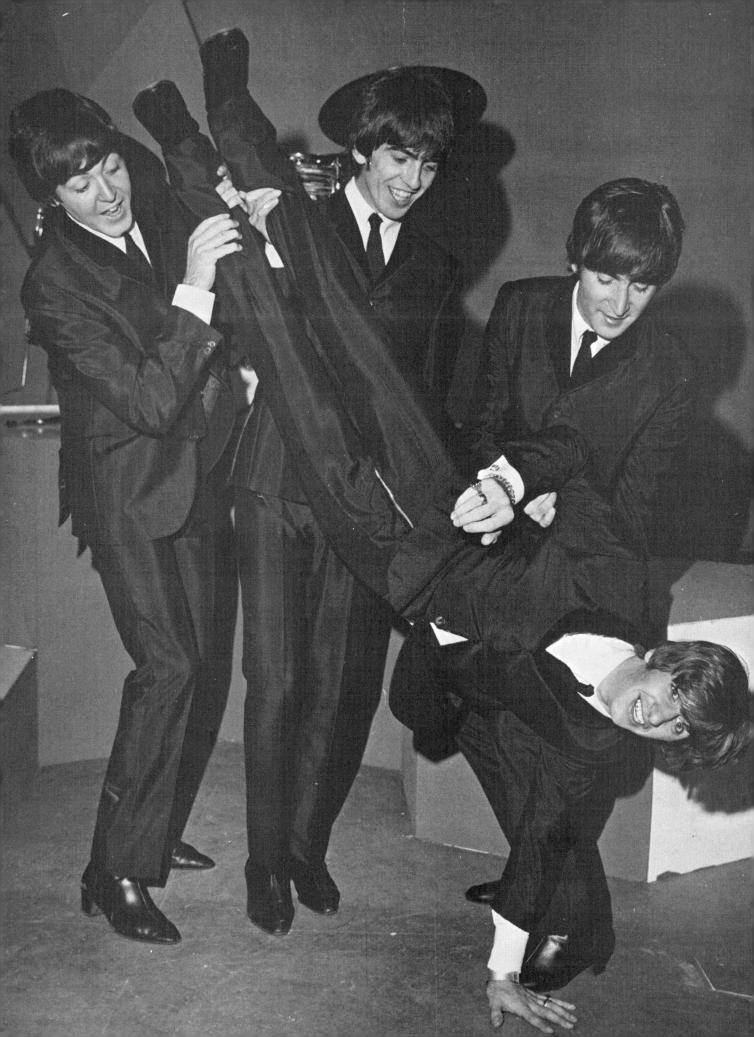

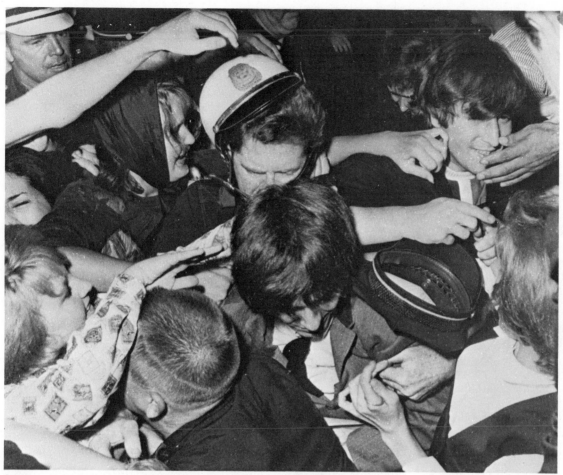

George and John surrounded by admirers in Dallas, September 1964 (Wide World Photos)

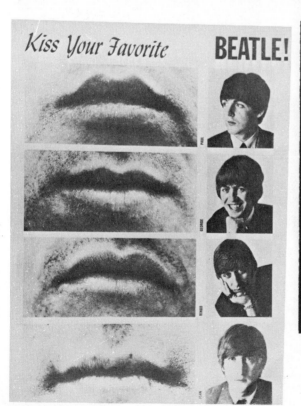

Kiss Your Favorite **BEATLE!**

(Courtesy, *16* Magazine)

Ringo and friends celebrating his 24th birthday July 7, 1964 (Keystone Press Agency)

Dishcloth

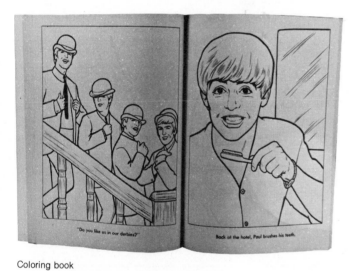

Coloring book

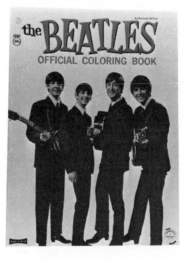

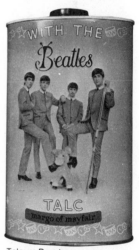

Talcum Powder

Bracelet

The Beatles' Hits—December 1962 through November 1964

TITLE AND LABEL	FIRST APPEARANCE	HIGHEST POSITION	WEEKS ON CHART
U.S. Top 100 Singles			
I Want To Hold Your Hand (Capitol)*	Jan. 18, 1964	1	15
She Loves You (Swan)*	Jan. 25, 1964	1	15
Please Please Me (V-J)	Feb. 1, 1964	3	13
I Saw Her Standing There (Capitol)	Feb. 8, 1964	14	11
My Bonnie (M.G.M.)	Feb. 15, 1964	26	6
From Me To You (V-J)	Feb. 29, 1964	41	6
Twist and Shout (Tollie)	March 14, 1964	2	11
Roll Over, Beethoven (Capitol/Canada)	March 21, 1964	68	4
Can't Buy Me Love (Capitol)*	March 28, 1964	1	10
All My Loving (Capitol/Canada)	March 28, 1964	45	6
Do You Want To Know a Secret (V-J)	March 28, 1964	2	11
You Can't Do That (Capitol)	April 4, 1964	48	4
Thank You Girl (V-J)	April 4, 1964	35	7
There's a Place (V-J)	April 11, 1964	74	1
Love Me Do (Tollie)	April 11, 1964	1	14
Why? (M.G.M.)	April 18, 1964	88	1
P.S. I Love You (Tollie)	May 9, 1964	10	8
E.P.: Roll Over Beethoven/Please Mr. Postman/All My Loving/This Boy (Capitol)	June 13, 1964	92	3
Sie Liebt Dich (Swan)	June 27, 1964	97	1
A Hard Day's Night (Capitol)*	July 18, 1964	1	13
Ain't She Sweet (Atco)	July 18, 1964	19	9
I Should Have Known Better (Capitol)	July 25, 1964	53	4
And I Love Her (Capitol)	July 25, 1964	12	9
I'll Cry Instead (Capitol)	Aug. 1, 1964	25	7
If I Fell (Capitol)	Aug. 1, 1964	53	9
I'm Happy Just To Dance With You (Capitol)	Aug. 1, 1964	95	1
Matchbox (Capitol)	Sept. 5, 1964	17	8
Slow Down (Capitol)	Sept. 5, 1964	25	7

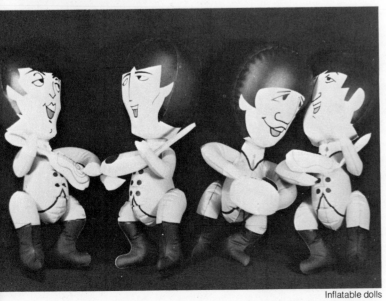

Inflatable dolls

U.S. Top 200 L.P.'s

Meet the Beatles (Capitol)*	Feb. 1, 1964	1	69
Introducing the Beatles (V-J)	Feb. 8, 1964	2	49
The Beatles—with Tony Sheridan and Guests (M.G.M.)	Feb. 15, 1964	68	14
Jolly What! The Beatles and Frank Ifield On Stage (V-J)	April 4, 1964	103	6
The Beatles' Second Album (Capitol)*	April 25, 1964	1	55
The Beatles' American Tour, with Ed Rudy (Radio Pulse Beat)	June 13, 1964	20	13
A Hard Day's Night (United Artists)*	July 18, 1964	1	51
Something New (Capitol)*	Aug. 8, 1964	2	41
The Beatles Vs. The Four Seasons (V-J)	Oct. 10, 1964	142	3
Songs, Pictures, And Stories Of the Fabulous Beatles (V-J)	Oct. 31, 1964	63	12

British Top Twenty Singles

Love Me Do (Parlophone)	Dec. 1, 1962	17	6
Please Please Me (Parlophone)	Feb. 1, 1963	2	11
From Me To You (Parlophone)	April 10, 1963	1	17
She Loves You (Parlophone)	Aug. 31, 1963	1	24
I Want To Hold Your Hand (Parlophone)	Dec. 7, 1963	1	12
Can't Buy Me Love (Parlophone)	Mar. 28, 1964	1	9
A Hard Day's Night (Parlophone)	July 18, 1964	1	10

(Chart positions according to *Billboard;* asterisk [*]: Record Industry Association of America certified Gold Record/Million Seller)

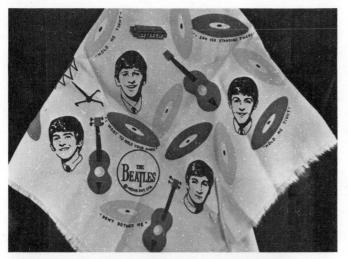

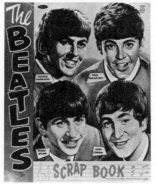

Beatlemaniacs storm Buckhingham Palace (UPI)

GETTING BETTER ALL THE TIME

. . . bliss the moment arrived
Apparition, four brown English
jacket christhair boys
Goofed Ringo battling bright
white drums
Silent George hair patient
Soul horse
Short black-skulled Paul
wit thin guitar
Lennon the captain, his mouth
a triangular smile,
all jump together to End
some tearful memory song
ancient two years
　　　—Allen Ginsberg
　　　　(from *"Portland Coliseum"*)

The songs that John and Paul wrote in the months following completion of *A Hard Day's Night,* which were to appear in America on *Beatles '65* and *Beatles VI,* and in the rest of Beatledom as *Beatles For Sale,* showed not only their growing musical sophistication and virtuosity, but that Lennon—an uncompromisingly honest, somewhat bitter man who felt uncomfortable with the notion that pop stars should radiate non-stop mindless good cheer—was beginning to explore his own emotions and imagination in his new lyrics.

The *Hard Day's Night* L.P. had already treated us to a fleeting glimpse of the real John: in "I'll Cry Instead," he had swept aside the usual saccharine to declare "a chip on my shoulder that's bigger than my feet." "A Hard Day's Night" was itself the first striking phrase to crop up in a Beatles' lyric; unsurprisingly, it was borrowed from one of John's "literary" endeavors ("Sad Michael," a piece in *In His Own Write*), and the rest of the song's words were typically unrevealing.

"To express myself," John recalled in *Rolling Stone* six years later, "I would write *Spaniard In the Works* or *In His Own Write,* the personal stories which were expressive of my personal emotions. I'd have a separate songwriting John Lennon who wrote songs for the sort of meat market, and I didn't consider them—the lyrics or anything—to have any depth at all. They were just a joke. Then I started being me about the songs, not writing them objectively, but subjectively."

The two Johns began to come together in the morose assortment of numbers Lennon contributed to *Beatles For Sale.* The free-wheeling imagery of *Sgt. Pepper* and the relentless soul-baring of *Plastic Ono Band* were still a long way away, but a kernel of the latter can be detected in "I'm a Loser," in which the ever-grinning moptop informed his fans:

Although I laugh and I act like a clown,
beneath this mask I am wearing a frown . . .

and in "Baby's In Black," the tale of a girl who refused to shed her mourning dress, we were treated to the first hint of the bizarre. "I Don't Want To Spoil the Party" was an unusually convincing account of being stood up, although like most pop songs of the time, including all the Beatles', these consist of the same phrases repeated again and

again until the obligatory two-and-a-half-odd minutes are up. And the lyrics were still in the boy-wins-or-loses-girl syndrome—but with the difference that when John told us he was losing, it sounded as if he meant it.

A 45-r.p.m. appetizer was excerpted from these sessions in November 1964 in the form of "I Feel Fine" and "She's a Woman." The demand was unprecedented, particularly in America, where five major albums and 16 45's had been issued in rapid succession over the first seven months of the year, making the ensuing gap seem like forever. All Beatlemaniacs were kept glued to their transistors during the agonizing 10 days between the songs' first appearance on the airwaves and their arrival in the shops, a ritual that would be re-enacted every time the Fabs came out with another record, and one that in the Beatles' more cosmic incarnations came to resemble that of disciples awaiting the latest Word. The D.J.'s quickly caught on to this fanaticism, and would keep us on edge—and tuned in to their station—with hints that the new songs might be aired any minute.

This single, like so many to come, had its share of surprises. "I Feel Fine" kicked off to a strange searing noise that many of us mistook for a mosquito, until it was revealed to be electric guitar feedback (an innovation that was later amplified by The Who, Jefferson Airplane, and Jimi Hendrix to become a staple of acid-rock). The song, which featured hazily mixed harmonies hovering over an insistent guitar riff that faded out to the sound of barking dogs (!), was their most innovative and mesmerizing recording yet. "She's a Woman," a mighty chunk of rock 'n' roll, had Paul belting away in his show-stopping "Long Tall Sally" voice for the first time on an original composition.

The L.P. tracks that followed included some successful reworkings of proven formulae, as in the bouncy "Eight Days a Week" (held off the American album to become the next big Stateside single), and the exuberantly interpreted '50's classics like "Rock and Roll Music" and "Kansas City" (which the Beatles welded together with Little Richard's "Hey Hey Hey"), perfected years before in the smoky cellar clubs of Liverpool and Hamburg. However, a touch of the unconventional was detectable not only in Lennon's lyrics, but in some of the instruments the boys were beginning to tinker with. Ringo could be heard bounding from tympani on

John Lennon: an uncompromisingly honest man who felt uncomfortable with the notion that pop stars should radiate mindless good cheer (*16* Magazine)

"Every Little Thing" to packing case on "Words of Love" to bongoes on "Mr. Moonlight," where he was joined by George's Arabian drum. Not only were the Beatles developing their knack for writing in a wide range of styles, they were also learning that similar material could be made to *sound* more varied and interesting by the use of a different line-up of instruments on each number.

On February 11, 1965, Ringo married Maureen Cox, thereby defying the conventional wisdom that the loss of an eligible bachelor must take its toll of a group's fans. Even Harrison had declared a year earlier: "I don't think the Beatles' image could stand another marriage." However, Ringo fans were apparently sturdy enough to absorb the shock—if any did defect, it must have been to the still-available Paul and George.

When Queen Elizabeth II granted the Beatles the coveted Member of the British Empire award on June 12 for their contribution to her kingdom's balance of trade, it represented something of an official surrender on the part of the class-conscious British Establishment. A few crusty hold-outs, however, sent back their medals in a fit of rage. A typical complaint was that of the old war hero who refused to be viewed "on the same level with vulgar nincompoops." John noted that all of those who complained had been honored "for killing people. We received ours for entertaining other people. I'd say we deserve ours more. Wouldn't you?"

For most Beatlemaniacs, who began to delight in addressing fan mail to Paul McCartney, M.B.E., the answer was an unqualified yes, although a few commentators suggested that rebellious fans might view the M.B.E.'s as a sell-out and defect to the Rolling Stones, who at around the same time had shored up their reputation for unwholesomeness when Jagger, Jones, and Wyman yanked out their you-know-whats and peed on a gas station whose attendant wouldn't let them use the W.C.

The Beatles seemed to take the M.B.E. escapade in stride. When they went to Buckingham Palace to pick up their medals, they punctured the solemnity of the occasion with their madcap humor (Queen: How long have you been together now? Ringo: Forty years). But later Lennon claimed that a case of nerves had sent them into one of the palace lavatories for a quick joint before the investiture.

A second collection of John's writings and drawings appeared, titled *A Spaniard In the Works* ("a spanner in the works" being a Britishism equivalent to "a fly in the ointment"). Although the book naturally received less publicity than the debut of "the literary Beatle," it was much pithier than *In His Own Write*. The word play was richer, the satire more pointed, and the stories unabashedly (and hilariously) bawdy. Included were an account of Britain's "general erection" and a macabre tale entitled "Last Will and Testicle." Pieces like these also provided early evidence of the disdain John felt for the political system, which would become more obvious as John's career progressed.

The title story starred Jesus El Pifco, a "garlic eating, stinking, little yellow greasy fascist bastard Catholic Spaniard" who "immigrateful" to Scotland to work in one Laird McAnus's stables. There the hero encounters and proposes to "wee Spastic Sporran the flighty chamberlain." The Laird's wedding present is "a special jar of secret ointment made by generators of his forefingers" to relieve the bride of crabs received from the Laird at the late Lady McAnus' wake. Needless to say, the pair are "overjoyced, and grapenut abun and beyond the call of duty . . . 'the only little crawly things we want are babies,' quipped Jesus."

The best, certainly the cruelest, piece in the book was the poem "Our Dad," which began

It wasn't long before old dad
was cumbersome—a drag.
He seemed to get the message and
began to pack his bag.

Maureen and Ringo with their first son, Zak, born September 13, 1965. The couple would produce one more boy, Jason, and a girl, Lee. (Keystone Press Agency)

L.P., Singapore, 1965 (Parlophone)

L.P., Australia, 1964 (Parlophone)

E.P., Britain, 1965 (Parlophone)

It was, of course, John's Daddy who'd left him, and Lennon clearly relished switching the roles to mercilessly hound the old geezer out of town in the ensuing stanzas.

The closest this fan ever got to the Beatles was when they whooshed past in their Rolls Royce on the way to the premiere of *Help!* in Piccadilly Circus. Thousands of us stood for hours to await their arrival; it was a ritual Beatlemaniacs enacted whenever the Beatles landed in or took off from an airport, or arrived at a local hotel. We all applauded as Princess Margaret breezed by in a convertible Bentley, waving the tips of her bejeweled fingers at the crowd; but when the shrill noise of screaming swept in from St. James Street we knew They were here. The sound was as deafening as at a Beatles concert, and legions of poker-faced bobbies kept us on the far side of the barricades. One glimpse of John and Paul waving out the window and—blink—they were gone.

The Beatles were such a national institution by this time that London's major newspapers devoted the whole front page that day to pictures of the Beatles and reviews of the new film.

As for the movie, which cost twice as much to make as *A Hard Day's Night* and made ten times that back in a jiffy . . . it was a treat and a half to see our heroes cavorting spiritedly on the Austrian Alps and the Bahaman beaches, in full color, too. Ringo, in particular, had lost none of his on-screen charisma, and the tunes were terrific. And yet, somehow, something seemed lacking in comparison with the first film.

Christmas 1964:
Songs Performed at the Beatles' Three-Week
Engagement at the Hammersmith Odeon, London
Twist and Shout (John, Lead vocal)
I'm A Loser (John)
Baby's In Black (John and Paul)
Everybody's Trying To Be My Baby (George)
Can't Buy Me Love (Paul)
Honey Don't (Ringo)
I Feel Fine (John)
She's A Woman (Paul)
A Hard Day's Night (John and Paul)
Rock and Roll Music (John)
Long Tall Sally (Paul)

The Beatles show off their new medals (Wide World Photos)

While much of *A Hard Day's Night's* charm lay in the quasi-documentary format, with the Beatles simulating the routines of their daily life—playing concerts, dueling with reporters and dodging fans—*Help!* was a surreal parody of the expensive gimmicky thrillers that were so popular at the time, such as *Goldfinger* and *Thunderball* (note how "The James Bond Theme" crops up in the *Help!* soundtrack). Sometimes the Beatles and their music didn't quite gel with the rest of the goings-on, and they never cared much for *Help!* themselves. Only a year later Lennon succinctly dismissed it with one word: "crap". More recently he elaborated somewhat, saying that director Richard Lester "forgot about who and what we were. And that's why the film didn't work. It was like having clams in a movie about frogs."

At least they didn't do *A Hard Day's Night* all over again in color, but they didn't feel prepared to play straight dramatic roles (a few months later they would nix plans to do just that, in a western called *A Talent For Loving*). Neither they nor their audience yet took themselves seriously enough for the sort of film the Beatles toyed with in 1967, *Shades of a Personality,* in which each of the boys was to represent one

L.P., Germany, 1965 (Odeon)

facet of a "quadrophonic" character (an idea that was eventually also scrapped, until its resurrection by Peter Townshend six years later in a "rock opera" by The Who). So the Beatles wound up playing themselves in an absurd, splashy Richard Lester comedy about bloodthirsty Hindus running around the world in search of a sacrificial ring that, willy nilly, turns up on Ringo's finger.

The film was "respectfully dedicated to the memory of Mr. Elias Howe who in 1846 invented the sewing machine"—the sort of startling nonsequitur the Beatles would soon delight in on their own albums.

Yet *Help!* did, in a rather offhand way, help initiate a new era in the music and lifestyle of at least one Beatle, and so, by extension, more than a few of the rest of us.

In the film's otherwise nondescript soundtrack instrumentals (especially familiar to American fans, as they usurped such Beatle tunes as "Yesterday" and "Act Naturally" on their *Help!* L.P.) the 21-stringed Hindustani sitar was utilized to create an eery effect. The instrument caught George Harrison's fancy, so he bought one for himself. Within a few months he was carting his new toy to the recording studios, embellishing John's "Norwegian Wood" with a simple sitar riff. That was only the beginning of an infatuation that was to result in the first major contribution of "the quiet Beatle" to the direction of his band.

The Beatles' experiments with outdoor concerts on their summer 1964 American tour had been so successful (financially, anyway) that for their cross-country blitz a year later Brian Epstein opted almost without exception for the hugest arenas available. The show at the 55,600-seat Shea Stadium in Flushing, New York was the most famous of the series, as it was the biggest of the bunch—never before in history had a concert of this magnitude been staged. This Beatlemaniac was lucky enough to get one of the tickets that were sold out within days of the announcement.

Fans began to stream in hours before the show was to begin, and lost no time in getting down to business. You could hear them scream half a mile down Van Wyck Expressway.

It had long been understood that nobody should expect to hear the Beatles at their concerts—after all, you could listen to the records at home (to an interviewer who asked why she didn't sit and listen at Shea, a girl replied: "We didn't pay $5.75 for nothing."). By now, however, a twist had been added, that you wouldn't be able to see them either. Even those blessed with front-row-center seats at Shea had to have opera glasses handy if they hoped to see anything larger than a quartet of flies, as the stage was located at second base, the baseball diamond a no-man's land zealously guarded by hundreds of New York's finest, at considerable cost to city taxpayers.

A blimp painted with Beatle slogans hovered overhead, as huge Union Jacks and bedsheets scrawled with such legends as "BEATLES M.B.E. 4-EVER" and "JOHN, DIVORCE CYNTHIA" billowed from the rafters. A layer of expectant shrieks and chants of "We Want the Beatles" obscured the noise of umpteen opening groups, some of whom featured the go-go girls that many people still thought indispensable to "beat music." Between acts, Ed Sullivan and every disk jockey in town managed to shuffle on stage to say their pieces, and the mere mention of the word "Beatles" would invariably make the rest of their schpiel inaudible through the ensuing eruption. Fat men wandered through the crowds, trying to hawk hot dogs and binoculars.

Meanwhile, the Beatles were flown from Manhattan to Flushing in a helicopter, then whisked into the stadium in an armored car, to the deafening noise of 55,600 Beatle-

Lennon in disguise on the set of *Help* (*16* Magazine)

THE PRINCESS MEETS A BEATLE London, July 30, 1965 (UPI): "Slightly different hair stylings are worn by Great Britain's *Princess Margaret* and Beatle *Paul McCartney* as they meet at the London Pavilion for the premiere of the Beatles' new film *Help*"

Early Summer 1965: Songs Performed on the Beatles' European Tour

Twist and Shout (John, lead vocal)
She's a Woman (Paul)
Ticket To Ride (John and Paul)
Can't Buy Me Love (Paul)
I'm a Loser (John)
I Wanna Be Your Man (Ringo)
A Hard Day's Night (John and Paul)
Baby's In Black (John and Paul)
Rock and Roll Music (John)
Everybody's Trying To Be My Baby (George)
Long Tall Sally (Paul)

Thousands of British Beatlemaniacs see Ringo, John, George, and Paul off at the airport before the third U.S. tour. (UPI)

E.P., France, 1965 (Odeon)

maniacs in the outer reaches of hysteria; and a twinkling galaxy of countless flashbulb-popping instamatics aimed at the Beatles from a hundred yards away. The first number was rumored to be "Twist and Shout."

The show was enlivened every few minutes when some particularly determined and ingenious young lady would successfully claw her way through the barricades and police, hurtling across the ballfield toward her idols until finally the blue meanies would manage to drag her, kicking and shrieking, out of Shea Stadium.

Girls who had fainted or collapsed, unable to handle the excitement of being in the same stadium with the Beatles, were carted out by the hundreds to nearby ambulances. The notoriously thick, sticky humidity of New York summers provided everyone with added incentive to pass out.

Those of us who were the wrong sex to carry on in so shameless a fashion listened to the murky rumble of the electric guitars—the only aspect of the music that was remotely audible—and played a challenging guessing game called What Song Are They Doing Now?

Of course, the actual performance of the inaudible and virtually invisible stars was hardly the point any more; the mere fact that it was a Beatle concert made it an Event that over 50,000 fanatics had united to celebrate. They were the real show.

After half an hour the concert was over, and the Beatles

rolled away in their armored car, $160,000 richer, their wages for the evening amounting to nearly $100 a second.

The songs of the Beatles, and almost everyone else on the pop scene, were by this point beginning to reflect the influence of a wiry Minnesotan troubador equipped with a nasal whine, a wheezing harmonica, and a definite way with words. Bob Dylan had, by the time of the Beatles' international emergence, already composed most of the budding civil rights and ban-the-bomb movements' major anthems: angry, haunting songs like "Blowin' In the Wind," "A Hard Rain's Gonna Fall," and "The Times They Are a-Changin'."

In the initial gush of Beatlemania, Dylan's and the Fabs' following were just about mutually exclusive. Bob was the object of a cult of earnest, socially concerned college students who sat at his concerts in awed silence, hanging on to their inscrutable prophet's every syllable. Few of them would have relished the thought of mingling with the frenzied apolitical teen-agers who packed stadiums in order to drown out the Beatles' music with their shrieks. To Dylan's original audience, as he was soon to learn, the electric guitar and the hit single were symbols of crass commercialism.

In 1964, the Beatles, like a great many other aware young Britishers, succumbed to Dylan's heady spell. The instant they heard one of his records, said John, "we all went potty on Dylan." Although many of his folkie pals were initially scornful of the Liverpudlians' bouncy sound and cuddly image, Dylan's shrewd instincts told him there was something happening here.

"They were doing things nobody was doing . . . [and] you could only do that with other musicians," Dylan told Anthony Scaduto years later, explaining how the Beatles made him consider using other accompaniment than just his own acoustic guitar. "There was a lot of hypocrisy all around, people saying it had to be either folk or rock. But I knew it didn't have to be like that."

That May, all four Beatles were in front-row attendance at Dylan's London concert. After the show, Dylan visited with them until the early hours, as he had done the previous summer, when the Beatles last played New York. At that first meeting, Dylan initiated them into the joys of a mind-expanding green herb that was then coming into favor with creative types. As John revealed years later: "He thought 'I Want to Hold Your Hand' when it goes, can't hide—he thought we were singing 'I get high'—so he turns up—and turns us on, and we had the biggest laugh all night."

Eventually Bob was to turn them on to a great deal more—and they him. And who would have guessed that this mutual infatuation would so revolutionize both the music of the rest of the decade, and the role that music would play in those crazy, turbulent years?

I wasn't too keen on lyrics in those days [1964]. I didn't think they counted. Dylan used to come out with his latest acetate and say "listen to the words, man." And I'd say, "I don't listen to the words."
—John Lennon

It took a quintet of young Californians called the Byrds to demonstrate conclusively that the worlds of Bob Dylan and the Beatles need not remain so far apart. Composed of veteran acoustic-guitar pickers, the Byrds decided, after seeing *A Hard Day's Night* and hearing George Harrison's electrified 12-string, that their future lay in pop music. However, the song they chose to embellish with electric guitars and Beatlesque harmonies for release as their first single was "Mr. Tambourine Man" by their old folk-singer friend Bob Dylan. In doing so they gave birth to a whole new genre of music, quickly dubbed "folk-rock" by *Billboard*, and by the summer of 1965 the single was perched atop the American and British charts.

George Harrison liked what he heard, reportedly anointing them "the American Beatles," and Derek Taylor, the Fabs' press agent, went to work for the Byrds, after parting company with the often tempestuous Epstein. Scores of other groups, such as Manfred Mann and the Turtles, began to raid the Dylan catalogue to great commercial advantage; many more woke up to the fact that no one was stopping them from "saying something" in their own songs. Foremost among these, of course, was the Beatles.

So, with the summer of 1965, we all began to take rock lyrics seriously for the first time. Thanks to Bobby D. and other renegade folkies, they received a sudden infusion of "poetry" and political commentary (and, as could be expected, opportunistic hacks lost no time in riding the New Wave with ponderous junk such as the million-selling "Eve of Destruction").

Over the next year or so, the established heart throbs of the teen music scene, none of whom had ever been asked for revelations more profound than their favorite color or how often they washed their hair, would get to show whether they had the talent, and their maturing fans the sophistication, to handle songs that had Something To Say. As it

Summer 1965: Songs performed on the Beatles' North American Tour

Twist and Shout (lead vocal, John)
She's a Woman (Paul)
I Feel Fine (John)†
Dizzy Miss Lizzy (John)
Ticket to Ride (John and Paul)†
Everybody's Trying To Be My Baby (George)
Can't Buy Me Love (Paul)
Baby's In Black (John and Paul)
Act Naturally (Ringo)*†
A Hard Day's Night (John and Paul)
Help! (John)†
I'm Down (Paul)†

*alternating with "I Wanna Be Your Man" (Ringo)
†performed, along with "Yesterday," on the Ed Sullivan Show, September 12, 1965

The Beatles at Shea Stadium (UPI)

(Wide World Photos)

E.P., France, 1965 (Parlophone)

turned out, the fans were most receptive, and the successful survivors of the '64 "English Invasion" were duly enshrined as the "spokesmen" and "prophets" of the "counterculture" that their fans were soon to build—on the foundations of their music.

Those groups that didn't have it in them to be arty or relevant, like Herman's Hermits, the Dave Clark Five, and Gerry and the Pacemakers, would rapidly fizzle, as others, like Eric Burdon and the Animals (who started out as a fine, earthy R & B combo), made buffoons of themselves trying. The Beatles, however, proved remarkably adept at staying a step or two ahead of the throng ("the pied pipers of their generation," they used to be called) and the Rolling Stones, the Kinks, the Who, and the Yardbirds were among the handful of bands that showed a similar capacity for growth.

Meanwhile, Dylan himself was changing his sound as drastically as the pop stars were revising their subject matter. At the Newport Folk Festival in the summer of 1965 he was hooted off stage when he emerged with his newly acquired electric guitar, rock combo, and Dylan's own adaptation of the Beatle hairstyle—a full head of Medusa locks. However, Bob may have felt vindicated a few weeks later when the pulsating single "Like A Rolling Stone" became

not only a Number One hit but virtual rock 'n' roll anthem (incidentally, that song, which rambled on for six minutes, did away with the unwritten law that hit singles must be kept under three minutes long, although it wasn't until the Beatles' "Hey Jude" three years later that D.J.'s had to cope with a *seven* minute single).

A stunning pair of Dylan albums, *Bringing It All Back Home* and *Highway 61 Revisited,* further enraged the Newport set, and inspired millions of others (including the Beatles) by coupling the heavy beat with introspective and wildly surreal lyrics that shunned overt political commitment.

The first Beatle tune in which Dylan's influence can be detected is "I'm A Loser," from the close of 1964. The folky chords are strummed acoustically, and blasts from John's harmonica punctuate his relatively penetrating lyrics. (Of course, the harmonica was hardly a Dylan rip-off; next to Mr. D., Lennon was the most notable reviver of the instrument, which can be heard on the Beatles' first three singles, and, with declining frequency, in most of their albums.) Lennon admitted the song was inspired by Dylan, but said "I could have made it even more Dylanish if I'd tried."

He did just that with "You've Got to Hide Your Love Away," which appeared a few months later. Nobody had to

46

guess too hard for the source of John's world-weary twang, or of those four repetitive acoustic guitar chords. But the imaginative substitution of flutes where one expected that harmonica to come careening in kept the resemblance from sounding indecent.

Henceforth, Dylan's influence would be less blatant—more one of example than of specific musical and lyrical style. By eloquently expressing himself in his songs, Dylan showed Lennon and McCartney that they could too, in *their* own way, and in *their* own style.

The other tunes that the Beatles released in the spring and summer of 1965 can be seen in retrospect as songs of transition, highlighted by a growing melodic inventiveness that would really blossom in *Rubber Soul* at the end of the year.

Their repertoire of American rock 'n' roll was plundered for the very last time, in a raucous pair of Larry Williams tunes ("Bad Boy" and "Dizzy Miss Lizzy") and Ringo's rockabilly "Act Naturally," a perfect showcase for the generally acknowledged star of *A Hard Day's Night* and *Help!* ("the biggest fool that ever hit the bigtime"). Ringo's real ambition had always been to be a cowboy—in 1961 he'd applied to the Houston Chamber of Commerce in hopes of finding employment in the prairie country. Luckily for us, he wound up getting a job in Liverpool playing drums for the Beatles; but his hillbilly yearnings still pervaded both the songs he chose to sing and the way he sang them. (Ringo may never have had much of a way with melody, but his Johnny-one-note deadpan vocals perfectly complemented his whimsical, self-effacing image, and the Beatles' tradition of awarding him one song per album insured that at least that one tune would smack of pure homey charm.)

The original numbers were for the most part relatively low key, with the exception of the rousing single "Ticket to Ride,"* and McCartney's frenzied "I'm Down," a rather blatant

*Whose U.S. edition bore the legend "from the United Artists release *Eight Arms to Hold You*"—that being the original title of *Help!*

rewrite of "Long Tall Sally," Paul's favorite Little Richard song which "I'm Down" replaced as the Beatles' concert finale.

The "folk-rock"-influenced "Help" was John's most honest, heart-felt, and autobiographical song yet, quite a contrast to the slick movie for which it served as a theme:

When I was younger, so much younger than today, I never needed anybody's help in any way, but now these days are gone I'm not so self-assured . . .
Please help me!

George Harrison began to emerge from the shadows, shattering the Lennon-McCartney songwriting monopoly with an otherwise unshattering pair of ditties, "You Like Me Too Much" and "I Need You."

But the most striking of the new songs, of course, was "Yesterday," which originally went by the name of "Scrambled Egg." It may not have been the first appearance of a string quartet on the planet, but for an English pop group to use one, especially in so baroque a manner, was a rare departure. What's more, if songs like "And I Love Her" had not convinced non-rockers that Paul McCartney was as facile a composer of haunting pop melodies as any, "Yesterday" certainly turned the trick. Little old ladies of all sexes lapped it up ("maybe there's something there after all") and all those countless starry-eyed hopeful Mrs. McCartneys were not disappointed to hear their angel-faced dreamdate in so sentimental a mood. Within the next decade, over a thousand recording artists around the world released versions of the tune, which not only makes "Yesterday" easily the most frequently "covered" song in Beatledom, but also one of the most oft-recorded tunes ever composed by anyone.

"Yesterday" has, like subsequent McCartney incursions into schmaltz, been cut down to size by rock-oriented writers. Yet it was undeniably a milestone for the Beatles. It marked the first occasion that outside musicians played a pivotal role in their music; the first time that a Beatle

(Courtesy, *16* Magazine)

L.P., Italy, 1965 (Parlophone)

Millions more fans watched the Beatles at Shea a few months later when the T.V. film was aired (Keystone Press Agency)

Beatle bubblebath came bottled in two varieties—Paul and Ringo, then the two most popular Beatles.

Lennon, McCartney, and Starr play with their spaghetti on the Italian stop of the Beatles' June 1965 European tour (*16* Magazine)

recorded solo (despite the fact that the song was credited to the group); and it was the first record whose sound could not be approximated in live concert by the boys alone (although due to its popularity the Beatles attempted a stringless version on their 1966 tour).

Perhaps the success of "Yesterday" hastened the day when the Beatles would augment their increasingly eclectic music with so many other musicians' horns, strings, woodwinds, and various hard-to-pronounce Indian instruments—often minus one, two, or even three Beatles—that any attempt at reproducing the results in person became out of the question.

The greatest triumph of Beatles '65 was the last one: the *Rubber Soul* album, issued just in time for Santa. This record, which perfectly summed up the year of folk-rock, was pervaded by a mellower, lower-voltage sound; acoustic guitars were everywhere, and the melodies and harmonies were unprecedentedly rich. (The only thing from these sessions that really attained a raw rock 'n' roll sound was "Day Tripper," released as a single.) Most importantly, with this L.P. the Beatles' lyrics were often equal to the music.

The Beatles had also now come to assume full control over all aspects of their "product" (except its American contents); they selected the covers, dreamed up the titles, and had the time and money to record at their own speed. Everything about the album showed the Beatles being consciously arty for the first time. Bob Freeman's front cover shot was daringly surreal for its day, with the Beatles' unsmiling faces distorted as though reflected in water (all

ears but Paul's now completely obscured by that creeping hair), and the by-now gratuitous label "Beatles" nowhere to be seen. This and the Beatles' subsequent L.P. covers effected quite a revolution in album artwork, which had heretofore been as cheap and unimaginatively garish as that on noodle boxes. Henceforth we would rarely be insulted with those dumb-dumb blurbs and liner notes, written in that hyped up language whose only article of punctuation seemed to be the exclamation mark.

As with anything a bit different, there were those who didn't catch on at first. *Melody Maker* said *Rubber Soul* was "not their best," even "monotonous." Fans wrote to the *Beatles Monthly,* complaining that the L.P. cover made their heroes look like corpses.

However, and despite the disconcerting fact that John and Paul wrote seven of the tunes in one fitful week, time has proven *Rubber Soul* as much of a "classic" as a pop record can be. Ten years after its initial release, Anne Murray and Gary Tom's Empire turned "You Won't See Me" and "Drive My Car," respectively, into big easy-listening and disco hits; and the words to "Norwegian Wood" were included in an anthology of classic British poetry.

And,
when I awoke,
I was alone,
this bird had flown,
So,
I lit a fire,
isn't it good?
Norwegian Wood.

E.P., France, 1965 (Odeon)

L.P. Italy, 1965, (Parlophone)

L.P., 1965 (Parlophone)

L.P., France, 1965 (Odeon)

L.P., Italy, 1965 (Parlophone)

This song, the one that introduced the sitar to the general English-speaking public (of which, more later), was also the first whose lyrics inspired debate over "hidden meanings": was the "wood" marijuana? The "bird" a lesbian?

"I was trying to write about an affair without letting me wife know," explained John years later. "So it was very gobble-degook."

Bob Dylan, by the way, recorded a parody of "Norwegian Wood," called "4th Time Around," on his next album, *Blonde on Blonde.* "I was very paranoid about that," said John.

Naturally, Capitol made sure to leave one of *Rubber Soul*'s choicest morsels off the record in America so it might release it there later as a hot "new" single. This time the honor went to "Nowhere Man" ("making all his nowhere plans for nobody"), the Beatles' first stab at social commentary, and their first lyric to completely depart from the subject of boy-girl relationships. The line "isn't he a bit like you and me" softened the put-down and kept "Nowhere Man" from sounding like a Son-of-Dylan's-"Mr.-Jones." The three folky chords may have been inspired by the man from Minnesota, but no trace of any Dylanesque snarl could be heard in those rich three-part harmonies, which John, Paul, and George handled like choirboys.

Lennon-McCartney were beginning to tell stories. "Drive My Car," about a would-be starlet who lets her boyfriend know that his place is behind the wheel of a limousine, was the first evidence of Paul's talent for wry irony. "I've got no car and it's breaking my heart/but I've found a driver, and that's a start." And in chime John and George in campy falsetto: "beep-beep, beep-beep, yeah!"

John's lyrics were becoming as varied as his and Paul's music. They could be nostalgic in "In My Life," sardonic in "Girl," and evangelistic ("I'm here to show everybody the light. . . .") in the first of the Lennon slogan songs, "The Word":

Say the Word and you'll be free
Say the Word and be like me
Say the Word I'm thinking of
Have you heard? The Word is Love.

—a message millions soon would take to heart.

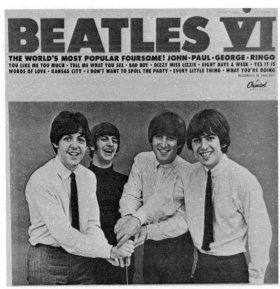

L.P., USA, 1965 (Capitol)

December 1965: Songs Performed on the Beatles' British Tour:

Dizzy Miss Lizzy (John, lead vocal)
I Feel Fine (John)
She's A Woman (Paul)
If I Needed Someone (George)
Ticket to Ride (John and Paul)
Act Naturally (Ringo)
Nowhere Man (John)
Baby's In Black (John and Paul)
Help! (John)
We Can Work It Out (John and Paul)
Day Tripper (John and Paul)
I'm Down (Paul)

The Beatles' Hits—December 1964 through February 1966

TITLE AND LABEL	FIRST APPEARANCE	HIGHEST POSITION	WEEKS ON CHART
U.S. Top 100 Singles			
I Feel Fine (Capitol)*	Dec. 5, 1964	1	11
She's a Woman (Capitol)	Dec. 5, 1964	4	9
Eight Days a Week (Capitol)*	Feb. 20, 1965	1	10
I Don't Want To Spoil the Party (Capitol)	Feb. 20, 1965	39	6
E.P.: Honey Don't/I'm a Loser/Mr. Moonlight/ Everybody's Trying To Be My Baby (Capitol)	Feb. 27, 1965	68	5
Ticket To Ride (Capitol)	April 24, 1965	1	11
Yes It Is (Capitol)	May 1, 1965	46	4
Help! (Capitol)*	Aug. 7, 1965	1	13
Yesterday (Capitol)*	Sept. 25, 1965	1	11
Act Naturally (Capitol)	Sept. 25, 1965	47	7
We Can Work It Out (Capitol)*	Dec. 18, 1965	1	12
Day Tripper (Capitol)	Dec. 18, 1965	5	10
U.S. Top 200 L.P.'s			
The Beatles' Story (Capitol)*	Dec. 12, 1964	7	17
Beatles '65 (Capitol)*	Jan. 2, 1965	1	70
The Early Beatles (Capitol)*	April 24, 1965	43	33
Beatles VI (Capitol)*	June 26, 1965	1	41
Help! (Capitol)*	Aug. 28, 1965	1	44
Rubber Soul (Capitol)*	Jan. 1, 1966	1	49
British Top Twenty Singles			
I Feel Fine (Parlophone)	Dec. 5, 1964	1	10
Ticket To Ride (Parlophone)	April 17, 1965	1	9
Help! (Parlophone)	July 31, 1965	1	10
Day Tripper/We Can Work It Out (Parlophone)	Dec. 11, 1965	1	10

(Chart position according to *Billboard;* asterisk [*]: Record Industry Association of America certified Gold Record/million seller)

E.P., Mexico, 1965 (Capitol)

Single, Japan, 1965 (Odeon)

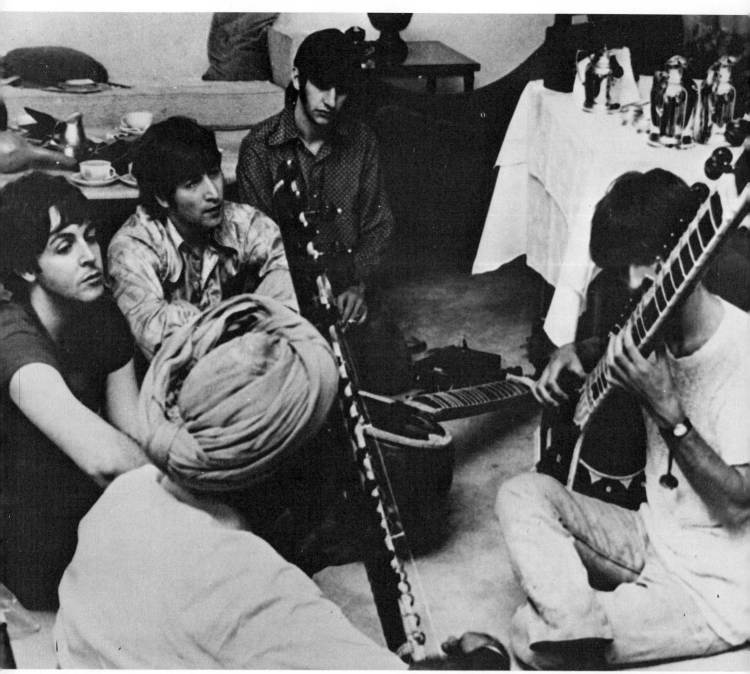

Sitar lesson for George (UPI)

LISTEN TO THE COLOR OF YOUR DREAMS

Psycho-politicians are using the Beatle music . . . to hypnotize American youth and prepare them for future submission to subversive control . . . a systematic plan geared to making a generation of American youth mentally ill and emotionally unstable.
—from *Communism, Hypnotism, and the Beatles,*
by Rev. David A. Noebel

The Beatles are a plot by the . . . ruling classes to distract . . . youngsters from politics and bitter pondering over disgraced and shattered hopes.
—from *Pravda*

In retrospect it can be seen that certain snatches of *Rubber Soul,* such as the sitar riffs on "Norwegian Wood," pointed toward directions previously uncharted in pop music; but in general that album represented a more mature and sophisticated version of the familiar trademark Beatles sound, softened and mellowed somewhat by the folky winds that had been blowin' throughout 1965. Lyrically, *Rubber Soul's* selections were, with some noteworthy exceptions, still fairly facile "love songs"; musically, the two-guitars-bass-and-drums lineup remained predominant. The songs were probably more accomplished than anything a teen-oriented pop group had heretofore achieved, but they could hardly be said to have pushed back the frontiers of popular music.

So most Beatle people were caught quite unawares by the strange new terrain their heroes would explore in 1966, a year when the Beatles really did begin to tear away so many of the conventions into which the pop song had been straight-jacketed, to inaugurate what has been called their "psychedelic" period. That adjective implies not only the influence of certain mind-altering chemicals, but also the freewheeling spectrum of wide-ranging colors that their new music seemed to evoke. 1966 certainly marked the end of, as one irate *Beatles Monthly* correspondent put it, "The Beatles we used to know before they went stark, raving mad."

In little over two years, the Beatles had created for themselves the most phenomenal success story in show-biz history. The list of records broken and precedents set by the Beatles in 1964 and 1965 could go on for pages. In the U.S. alone, they netted 19 gold discs (each marking sales of over a million), and 18 Number Ones, in two years. They became the only artists ever to sell a million copies of one album *(With the Beatles)* in Britain, which means that about two per cent of that country's entire population saw fit to go out and buy the record. Before the Beatles arrived on the scene, it would have seemed unimaginable that a single rock combo could ever occupy simultaneously the top five positions in the U.S. Hit Parade, or lure 55,000 paying fans to a performance at Shea Stadium. The Beatles accomplished all this by creating an original brand of light entertainment that succeeded in making millions of people happy.

They could very easily have left it at that, and, eventually, most of us might have outgrown Beatlemania, letting it fade into a pleasant memory of early adolescence—a wacky fad that may have left as its legacy little more than an abundance of male hair, and, perhaps, a few tunes of lasting merit. But it was one of the miracles of growing up in the 1960's that the same four fellows who had instigated Beatlemania were not only willing and able to evolve and mature, but also happened to possess latent genius as composers and lyricists of real imagination, originality, versatility, and sophistication. In 1966, the Beatles' genius began to flower to an extent that surprised even their most optimistic admirers.

Adolescence is a time of rapid transition. The flighty fads and phases that might so engross a thirteen- or fourteen-year-old are generally discarded in favor of more sophisticated interests as he or she approaches the later teens. But Beatlemaniacs did not have to look very far to find someone to replace the happy, cuddly moptops and bouncy, mindless music that had helped get them through 1964 and 1965, for the Beatles were changing along with them. Said Paul: "We're so well established that we can bring our fans with us and stretch the limits of pop." As they did so, the Beatles fashioned a popular art form which was thought-provoking as well as entertaining, and which managed to mirror so many of its listeners' unarticulated feelings.

Perhaps this can help explain the remarkable awe with which the Beatles came to be viewed by millions of kids throughout the second half of the decade. Of course there were some fans—like the girl who complained to the *Beatles Monthly*—who might have preferred it had the Beatles remained the same cheery entertainers Americans had first glimpsed on the Ed Sullivan Show in February 1964. But to the vast majority there was something uncanny, almost magical, about the Beatles' startling evolution. John, Paul, George, and Ringo seemed to have an unerring knack for staying one jump ahead of their fans, so we made them our leaders and spokesmen, fondly imagining they had all the answers.

In the music the boys recorded in the spring of 1966, they rarely sacrificed that basic Beatles ingredient of a catchy tune of between two and four minutes' length. By seducing

George, John, Ringo, and Paul shortly before a lengthly retirement from public performances (*16* Magazine)

E.P., France, 1966 (Odeon)

listeners with an accessible melody, they were all the more able to slip in the innovations without losing too many fans along the way.

The two drastic changes were in lyrical content and musical arrangement. Formula "love songs" were abandoned almost overnight; of the forty-six numbers they would write and record in the next two years or so, only 10 could be remotely construed as dealing with love affairs, and then always either ironically or with genuine lyricism. Suddenly their writing began to touch on a wide range of subjects, many of them bizarre or downright fantastic. To get their new visions across, the Beatles began to make use of unlikely resources: a jazz quintet here, a French horn there, sound effects, and a great deal of advanced studio manipulation.

This juncture in the Beatles' recording career is comparable to the part of the movie *The Wizard of Oz,* where, when Dorothy discovers herself transported from Kansas to Oz, the film dramatically changes from black-and-white to glorious technicolor.

The Beatles were, of course, fortunate to have the cash to experiment at an increasingly leisurely pace—usually

between 10 at night and seven in the morning—in Britain's finest recording studios, sometimes using whole symphony orchestras as their guinea pigs—and to have the clout to assure automatic commercial interest in their costly enterprises. Most of all, they were lucky to have a brilliant and sympathetic technician like George Martin in the producer's box.

On June 10, 1966, we were treated to a sampler of the Beatles' new sounds, in the form of a single of Paul's "Paperback Writer" and John's "Rain."

The A side concerned a struggling hack writer trying to peddle his wares ("Dear Sir or Madam will you read my book/It took me years to write, will you take a look?"). Paul no doubt drew upon his experience of a few years before, when it had been his responsibility to compose beguiling hype to mail out on behalf of the then-struggling Beatles.

Musically, the hooks of "Paperback Writer" included a riff of authoritative chords in the style of The Who's "Substitute" ("Dylan . . . and The Who," Paul had announced not long before, "are [our] two great influences") and intricate four-part harmonies that vanish in a haze of reverberation at the climax of each verse.

The hypnotic "Rain" was the first articulation of a philosophy John and George were to expound repeatedly in their work over the next few years: that the outward manifestations of the material world are all nothing more than a "wall of illusion":

If the rain comes
they run and hide their heads,
they might as well be dead.

When the sun shines,
they slip into the shade,
and sip their lemonade.

But it's all "just a state of mind," John assures us, so

Rain! I don't mind.
Shine! The weather's fine.

George managed a quasi-Eastern sound on his heavily distorted guitar, and Ringo's inventive drumming gave the lie to insinuations that he was an incompetent dolt only along for the ride. Yet another innovation surfaces toward the end of the song. John derived those eery-sounding nonsense syllables, such as "nair," from feeding a reprise of his vocal track over the instrumental coda—backward. "I got home about five in the morning, stoned out of me head," John later told *Rolling Stone*'s Jonathan Cott. "I staggered up to me tape recorder and put it ['Rain'] on, and I was in a trance in the earphones, what *is* it, what *is* it. Too *much,* you know, and I really wanted the whole song backwards . . . so we tagged it onto the end. I just happened to have the tape the wrong way round."

1966 was also the last year of live Beatles performances. That summer they launched on a two-part world tour that proved to be both their most lucrative and their most controversial.

It began calmly enough on June 23 in Germany, where three dates included a triumphant return to Hamburg. Four days later the Beatles flew to Tokyo for three concerts at the Budo Kan judo arena, at which the presence of 3,000 policemen insured good behavior on the part of 9,000 fans in the audience. One of these concerts was filmed in color for Japanese television; the result is the finest, and rarest, of the Beatles' concert films.

The Philippines were next on the agenda; there the Beatles got their first taste of mass hostility. Coping with hysterical mobs was, of course, almost part of their daily routine, but until now it had always been adulation that made people want to tear them apart. In Manila, however, the afternoon after a successful pair of concerts at the Aranita Coliseum, they were shown to the airport by kicking, screaming hordes who were literally after their blood.

Apparently, Mrs. Marcos, the wife of the President, had invited and expected the Beatles for lunch. When the Beatles didn't show up, they gave thousands of Filipinos an opportunity to vent their nationalistic ire at what was considered an unpardonable slight to their First Lady. The boys claimed they never even received an invitation, and escaped to New Delhi with minor injuries.

There George indulged his growing infatuation with Indian sounds by snapping up practically a museumful of Hindustani instruments at the esteemed Rikhi Ram & Sons music emporium. Press photographers, present in droves despite the supposed secrecy of the Indian stopover (which was arranged at Harrison's request), popped flashbulbs as John and Paul each selected a sitar while the Rams provided music lessons and tea.

Meanwhile, on the other side of the Pacific, controversy was brewing over an L.P. cover. We have noted the insatia-ble appetite of the boys' U.S. record company; as *Rubber Soul* had tumbled back down the charts after five weeks at Number One and two million copies sold, and as Capitol was sitting on the songs it had excised from the record's British edition, as well as a string of uncollected singles, all signs seemed in ideal conjunction for the release of a new Beatles album.

Accordingly, the title *Yesterday and Today* was hastily dreamed up ("Yesterday" being a highlight of the new collection), and tapes of three brand new tunes were flown in from Britain to fill out the program. Now the only remaining prerequisite for a certain smash was an album jacket in which to ship the new disc out to a million waiting fans.

But *Yesterday and Today* proved to be the first and only Beatles L.P. to actually *lose* money for Capitol, despite the fact that it topped the charts for most of the summer. It was all on account of its original cover, which has since become the most legendary and sought after of all Beatles memorabilia. Capitol may have expected another shot of four happy, docile cherubs such as the boys had furnished for previous amputations like *Beatles VI,* but this time the Fab Four were serving up an entirely different dish: slabs of raw, red meat and decapitated baby dolls, which they clutched with a sadistic leer on their faces before a sickly scarlet backdrop. All this seven years before Alice Cooper and *Billion Dollar Babies,* back in an era when just about the only arty or offbeat record jacket around was the Beatles' own *Rubber Soul.*

It seems surprising that Robert Whitaker's gory photograph passed the image-conscious Brian Epstein's scrutiny, but by this time the Beatles were making most of their own decisions. Also, according to Epstein's assistant Geoffrey Ellis, *Yesterday and Today* "was not considered a major release," so wasn't given that much thought, and the Beatles themselves were "very keen" on the butcher picture. It also appeared in all the British music papers in full-page ads for "Paperback Writer." An equally gory full-color "out-take" from the butcher sessions adorned the cover of the June 11, 1966 issue of *Disc,* occasioning one crusty columnist to rail against the importation of American "sick humor" into the United Kingdom.

But back in the sickly humorous U.S.A. many influential citizens also found the taste of the Beatles' meat unappetizing. As soon as the original *Yesterday and Today* jackets made it safely from the printers and into the hot hands of America's disk jockeys, reactions of aghast disbelief began to flood Capitol's offices. High-level meetings were called, trans-Atlantic phone-calls lodged, and it was decided that the butchers had to go.

Although the Beatles themselves stuck to their hatchets (John retorted that their cover was "as relevant as Vietnam," and Paul, who had dubbed it "very tasty meat," called its detractors "soft"), Capitol issued an apology for the ill-starred "attempt at pop-art satire." Streamers and other printed promotional material had to be junked, and Capitol employees were detained over the weekend and kept busy extricating 750,000 records from their "butcher covers," destroying the latter at a cost of over $200,000. Some of the workers, however, were apparently a bit lazy and saved themselves trouble by merely pasting the new L.P. jacket over the old.

So an indeterminate number of the originals actually did make it to the shops in disguise. Many fans who unsuspectingly purchased these copies weren't, and maybe still aren't, aware that under that bland picture of the Beatles posed around a trunk, which replaced the original, lurks hidden treasure. For the "butcher cover" has since become a status

Japanese souvenir program

A second scrapped *Yesterday and Today,* jacket, slightly more reminiscent of the one actually released

The Beatles with Brian Epstein (Keystone Press Agency)

symbol for Beatles collectors, an indispensable cornerstone to any serious collection of memorabilia, and its value has risen dramatically over the ensuing decade. At Philadelphia's 1976 Beatlefest, a copy was auctioned off for $301.

Since *Yesterday and Today,* banned rock L.P. covers have become a staple of the business, often bestowing some welcome publicity on unknown or flagging artists. Eric Clapton's Blind Faith, Mom's Apple Pie, and Roxy Music all became embroiled in controversies about tabu parts of young ladies' anatomies; Golden Earring got themselves in trouble with a naked boy. The Rolling Stones' record company refused to ship *Beggars Banquet* in a jacket depicting a toilet and some unsavory graffiti. And, of course, there would be John and Yoko Lennon's *Two Virgins.* As usual, however, the Beatles were the first.

(The only precedent of sorts had occurred in early 1965 when someone noticed some unorthodox advice in Andrew Loog Oldham's longwinded and unreadable *Clockwork Orange*-inspired notes for *Rolling Stones, Now!,* where fans were instructed to knock blind beggars on the head, steal

their money, and spend it on Stones records. The offending passage was hastily obscured with a sticker, and eliminated altogether on subsequently printed copies.)

Buried Treasure

Rich Friedland, editor of an excellent Beatles fanzine called *The Inner Light,* offers the following advice on how to tell whether your copy of *Yesterday and Today* conceals a "butcher cover"—and if so, how to go about extricating it. You may find this even more entertaining—and profitable—than scraping instant lottery tickets.

"Look at the [trunk] cover very closely, at the white parts around the Beatles. If you see a picture underneath, you've got one! A good place to look for the photo to see where it stands out the most is 3½ inches under the 'y' in 'Today.' On the original, you'll notice Ringo's collar from his coat really stands out.

"If you've got the 'butcher cover,' there are two ways to get the top picture off without ruining the bottom one. One way is to steam it off, but that way usually does a bit of tearing to the photo underneath. The other way, which is much more

56

time consuming, is to peel it off with tape. By taking ordinary Scotch tape and sticking it on the top picture so that it completely covers it, and peeling it all off again, you can get a lot of the top picture off. It will come off in layers so you might have to do this two, three, or even four times before you can get right down to the picture underneath.

"Caution: don't go down too far! As soon as you notice there is just a very thin layer of paper between you and the "butcher cover," STOP! Get a pencil eraser and slowly peel more of the remaining picture away. After you've done this, rub away the rest of the pieces with 100-proof gin. If there's any gin left over when you're finished, you can drink it, *but not before you're done.*"

If you don't follow Rich's advice you may destroy your "butcher cover"—as I did with soap and water back in '66, little supposing I was ruining a collectors' item that within 10 years could have been worth up to $301.

But by the time the Beatles touched down in Chicago, the butcher smocks were virtually forgotten in the wake of the new controversy that greeted them. Poor Brian Epstein—he had gotten the Beatles to shed their black leather and clean up their act, but nothing would ever keep John Lennon from shooting his mouth off in the presence of reporters. And, as John later complained, when you're famous you can be held accountable for the sort of off-the-cuff remarks ordinary mortals get to tell their buddies over a pint of lager.

By mid 1966 the Beatles had managed to air quite a few flamboyant opinions in the press (sample: "Show business belongs to the Jews, it's a part of the Jewish religion"). Reporters always in search of a good story egged them on. In mid 1965, *Playboy* ran a lengthy interview with the Beatles, plying them with queries about their religious beliefs and the "homosexual problem" in England. They came out for agnosticism, and George informed *Playboy*'s readers that the U.S. was full of homosexuals, only "they've got crewcuts in America. You can't spot 'em."

But nothing caused quite the flap of these observations of John's: "Christianity will go. It will vanish and shrink. I needn't argue about that, I'm right and will be proved right. We're more popular than Jesus Christ now. I don't know which will go first, rock 'n' roll or Christianity. Jesus was all right, but his disciples were thick and ordinary. It's them twisting it that ruins it for me."

Actually these comments were made back in February for the *London Evening Standard,* whose readers evidently shrugged them off as just another Lennonism. But when *Datebook,* an American teen-age magazine, chose to reprint them just prior to the boys' visit, Lennon's five-month-old comments became a hot news flash, and God-fearing disk jockeys, church leaders, and right-wing politicians across the old Confederacy decided the time had come to stamp the Beatles out for good.

Throughout the first two weeks of August, papers carried lurid reports that read like scenes from Ray Bradbury's *Fahrenheit 451,* of rallies around bonfires into which were dumped large quantities of Beatle records and memorabilia, and sometimes even effigies of the Fab Four. Birmingham's WAQY hired a giant tree-grinding machine with which to pulverize its listeners' Beatles albums to dust. Another station donated garbage cans that bore the legend "place Beatle trash here." Although one anti-Beatle station—KLUE of Longview, Texas—was struck by lightning and knocked off the air for the night, its disk jockeys refused to take that as a

A Beatle bonfire in Ft. Oglethorpe, Georgia (Wide World Photos)

SID BERNSTEIN
PRESENTS THE

BEATLES

IN PERSON

PLUS ALL STAR SHOW
SHEA STADIUM
TUES. 7:30 P.M. AUG. 23

ALL SEATS RESERVED: $4.50, 5.00, 5.75 phone 265-2280 FOR INFORMATION
TICKETS NOW AT
SINGER SHOP, RECORD DEP'T. Rockefeller Center Promenade, 49th-50th Sts. on Fifth Ave.

Sid Bernstein declined an offer of $400 for his last copy of this poster

message from heaven and resumed the crusade the following morning.

A flu-smitten Epstein rose from his sickbed and jetted to the States nearly two weeks before his clients were due, in order to "clarify" Lennon's statement. John, Brian insisted, was only expressing his "deep concern" at the decline of interest in religion.

Nonetheless, the fever rapidly spread from the Bible Belt to the Midwest, and even to Spain and that citadel of Christian morality South Africa, where the Beatles were banned from the airwaves for the next five years (when the group split in 1970, local fans could once again be serenaded by the voices of Paul, George, and Ringo—but not John). The Vatican mouthpiece L'Osservatore Romano warned that "some subjects must not be dealt with profanely, not even in the world of beatniks." Even the stock market was affected: the value of a share in the Beatles' Northern Songs slumped from $1.64 to $1.26 in a week.

Some stations, however, came to the Beatles' defense and played more of their music than before, in one case to "show contempt for hypocrisy." Back in London, Melody Maker ran a rare editorial to say that "much of the fantastically unreasoned reaction to Lennon merely adds

weight to his statement that some of Jesus' followers are 'a bit thick.'" For most fans, the attacks on John merely served to strengthen their loyalty, and record sales weren't harmed any: the butcherless Yesterday and Today clung to Billboard's Number One slot throughout August.

Actually, John's comments, which seemed so off-the-wall in 1966, soon proved to be almost prophetic. The seriousness with which fans took the Beatles was about to increase dramatically, at a time when traditional religious, moral, and patriotic values were being discarded wholesale. For young people left with little to believe in, infatuation with rock stars in the late '60's—especially Dylan and the Beatles—often assumed the characteristics of a mystical cult. Little over two years after the John-Jesus flap, Timothy Leary would tell his thousands of followers the Beatles were nothing less than "Divine Messiahs," and Charlie Manson's singularly warped interpretation of the gospel according to the "four angels" would lead to the most bizarre and gruesome murder case of the Sixties.

When the Beatles themselves arrived in Chicago on August 12, a rather pale and nervous Lennon found a great many microphones and T.V. cameras aimed in his direction, and did his best to apologize without selling himself out: "I suppose if I had said television was more popular than Jesus, I would have gotten away with it. I'm sorry I opened my mouth. I'm not anti-God, anti-Christ, or anti-religion. I was not knocking it. I was not saying we are greater or better."

In the Vatican, the Osservatore editorially accepted Lennon's apology. An editorial in the staid New York Times declared the case closed, adding that "the wonder is that such an articulate young man could have expressed himself imprecisely in the first place."

Despite a unanimous vote of the Memphis city council requesting the Beatles to stay away, and a demonstration by the Ku Klux Klan when the Beatles played there anyway, the tour proceeded on schedule and without mishap. The Beatles even courted further controversy at their New York City press conference when they all defied their manager's instructions and denounced the Vietnam war as "wrong"— an opinion not shared by 90 per cent of the American population at the time.

Later that afternoon midtown traffic was tied up by the spectacle of two somewhat over-zealous Beatlemaniacs poised precariously on a 22nd-story ledge. Their plan was to hurl themselves into Sixth Avenue if the Beatles wouldn't pay them a visit. Police managed to rescue the young ladies and commit them to a hospital.

Meanwhile, outside the Beatles' digs at the Warwick Hotel, Christian demonstrators jostled with screaming fans; both sides were liberally armed with placards, Beatles 4-Ever vs. Stamp Out the Beatles. Aloof from the holy war, a young man stood on the street corner, solemnly holding up a sign that read "John Is A Lesbian."

At the Beatles' return to Shea Stadium that night there were, unlike the year before, a few vacant rows in the back rafters. Still, the Beatles had managed to sell nearly 50,000 tickets to one performance, a feat nobody else at the time could have come near to duplicating.

The screaming had also abated somewhat—one could occasionally even hear snatches of music, mostly dating back to the Beatles for Sale/Help era. To the Beatles, playing such concerts had become a charade so remote from the new directions they were pursuing that not a single tune was attempted from the just-released Revolver L.P., whose arrangements were for the most part impossible to reproduce with the limitations imposed by their two-guitars-

A poster advertising the last Beatles' concert

bass-and-drums stage lineup anyway.

Hopping from one acoustically disastrous coliseum to the next, the Beatles performed like robots, cranking out a half-hour program of old hits pretty much by rote. Only the ever-professional McCartney, who sang lead for the bulk of the show, seemed to put much heart in the proceedings, belting away "She's A Woman" and "I'm Down" with considerable gusto. But on other songs, as recently surfaced bootleg recordings attest, they didn't even bother to get their own lyrics straight.

However, most Beatlemaniacs still had a screaming good time, which was documented by an enterprising independent label called Audio Journal in a hard-to-find L.P. entitled *Beatles Blast at Stadium Described by Erupting Fans.* This album, which consists of fan reaction recorded before, during, and after the 1966 Shea concert, is a unique souvenir of Beatlemania.

"I'm gonna die," sobs one young lady as she finds her seat. "You're so stupid, Magdalen, so dumb," says her friend.

The first sounds from on-stage—"1, 2, 3, 4, this is an audio test"—are followed by a cascade of screams.

As the Beatles hit the stage to total pandemonium, a girl shrieks at the interviewer: "how can you just sit there when they're in our atmosphere?"

Others eagerly explain the Beatles' appeal: "They have everything—talent and good looks and the English accents everybody looks for." "The Beatles are the greatest guys that ever existed." "I'm a schoolteacher so I came and brought my students . . . they're good showmen, they're honest."

A Londoner studying business at Harvard is there because "these people are one of the greatest exports Britain's had in many, many years."

Those who didn't have to pay to get in are less enthusiastic. A black janitor notices the Beatles' debt to black

music, but "the way they play . . . doesn't make sense to me." A cop says "dey stink. Dey da woist."

After the show, one fan defends John: "more people pay more attention to their social life than God. You pay more attention coming here than going to church." A girl ejected from the stadium for rushing the stage explains what she would have done had she made it to the Beatles: "I'd get ahold of their hair and pull it out."

"What would you do that for? You'd hurt 'em," intervenes another fan.

"Tough. I like 'em."

On August 29, 1966, San Francisco's Candlestick Park was the site of the last concert the Beatles would ever play. For them, at least, the screaming was over.

The frenzied crowds, the one-night stands, the siege-like accommodations, the farcical acoustics of the sports arenas, the audiences deafened by their own hysteria . . . the Beatles had had it with the lot. One of them told *Beatles Monthly* publisher Sean O'Mahoney that the pressures of such an existence were making them age twice as fast as ordinary mortals.

Says Ringo on *The Beatles Tapes* (released on British Polydor in 1976): "It was the worst time and the best time of my life. The best time because we played a lot of good music and had a lot of good times. The worst time . . . where it was like 24 hours a day, without a break: press, people fighting to get into your hotel room, climbing 25 stories up drainpipes. And it never stopped. . . . If it had carried on, I personally would have gone insane."

In addition, they felt quite fed up with their original musical style. John told *Music Maker:* "I can't stand listening to most of our early stuff . . . songs like 'Eight Days A Week' and 'She Loves You' sound like big drags to me now. I turn the radio off if they're ever on."

Summer 1966:
Songs Performed on the Beatles' World Tour

Rock and Roll Music (John, lead vocal)
She's A Woman (Paul)
If I Needed Someone (George)
Baby's In Black (John and Paul)
Day Tripper (John and Paul)
I Feel Fine (John)
Yesterday (Paul)
I Wanna Be Your Man (Ringo)
Nowhere Man (John)
Paperback Writer (Paul)
I'm Down (Paul)

A ticket to the last Beatle concert

There were now three prolific songwriting Beatles—from left: George, John, and Paul (*16* Magazine)

As the Beatles trotted from one continent to the next, going through the motions of performing a style of music they had decided to discard, they spoke excitedly at every opportunity of the music they really cared about—the songs that were about to be unveiled as *Revolver*. Gushed Paul: "They are sounds that nobody else had done yet—I mean nobody . . . ever."

The Beatles were equally enthusiastic about their new lyrics. Paul waxed a bit more sardonic in explaining the sudden preoccupation with words: "My Auntie Lil said to me: why do you always write songs about love? Can't you ever write about a horse or a summit conference or something interesting? So I thought, all right Auntie Lil." The two *Revolver* tracks chosen to precede the L.P. as a single release presumably met Auntie Lil's requirements for interesting

subject matter. One was about a yellow submarine and the other described the lonely life and death of a spinster named Eleanor Rigby.

There is a recurring music-business phenomenon known as the novelty hit. Every so often an absurd, gimmicky record without the slightest connection to prevailing musical fashion catches the fancy of the masses in a big way. A chorus of dogs barking "Jingle Bells," an ensemble of bagpipes playing "Amazing Grace," one gentleman babbling about nice men in white coming to take him away, ho ho hee hee, to the funny farm, backed by the steady clip of a single

"Taxman" hinted that George hadn't shed his fascination with money (*16* Magazine)

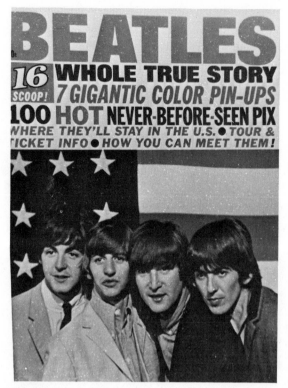

(Courtesy, *16* Magazine)

arranged by Paul and George Martin. The only other thing "Rigby" had in common with "Submarine" was that it sounded nothing like a Beatles record. Whereas "Yellow Submarine" was the most flippant and outrageous piece the Beatles would ever produce, "Eleanor Rigby" remains the most relentlessly tragic song the group attempted. Its chorus bemoans "all the lonely people"; in the verses Paul focuses on two of them: Eleanor Rigby, waiting hopelessly by her window, and Father McKenzie, writing "a sermon that no one will hear." Has he lost his congregation? Is this another comment on the waning influence of Christianity? Or on people's inability to communicate and listen, everyone locked into his or her own lonely existence? Such lines would keep sociologists, who were beginning to view the Beatles as "spokesmen for their generation," busy for years.

The song's two characters come together in the end:

*Eleanor Rigby died in a church
and was buried along with her name;
nobody came.
Father McKenzie, wiping the dirt
from his hands as he walks from the grave—
no one was saved.*

"Eleanor Rigby" has its trite lines, such as that last one, and some critics have charged that its pathos veers rather close to bathos. The song's lasting strength lies in its haunting ambiguities: is the face that Eleanor "keeps in a jar" her make-up? or pure surrealism? A year later Paul would compose a similar piece about a young runaway, with a far more literal lyric and a rather less successful impact.

Liverpudlian musician and author George Melly comments (in *Revolt Into Style*): "As James Joyce reconstructed the Dublin he had fled from, so the Beatles rebuilt the Liverpool of their own anonymous childhoods. I can vouch for the imaginative truth of 'Eleanor Rigby': the big soot-black sandstone Catholic churches with the trams rattling past, the redbrick terrace houses with lace curtains and holystone steps, the parchment-faced old spinsters who kept a canary, did a bit of dress-making, or had been 'in service'—all the lonely people." On their next single, the Beatles would add some more scenes to their *Liverpudlians*.

maddening drumbeat, another babbling pro-American sentiments to the soupy backdrop of a patriotic tune—all proved to be the stuff out of which gold records can be wrought. Like most novelty hits, all were perpetrated by unknowns who were never heard from again.

However, with "Yellow Submarine," the Beatles, the biggest stars in the world, created one of the biggest novelty hits ever. John and Paul coupled some incredibly disarming and idiotic lyrics about their improbable conveyance with an equally simple and ridiculous melody, and it proved to be the perfect vehicle for Ringo's goofy, toneless voice. A few chords strummed on an acoustic guitar and a few kicks aimed in the direction of a bass drum completed the Beatles' instrumental involvement in the piece.

The rest of the background was provided by sound effects, such as waves on "so we sailed unto the sun" (these were actually Ringo pushing rags around in a bucket of water) and clinking glasses on "and our friends are all aboard," and, for five seconds, a military brass band. Since George Harrison had no leads, his contribution to the song was to blow bubbles through a straw. Everyone in sight, including engineers and roadies, was hauled before microphones to bray along on the chorus.

George Martin, who had made his original splash in the record biz producing Peter Sellers' records, must have felt right at home in the yellow sub. The tune was one of the Beatles' first experiments with the musical collage, which they would repeat to weightier effect on *Sgt. Pepper* and in "I Am the Walrus." Whether you loved it or hated it, the "Yellow Submarine," once lodged in the brain, was impossible to get rid of. Everywhere you went in the latter half of 1966, you could hear people whistling it.

The Beatles may have gotten a laugh out of releasing a record on which their instrumental contribution was practically zilch. For the flip side, "Eleanor Rigby," none of them played a note. Their place was taken by a string octet

Single, Italy, 1966 (Parlophone)

L.P., Germany, 1966 (Odeon)

It is interesting in retrospect that, for all John's later political involvement, the songs most closely resembling social commentary in 1966 and 1967 ("Rigby," "Penny Lane," "She's Leaving Home") were mainly Paul's handiwork. John was far more interested in what was going on inside his head than in the world around him.

Whatever "Eleanor Rigby"'s defects, who would have guessed two years before that the Beatles could and would bestow so touching and poetic a tale on the AM airwaves? In any case, "Rigby," "Submarine," and the other songs on *Revolver* represented a remarkable break with their own past.

On most of the Beatles' earlier hits, George's lead guitar assumed a thin, tinny sound that fit snugly into the harmonics of John's jangling rhythm guitar; and Paul's bass and Ringo's drums provided an indistinct, pulsating bottom to the wall of noise. The vocals were often handled by two or three Beatles, singing in unison and recorded at equal volume. All the parts, then, were swallowed up by the whole to create a single monolithic din, and when you heard the records on the radio it was often impossible to make out clearly the separate voices and instruments.

By 1966 the Beatles had all developed as individuals, in their singing and musicianship as well as in their life styles. Each instrumentalist began to take on a meatier, more distinct recorded sound, and they started to play in more diverse styles. Furthermore, the guitars and drums were often submerged or altogether replaced on *Revolver* and subsequent recordings by the unusual array of instruments they began to incorporate into their palate; the strings on "Rigby," the blaring trumpets and saxes of five top British jazzmen on "Got to Get You Into My Life," the Indian instruments on "Love You To."

Another reason why the Beatles would henceforth lack a consistent collective "sound" or style is that the Lennon-McCartney songwriting partnership had pretty well dissolved. Although they would occasionally help each other out (John contributed to the lyrics of "Eleanor Rigby"), and although their songs would continue to be credited to "Lennon-McCartney" until the band broke up, John and Paul were beginning to pursue separate directions in both their words and their music; and they stopped singing together except to provide background harmonies to one another's lead vocals. Aside from "Yellow Submarine," "With A Little Help From My Friends," and "Goodnight," which they concocted for Ringo, you could from now on always tell who wrote a Lennon-McCartney song by which of the two sang it.

Revolver also offered ample indication that there were now three prolific songwriting Beatles. Three of the tracks were George Harrison compositions, the outstanding one being "Taxman," which opened the album.

Although George would soon develop an image as the Beatles' resident expert on all things Eastern, his rock 'n' rolling "Taxman" hinted that he hadn't yet shed his earlier yen for money. Since George had been the one Beatle to show a keen interest in the financial aspects of their career, he was well equipped to deliver a caustic attack on the Man who was taking away (he claimed) all but five per cent of his earnings, British taxes being what they were—and are. (The weather isn't the only reason why so many British rock stars currently reside in California.) In the middle of his harangue George graciously steps back to give Paul a chance to add his two cents on lead guitar.

Auntie Lil notwithstanding, most of Paul's contributions to *Revolver* (apart from "Eleanor Rigby") were good old-fashioned love songs. Two of them—"Here There And Everywhere" and "For No One"—further showcased McCartney's flair for ballads, and have since become standards, with poignant lyrics to do justice to exquisitely delicate melodies. Along with "Eleanor Rigby" they proved to be the overwhelming favorites in the *Beatles Monthly* "Revolver poll."

John Lennon's numbers were a different kettle of fish entirely. Unbeknownst to the subscribers of *16* and *Beatles Monthly,* John had whiled away many an evening over the past year under the influence of a mysterious, not yet illegalized wonder drug called L.S.D., which the other Beatles had also sampled in less immoderate doses. Lennon's 1966 compositions all bear the stamp of the "acid" experience, though it took a while for most of the rest of us to catch the references. At the time some people thought Lennon was spouting incomprehensible gibberish, and concluded that the poor lad had slid off the deep end. The real reason for this apparent crackup was kept a carefully guarded secret for another year or so.

Some of his songs from this period still seem oblique. "And Your Bird Can Sing," musically, is a rousing number almost in the old Beatles tradition, played on two electric guitars, bass, and drums, with a minimum of studio shenanigans. They could even have done it on tour that summer. But what was/is one to make of lines like "You say you've seen seven wonders/and your bird is green/but you don't see me. . . ."? Perhaps John was still under the influence of Bob Dylan, who at the time seemed to take pleasure in confounding dissectors of his "message" with cryptic lyrics that made no sense at all.

In "She Said She Said," the "she," it was later revealed, was actually Peter Fonda, who had joined the Beatles for an acid trip during which Fonda had kept mumbling "I know what it's like to be dead." John's response, for the record, anyway: "You're making me feel like I've never been born." To churning, distorted guitar music the song's protagonists continue their repartee, delivered in the sort of inscrutable riddles that become instantly recognizable as revelations once a little L.S.D. is added to the bloodstream.

"Doctor Robert," evidently, was the fellow who gave Lennon his new perspective on life. His prescriptions, John avows, can make you "a new and better man":

If you're down he'll pick you up,
take a drink from his special cup. . . .

Then the gritty rock beat dissolves into celestial organ music as the Beatles sing "Well, well, well, you're feeling fine."

For "I'm Only Sleeping," John's wonderful lethargic paean to the joys of staying in bed all day, George worked out guitar sections that were fed backwards into the mix to create a yawning, hypnotic effect.

This device and images of floating up and down streams reappear on "Tomorrow Never Knows," which was originally entitled "The Void" and which makes the rest of the album seem conventional in comparison. John said he wanted to have a thousand Tibetan monks chanting along on this number, but for once Mr. Martin couldn't fill the order. Instead, each Beatle worked at home inventing other-worldly sounds on their tape recorders. These were added at various speeds and in various directions (mostly backwards) onto a repetitious drumbeat and droning tanpuras (an Indian instrument introduced by Harrison), to create noises that evoked a stampeding herd of elephants gone mad.

Lording over this peculiar cacophony was the voice of John Lennon (sounding quite unlike the one that had just belted "Let me hear some rock 'n' roll music . . . if you wanna dance with me" to stadiums full of screaming girls) distorted as though it were blasting out of a distant foghorn, telling us to "turn off your mind," "lay down all thought," "surrender to the void," and "listen to the color of your dreams."

Fans who found it difficult to comply with these instructions probably hadn't read the works of Dr. Timothy Leary (hallucinogenic drugs, y'see, tend to juggle sense impressions, enabling the initiate to "hear" colors and "see" sounds). The credo Lennon had set forth in "The Word"

reappeared on "Tomorrow Never Knows." This time it went "love is all and love is everyone." Soon people would begin getting the hint.

"Tomorrow Never Knows" was a bold experiment. Depending on backward tapes is a chancy proposition, as when you record them there's no telling what they'll sound like in reverse. Two other novel things about this psychedelic temple chant are that it attempted to do without both rhymes and chords. Most of the lyrics were inspired by *The Psychedelic Experience,* Timothy Leary and Richard Alpert's lysergic reading of *The Tibetan Book of the Dead;* and far more than "Eleanor Rigby"'s they stumbled into the trap that often awaits unrelieved earnestness. But as experiments by definition bring uncertain results, one could forgive John some ludicrously ponderous words. Still, it ain't easy to "turn off your mind, relax, and float downstream" in the company of mad elephants.

Almost everyone was impressed by *Revolver,* with the exception of pop-star-turned-pundit Jonathan King, who thought a lot of it was "pseudo-intellectual rubbish," and a few conservative Beatlemaniacs who began to yearn for the uncomplicated days of "She Loves You." *Melody Maker,* whose reviewers had been out to lunch when *Rubber Soul* came out, hailed *Revolver* as "a brilliant album which underlines once and for all that the Beatles have definitely broken the bounds of what we used to call pop."

Many critics and connoisseurs still feel that, as a collection of diverse songs, *Revolver*—the unexpurgated British version—remains the Beatles' finest achievement. Subsequent albums such as *Sgt. Pepper* and *Abbey Road* may have been more powerful in their overall impact, but many of the selections on them are just fragments of a collage, and don't make it outside the context of the whole album. Nearly everything on *Revolver* could, and still does, stand on its own.

Unfortunately, however, the American release is marred by the omission of the three key Lennon tunes that were used to fill out *Yesterday and Today,* heavily weighting the U.S. *Revolver* in favor of McCartney's more conventional material. So American fans got a rather lopsided view of this important crossroads of the Beatles' career, although henceforth all their L.P.'s would make it across the Atlantic intact.

With their touring days behind them, and their masterpiece in the shops, the Beatles went their separate ways for a season, with each (except for Ringo) trying his hand at something new in a different far-flung corner of the globe.

John cut his hair off and became the first Beatle to appear without the others in a feature-length movie. He did reasonably well as Private Gripweed in Richard Lester's anti-war black comedy, *How I Won the War,* which was filmed in Spain. Shortly afterward, Lennon played a lavatory attendant in a Peter Cook and Dudley Moore T.V. show, "Not Only—But Also."

Paul lingered in London, composing a lush orchestral score (arranged by George Martin) for another film, the Boulton Brothers' *The Family Way.* The generally overlooked soundtrack L.P. might be considered the first Beatle solo release. In his spare time he read widely, checked out "classical" composers from Bach to Stockhausen, took music lessons, and began dabbling in film-making. Then he embarked on a Kenyan safari with Jane Asher, a well-heeled young actress with a promising career of her own (she appeared in the Michael Caine film *Alfie,* on numerous

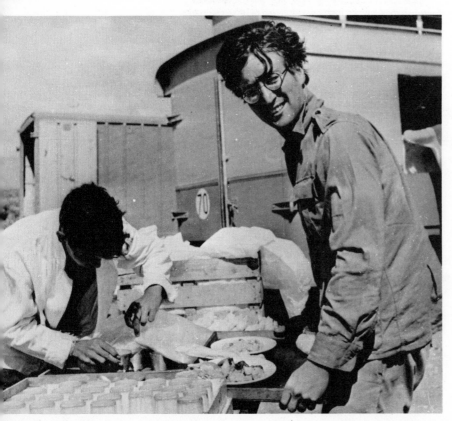

John Lennon in chow line for *How I Won the War* (UPI)

Rare American singles sleeves, 1964–65. For the complete set, see the section, "All Together Now."

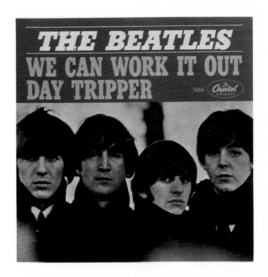

Two more American
singles sleeves,
1967 (left),
1969 (right)

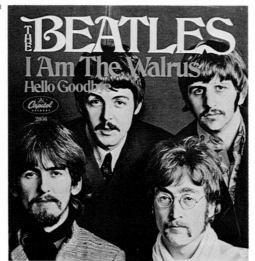

The banned L.P. jacket,
Yesterday and Today,
750,000 of which were
to have been destroyed,
but a few survived to
become collector's items

Film poster, (© 1968, King Features Syndicate Inc. 1968)

Yellow Submarine memorabilia:
Corgi Toy submarine, party coasters, lunchbox and candle,
(© 1968, King Features Syndicate Inc. 1968)

T.V. programs, and in plays ranging from *Pygmalion* to Shakespeare). Under her genteel influence Paul was developing into the most suave and sophisticated Beatle, becoming both a social butterfly and a culture-vulture. Paul got into the habit of checking out most of London's theatrical productions and art exhibits, usually with Jane. "I vaguely mind anyone knowing anything I don't know," he declared at the time. And he told the London *Evening Standard:* "I'm trying to cram everything in, all the things that I've missed. People are saying things and painting things and writing things and composing things that are great, and I must know . . ."

Jane's relationship with Paul became a staple of gossip columns, and she became accustomed to threats and abuse from jealous girls, who kept reading in trashy periodicals that Jane was about to become the fourth Mrs. Beatle, George Harrison having wedded *Hard Day's Night* starlet Patti Boyd earlier in 1966.

George went off to India, where, like thousands of young Westerners since, he evidently managed to "find himself." This was at a time when, back home in Britain, and to a lesser degree in the U.S., an unusual sound he had instigated was becoming a major element on the music scene. The trades, characteristically quick with their labels, called it "raga-rock." However, aside from the Indian instruments it exploited, most commonly the sitar, it actually owed far more to rock than to classical Indian music forms such as the raga.

John Lennon as a snappily dressed W.C. attendant in *Not Only . . . But Also* (Keystone Press Agency)

Paul McCartney with Jane Asher at the premiere of *"How I Won the War"* (UPI)

George was swiftly anointed the maharaja of raga-rock, a genre which he had launched with his sitar tinkerings on "Norwegian Wood." Throughout 1966, the youngest Beatle developed a fanatical obsession for Indian music, and soon other stars were catching his bug.

He became prone to making pronouncements such as the one that, if he could be granted one wish, it would be to spend an evening inside the gourd of Ravi Shankar's sitar when the Indian master musician was performing a concert. In much the same way as a Beatle endorsement had once spurred sales of jelly babies, now fans and fellow musicians started to investigate Indian music. To some of the latter, the strange scales and hypnotic drone seemed to suggest whole new possibilities for their compositions.

Suddenly the "quiet Beatle" began, for the first time, to inspire as much spicy copy as any of the others. Stories emerged of Beatle George sitting cross-legged upon the floor of an incense-filled room of his multi-colored bungalow in Esher for hours at a time, sitar balanced on the arch of his left foot as he practiced to tapes of Ravi Shankar's sitar lessons. On those rare occasions when George would receive reporters, his conversation was often laced with mysterious sounding words like *karma* and *sansara.* If the reporter was lucky enough, he might also hear Harrison expound on "people living on Venus in a different physical plane," or on the imminent arrival of the New Messiah: "Anyone who doesn't believe that He's the one, then He'll

just show 'em. He's just gonna come down and zap 'em all." Unusual stuff—back then.

Although to this day, George (like the other Beatles) remains ignorant of written Western music, he became conversant with Indian notation in order to transcribe his arrangements for such pieces as "Within You Without You" for his turbaned accompanists.

It is probably accurate to say that other artists were more successful in incorporating Indian sounds into Western pop—even that little Beatles music of note emerged from George's affair with the sitar. Its real contribution to the Beatles was that it gave George an identity. John, Paul, and Ringo had all projected strong public images from the beginning, but George was often deemed relatively bland and unexceptional. He earned a few accolades as the Beatles' most disciplined musician, yet always seemed considerably less creative than John and Paul, less striking than Ringo, and less witty or personable than any of them.

A fragile four-foot, 21-stringed instrument most people had never heard of before changed all that. In a few twangy strokes, George was transformed into as much of an individual as the others, and, more important to him, found new direction in his life and career. Indian music led him to an intense study of, and belief in, Indian religion, which gave him a new serenity and self-confidence—and which still permeates his lyrics and his life style even though he has evidently concluded that his karma does not include becoming a master of the sitar after all. (George continues, however, to top the "miscellaneous" category of music polls for his work on an instrument he hasn't played since around 1969.)

George first met Ravi Shankar in June 1966, and the sitarist accepted an invitation to visit his Beatle admirer in Esher. There George received his first formal sitar lessons, and Shankar returned a few days later with his tabla player, Alla Rakha, to give a private recital for the four Beatles and their friends. After the final tour, when the Beatles were all able to take their well-deserved sabbaticals from the group, George and Patti joined Shankar in Bombay in the hopes of undertaking an intensive study of Indian music. However, despite the fact that Harrison had cut off his famous hair and sprouted a moustache, his hotel was soon surrounded by local fans who had somehow got a premonition of the Beatle's visit. The non-stop screaming from the street made it impossible for George to study, so finally the entourage was obliged to flee to the relative tranquility of Kashmir.

It is unlikely that as prestigious and busy an artist as Shankar would have given so much time to just any 24-year-old Western novice, but Ravi (like the Maharishi a year later) was probably astute enough to understand how the publicity derived from his Beatle connection could further his lifelong crusade to turn the West on to the wonders of Indian music. He and George did seem to develop warm personal rapport, with Shankar playing the fatherly mentor figure to Harrison, who deferred to his "guru" (another word added to our vocabulary at this juncture) with unaccustomed humility.

However, Shankar's more traditionally-minded colleagues looked somewhat askance at Ravi's escapades with George and with his youthful new audiences. Even his brother-in-law, sarod virtuoso Ali Akbar Khan, cracked that Ravi was attempting to teach the Beatles sitar by telephone. Since both he and Ravi had spent many years of 12-hour-a-day training with Khan's father before they dared play their instruments in public, such skepticism was understandable.

Whatever Shankar's intentions, his link with Harrison certainly helped bring to his work success in Britain and the United States that was without precedent for so alien a style of music. His concerts, which had heretofore been intimate gatherings of Indian expatriates and ethnomusicologists, moved to large halls full of long-haired youths. He accepted invitations to play at all the famous large outdoor "rock festivals" of the late Sixties, beginning with the one at Monterey in the summer of 1967. An album of that performance actually made the hit parade.

However, many of Shankar's new fans failed to receive his art with the purity of mind and body he felt it demanded. Ravi was mortified to learn that his music was frequently thought one of a piece with Kama-Sutra-style sex and Himalayan hash, and he often interrupted his program to request that people stop necking and smoking.

Nonetheless, the sinuous sound of the sitar was usually used in rock to give a sensual, narcotic feel to the proceedings. "Norwegian Wood," however obliquely, had to do with sex and drugs. George's own sitar showcase on *Revolver*, "Love You To," advised the listener to "make love all day long/make love singing songs"—a difficult feat to pull off in any case.

Dozens of instruments enjoy a comparable prominence in India, yet the sitar probably appealed to guitarists like George, the Stones' Brian Jones, and Donovan, because of its relative similarity to the guitar: it has frets, and is played with a pick. But, like all Indian instruments, it is not designed to play chords, and the presence of resonant sympathetic strings, tuned to the scale of the piece being performed,

L.P., USA, 1967 (London)

gave the sitar a zingy sound that seemed wonderfully weird and mind-blowing to young Westerners in 1966. So did the fact that it is far easier to "bend" notes on the sitar than on an acoustic guitar (Indian music makes extensive use of quartertones); the widespread subsequent use of this technique by rock's electric guitarists, like Jimi Hendrix, not to mention George himself, probably owed a great deal to Indian music. As did the burgeoning fad for endless guitar improvisations, which usually lacked any of the disciplined structure of Indian ragas, and which the Beatles themselves had the sense never to succumb to.

By early 1967 the sitar itself had become an indispensable addition to the sound of many pop idols who were following the Beatles in attempting to become more poetic, eclectic, and even "cosmic." A naive belief that the mere welding of some rudimentary sitar licks to a song more often than not packed with muddled, fourth-hand scraps of "Hindu" philosophy can somehow add up to a work of spiritual profundity resulted in some of the most pretentious records ever made. The Animals' "Winds of Change" and "All Is One," the Hollies' "Maker," Chad and Jeremy's "Progress Suite," and a whole string of Moody Blues tunes must (one hopes) make their perpetrators wince today. Some unkindly souls would include Harrison's own compositions in the same category.

A growing disillusionment with their own society and culture made the sitar, and many other things Eastern, fascinating to pop stars and audiences at the time, but there were two distinct attitudes musicians might take toward their new toy. The sitar *could* be fortuitously used in rock arrangements when it was merely viewed as an attractive, exotic-sounding addition to an artist's palate, particularly if a song featured dreamlike, fantastic, or even "Eastern" imagery. "Norwegian Wood" was a successful example of this.

Most of the songs on Donovan's exquisite *Sunshine Superman* album, his finest achievement, feature a sitar, as do the Rolling Stones' nihilistic "Paint It Black" and such delightful fantasies as Traffic's "Paper Sun" and "Hole In My Shoe," and the Incredible String Band's "The Iron Stone." The "East" presented in many of these pieces is, of course, a fabrication, but that's legitimate. a venerable line of eccentric British authors from William Beckford to Ernest

Bramah made their reputations writing about an Orient they didn't even pretend to know anything about.

But in the late 1960's many young Westerners were searching for philosophical answers they felt could not be found at home, and demanded from the sitar something more spiritually uplifting than exotic dreamscapes. They read that Ravi Shankar comes from a tradition that views the sound of music as a means of attaining oneness with God, and George Harrison and his imitators seemed to imagine they could do just that. But in their rush to manufacture instant karma, they managed to overlook the fine print that specifies three lifetimes' worth of rigorous musical and spiritual discipline before such miracles might be achieved.

George's introduction of the sitar into rock was a wonderful stroke of imagination, but he became too caught up in his new discoveries to stop there. Not only would he solemnly try to regurgitate *The Bhagavad Gita* on three minutes' worth of vinyl, he also would abandon his intimate knowledge of pop music on such compositions, attempting to use only Indian instruments in his arrangements.

"Love You To" is sprawling and listless in just about every way, but the subsequent "Within You Without You" and "The Inner Light" feature haunting, exquisitely lovely melodies. Had Harrison not given the other Beatles the day off when he recorded them instead of hiring Indian sidemen, they might have wound up as two of his greatest achievements.

But the Beatles never comfortably assimilated the sitar into their work. When they weren't letting George indulge in quasi-Indian overkill in his lyrics and arrangements, Harrison would at most strum a couple of subservient notes on his sitar way in the background, as in "Lucy In the Sky With Diamonds." "Norwegian Wood," although it was the first, remains the best when it comes to Beatle raga-rock, even if George didn't know how to hold his sitar properly when the song was recorded.

Yet, whatever the shortcomings of Harrison's own contributions to the genre—and despite the fact that, unlike most ascetics, he had a million in the bank in case the karma turned sour—George seemed to personify an increasingly fashionable outlook on life and the most anonymous Beatle became the youth culture's number one mystic and sage (typically, one of those to whom Eric Burdon dedicated his insufferably cosmic *Winds of Change* was Harrison, "from whom I learn from being in the same room"). If John gave to the Beatles' music a restless mind, and Paul the tender heart, George now contributed some holy spirit.

He could thank his lucky sitar for all that, and many of the rest of us can thank him for leading us toward the real thing: the shimmering, effervescent beauties of real Indian music.

It was not until December 1966 that the Beatles regrouped in a London studio to devise a follow-up to *Revolver.* Despite assurances to the contrary, their usual Christmas present to the world did not materialize, and in Britain E.M.I. tried to fill the gap with *A Collection Of Beatles Oldies* (strangely, there was no American counterpart).

Fans were obliged to wait an unprecedented six months for new Beatle product; finally, in February 1967, a single appeared: "Penny Lane" and "Strawberry Fields Forever." This was a "double A side" if ever there was one. Each of the pair has often been cited as one of the Beatles' greatest accomplishments, and certainly no single ever excelled it in presenting, back to back, the most fully realized talents of Paul McCartney and John Lennon. Although it was a remarkably innovative and ambitious single, the lyrics on both sides reflected a nostalgic yearning for the Liverpool of their childhood, which was underscored by the appearance of Beatle baby pictures on the record jacket.

L.P., Germany, 1967 (Odeon) Depicting a scene from the *Strawberry Fields* film

E.P., France, 1967 (Odeon)

"Penny Lane," named after a bustling Liverpool street, may have been inspired by "Fern Hill," a poem by Dylan Thomas, whom Paul revealed he had been reading. In "Fern Hill" Thomas reminisces nostalgically about his youth in the Welsh countryside, where he had been "happy as the grass was green."

With "Penny Lane," Paul created a similar situation. Sitting "beneath the blue suburban skies" of his present life, the singer recalls that rainy spot where, it seems, he had once been happy as the skies were gray. Penny Lane is portrayed as an idyllic, friendly place where "all the people that come and go stop and say hello," among them a barber who shows "photographs of every head he's had the pleasure to know," a banker who "never wears a mac in the pouring rain," and a fireman who treasures a "portrait of the Queen" in his pocket.

"Penny Lane"'s lyrics succeeded in blending wry wit and nostalgic pathos with the Beatles' growing penchant for the surreal. They featured a few bawdy touches as well: Paul later confessed that he had more than fire engines in mind when he sang of that patriotic fireman keeping his "machine" clean; and "fish and finger pie" turns out to be Liverpudlian for a delicacy not to be found on the menu of any fish-and-chips joint.

The music also managed to be at once lilting and good-timey, and that recurring chorus "Penny Lane is in my ears and in my eyes" provided the unforgettable hook that enabled "Penny Lane" to hitch itself so quickly to the top of the hit parade. The song was enhanced by some highly melodic trumpet obbligatos, which McCartney hummed to George Martin, who transcribed them on paper for the benefit of the hired trumpeteers. (Collectors' note: some disk jockey copies of the single feature a trumpet coda that was lopped off the commercially-released version, and which makes said copies worth a great deal to hard-core completists. One crank recently placed an ad offering one for $150.)

"Strawberry Fields Forever" provides a choice example of the role Lady Luck could play in the Beatles' creations. They reportedly had recorded two renditions, in differing keys and tempos, but neither quite seemed to make the grade. Then George Martin chanced upon the discovery that the tape of the faster version could be slowed down to correspond exactly to the tempo *and* key of the other. As if by magic, the puzzle fell together, and the two tapes were combined in the final mix.

Martin and the Beatles seemed to have learned a few lessons from the experimentation on "Tomorrow Never Knows," and in "Strawberry Fields," they created a far more successful montage with studio technology and unconventional arrangements. The vocal track was culled from the slowed-down tape, and the hesitant, eery lethargy this gave John's delivery proved an ideal match for the dazed, stream-of-consciousness lyrics. Mellotrons and cellos evoked swirling, languid textures to be abruptly dispelled by feverish horns.

"Strawberry Fields" also introduced what would become a favorite device—the trick ending—to the Beatles' repertoire. The "surprise" coda is preceded by several seconds of nothing, occasioning perhaps the first time silence was aired on the Top Forty radio stations' non-stop barrage of music, patter, and commercials.

"Strawberry Fields" came to earn a reputation for being a drug anthem, and it is probable that, as with most of Lennon's writing from this period, it was largely inspired by L.S.D. However, the title was derived from a grim Liverpool orphanage called Strawberry Fields, and the song is no starry-eyed Utopian vision either. The trip Lennon takes us on is a lonely, frightened, and confused one. Even after John publicly abdicated his role as "the dreamweaver," he called "Strawberry Fields" one of his two or three best and most honest Beatle songs.

In his lyrics, which make almost no use of rhymes, John seems to be trying now desperately to make sense out of his confusion, but can only contradict himself at every turn:

No one I think is in my tree,
I mean it must be high or low,
that is you can't, you know, tune in,
but, it's all right.
That is, I think it's not too bad.

The only way out of this maze, apparently, is the hazy oblivion of Strawberry Fields, where "nothing is real . . . nothing to get hung about."

"Strawberry Fields Forever" provided quite a contrast to the tidy imagery of "Penny Lane." John's song, on the surface, makes little sense, but that itself seems to be the point of the lyrics—that life often yields no sense either.

The Beatles returned to Liverpool in January to make a short film with which to promote the songs on T.V., as they obviously weren't going to attempt to perform them live. The film showed the Beatles, to the sound of their new songs, ambling down Penny Lane and trotting through strawberry fields on horseback. Some fans were startled to note that their idols had sprouted moustaches since the last time they had seen them.

E.P., Japan, 1967 (Odeon)

The Beatles' Hits—March 1966 through May 1967

TITLE AND LABEL	FIRST APPEARANCE	HIGHEST POSITION	WEEKS ON CHART
U.S. Top 100 Singles			
Nowhere Man (Capitol)*	March 5, 1966	3	9
What Goes On (Capitol)	March 12, 1966	81	2
Paperback Writer (Capitol)*	June 11, 1966	1	10
Rain (Capitol)	June 11, 1966	23	7
Yellow Submarine (Capitol)*	Aug. 20, 1966	2	9
Eleanor Rigby (Capitol)	Aug. 27, 1966	11	8
Strawberry Fields Forever (Capitol)	Feb. 25, 1967	8	9
Penny Lane (Capitol)*	Feb. 25, 1967	1	10
U.S. Top 200 L.P.'s			
Yesterday . . . and Today (Capitol)*	July 9, 1966	1	31
Revolver (Capitol)*	Sept. 3, 1966	1	77
British Top Twenty Singles			
Paperback Writer (Parlophone)	June 18, 1966	1	7
Yellow Submarine/Eleanor Rigby (Parlophone)	Aug. 13, 1966	1	8
Penny Lane/Strawberry Fields Forever (Parlophone)	Feb. 25, 1967	2	8

(Chart positions according to *Billboard;* asterisk [*]: Record Industry Association of America certified Gold Record/Million Seller)

George and Ringo at the Maharishi's feet (Transworld Feature Syndicate)

I'D LOVE TO TURN YOU ON

The Beatles are Divine Messiahs. The wisest, holiest, most effective avatars (Divine Incarnate, God Agents) that the human race has yet produced. . . . I declare that John Lennon, George Harrison, Paul McCartney, and Ringo Starr are mutants. Prototypes of a new race of laughing freemen. Evolutionary agents sent by God, endowed with a mysterious power to create a new human species.
—Timothy Leary

The names—or numbers—of certain years can express a unique meaning of their own. For instance, 1984, thanks to George Orwell, is often used to evoke a nightmarish fusion of technology and totalitarianism. For millions of us, 1967 has an equally evocative ring, but its connotations are quite the opposite from the regimentation and hopelessness conveyed by 1984.

Those of us who were in our teens and twenties in the late 1960's were probably the most affluent and best-educated generation of brats our society had ever produced. Thanks to the hard work of our elders, millions of us were blessed with the money, the leisure, and the sophistication to indulge our hedonistic whims on an unprecedentedly grand scale, and to question the materialism, violence, and vapidity of the very culture that had nurtured us.

In 1967, the links between Them and Us suddenly seemed to snap like rotten thread. Kids began to drop out of the "straight" world in epidemic numbers, to coalesce into a class of their own within society—one defined not by income or breeding, but by youth—a so-called "counterculture" that defied, and aspired to replace, just about everything "the system" seemed to stand for.

As far as many older people were concerned, an awful lot of their offspring had somehow gone quite round the bend. But those who reveled in the contagious madness that began to sweep the world in 1967 were convinced that it was in the stars for a new and better order to prevail out of all the craziness. The earth, it was proclaimed, was at last passing out of a thousand years under the divisive sign of Pisces (two fish swimming in opposite directions) and into the golden age of Aquarius. It seemed a prophetic metaphor, even to the few renegades who didn't take the newly fashionable "science" of astrology literally. Thanks to "the bright, sensitive children of the affluent middle class," Charles Reich would proclaim in his million-selling *Greening of America:* "There is a revolution coming . . . a 'new head'—a new way of living—a new man."

In fashioning that "new man," boys forgot barbers, and girls their bras, and their clothes became almost interchangeable. Those of us who had once let our hair grow out in honor of the Beatles no longer seemed so queer to everyone else in the class, as some of last year's jocks

began to make the Fab Four look like U.S. Marines by comparison. As the sexes became less sharply defined, the rigid roles society had pigeonholed us all into also grew more open to question. And the taboos against sex itself were increasingly perceived as unnecessary, and easily overturned, barriers to good, clean fun.

University campuses and the "liberated" ghettos of St. Mark's Place and Haight Ashbury turned into a dazzle of bright colors. Greens, oranges, and purples blared from the bell bottoms and paisley shirts that swept male fashions; rock 'n' roll heroes and otherworldly scenery phosphoresced on psychedelic dayglo posters; and flowers were inescapable, handed by long-haired teenagers to passing strangers, even nonchalantly inserted by demonstrators into the barrels of National Guardsmen's guns.

"Peace" and "Love" were the two most popular words in the language then, and all the trappings of the counterculture were expected to somehow turn them into a universal reality. The summer of '67—which has now passed into nostalgia as "the summer of love"—was a time when millions began to imagine that they were reaching together toward a plateau of consciousness far higher than the one they were brought up on. It was music, more than anything else, that brought about this state of affairs—music and the personalities behind it.

Mass communications, particularly television and popular music, have unquestionably played a major role in shaping the attitudes of those born since the last world war. But whereas young people in the 1960's developed a cynicism toward the boob tube (even as they glued themselves to it every day), the music business seemed far more responsive. While T.V. seldom strayed far from the concerns and values of middle-class adults, it was mostly the kids who tuned in to Top-40 radio, bought the records and made them hits, and turned performers not much older than themselves into filthy-rich demigods. Pop music was youth's own medium.

When rock 'n' roll appeared in the 1950's, it represented, however inarticulately, young energy, defiantly flaunted in the withered face of Responsibility. Around 1964, the Beatles and their bandwagon brought rock 'n' roll, an outgrowth of the musical expression of discontented American

John Lennon at home (Keystone Press Agency)

blacks, to new flights of popularity. At the same time, Bob Dylan and his ilk were finding an affluent young audience for their updating of another anti-Establishment form: the topical folk ballads with which the likes of Woody Guthrie used to galvanize the downtrodden working classes.

When rock 'n' roll and folk music began to fertilize one another—as Dylan started to use the rock beat to pound his increasingly elliptical visions into the mass consciousness, and the Beatles and other teen idols, inspired by Dylan's example, began to write lyrics worth listening to—the impact was even more powerful than either folk or rock could manage on its own.

A vital new popular art form arrived, almost a 20th-century incarnation of the ancient bardic tradition when literature was passed down orally and chanted to repetitious music. Artists like Dylan and the Beatles were turning millions of people, for whom "real" poetry had become overly cerebral, unmusical, and unmagical, onto the power of words. And for those members of the T.V. generation who seldom found much time or inclination for reading, records proved to offer a far more digestible taste of the poetic muse than could the printed page. "I haven't written poetry . . . ," said John

Lennon. "I sing my poetry. I consider it poetry, I just sing it. . . . There's no time to read it, but there's time for listening." Technology had in a sense brought matters full circle: back to the days before the printing press.

Only now the magic wasn't limited to a few lucky souls huddled round some wandering troubador, for records and radio transmitted the new rock into the lives of everyone who asked for it, and many more who didn't, repeatedly hammering its messages into the subconsciouses of even those who weren't particularly listening.

By 1967 it seemed that no subject could be too controversial, bizarre, or profound for rock lyrics to tackle. Hit songs like "Eleanor Rigby" and "Strawberry Fields Forever," or "Mr. Tambourine Man" and "Like a Rolling Stone," had shattered the convention that popular lyrics should be sung but not heard. Although many rock 'n' rollers were content to stick to monosyllabic grunts, commercial success was now within range of songwriters who questioned established attitudes toward sex, drugs, politics, parents, and religion in an increasingly articulate and poetic way. For many, rock lyrics became a major source of input on what was going on in the world outside.

For the most part, rock's roots remained in the insistent, sexual rhythms of black American music, amplified to the nth degree by the electric power of white technology. But mass communications—and the pioneering efforts of artists like the Beatles—enabled many of the global village's new bards to embroider their musical settings with such far-flung influences as Indian ragas, English folk ballads, European 'concert music,' and electronic gurgles. The Beatles and a handful of others made it possible for rock to be literature and social commentary; to stray into the domain of symphony, opera and experimental music. It certainly wasn't mandatory for all rock to dither with such ambitions and more often than not the music fell far short of the mark when it did. Nonetheless, in 1967, the possibilities and potential of rock music suddenly seemed unlimited.

No popular art form with such pretensions to Importance had ever before reached and so gripped so many impressionable millions as rock did, and its effect was extraordinarily powerful on those it captivated. It belonged to us, the children of the age of mass communications; it was our own, and, whether or not much of it was as brilliant as it seemed at the time, we took it very seriously.

Of course, much of the rock stars' contributions to the counterculture life style had little directly to do with their words and music. Those represent only two dimensions of rock: "image" is the third. What we see, read, and hear about artists can be as central to their impact as their songs. Figures like Dylan and Lennon learned how to turn their lives into performances, maybe even works of art. And when Lennon badmouthed the Church, or Dylan carried a huge lightbulb wherever he went, thousands were bound to do the same.

When the Beatles first arrived on the American scene, their most spellbinding hook was neither a catchy guitar riff nor a clever turn of lyric—it was their hair. Those long (for 1964) locks captivated most of the kids, and made most of the adults uptight, but nobody seemed able to ignore them. And so the Beatles gave young people their most effective symbol of rebellion without ever mentioning long hair in a lyric until 1969's "Come Together."

When the Beatles, Dylan, the Stones, and the Who began around 1965 to parade about in multi-colored "pop-art" outfits, these too were adopted by thousands of us despite the teachers who castigated us for wearing pajamas to class, and the other boys who called us fairies. By 1967, clothes that were flamboyant yet casual had become, like long hair, an extremely popular means of visual warfare against the drabness and conformity of the suit, tie, and crewcut Establishment. Without really planning it that way, the Beatles, Dylan, and the rest succeeded in molding millions of youths more or less in their own image. Around 1967 an awful lot of these "freaks" (originally a derogatory label which stuck as a badge of pride) began to sense that they had far more in common with each other than with the rest of society.

Certainly, there were additional reasons for that feeling of fraternity that had little to do with rock; we'll leave the job of unraveling them to those who'll doubtless write many fat volumes on the Sixties. However, it's difficult even to touch on the subject of the counterculture without mentioning Vietnam.

The world we inherited from our elders was an unsettling one to begin with; we were the first generation to grow up haunted by nightmares of mushroom clouds that could wipe the earth out in a day. Just as rock music was evolving into so influential a medium, the U.S. was busy "escalating" its devastation of an obscure country 6,000 miles away; and nobody could convincingly explain why. The endless

magazine covers and T.V. newsreels of ruined villages and napalmed babies made quite a few of us question whether there might be something incredibly twisted about our society's values. The ultimate horror for young American men was the draft, through which they were being compelled to kill—and maybe die—for the government's misadventures. The Vietnam war became a symbol of everything perceived as barbaric and grotesque about the Establishment; it played a tremendous part in turning millions of teenagers and young adults off "the system."

With the counterculture there emerged a sensibility that might be described as a wholesale rejection of everything "straight" society considered logical, rational, or sober. This went far deeper than a desire to enliven the drab landscape with bright, dizzy colors, or disgust with the political system that had brought us the Vietnam war.

Young people began to sense that the pragmatic, materialistic way of life stressed by modern Western society was spiritually barren, and offered little that was truly meaningful—and that the established way of thinking resulted in more that was destructive than constructive. This backlash against technology, regimentation, and cold logic ushered in a surge of intense fascination with the mysticism of remote cultures and of our own culture's distant past, with astrology and the occult, fairy-tales and mythology; with Alternative States of Consciousness; and also with the surreal, the absurd, and the meaningless. If some of these dislocations of "reality," such as those toward the end of the list, did not exactly promise a path to spiritual enlightenment, they at least helped to reinforce a growing conviction that present-day society was nothing less than an oversized madhouse. It all contributed toward a renaissance of imagination and fantasy and mysticism that was particularly evident in the arts, and nowhere more so than in the popular music of the day.

As George Harrison put it in a 1967 interview: "Everybody lives their lives thinking 'this is reality' and then say to people like us, 'oh, you're just escaping from reality.' They seriously term this scene of waking up, going out to work, going home again . . . and all that—reality!"

In keeping with that attitude, the two most widely read and admired books on college campuses and in hippie ghettos were Hermann Hesse's *Siddhartha* and J.R.R. Tolkien's *Lord Of the Rings.* The former is a parable about a youth's quest for enlightenment in ancient India, which includes rejection, one by one, of parents, established religion, material gain—and even the opportunity to follow the Buddha himself on a new, iconoclastic path. In *Siddhartha* young Westerners found an idealization of individuality, as well as a vision of the exotic and mysterious East (which George Harrison was helping to glamorize).

Even more popular was *Lord Of the Rings,* a 1300-page epic escape into a magical, mythical past populated largely by the elves, dwarves, wizards, and dragons of Norse and Arthurian legend. With its detailed maps, "historical" footnotes, and imaginary languages, Tolkien's "Middle-Earth" provided a self-contained fantasy world that millions of young people vastly preferred to their own. Although Tolkien's work won almost universal acclaim from high-brow critics, Middle-Earth became a popular cult almost comparable to the Beatles, complete with posters, buttons, and fan magazines.

The Beatles themselves were evidently so taken with *Lord Of the Rings* that they gave serious consideration to tackling the near-impossible task of adapting it into a movie. Paul, speculated *Disc,* would most likely be cast as Frodo, the book's saintly hobbit hero, with Ringo playing Sam,

Frodo's simple and faithful servant. The role of Gandalf, the wise wizard, would fall to George, and John would play a slithering creature named Gollum. The film, however, never got past the talking stage.

Scores of other books with mystical and/or fantastic themes also suddenly became extraordinarily popular. Many of these were "children's stories," like C. S. Lewis' *Narnia* series, or Lewis Carroll's *Alice* books. Apparently people began to wonder whether a childlike vision of the world might not be more receptive to truth and beauty than the viewpoint of a typical modern adult.

In favor, too, were painters like Magritte, Dali, Escher, and their contemporary disciples, whose distortions of logic began to proliferate on mass-produced posters and even L.P. covers. And talk of the zodiac, Tarot cards, the I Ching, witchcraft, and yogis was in the air as never before in the industrial West. Rock songwriters were among the first to pick up on this trend—and to broadcast it to the rest of the world.

Bob Dylan was the first major songwriter to take contemporary music "through the smokerings of the mind" and "down the foggy ruins of time." When he did so, much of his original following reviled him for abandoning political protest. Actually, however, Dylan had become far more radical than they, for in his enigmatic imagery and stream-of-subconsciousness narratives he was challenging people's preconceptions of reality itself.

The Beatles, especially John Lennon, were among the earliest to catch on to what Dylan was up to and to express it in their own way. Their forthcoming *Sgt. Pepper's Lonely Hearts Club Band* would amount to a virtual encyclopedia of the ways one might juggle with reality. But a year before its appearance they had already noted (in "Rain") that external events are "just a state of mind," and released messages from the subconscious (such as "Norwegian Wood"), whose dreamlike meanderings offered little for the literally minded to hang their hats on. Also, like Dylan, John began to goof on people's expectations of "sense" by sticking the most absurd non sequiturs he could think of into his songs. And from now on . . . especially in 1967 . . . odd-chord progressions, elusive lyrics, unusual instruments and bizarre studio effects would lend to the Beatles' music a sense of magic and mystery that defied rational interpretation.

Of course, there was no shortage of long-haired hippie Mr. Joneses ("you know something's happening, but you don't know what it is. . . .") who simply couldn't deal with the fact that art didn't necessarily have to *mean* anything at all. A. J. Weberman made a career out of cracking the "code" he insisted Dylan's cryptic lyrics must be written in; his tools included a phonebook-sized concordance containing cross-references to every word Dylan wrote, and well-publicized rummagings through the bard's trash cans in search of evidence.

The Beatles also had more than their share of fans who persisted (as the tragedy of the Manson murders and the high comedy of the "Paul Is Dead" rumors would dramatize) in hunting for elaborate metaphors, hidden meanings, and "clues" in order to make logical, coherent "sense" out of their more elusive songs—whose very "point," if any, was that there was none to be had. That there were other answers than those available to the sober probing analysis of the wide-awake modern Western adult mind.

As John Lennon would sing many years later:

Intuition takes me there,
Intuition takes me anywhere.

The easiest and fastest route to Alternate States of Consciousness, as countless young Westerners learned around this juncture, was provided by "mind-expanding" drugs. As Aldous Huxley once wrote: "When, for whatever reason, men and women fail to transcend themselves by means of worship, good works, and spiritual exercises, they are apt to resort to religion's spiritual surrogates." L.S.D., peyote, and other hallucinogens, and, to a lesser degree, marijuana and hashish, enabled anyone to play Alice, transform his or her environment into a Wonderland, and simulate a mystical experience in the process—almost as effortlessly and instantaneously as he or she might switch on a T.V. program.

Indeed, these substances were destined to become a virtually unavoidable facet of the counterculture (which was often tagged "the drug subculture"). So much so that a case can be made for many of the attitudes and trends summarized in the preceding pages being as much inspired by the influence of pot and hallucinogens as the other way around. "Progressive" rock, in particular, began to reflect—and glamorize—the drug experience to the point where many pot- and acid-heads would insist it impossible to understand the music without the right chemical orientation.

With mind-bending drugs, thousands of people began to snap the bonds of empirical logic, to overwhelm their senses with heightened perceptions, and bring to their waking hours many of the sensations and images of dream sleep. (Needless to say, there were other drugs that did not pretend to do anything more than to give one a lift, or slow one down; but in the Sixties the fashionable drugs were those said to expand awareness, even induce profound revelations.)

Of course, "straight" society did not relish the proliferation of these substances, and reacted with countless hysterical exposés of the perils they posed. Hallucinogens were outlawed and savage penalties enforced even for possession of the relatively harmless weed. Although even most L.S.D. enthusiasts (if not Timothy Leary) conceded that an acid trip gone awry could prove a harrowing experience, the relative benefits and dangers of pot and acid became a subject of sharp disagreement between the counterculture and straight society.

Marijuana and hashish had long been in favor among certain artists, bohemians, and segments of the black community; but L.S.D. did not start to become the sacrament of a substantial cult within our society until the early Sixties, when figures like Dr. Leary began to extoll its miraculous and mystical powers. The L.S.D. pioneers were among the first to really let their hair go, wear flamboyant clothes, and flaunt their defiance of straight values. Unsurprisingly, many of them had a soft spot in their hearts for the Beatles, and sensed in them (as Leary would put it) "prototypes of a new young race of laughing freemen," even before receiving songs like "Tomorrow Never Knows" and "Strawberry Fields Forever" with what must have been a familiar rush.

A fascinating account of an early acid cult's encounter with Beatlemania can be found in Tom Wolfe's *The Electric Kool-Aid Acid Test,* which became a number one bestseller and instant counterculture classic when it appeared in 1968 (electric kool-aid being a heady brew whose active ingredient is L.S.D.).

The book chronicles the escapades of author Ken Kesey (whose book *One Flew Over the Cuckoo's Nest* was inspired by an L.S.D. trip) and his entourage, the Merry Pranksters, as they cavort through 1965 dousing their brains, and those of almost everyone they chance to meet, with acid. Much of their time is spent cruising around America in a dayglo painted bus, zonked out of their skulls and filming everything in sight (a program the Beatles would eventually follow on a similar romp through England). The Pranksters' bus is wired for music, and when their own band

Ringo and Paul in Greece, July 1967 (UPI)

isn't playing, Beatle and Dylan records often provide the sound track for their merry trips.

When the Fab Four come to San Francisco, Kesey and friends hang a huge sign outside their La Honda commune, welcoming the Beatles, who, they hope, might be sufficiently attuned to the Prankster wavelength to drop by for a glass of kool-aid. They also manage to wrangle thirty choice tickets to the Beatles' show at the Cow Palace from an influential L.S.D. peddler, and turn up for the performance in the psychedelic bus, blasted out of their gourds. "It was one of the great, fantastic experiences of my life," Kesey recalled recently.

But despite Kesey's view that the Beatles "represented, each of them, one of the four letters of 'love'," the revelations he and his friends receive that night are not all pleasant ones. From the moment the Beatles hit the stage to a twinkling galaxy of Instamatic flashbulbs, the audience seems transformed into one "enormous organism," or as Wolfe would put it:

a single . . . animal with a thousand waving pink tentacles—

vibrating poison madness and filling the universe with the teeny agony torn out of them. One of the Beatles . . . dips his long electric guitar handle in one direction and the whole teeny horde ripples precisely along the line he sets off . . . it causes them to grin, John and Paul and George and Ringo, rippling the huge freaked teeny beast this way and that.

"I saw them create," says Kesey, "the pyramid that our Western consciousness is still built upon. *I've* felt it when you get up and talk to a college and look out to see these banks and banks of faces . . . relinquish their consciousnesses to you. . . . This intersection of attention is where you'll always find Hemingway and Janis Joplin and Malcolm X and Kennedy. . . . All these people looking to this one place to find an answer to their scene, and they're giving to him powers that no man has a right to have. . . .

"When I saw the Beatles up there, I saw that pyramid of concentration and power like nothing ever before that I can imagine like that, as far back as you want to go, in *The Bible,* 'cause there wasn't that many people into Christ that could build up that kind of attention."

For the first few numbers, the Beatles seem to have total power over the multitudes; but soon the thousand-tentacled monster begins to rage wildly out of control. The kids storm the stage en masse and the cops hurl them back as the Beatles play on.

"What you have is a cancer that's aware of what it's doing but can't stop doing it," says Kesey. "There was not enough cops to hold this thing that was pushing forward . . . and people who were up close were on a bummer because they were being crushed, and the people in the back, all they knew was to get close to this thing that they loved, to push forward toward it."

To the deafening combination of teenage screeches and muddy rock 'n' roll is added the noise of folding chairs cracked to splinters by the surging mob.

And then the girls start fainting, like suffocation, and getting tromped on, and they start handing out . . . the bodies of little teeny freaks being shuttled out over the pitched sea like squashed lice picked off the beast, screaming and fainting and *Ghhhhwooooooowwwwww* again up against the cop fence while the Beatles cheese and mince at them in the dumb show, utterly helpless to ripple them or anything else now, with no control left.

The bad vibes become too much for the Pranksters' highly strung lysergic sensibilities, and they troop out midshow. "These guys could have got up there," says Kesey, "and started coming on together with the kind of power they played with, saying . . . what you want is yourself and the guy standing next to you, to stop turning it toward us and turn it out there. . . . They could have taken this roomful of kids and snapped them and they would have left that place enlightened, mature people that would never have been quite the same again. But they couldn't, because they couldn't do anything but what they'd learned to do. . . . They had the power to bring off this new consciousness to people, but they couldn't do it."

Yet by 1967 the Pranksters' early intuition of an affinity between themselves and the "four vinyl imported dolls" (as the Beatles seemed at the concert) would prove somewhat clairvoyant. The Beatles would manage to channel enough of that "power to bring off a new consciousness" to help effect quite a transformation in that thousand-tentacled teeny beast that so horrified Kesey's entourage at the Cow Palace. In the process, the Fab Four would take from Kesey and Leary the distinction of being the world's most famous acid-heads. Kesey would wind up setting up shop at the Beatles' Apple Records headquarters, and Leary singing along on Lennon's single "Give Peace a Chance."

The Beatles had in fact been initiated into L.S.D. some months before the Merry Pranksters attended their Cow Palace concert. Lennon and Harrison first took acid earlier in 1965 when a dentist friend secretly slipped some into their coffee. As George told biographer Hunter Davies, "It was as if I'd never tasted, talked, seen, thought, or heard properly before. For the first time in my life I wasn't conscious of ego."

He and John lost little time in turning Paul and Ringo onto their new discovery, and soon all of them became accustomed to tripping regularly. Particularly John Lennon, who years later would reminisce: "I must have had a thousand trips. I used to just eat it all the time." The drug was a major inspiration for the new artistic vision that surfaced with *Revolver,* as well as being the subject matter of a number of the songs on that L.P.

Not that acid was all "rocking horse people with marshmallow pies" for the Beatles. John especially found that it often made him "paranoid" and unable to communicate with other people. But it was some time before he would conclude that all the insights, inspirations, and kicks were no longer worth that price.

George Kelly, a veteran of 16 years of service in the Royal Army who went on to become butler and chauffeur at some of Britain's most stately homes before being hired by Paul McCartney in 1966, recalls with distaste in his memoirs having to bring morning tea for two to Paul's bedroom when Jane was away, and having to endure the sight of the Beatle stubbing out ciggies on his silver Ivor Novella awards. But nothing seems to have unhinged Kelly more than the time he accidentally stumbled in on "one of the most bizarre scenes I have ever witnessed. There, in front of the television set, were the highest paid pop group in the world and their manager, bowing down and salaaming, chanting and dancing with one another!"

Kelly recalls making his way through billowing incense and flashing colored strobelights to give Paul a message, but "nobody took the slightest notice of me. They were all on their own little clouds. So as the Eastern music . . . grew louder, I just left the room quietly."

Shortly afterward, the butler handed in his notice, but not before receiving lectures from his employer about the benefits of L.S.D.: "Your whole life flashes before you and you realize all the mistakes you have made."

Yet despite the extent to which they felt acid had opened up their artistic perspective and changed their lives, it wasn't until 1967 that the Beatles came out of the closet. Understandably so: even in that year, for the vast majority of the population, the mere mention of drugs, any kind of drugs, conjured up squalid visions of dirty needles, addiction, desperation, and certain death. Had the loveable moptops of 1965 let the world know about their shenanigans, their career would probably have plummeted to an untimely end.

Even as late as May 1967, *Beatles Monthly* awarded a free subscription to a fan who wrote how proud she was that the Beatles hadn't got "mixed up in this drugs business. . . . I know if Paul took drugs I'd be worried sick, but I know he's too sensible." Her letter was printed in large, specially-colored blue type so nobody would miss it, which suggests that the editors might have been somewhat out of touch with their subjects by that point.

That letter, ironically, was published the very month that Paul let slip his secret to a reporter who promptly passed it on to *Life* magazine's millions of readers. McCartney would later insist that he merely gave an honest answer to a question about whether he had tried L.S.D.; nonetheless, his response included this elaboration: "It opened my eyes. We only use one tenth of our brain. Just think what we could accomplish if we could only tap that hidden part! It would mean a whole new world if the politicians would take L.S.D. There wouldn't be any more war or poverty or famine. A few days later Paul went on to inform another reporter that acid had made him "a better, more honest, more tolerant member of society . . . brought closer to God."

Unsurprisingly, these remarks set off a storm almost comparable to the John and Jesus affair of a year earlier. In London, *The Mirror* editorially labeled Paul "an irresponsible idiot." Billy Graham, who did not relish the thought of being replaced by a chemical, declared that L.S.D. should be "shunned like the plague" by Beatle fans. At every opportunity, reporters needled Paul with questions about his obligations toward impressionable children, to which he finally retorted: "It's you who've got the responsibility not to spread this. . . . If you'll shut up about it I will!"

Nevertheless, the Beatles and Brian Epstein soon saw fit to attach their names to a full-page advertisement to appear in the July 24, 1967 issue of the prestigious *London Times,*

A yellow sub for peace

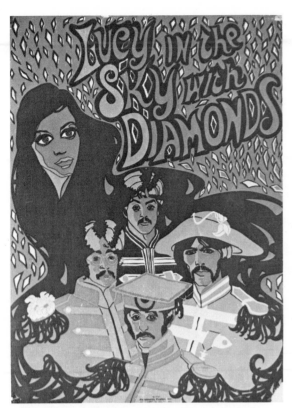

Personality Posters' dayglo interpretation of "Lucy in the Sky"

calling for the legalization of marijuana. But by that time the Beatles hardly needed to resort to interviews and newspaper ads to get the message across. Their new collection of songs of innocence and experience, *Sgt. Pepper's Lonely Hearts Club Band,* had been unleashed the month before. Aside from being their most influential record ever, and an uncannily timely evocation of almost every other aspect of the emerging counterculture, *Sgt. Pepper* was loaded with unmistakeable references to pot and L.S.D.

"Then I hope your finger is better now?" Alice said very politely, as she crossed the brook after the Queen.

"Oh, much better!" cried the Queen, her voice rising into a squeak as she went on. "Much be-etter! Be-e-e-etter! Be-e-ehh!" The last word ended in a long bleat, so like a sheep that Alice quite started.

She looked at the queen, who seemed to have suddenly wrapped herself up in wool. Alice rubbed her eyes, and looked again. She couldn't make out what had happened at all. Was she in a shop? And was that really—was it really a *sheep* that was sitting on the other side of the counter?

—from *Through the Looking Glass,* by Lewis Carroll, whom John Lennon called his "favorite author" and "greatest influence."

Although *Sgt. Pepper* was one of the first rock L.P.'s to attempt a semblance of thematic unity, it also ranked among the most varied collections of songs anyone had ever pieced together, a crazy quilt of rock 'n' roll, sound-effects, electronic noodling, and Indian, folk, baroque, classical, and music-hall influences. The Beatles managed to pull off this paradox by devising the entire album as a hallucinatory cabaret revue—McCartney billed it a "magic presentation"—in which anything was likely to happen next, and the more unexpected or incongruous, the better.

To create the illusion of a show, *Sgt. Pepper* was also one of the first rock albums to dispense with those bands of silence that traditionally separate one L.P. selection from

the next. Instead, each tune on *Sgt. Pepper* blends into its successor like one dream dissolving into another, in quite the same way Carroll's White Queen turned into a sheep before Alice's startled eyes. This device, and the concept of a "concept album," have been widely imitated ever since.

Even within the individual songs, unexpected changes in rhythm, key, and time signatures abound. "Lucy In the Sky With Diamonds" shifts abruptly from a languid 3/4 on the verses into an upbeat 4/4 on the chorus, and the instrumental break of "Within You Without You" coasts from 4/4 into 5/8. The 1967 Beatles were especially fond of slipping out of racy syncopations into the most brittle, robot-like rhythm imaginable; the verse and chorus of the "Sgt. Pepper" theme provide a typical example of this new Beatle trademark, as do portions of "Mr. Kite," "A Day In the Life," and "I Am the Walrus." None of which was very helpful to dancers.

One thing that can be said of all 24 eclectic songs the Beatles issued in 1967 is that they seemed entirely to shake off the black influences that had given birth to rock 'n' roll in the first place. Psychedelia was, by and large, a white trip, and much, though certainly not all, of the new rock music reflected that fact.

Sgt. Pepper's Lonely Hearts Club Band, which required four months and about $100,000 to realize, starts with the sounds of an expectant crowd and an orchestra tuning up. Then the show begins with the brassy title song, in which Sgt. Pepper's Band introduces itself to dispense show-bizzy pleasantries:

Sit back and let the evening go . . .
You're such a lovely audience
we'd like to take you home with us. . . .

Horns come blaring out from the 17th century; the invisible crowd breaks into ripples of applause; and the spotlight falls on Ringo Starr (introduced as "Billy Shears") as the title song segues into "With a Little Help From My Friends."

Ringo's role in the Sgt. Pepper revue is, characteristically, that of a disarmingly incompetent buffoon. He admits that it's no easy matter for him "not to sing out of key," but, with a little help from his friends, he'll "get by." And "get high" into the bargain. (For that last reference Vice President Spiro Agnew in 1970 would launch an unsuccessful campaign to have the song banned from the American airwaves.)

Having gotten Mr. Shears good and high, Sgt. Pepper's Band invite their lovely audience to join them on a trip through the looking glass:

Climb in the back with your head in the clouds,
and you're gone. . . .

Clever people quickly detected the acrostic spelt out by "*L*ucy In the *S*ky With *D*iamonds," and weren't about to be taken in by the Beatles' explanation that the title had been dreamed up by four-year-old Julian Lennon for one of his own paintings.

But if the Beatles *weren't* pulling our legs—and the reliably candid Lennon *still* sticks by the original story—it would only be in keeping with the equally unusual catalysts for John's other contributions to *Sgt. Pepper:* a Victorian carnival poster, a T.V. cornflakes commercial, and a *Daily Mail* clipping about holes in Blackburn, Lancashire inspired, respectively, "Being For the Benefit Of Mr. Kite," "Good Morning, Good Morning," and "A Day In the Life."

In any case, "Lucy" contains some of the most wondrous imagery ever to turn up in a popular song. Those "plasticine porters with looking glass ties" and "rocking-horse people with marshmallow pies" may owe as much to John's lifelong love of Lewis Carroll as to his recent chemical experiments.

L.P., 1967 (Capitol)

(Nonetheless, Agnew also proposed a ban on "Lucy In the Sky.") The theme of drifting passively "in a boat on a river" while marvels unfold from the shore (which John had earlier toyed with on "Tomorrow Never Knows") has always been a favorite with dreamweavers and visionaries. It turns up in Carroll's *Alice In Wonderland* and dominates Rimbaud's long poem "The Drunken Boat," Lord Dunsany's "Idle Days On the Yaan," and many other classic literary fantasies.

Paul contributes to the air of unreality by dubbing over his bass (which he plays here like a dotty old lady) languid riffs on an organ that has been doctored to sound like a celesta. *Sgt. Pepper* established McCartney as the resident Mr. Versatility. Elsewhere on the album he showcases on harpsichord, piano, lead guitar, and comb-and-paper. The others began joking that some day he should make an album by himself, overdubbing all the instruments. One day he would.

"Lucy" gives way to two of Paul's more upbeat numbers: "Getting Better" (oh, the optimism of 1967), and "Fixing a Hole." Some listeners concluded that that one was about a junkie, but Paul insisted not. "This song is about the hole in

your makeup which lets the rain in and stops your mind from going where it will. . . . When I wrote it I meant if there's a crack, or the room is uncolorful, then I'll paint it."

A harp (the kind angels play) ushers in "She's Leaving Home," Paul's miniature soap opera. Melodramatic strings accompany a tale of a young runaway who escapes from her middle-class upbringing. The mum and dad who'd given her "everything money could buy" wring their hands, uncomprehending: "what did we do that was wrong/we didn't know it was wrong"—but, for the first time in her life, their daughter is having "fun." A bit contrived, perhaps; but it couldn't have been more timely. In 1967 running away from bourgeois parents and straight society was suddenly a highly popular pastime. Although based on a hokey waltz, the melody is exquisitely detailed. Complete with unusual (for rock) experiments in vocal counterpoint, the music recalls and elaborates upon the earlier "Eleanor Rigby." (No Beatle plays an instrument in "She's Leaving Home" either.) The lyrics, however, are too trite to be as affecting as those of "Rigby". Then again, soap operas usually are trite.

Side One concludes on a festive note with "Being For the Benefit of Mr. Kite," John's surreal vision of a Victorian carnival. At the words "of course Henry the Horse dances the waltz!" the music does just that, careening out of a prim 4/4 into one of the most madcap waltzes ever committed to record. Lennon wanted an authentic old steam organ to give the piece the correct period feel, but settled instead for what assistants Mal Evans and Neil Aspinall described with only slight exaggeration as "various organ recordings speeded up, slowed down, electronically distorted, played backwards, and dipped in a bottle of coke." Some of these were in fact cut into 15-inch strips that were hurled into the air and stitched back together at random. It all helped "Mr. Kite" to come across as a high-flying character as his name implies.

Like Ringo the buffoon, George the mystic is allowed one star performance in a show primarily designed by and for Lennon and McCartney. As the swirling sounds of cellos and an Indian dilruba rise from the droning tanpuras like so much jasmine and sandalwood, Harrison delivers himself of the lengthy sermon that opens Side Two. "People who hide themselves behind a wall of illusion never glimpse the truth." "With our love, with our love, we could save the world." Steven Stills found these lyrics so stirring that when

he himself became a rich superstar he decided to have them carved on a stone monument in his garden.

Just when it begins to send us into a trance—or to sleep— the lugubrious raga-rock is abruptly dispelled by peals of raucous laughter, and we find ourselves among the clarinets of a 1930's vaudeville revue. And what could be further, more absurdly removed from the land of elephants, snake charmers, yogis, and levitation evoked by George's "Within You Without You" than the sound of Noel Coward (no! Paul McCartney) serenading us with the glib patter of:

When I get older, losing my hair,
many years from now,
will you still be sending me a Valentine?

So much of *Sgt. Pepper* is program music: melodies and arrangements paint pictures that illustrate the lyrics. When John sings "and you're gone" on "Lucy," a wash of chords is followed by silence. Henry the Horse's waltz brings on demented carousel music. George's mystical meanderings are complemented by Indian temple instruments. Now Paul describes old age with the most old-hat music yet to turn up on a rock L.P. (The song was written for his dad, who'd recently turned 64.) The effect is as touching as it is hilarious.

WHO'S WHO IN SGT. PEPPER'S BAND

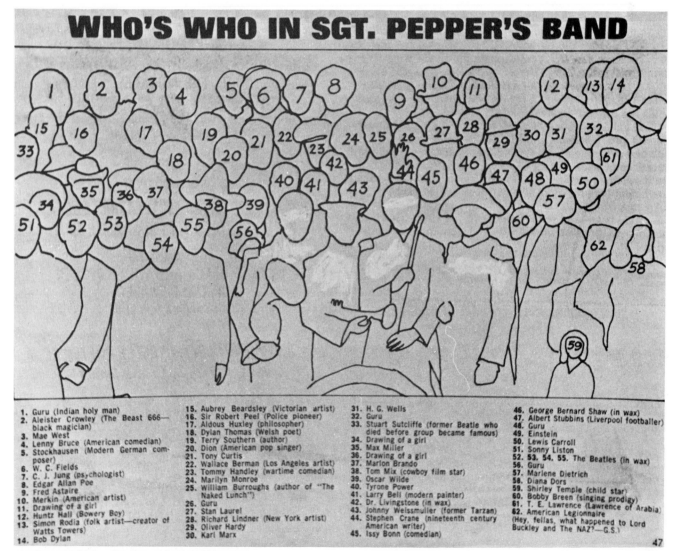

1. Guru (Indian holy man)
2. Aleister Crowley (The Beast 666— black magician)
3. Mae West
4. Lenny Bruce (American comedian)
5. Stockhausen (Modern German composer)
6. W. C. Fields
7. C. J. Jung (psychologist)
8. Edgar Allan Poe
9. Fred Astaire
10. Merkin (American artist)
11. Drawing of a girl
12. Huntz Hall (Bowery Boy)
13. Simon Rodia (folk artist—creator of Watts Towers)
14. Bob Dylan

15. Aubrey Beardsley (Victorian artist)
16. Sir Robert Peel (Police pioneer)
17. Aldous Huxley (philosopher)
18. Dylan Thomas (Welsh poet)
19. Terry Southern (author)
20. Dion (American pop singer)
21. Tony Curtis
22. Wallace Berman (Los Angeles artist)
23. Tommy Handley (wartime comedian)
24. Marilyn Monroe
25. William Burroughs (author of "The Naked Lunch")
26. Guru
27. Stan Laurel
28. Richard Lindner (New York artist)
29. Oliver Hardy
30. Karl Marx

31. H. G. Wells
32. Guru
33. Stuart Sutcliffe (former Beatle who died before group became famous)
34. Drawing of a girl
35. Max Miller
36. Drawing of a girl
37. Marlon Brando
38. Tom Mix (cowboy film star)
39. Oscar Wilde
40. Tyrone Power
41. Larry Bell (modern painter)
42. Dr. Livingstone (in wax)
43. Johnny Weissmuller (former Tarzan)
44. Stephen Crane (nineteenth century American writer)
45. Issy Bonn (comedian)

46. George Bernard Shaw (in wax)
47. Albert Stubbins (Liverpool footballer)
48. Guru
49. Einstein
50. Lewis Carroll
51. Sonny Liston
52. 53, 54, 55. The Beatles (in wax)
56. Guru
57. Marlene Dietrich
58. Diana Dors
59. Shirley Temple (child star)
60. Bobby Breen (singing prodigy)
61. T. E. Lawrence (Lawrence of Arabia)
62. American Legionnaire
(Hey, fellas, what happened to Lord Buckley and The NAZ?—G.S.)

47

Key to personalities on *Sgt. Pepper's* jacket (16 Magazine)

79

"When I'm 64," and "Lovely Rita," which follows, provide some of the best-ever examples of McCartney's occasional capacity for urbanely campy wit. "When I'm 64" emulates songwriters like Coward and Cole Porter who, instead of saying nothing earnestly, as was customary in the popular songs of their era, developed the fine art of making light of their vacuous subject matter by using the traditional clichés ironically. Like Paul here, they were fond of absurd rhymes like "will you still need me/will you still feed me." However, their patter never did quite take the surreal turn of "Lovely Rita," McCartney's jaunty tribute to a meter maid.

A crowing cock heralds "Good Morning, Good Morning," in which John raucously parrots some of the vapid pleasantries most of us take refuge in to disguise a lack of real communication. As in later works like "Cold Turkey," Lennon feels no qualms about using unpleasant music to complement a bleak message. By the end of the song, nothing is left but a cacophony of animal noises.

The last note of the piece, the clucking of a chicken, turns into the sound of a guitar (a conjuring trick for which Mr. Martin has received many compliments) and we're back

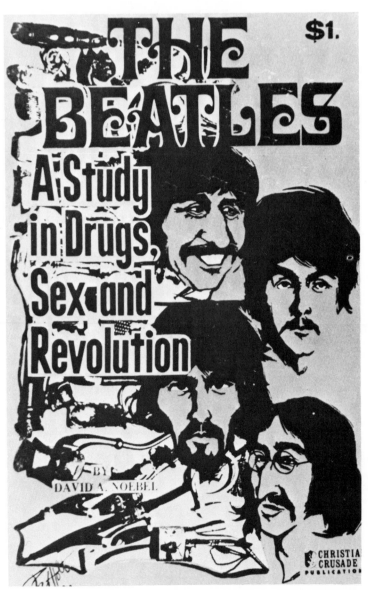

An anti-Beatle booklet

where we began, with a reprise of the album's theme song. Only now Sgt. Pepper's Lonely Hearts Club Band sound more like a psychedelic marching band, and their signal tune a relentless blitzkrieg of electric noise. The lyrics tell us that the show's over and thank us for listening, but in fact Sgt. Pepper's Band still have one last coup up their sleeves—the most incredible of them all.

Like much of the Beatles' finest work, the encore, "A Day In the Life," owes a great deal to chance. John and Paul had each gotten bogged down writing two separate songs that neither could finish. So they decided to see what would happen if they welded the two fragments together, and, as Paul once said, "Bang: you have the jigsaw puzzle!" From that arbitrary juxtaposition evolved what many consider the greatest song the Beatles ever created.

To a stark, rather bland musical setting, John's eerily detached voice intones the opening lines:

I read the news today, oh boy . . .
and though the news was rather sad,
well I just had to laugh . . .

Lennon's black humor runs like cold blood through his unsettling collage of news clippings:

I saw the photograph,
he blew his mind out in a car,
he didn't notice that the lights had changed.
A crowd of people stood and stared,
they'd seen his face before. . . .

The scene splices to a screening of *How I Won the War*, the gory black comedy in which John had recently played a part. Then Lennon breaks off his recitation to chant those magic words, "I'd love to tu-u-u-u-u-urn you-ou-ou-ou-ou-ou ah-ah-ah-on." The bleak panorama explodes into the sound of the Royal Philharmonic Orchestra gone berserk, each of the 41 instruments playing as if on a different wavelength from all the others. They build up to a climactic rush—then are suddenly switched off on an unexpected beat. The music instantly contracts to a cramped, claustrophobic space, inhabited at first by a single piano.

As if to suggest that the first part of the piece had been just someone's bad dream, an alarm clock goes off. Someone's day begins:

Woke up, fell out of bed,
dragged a comb across my head,
found my way downstairs and drank a cup . . .

Typically, Paul follows John's impressionistic imagery by describing in his section a more humdrum, external side of a day in our lives—getting up to face the nine-to-five grind. He lurches out to catch his bus in seconds flat, makes his way to the top level of the double-decker (the smoking section on British buses), and lights up a joint.

Somebody spoke
and I went into a dream . . .

The musical space opens up again, to drifting voices and a burst of strings.

When John resumes the narrative, all semblances of reality and logic have been swept aside. He babbles about filling the Albert Hall with holes, concluding once more: "I'd love to turn you on." After a second orgasmic crescendo from the mad orchestra, "A Day In the Life" melts away on 42 seconds of harmonics from the final, doom-laden chord.

Nothing quite like "A Day In the Life" had been attempted before in so-called popular music—not even in the 11 songs that preceded it on this unusually adventurous album. Its use of dynamics and tricks of rhythm, and of space and stereo effect, and its deft intermingling of scenes from

The Beatles as kiddie cartoon characters
(King Features)

dream, reality, and shades in between, seemed especially daring back in 1967. Even more so than the rest of *Sgt. Pepper,* "A Day In the Life" was so visually evocative it seemed more like a film than a mere song. Except that the pictures were all in our heads.

The Beatles and their entourage took exceptional pains to create for the *Sgt. Pepper* jacket a collage as colorful, imaginative, and intriguing as the record itself. Burman's theatrical agency was commissioned to tailor, out of the most lurid shades of satin available, special Lonely Hearts Club Band uniforms for the Beatles to pose in. The boys drew up a list of about sixty personalities they wished to have pose with them, names ranging from Edgar Allan Poe to Marilyn Monroe to Bob Dylan. Photographs had to be found of each one, then blown up to the proper scale. Madame Tussaud's wax effigies of Diana Dors, Sonny Liston, Lawrence of Arabia, and the Beatles themselves also found their way into the improbable mob.

A garden 12 feet square was built especially for the photo sessions. Over loose dirt that suggested a newly-dug grave, flowers were planted to spell out the word Beatles, and to form the shape of a guitar. The boys contributed from their personal collections various statues and ornaments to be strewn among the potted palms and marijuana plants. Only then were the brilliantly outfitted Beatles, with trumpets in hand and medals pinned proudly to their chests, finally prepared to take their place center-stage among the motley crowd of faces.

The album also came with a sheet of cardboard cut-outs; and, for the first time on a major pop release, the words to all the songs were printed on the back of the sleeve. The sheet-music publishers were decidedly nervous at the idea (it has since become quite commonplace), but the Beatles were adamant that none of their new lyrics slip past their audience.

Nobody had ever before invested so much trouble and expense in an album jacket, but it was worth it for reasons that went beyond *Sgt. Pepper:* never again would any respectable rock star dare put out a dull L.P. cover.

It is likely that much of *Sgt. Pepper,* like the rest of the Beatles' finest work, will show staying power, be anointed "classics," and entertain and even inspire people for quite some time. "A Day In the Life," for instance, should survive as a brilliant recording, and "With a Little Help From My Friends" as just one hell of a catchy tune (even Agnew admitted it was that). On the other hand, some songs may increasingly come to seem like quaint period pieces.

But even now it is quite impossible for those of us who shared our lives with *Sgt. Pepper* to fairly unravel the artistic merit from the social history of the time. For, with uncanny accuracy, the album managed to evoke almost every facet of the emerging youth subculture. *Sgt. Pepper* was the most powerful piece of propaganda the counterculture could have had; the album carried a slice of it into millions of homes and played a part in shaping the attitudes of countless listeners.

When the B.B.C. refused to let "A Day In the Life" be heard on the British airwaves on the grounds that it might encourage people to smoke illicit weeds, one despised the old farts for wanting to suppress such a great song. And yet their crusty logic was probably sound (although they were unable to prevent anyone from buying or hearing the record itself).

Of course "A Day In the Life" was much more than just an advertisement for dope. Parts of it had indeed been "written as a deliberate provocation, a stick-that-in-your-pipe," Mc-Cartney admitted at the time. "But what we want is to turn you on to the truth, rather than pot."

That last comment was typical of the rather earnest manner Paul sometimes assumed in 1967, but "A Day In the Life" did evoke so well the numbing confusion and apathy felt by much of the post-war generation. As did "She's Leaving Home" the generation gap (as they called it then), and "Good Morning, Good Morning" the difficulty of communicating even with one's own peers.

Other songs on *Sgt. Pepper* seemed to sum up so aptly the various ways and means with which young people were trying to transcend, transform, or escape from straight society: the Indian mysticism and the peace, love, and flowers;

the fantasy and the surrealism, and, of course, the mind-expanding drugs. "Within You, Without You" and "Lucy In the Sky With Diamonds" were almost miniature pop versions of *Siddhartha* and *Lord Of the Rings.* Not the actual books themselves, but the spirit they evoked in their youthful readers.

Sgt. Pepper seemed to say it all, to capture everything that had been emerging—in part because of what the Beatles had done before—in the isolated pockets of university towns and hippie ghettos. It helped bring millions in touch with the new developments; and the lives of those who had already, in Dr. Timothy Leary's famous phrase, "turned on, tuned in, and dropped out," couldn't have had a more apt soundtrack—although a few of them did have mixed feelings about what seemed the commercialization and popularization of their life style.

But Leary himself was thrilled. L.S.D.'s most influential champion hailed the Beatles as "the wisest, holiest, most effective avatars (Divine Incarnate, God Agents) that the human race has ever produced." Dr. Leary, despite his advanced years, was a fervent believer in the cosmic powers of the new rock. The essay on the Beatles that he would write ("Thank God For the Beatles" © 1968, League For

Spiritual Discovery) would exaggerate only slightly the sentiments many other fans cherished at the time:

The *Sgt. Pepper* album . . . compresses the evolutionary development of musicology and much of the history of Eastern and Western sound in a new tympanic complexity.

Then add psychedelic drugs. Millions of kids turned-on pharmacologically, listening to stoned-out electronic music designed specifically for the suggestible, psychedelicized nervous system by stoned-out, long-haired minstrels.

This . . . is the most powerful brainwashing device our planet has ever known. Indeed, if you were an observer from a more highly evolved planet wondering how to change human psychology and human cultural development (in other words if you were a divine messenger), would you not inevitably combine electrical energies from outside with biochemical catalysts inside to accomplish your mutation?

Leary's "brainwashing" theories weren't all that far removed from those of a less sympathetic group of Beatle-watchers that included right-wing Christian evangelists and members of the John Birch Society. Recent developments seemed to confirm what many of them had suspected from the start: that the Beatles were a Communist conspiracy. One of their spokesmen was Dr. Joseph Crow, billed as

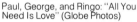

Paul, George, and Ringo: "All You Need Is Love" (Globe Photos)

America's "Number One expert on musical subversion," who charged:

Some of the newer Beatles songs . . . show an acute awareness of the principles of rhythm and brainwashing. Neither Lennon nor McCartney were world-beaters in school, nor have they had technical training in music. For them to have written some of their songs is like someone who had not had physics or math inventing the A-bomb. . . . Because of its technical excellence it is possible that this music is put together by behavioral scentists in some "think tank". . . . I have no idea whether the Beatles know what they are doing or whether they are being used by some enormously sophisticated people, but it really doesn't make any difference. It's results that count, and the Beatles are the leading pied pipers creating promiscuity, an epidemic of drugs, youth class-consciousness, and an atmosphere for social revolution.

Whether or not John, Paul, George, and Ringo were "agents" of either God or the Kremlin, the Beatle cult had certainly come a long way in three years. The sacrament had been changed from jelly beans to marijuana, the effigies from blow up dolls to op-art posters, the gospel from "I'm Happy Just To Dance With You" to "I'd Love To Turn You On." Beatle records, once unabashedly frivolous mass entertainments, had evolved into stereophonic fantasy worlds where listeners imagined themselves likely to chance upon profound revelations. It even became not uncommon for impressionable fans, often fortified by Electric Kool-Aid, to "find God" while hearing *Sgt. Pepper.* When, a long year-and-a-half before, John Lennon had said that the Beatles' popularity was eclipsing Christ's, perhaps there had been more truth to his words than anyone had cared to perceive at the time.

Two years later, while crusading for peace with Yoko Ono, John Lennon would offhandedly try to abolish the Christian calendar by renaming 1970 A.D. "Year One." However, as far as many of his admirers were concerned, the real Year One began with the start of 1964; those colorless and unliberated pre-Beatle years seemed, by comparison, the Dark Ages.

Outwardly, at least, the Beatles wore their new status as gurus and poet laureates of their generation quite lightly. George Harrison called the whole phenomenon a "cosmic joke." For one thing apparently hadn't changed much: the Beatles were still, in that phrase coined by bemused commentators way back in 1964, "laughing all the way to the bank."

Sgt. Pepper also solidified for the Beatles a more staid audience of middle-aged intellectuals eager to tune in to what "the young" were up to. Liking the Beatles, no doubt, helped them feel more youthful, vital, and "with it" themselves.

The benign condescension with which "serious" composers, writers, and critics had originally approached Beatlemania had gradually melted into admiration as they succumbed to the charm of the films, the literary inventiveness of John's books, and the tunefulness and lyricism of songs like "Eleanor Rigby." With the release of *Sgt. Pepper,* elaborate dissertations on the Beatles and rock music became a staple of the most highbrow of publications. In *The New York Review Of Books,* for instance, composer Ned Rorem anointed the Fab Four with Mozart's "magic of genius," and suggested that "the Beatles exemplify . . . a new and golden renaissance of song." Gentlemen and scholars ranging from Leonard Bernstein and Aaron Copland to Allen Ginsberg and John Cage chimed in with extravagant praise.

With the reaction to *Sgt. Pepper,* serious rock criticism really came into its own. The record consolidated rock

Yale Literary Magazine
March 1968 $1.00

Academia adopts the Fab Four

music's pretensions to "art," and henceforth every major album could expect the same sort of critical scrutiny and analysis accorded an important new novel.

Needless to say, the genre of rock criticism was not inaugurated by distinguished intellectuals who pondered the Beatles' affinities with Monteverdi or T.S. Eliot. For the most part, it emerged out of dozens of "underground" publications that were being launched at the time by enterprising young writers. The two finest and most successful of these proved to be San Francisco's *Rolling Stone* and Boston's *Crawdaddy,* both of which were initially devoted almost exclusively to coverage and analysis of the rock scene.

Perhaps no rock L.P. has ever garnered such near-unanimous raves as did *Sgt. Pepper.* Tom Philips echoed dozens of critics when he proclaimed in New York's *Village Voice* that *Sgt. Pepper* was "the most ambitious and most successful record album ever issued." The one notorious dissent appeared in a review by Richard Goldstein in *The New York Times,* where he dismissed most of the songs as

Single, Italy, 1967 (Parlophone)

Single, Japan, 1967 (Odeon)

pretentious and gimmicky. Goldstein's piece got so many bad reviews in turn that the critic was kept busy for months defending himself. "We must keep our heads on [the Beatles'] music, not on their incarnations," he protested. However, for most people the two were inseparable ingredients of the Beatles' schtik.

The only other sour notes came from writers, who, while conceding *Sgt. Pepper*'s brilliance, saw it as a prelude to the inevitable commercial exploitation of the counterculture. Commented Robert Somma in *Crawdaddy*: "They [the Beatles] tidied up the drug scene, made psychedelia as palatable and mind-blowing as Congress."

Meanwhile, the Beatles just about evaporated from the pages of slick teen-age magazines like *16* and *Datebook*. Beatle people had apparently grown too sophisticated for such publications, and all the "scoops" and "pix" were inherited by the newest teen sensation, the Monkees, a pre-fabricated quartet with a weekly T.V. show who had been programmed to look, sound, and act as much like the Beatles of *A Hard Day's Night* as possible. (For the very young Beatle loyalists, however, there was a Beatle cartoon show every Saturday morning courtesy of King Features, which was gearing up to produce a full-length animated *Yellow Submarine*.)

In the wake of *Sgt. Pepper*, the rock music scene exploded wide open. The record business went over the top as a billion-dollar industry, yet, thanks to the Beatles and a few others, its rigid standards of what was or wasn't commercial were largely discarded. The counterculture encouraged extremes of nonconformity, individuality, even eccentricity, and rock stars were particularly expected to personify these qualities.

Pop music enjoyed a brief period of unprecedented freedom of expression. Anything went. Songs could be one minute long or 20—invoke incest, magic carpet rides, or the Second Coming—incorporate just about any unlikely musical instrument or style—and still sell. Titles like *Aomoxomoa* (the Grateful Dead), or *My People Were Fair and Had Sky In Their Hair, But Now They're Content To Wear Stars On Their Brows* (Tyrannosaurus Rex) became almost humdrum.

In the music business, at least, a revolution really had taken place. It all happened so fast that the industry's hot shots, so accustomed to slick formulas of their own invention, were thrown quite off-balance. As they groped blindly for a lucrative piece of a scene few of them had the slightest understanding of, new artists were snapped up, not on the basis of how well they fit some clearly defined lowest common denominator, but on the strength of their uniqueness, even strangeness.

Some of these newcomers, like Pink Floyd with *Piper At the Gates of Dawn,* and the Incredible String Band with *5,000 Spirits, Or Layers Of the Onion,* convincingly emulated *Sgt. Pepper's* eclecticism, mysticism, and escapism. San Francisco, in particular, spawned many inventive groups, the most successful being Jefferson Airplane. The Airplane's big hit "White Rabbit" went "Lucy In the Sky With Diamonds" one better by explicitly depicting an L.S.D. trip in terms of scenes from Lewis Carroll. Not, of course, that the new music was all great stuff: somewhat less tasteful morsels of psychedelia—and heaps of pretentious word salad masquerading as "poetry"—were generously doled out by groups with names like Strawberry Alarm Clock, Peanut Butter Conspiracy, Vanilla Fudge, and the Electric Prunes. As George Melly put it: "The point about acid, about any drug used as a way to creativity, is that while it makes its communicants feel they have got the world in a jug, what they're able to 'bring back home' depends on what sort of mind they have in the first place."

Concert-goers began to fill the air with marijuana smoke instead of shrieks, and it became customary for isolated fans to take off all their clothes and freak out in the aisles. New venues, such as Bill Graham's Fillmores West and East, sprang up specifically to present what the label makers now called "acid-rock."

No longer were fans kept in the dark about their heroes' affairs with pot, pills, and cocaine. Instead, everyone was encouraged to believe that drugs were the ambrosia no respectable rock 'n' roll god could do without. Lurid headlines announced the drug arrests of numerous rock stars, most notoriously Mick Jagger and Keith Richard, who were even briefly tucked away behind bars. When they

The Beatles arriving in Bangor, Wales with their new guru (Wide World Photos)

Listening to their new teacher (Keystone Press Agency)

emerged from prison, the Stones recorded a sardonic ditty called "We Love You." The song featured the sounds of clanking chains and pals Lennon and McCartney on vocal harmonies.

On a June 1967 weekend in Monterey, California, thousands of fans gathered on the grass to celebrate the first great outdoor rock festival. Although the Beatles declined to perform, McCartney was listed on the board of advisers. The event, and the movie that was made of it, assured a place in contemporary mythology for Janis Joplin, and for Jimi Hendrix, who set his guitar on fire moments after the Who's Pete Townshend smashed his to splinters.

Of course, the hippie scene was readily exploited by the media and commercialized by capitalist infiltrators. By October, *Melody Maker,* which earlier in 1967 had featured a "Test Your Flower Power Rating" quiz (top scores meant "Paul McCartney's proud of you"), was running mournful headlines like "Who Killed Flower Power?"

Meanwhile, established artists took up the challenge of matching *Sgt. Pepper.* The ever-inventive Who plunged into work on a two-record magnum opus about a deaf, dumb, and blind boy named Tommy, and his search for the truth. For the interim, they released *The Who Sell Out,* a concept based on pop radio, complete with sardonic jingles.

In an attempt to evoke the darker side of the psychedelic experience, the Rolling Stones created *Their Satanic Majesties Request,* which arrived complete with 3-D cover (designed by Michael Cooper of *Sgt. Pepper* fame) depicting the band in outlandish costumes before a fairy-tale palace—with the heads of the Beatles glimmering in the shrubbery. (This last was to return the tribute of the doll with

the Rolling Stones T-shirt on the *Sgt. Pepper* cover.) *Satanic Majesties,* however, was savagely panned as a *Sgt. Pepper* rip-off, and the Stones promptly dropped out of the cosmos to get back down to good old rock 'n' roll with "Jumpin' Jack Flash" and *Beggars Banquet.*

All the while, Dylan stayed mum in Woodstock, recovering from a motorcycle accident and becoming more mythical with each month he remained in hiding. Some people theorized that he had secretly died; others eagerly awaited the extravagant coup with which he might outdazzle the competition upon his return.

But nobody aroused higher expectations and awe than the Beatles. Jann Wenner reported in *Rolling Stone* a debate among San Francisco's cognoscenti "about what the Beatles might do after *Sgt. Pepper.* Someone suggested that they would set the Bible to music. 'Ah no,' was the reply. 'They'll write their own.' And the reply to that was that if we had just come up with the idea, the Beatles would be doing something well beyond that." The Beatles themselves seemed equally optimistic about their career. Said George: "the future stretches out beyond our imagination."

Actually, however, the Beatles' experimentation, influence and stature reached their peak with *Sgt. Pepper.* In the next few years, they would keep their output at the high level of quality people expected from them, but the surprises and innovations would be largely replaced by a consolidation of what had come before. Nonetheless, in 1967 fans imagined that the almost mathematical progression of the Beatles' work (i.e., *Help* to *Rubber Soul* to *Revolver* to *Sgt. Pepper*) could continue indefinitely.

In the meantime, lots of joss sticks burned and lots of

strobelights flashed, as the rock stars and their fans all strived, in the catch-phrase of the time, to "do their own thing."

While they were still laboring over *Sgt. Pepper,* the Beatles accepted an invitation to represent Britain on the landmark international television program "Our World." Their appearance would be broadcast by satellite on June 25 to almost every imaginable country.

It was suggested that the occasion merited a special new song with lyrics basic enough for the multi-lingual audience to grasp. Following these instructions, John popped up with "All You Need Is Love." The music seemed equally simple, even as it romped in and out of 7/8 time.

While rehearsing for the show, the Beatles recorded a studio version featuring 13 session men on assorted strings and horns, with George Harrison chipping in an additional violin (his first fling with the instrument). The boys were so pleased with the result that on the day before their "Our World" appearance it was decreed that "All You Need Is Love" should nudge aside "Magical Mystery Tour" as the next Beatle single—and be released immediately.

"All You Need Is Love," which kicks off to the strains of the French National Anthem and ends with a sardonic reprise of "She Loves You," was tailor-made not only to the spirit and demands of the "Our World" spectacular, but also the "Summer of Love," of which it managed to be both an anthem and a parody. The Beatles could still be irreverent as ever, in this case about themselves, their earlier exhortations to "say the word love," and the flower children who had so taken "The Word" to heart. Decked out as the four letters of love in beads and multi-colored costumes, the Beatles previewed their new record for literally hundreds of millions of people—accompanied by a parade of signs translating the magic word into all kinds of languages.

In early August, after a stay on Hollywood's Blue Jay Way that he instantly immortalized in song, George Harrison decided to personally check out San Francisco's Haight Ashbury, which was being billed by the media as the hippie capital of the world. Followed like the Pied Piper by a growing train of adoring flower children, and wearing rose-tinted glasses shaped like a pair of valentines, George ambled past the head shops and free-food clinics of "Hashbury," strumming a guitar and singing "Baby You're a Rich Man."

This song, which appeared on the reverse of the single, is an off-the-wall snippet of vintage Lennonian psychedelia that had originally been stashed aside for the forthcoming *Yellow Submarine* soundtrack. However, as no other suitable B-sides lingered in the can, the Beatles played Indian givers with King Features.

"Rich Man" introduced yet another strange instrument to the pop scene: that noisome piping doing the leads is an electronic keyboard wonder known as the clavioline, played by Mr. Lennon. John's irrepressible originality and unconventionality are also evident in the lyrics, most of which take the form of a cryptic self-interview:

Q: Have you travelled very far?
A: Far as the eye can see.

Q: How often have you been there?
A: Often enough to know.

Q: What did you see when you were there?
A: Nothing that doesn't show.

Many at the time were content to explain away these riddles by concluding that Electric Kool-Aid still flowed more freely than wine in Pepperland.

But it wouldn't for much longer, for His Holiness the Maharishi Mahesh Yogi was about to arrive on the scene.

"There's high, and there's high, and to get really high—I mean so high that you can walk on the water, that high—that's where I'm goin'." —George Harrison

For the next eight months or so, the Beatles would imagine that their quest for spiritual meaning had at last ended at the Maharishi's shoeless feet. Their dozens of L.S.D. trips had been getting redundant. The visions of an acid trip can awaken a sense of spiritual discovery, but, like "Strawberry Fields Forever" and "Baby You're a Rich Man," they tend to provide more riddles than solutions. L.S.D., George Harrison explained, "could heighten your perception a little" and "let you see yourself from a different point of view." But "it's no good believing in hallucinations."

Acid proved to be, in George's words, "a key that opened the door and showed a lot of things on the other side," and doors, by definition, are there to be passed through. Hallucinogens can rip from your skull a great many preconceptions and notions of reality, but they leave it to you to piece together new frames of reference on your own. Some acid-heads were cruelly unhinged by the drug, and wound up falling out of windows or landing in mental institutions. The Beatles stopped taking it and moved on to other things.

They preceded legions of other L.S.D. buffs in fancying that more solid spiritual answers might be found in the religions of the East. (A similar case was that of Dr. Leary's top sidekick, Richard Albert, who is now known as Baba Ram Dass and as America's most successful home-grown Hindu-style guru.) Judaism and Christianity, tainted by association with the society that the counterculture imagined it had outgrown, held little magnetism for most young seekers in the late Sixties. The exotic and mysterious East seemed far more promising.

At first the Beatles had been content to explore Indian mysticism secondhand, through books. They paraphrased their reading in songs like "Tomorrow Never Knows" and "Within You Without You"; and in early 1967 John Lennon said he considered himself a Buddhist.

Then George began to try out various gurus for size. One kept him up several nights climbing a hill in Cornwall. But none seemed to quite fit until Patti Harrison turned her husband onto the Maharishi. Captivated by his personal charm and his remarkably simple technique for spiritual advancement, the Beatles all decided to attend an August weekend

George and John rap with David Frost about L.S.D. and T.M. (UPI)

The Beatles' entourage at Rishikesh (from left, George, Paul, unidentified pal, Donovan, Patti Harrison, John, and Paul Horn). Ringo left because the food was too spicy. (*16* Magazine)

conference of the Maharishi's Spiritual Regeneration League in Bangor, Wales.

Typically, that expedition was transformed into a carnival by the media. Hundreds of reporters, photographers, and fans—and bobbies to keep them in line—turned out to watch the Beatles board the train to Bangor. Many who had never even heard of the destination clambered aboard in order to be within reach of their idols. Meditators who had signed up for the conference were unable to get on the train; and even Cynthia Lennon was barred by a policeman who found her line about being John's wife unconvincing.

During the journey, the Maharishi gave each Beatle (and Mick Jagger, who was along for the ride) a mantra. As George explained a few weeks later, "each person's life pulsates in a certain rhythm, so they give you a word or sound, known as a mantra, which pulsates with that rhythm. By using the mantra . . . to transcend to the subtlest level of thought . . . the mantra becomes more subtle and more subtle, until finally you've lost even the mantra, and then you find yourself at that level of pure consciousness."

Transcendental Meditation provides an effortless escape from stress. When repeated as a twice-daily ritual, T.M., according to its partisans, gradually transforms practitioners into happier, more fulfilled individuals. The Beatles were instantly sold on it, and in the world's eyes the Fifth Beatle was, all of a sudden, a wizened, diminutive, scraggly-haired Hindu monk whose perpetual fits of the giggles dominate even his discourses on the meaning of life.

Many years before, after earning a university degree in physics, young Mahesh had sensed that his skills might be profitably employed in devising a blend of Western science and Indian mysticism. He learned Sanskrit and studied the scriptures with Guru Dev (who is invoked in the Beatles' "Across the Universe" and at every T.M. initiation to this

day), and adopted the title Maharishi, meaning saint, sage, or seer. After Guru Dev passed on, the Maharishi set up shop in Britain in 1959 to market his brand of instant karma to the West. For eight years he was only moderately successful—until the attentions of a rock group whose music he had never even heard gave him all the publicity he could ever have dreamed of. At a time when the last vestiges of traditional Western belief were being discarded by growing numbers of disoriented young people, they were particularly susceptible to any sage (or charlatan) who seemed to offer a convincing replacement.

T.M. became wildly fashionable, especially among pop stars. Donovan, Brian Jones, the Doors, and the Beach Boys—who still remain the Maharishi's most loyal advocates in rock—all followed the Beatles in clamoring for their mantras. Transcendental meditation promised the instant gratification that even the most cosmically oriented young Westerners continued to expect, packaged with the trappings of the mysterious and exotic East. Like raga-rock, T.M. perhaps offered of an ancient and complex discipline only the frosting to the cake. Nonetheless, Westerners could find even in Maharishi's simplified version of Eastern mysticism much that was instructive, beneficial, and new.

The giggling guru has been roundly condemned as a quack by his more traditionally minded competitors. T.M., they say, is superficial and amoral. The Maharishi does not even insist that his followers cut down on sex, booze, meat, or material gain, although he suggests that drug use may be physiologically incompatible with meditation and is himself supposedly a celibate teetotaling vegetarian. T.M.'s adherents call it a simple nonsectarian technique designed to tap the wells of latent energy that exist in everyone. They say it makes them do what they already do better, to become more efficient musicians or Christians, businessmen

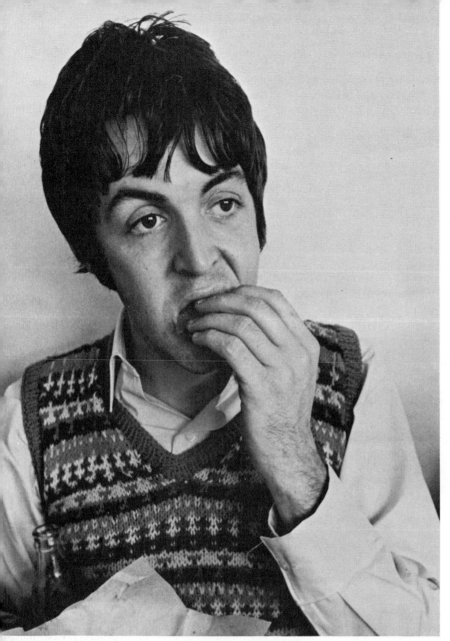

Fish and chips on the Mystery Tour (Keystone Press Agency)

custom-made mantra. T.M. courses were instituted in high schools, drug clinics, and the military. General Franklin Davis, Apollo 11 astronaut Michael Collins, and Los Angeles' reactionary Mayor Sam Yorty began to extoll the miraculous powers of T.M.

These gentlemen, like many of today's meditators, may not have ranked among the Beatles' warmest admirers, but if it weren't for the Fab Four they probably would never have received their mantras, and might still be victims of high blood pressure, alcoholism, or irritability. For, as Martin Ebon wrote in his book *Maharishi,* "[the linking of] the Maharishi's name . . . with that of the Beatles . . . was extremely important, for it permanently established the Maharishi in the public eye." Thanks in large part to the Beatles, nearly two million Westerners have been turned on to something that many of them swear has given them a new lease on life.

Many musicians have attempted to describe and eulogize transcendental meditation in song, but none have improved on one of the first of these efforts: John Lennon's "Across the Universe," which he wrote in 1967 under the spell of his mantra. (Because of his dissatisfaction with the Beatles' many attempts to record it, it wasn't widely released until its 1970 appearance on *Let It Be.*) One of the most iridescently beautiful of all John's songs, it exquisitely conveys some of the sensations of meditation:

Images of broken light which dance before me like a million suns,
they call me on and on across the universe;
thoughts meander like a restless wind inside a letter box,
they tumble blindly as they make their way across the universe.

Yet less than a year after their initiation, the Beatles moved away from the Maharishi and T.M. To get ahead of the tale a bit, the Beatles, after months of rhapsodizing about meditation on T.V. and in the press (they even talked of financing both a T.M. university in London, and a film starring His Holiness), all joined the Maharishi for an advanced training course in February 1968 at his retreat in Rishikesh, India. Thanks either to the miraculous powers of T.M., or simply to the lack of distraction, the Beatles were amazingly prolific in Rishikesh, turning out 30 new songs. (John and Paul also made a movie of the experience, intermingling scenes of the Maharishi, themselves, fellow meditators, and copulating monkeys.) However, despite the fact that the Maharishi had slashed the course's length to only three months especially for them, none of the Beatles stuck it out even that long.

After only 10 days, Ringo decided to go home, complaining that the retreat reminded him of Butlin's (the British holiday camp for working-class kids) and that the food was too spicy. A few weeks later, Paul and Jane also got bored and left. "He's a nice fellow," said Paul. "We're just not going out with him any more."

The other two almost saw the course through—until John thought he discovered evidence of His Holiness's lecherous designs on fellow student Mia Farrow. John responded to what he considered the monk's blatant hypocrisy by flying home (with George) to compose a scathing indictment for the next Beatle album. The tune was originally called "Maharishi," but after John's ire subsided he changed the title (and the gender of the protagonist) to "Sexy Sadie":

Sexy Sadie, what have you done,
you made a fool of everyone. . . .

One sunny day the world was waiting for a lover,
she came to turn on everyone,
Sexy Sadie, the latest and the greatest
of them all.

or soldiers. Purists wonder whether a system that caters to executives and generals can also furnish a path to enlightenment. But this cosmopolitanism is precisely why T.M. proved ideal for the competitive and materialistic West, and why it easily eclipsed its more demanding, Indian-imported rivals.

Most of T.M.'s late-Sixties recruits, such as the Beatles, seemed to view it as an initiation into the mysteries of the East, and accordingly donned flowing robes and strings of beads and filled the air with incense. But His Holiness, who is given to blue-printing World Plans with the ultimate aim of turning every last human being onto T.M., was astute enough to notice that the counterculture contained but a fraction of his envisaged constituency. T.M.'s young teacher/salesmen were requested to cut their hair short, wear suits and ties, and spread the word to Middle America, where people were less concerned with talk of "cosmic consciousness" than with quick relief from fatigue, stress, and high blood pressure (which, nonpartisan studies indicate, T.M. can provide).

In steadily increasing numbers, people in all walks of life began to follow the flower children in trading $125 and an offering of fruits, flowers and a clean white hanky for a

John also changed his opinion of the meditation itself, concluding that any beneficial effects were due to wishful thinking. T.M. was nothing more than "colored water," and "a waste of time." George disagreed. He thought T.M. was a fine enough introduction to the spiritual plane, only he himself was now prepared to graduate to even loftier paths.

For John, the defection from the Maharishi marked a return to his restless public quest for meaning and identity. George increasingly immersed himself in the more intense and traditional dogmas of Krishna Consciousness (although he declined to shave his head and wear the prescription orange robes, and didn't feel he could live without coffee and cigarets), while Paul began to retreat toward the security of more bourgeois preoccupations.

True to their mythological status, the Beatles provided an almost archetypal cross section of the thousands of acid-heads of the 1960's who went on to embrace Indian mysticism. For some of them, like George, the fervor intensified; for them the East would always have all the answers. Others, like John, continued to drift from one unconventional self-awareness trip to another. Yet others joined Paul in concluding that the whole business of consciousness expansion wasn't worth the trouble, and that the straight world wasn't so distasteful after all.

John, Paul, and George emerged out of acid and meditation three very different personalities who seldom saw eye-to-eye any more. Each had developed strong individual identities, and sharply contrasting musical styles to match. The trip to India was the last one the Beatles ever took together.

The disintegration of the group as a tightly-knit unit was probably hastened by Brian Epstein's death from an overdose of bromide on August 27, 1967, while the Beatles were off on their first fling with the Maharishi. At the age of 32, their manager became the first major casualty of an era of popular music that he had been instrumental in bringing about.

Epstein's critics have faulted his business expertise, contending that under a tougher and more experienced manager the Beatles might have piled up even more money than they did. But Brian deserves tremendous credit for having recognized the Beatles' potential, and for having stuck with them, long before anyone in the music industry would take them seriously—as well as for his part in refining the image with which the Beatles captivated the world in 1963 and 1964.

The Beatles did not, at first, attempt to find a new manager. "No one could possibly replace Brian," said Paul, who himself assumed the task of holding the Beatles together, keeping an eye on their finances, and piloting the group's career. The first project they embarked upon after Epstein's death was one largely of Paul's own invention: *Magical Mystery Tour,* an hour-long color film, starring the Beatles and written and directed by themselves, to be shown on T.V. around Christmas time. According to the press releases, the gist of the film would go something like this:

Away in the sky, beyond the clouds, live four or five magicians. By casting Wonderful Spells they turn the Most Ordinary Coach Trip into a Magical Mystery Tour. . . .

For the rest of the group's career, the Beatles, like Dylan, would find themselves in an unusual position. Ordinarily, pop stars who do not make regular personal appearances are swiftly forgotten by the public. But by the late Sixties, the Beatles and Dylan had accumulated so much mystique that for them to have appeared on stage like ordinary mortals might have actually proven anticlimactic.

Most artists could have attained that status in only one way—the way Jimi Hendrix and Janis Joplin chose. But Dylan and the Beatles vanished from public display when their popularity, prestige, and influence were at such a peak that their inaccessibility made them even more intriguing. Dylan became literally a Howard Hughes figure: a mythical recluse, utterly beyond public reach. Individually, John, Paul, George, and Ringo did remain relatively visible, and available to the media; but the *group* would virtually disappear from public view. With the exceptions of *Magical Mystery Tour, Let It Be,* and a smattering of brief T.V. spots, the Beatles would henceforth limit their performances to the recording studio, behind closed doors.

In 1967, however, fans were still eagerly awaiting a new series of concert tours. The Beatles at first felt obliged to find some way to meet these expectations, and hinted that they might play live once they figured out how to present their new music onstage. Of course they never did, and that is probably just as well. It would have been next to impossible for them to reproduce in the flesh the fantasmagoria that *Sgt. Pepper* evoked in the imaginations of its listeners.

Bands like Jefferson Airplane and the Grateful Dead *were*

(Keystone Press Agency)

beginning to utilize stroboscopes, films, and psychedelic light shows in an attempt to augment their record-breaking decibel counts with multi-media spectaculars. But these seldom amounted to much more than superficial gimmicks. It would be another six years before David Bowie would succeed in complementing his ambitious concept albums with elaborate sets and sophisticated theatrics, and before Pink Floyd would manage to reproduce faithfully a complicated recording as dominated by sound effects and studio electronics as their *Dark Side Of the Moon.* In 1967 all that was still too many light years away from the sorts of concerts the Beatles had been wont to give only a year before, so they declined the challenge of trying to do *Sgt. Pepper* justice in live performance. (According to *Rolling Stone,* the Beatles' representatives *did* briefly try to negotiate a concert linkup with Leonard Bernstein and the New York Philharmonic.)

The Beatles proposed instead to devise what John called "a film vehicle to go with the new music." The ingredients, he announced, would be "a lot of laughs, some off-beat characters, a few very glamorous girls, a bit of dancing, and quite a bit of magic." As it turned out, however, *Magical Mystery Tour* did not prove to be the ideal means of keeping

the Beatles in the public eye—not that the world was likely to forget them anyway.

At the time John seemed as enthusiastic about the show as anybody, but he later insisted in a *Rolling Stone* interview that the *Mystery Tour* was strictly Paul's trip: "I thought, fuckin' ADA, I've never made a film, what's he mean, write a script. . . . And then George and I were sort of grumbling, you know, 'fuckin' movie, oh well, we better do it,' feeling that we owed the public, that we should do these things."

In any case, all the Beatles went along for the ride as Paul rented a bus and filled it with weirdos. In best Merry Prankster style, the Beatles and their entourage careened around the English countryside, filming whatever happened to happen, and occasionally staging premeditated happenings along the way.

The result was a colorful home movie, with plenty of cute glimpses of the Beatles goofing it up in wizards' outfits and white tuxedos. It was also riddled with the sorts of gimmicks—lots of slow and fast motion, dizzy zooms in and out of close-up, and superimpositions of images—that give the impression of clever kids playing with a new toy. The incoherent editing did not evoke the unpredictable hallucinations of a "mystery trip" nearly so well as had the lyrical and musical non sequiturs of songs like "Strawberry Fields" or "A Day In the Life."

To be able to dream is one thing, but for artists to successfully convey their visions to viewers, readers, or listeners also requires great self-discipline and talent. When it came to making imaginative pop music, the Beatles were pros. No matter how fanciful or experimental their ideas, the Beatles, unlike many of their late-Sixties imitators, were able in the recording studios to realize them tastefully, succinctly, and in a way that was accessible to millions. But they proved to be somewhat less well equipped to capture their whims and fantasies on film; and *Magical Mystery Tour,* despite its fleeting charms, struck even many fans as being, as often as not, more tedious than mysterious.

The show was aired to about fifteen million Britons on December 26; the morning after, the critics pounced like vultures. They clearly relished the first real opportunity they'd had in years to tear the Beatle myth down to size, and overreacted accordingly. "The harder they come, the harder they fall. . . ." read a front-page attack in the London *Daily Express.* "I cannot ever remember seeing such blatant rubbish." Other verdicts included "chaotic," "appalling," and "a colossal conceit."

A million-dollar deal for American broadcast rights was withdrawn, so *Magical Mystery Tour* has become something of a cult item in the U.S., surfacing occasionally at Beatle fan conventions or as a midnight special in hip movie theatres. In that capacity, it holds up much better than it did when millions of Britons were led to believe it would be the event of the season. (Paul's idea for a sequel depicting the Beatles at an Edwardian picnic was permanently shelved.)

The score, unsurprisingly, was received with considerably more enthusiasm than the film itself. For their *Mystery* music, the Beatles utilized for just about the last time the extravagantly varied palette with which they had created *Revolver* and *Sgt. Pepper:* the strings, woodwinds, sound effects, electronics, and the rest. The results ranged from some rather blatant *Sgt. Pepper* rehashes to two of the most impressive Beatle songs ever.

Paul's "Magical Mystery Tour" theme song is little more than a motif, catchy but undeveloped—like its counterpart on *Sgt. Pepper,* an exhortation to listeners to snap into the spirit of the Beatles' presentation. "Sit back and let the evening go" has become "roll up for the mystery tour . . . satisfaction guaranteed," and as in "Sgt. Pepper's Lonely Hearts

Club Band," trumpeteers are brought in to add some razzle-dazzle to the proceedings. Similarly, "Your Mother Should Know" (also McCartney's) is a lyrical and musical Xerox of "When I'm 64," and, as is often the case with Xeroxes, somewhat less focused than the original. Among the details missing here are the bittersweet wit of "64," and the clarinets. Paul would retrieve both a year later with "Honey Pie," the next in his series of excursions into pre-World War II nostalgia.

In "Flying," the third of *Mystery Tour*'s charming off-the-cuff-ers, and the first composition credited to all four Beatles, they uncharacteristically manage without words. Instead, all four chant "la-la-la's" over an instrumental track that evolved largely out of studio jamming. John plays the leads on his Mellotron (a new keyboard wonder that could be programmed to sound like almost any instrument, and which would soon become popular with producers too cheap to hire real strings) and the coda includes another collection of those famous backward recordings and tape loops, here courtesy of John and Ringo.

Although few would file it under the Beatles' Great Works, "Flying" has received more radio exposure than all but a handful of their songs. For countless disk jockeys soon discovered in this ethereal, infectious theme an ideal way to fill up those awkward odd moments before the hourly news: because there were no words, it didn't seem rude to chatter at the same time, or to phase it out mid-song.

With "Blue Jay Way" George finally attempts to adapt some of his Indian-derived ideas to a more Western setting. The sitar and tabla are replaced by a murky-sounding cello and Ringo's drums, and the lyrical setting is "a fog upon L.A." (Liberal use of "phasing" gives the production an unusually foggy texture.) Harrison retains his mystical drone, supplied here by his Hammond organ instead of the customary tanpuras, and it does help evoke both the fog and the monotony of waiting all night for those who've lost themselves in it.

"Blue Jay Way" may be a metaphor of those people who "lose their souls" in the fog of materialism, whom we'd heard tell of in "Within You Without You"; but because it is less obvious and preachy, it is much more intriguing. However, although George's songwriting may be improving, he still doesn't know when enough is enough. Which is particularly unfortunate when the phrase he chooses to repeat 29 times is "don't be long."

"The Fool On the Hill" proved to be one of the most irresistible, universal, and widely recorded of all Paul's ballads. The notion that a fool, in his simplicity, might be far wiser than the sophisticates who scorn him has always touched people; it can be traced back to numerous fairy tales, and accounts of kings who valued the counsel of their court fool above all others', through Dostoevski, whose Prince Myshkin *(The Idiot)* is one of the most beloved characters in literature. In "The Fool On the Hill," McCartney succeeds in adapting this somewhat mystical theme simply and well to the format of a three-minute pop ballad. His song was particularly popular with the growing segment of the population that was trying to recapture a sense of childlike innocence. The melody and arrangement are kept appropriately simple, although Paul takes the liberty of adding flute and recorder to the long list of instruments he can be heard playing on Beatle records.

In "I Am the Walrus"—one of John's most remarkable creations, certainly the most utterly mad—the Beatles yank out all the stops. From its ominously orchestrated entry, "the Walrus" advances relentlessly, each beat of its robot-like meter driving the listener one step further into total absurdity, hallucination, and chaos. Like demented geniuses,

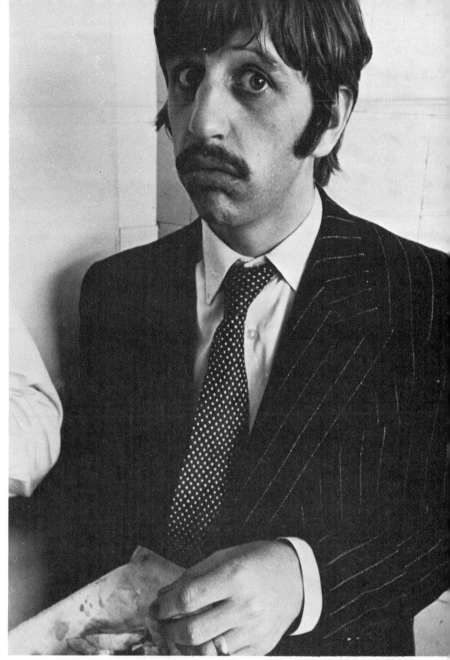

(Keystone Press Agency)

the Beatles and George Martin pile on layers of cellos, violins, horns, and then finally a full-scale choir chanting "oompah, oompah, everybody's got one," as John harangues us with an extraordinary combination of *A Spaniard in the Works'* outrageous wordplay and *Sgt. Pepper's* psychedelic derangements.

An inspiration for "I Am the Walrus" can be found in those famous lines of nonsense verse from Lewis Carroll's *Through the Looking Glass:*

"The time has come," the Walrus said,
  "To talk of many things:
Of shoes—and ships—and sealing wax—
  Of cabbages—and kings—
And why the sea is boiling hot—
  And whether pigs have wings."

This Walrus talks—rather, rants—of many things indeed, from Indian philosophy:

I am he
as you are he
as you are me
and we are all together,

Magical Mystery Tour: "Satisfaction guaranteed . . ." (Keystone Press Agency)

Single, Japan, 1967 (Odeon)

to indecent exposure:

*. . . pornographic priestess,
boy you've been a naughty girl,
you let your knickers down.*

(For that, "I Am the Walrus" was added to the B.B.C.'s list of songs unsuitable for airplay.)

Along the way, the Walrus offers flights of fancy that range from such grue as:

*Yellow matter custard
dripping from a dead dog's eye*

to the sheer lunacy of:

*Elementary penguins singing Hare Krishna,
Man, you should have seen them
kicking Edgar Allan Poe.*

Throughout the second half of the record, crackling voices drift in and out of the mix, as if someone were fiddling with a radio dial. But when the music finally fades away the voices briefly linger, and we find we have been listening all along to

a dramatization of Shakespeare's *King Lear* (Act IV, Scene 6).

The six *Magical Mystery Tour* numbers were released in Britain in a package containing two seven-inch E.P.'s and a lavish 24-page booklet containing stills and cartoon-strip adaptations of the show. For the Americans, however, Capitol concocted a *Magical Mystery Tour* L.P. by adding all the Beatles' 1967 singles, including the latest, Paul's innocuous and highly commercial "Hello Goodbye." This in itself was fine—better a padded *Mystery Tour* than a butchered *Revolver*—and the booklet proved to be even more psychedelic when blown up to 12 inches square from seven. (Those odd creatures on the record jackets are, of course, the Walrus and his Eggmen: from left to right, Paul, George, and Ringo.)

Unfortunately, however, Capitol didn't bother to acquire the stereo masters of most of these tacked-on singles before rushing out its Christmas bonanza; consequently, tunes like "Penny Lane" and "Baby You're a Rich Man" are

The unveiling of Apple (Globe Photos)

John after giving his Rolls a new look (Keystone Press Agency)

only heard in "electronically reprocessed" stereo. Which means that the highs are filtered from one channel of the monaural masters and the lows from the other, to create the illusion of stereo by substituting two low-fidelity tracks for one high-fidelity mono recording. As the imaginative use of stereo was an important (and innovative) facet of the Beatles' 1967 productions, Capitol's sloppiness in this case is particularly annoying. Fans who wish to hear the songs in their full stereophonic glory are advised to hunt for the overseas pressings.

On December 5, 1967, the Beatles unveiled their boutique on London's busy Baker Street, called "Apple" (a word that was destined to become almost synonymous with "Beatles"; *Mystery Tour* was also billed an Apple presentation). Perhaps this shouldn't have come as a surprise, as the Beatles had always been fashion trend-setters. So that Apple might be, in Paul's words, "a beautiful place where you could buy beautiful things," the shop was liberally stocked with the sort of orgasmic fashions then in favor with the Beatles themselves. Items included cloth from India and beads from Greece, stitched together to create costumes

depicting "Water," "Fire," or "Space"; and the Fool (a quartet of Dutch designers), who created most of the expensive merchandise, were also hired to emblazon the outside of the building with brightly-colored planets, clouds, rainbows, and mystical symbols. Staid neighboring businesses sued in vain to have 94 Baker Street repainted more conservatively. The Fool owed most of their brief fame as designers and painters of psychedelic fantasy to projects commissioned by the Beatles. Their other works included the exteriors of George Harrison's Esher bungalow and of John Lennon's piano.

Around this time John also had his Rolls Royce coated with outrageous psychedelic designs. It swiftly became one of the most notorious cars in the world, and a top draw at automobile shows on both sides of the Atlantic. Lennon's Rolls even prompted a denouncement in the English press by a traffic expert, who contended that its startling appearance posed a hazard to unsuspecting drivers. As 1967's King Ludwigs, the Beatles made certain that every last facet of their lives from their appearance and their music to their houses and their chauffeured limousines, would be as color-

L.P., Germany, 1968 (Apple)

ful, as outlandish, or as magical as possible. Their image and their bank accounts permitted them to satisfy all their off-beat whims, including a psychedelic boutique.

Even the timetable on the much-coveted invitations to the party with which Apple was launched featured a touch of Beatlesque surrealism: "Come at 7:46. Fashion show at 8:16. . . ." Only two Beatles, John and George, turned up to sip apple juice and mingle with the star-studded throng, as Paul decided to repair to his new farm in Scotland and hide from the world (an increasingly characteristic habit). Ringo was in Rome, starring in a film, for the first time, minus the others (he played a Mexican gardener in a tepidly received adaptation of Terry Southern's *Candy*).

Like many of the Beatles' other impulsive brain waves, however, the boutique soon lost its novelty and turned into a headache. Less than eight months after Apple's well-publicized opening, the Beatles scored even bigger headlines with the way they summarily abandoned the enterprise.

On the morning of July 30, 1968, Apple's cashiers informed startled customers that they needn't trouble to pay. At first passersby on the street were collared and offered free tangerine velvet capes; then news of the sale of the century quickly spread by word of mouth. By the time it reached the airwaves and the afternoon tabloids, the scene on Baker Street was pandemonium.

"We decided . . . the retail business wasn't our particular scene," explained Paul. "So we went along, chose all the stuff that we wanted—I got a smashing overcoat—and then told our friends. Now everything that's left is for the public."

By the end of the day, nothing was left of about $25,000 worth of the Fool's quasi-medieval designs, and the boutique was shut down for good. The name "Apple," however, would shortly be revived for even more implausible schemes.

Before leaving for the Maharishi's Indian retreat on February 21, 1968, the Beatles recorded four more songs, including "Hey Bulldog," which, along with three unreleased earlier numbers, was stashed aside for *Yellow Submarine*. In selecting a single to hold the fort in their absence, the Beatles initially plumped for John's appropriately transcendental "Across the Universe"; but when Lennon, hurt at McCartney's lackluster contribution, decided that the

particular version wasn't suitable for release, the honor went to Paul's "Lady Madonna." (The original rendition of "Universe" was donated to an all-star charity L.P. entitled *No One's Gonna Change Our World,* benefiting the World Wildlife Fund.)

Musically, "Lady Madonna" represented a return to the sort of black-influenced rock 'n' roll that the Beatles had not bothered with since 1966's "Got To Get You Into My Life." They frankly admitted that "Madonna"'s melody and arrangement were based on an old record called "Bad Penny Blues." Like "Got To Get You . . .," "Madonna" is goosed along by a sassy horn section, and McCartney belts away in the manner of such vintage rockers as Elvis Presley or Fats Domino (who eventually had a success with "Madonna" himself).

The lyrics, however, are as tantalizingly cryptic as anything the Beatles had written over the previous year. A favorite interpretation at the time was that Lady Madonna manages to make ends meet by entertaining gentlemen callers, who are described according to the times of their appointments:

Friday night arrives without a suitcase,
Sunday morning creeps in like a nun. . . .

The B-side offers a considerably more transcendental message, as John and Paul finally agreed to allow George's budding songwriting talents onto a Beatles single. "The Inner Light" proved to be the best—and last—of George's attempts to incorporate Indian music into the context of the Beatles, though the lyrics were pinched almost verbatim from a Chinese poem from the *Tao Te Ching,* some of which reads as follows:

Without going out of his door, he knows everything in the world, without looking out of his window, he knows the way to heaven. The farther we go, the less we learn.

"The Inner Light"'s instrumental track was recorded with some authentic Indian classical virtuosos in Bombay, where George had flown in January to supervise recording of his *Wonderwall* film soundtrack. Paul professed to be delighted with his junior colleague's progress: "Forget the Indian music and listen to the melody. Don't you think it's a beautiful melody? It's really lovely."

But George later insisted that persuading the others to take his material seriously had never been easy. John and Paul always seemed to consider Harrison compositions a rather low priority on the Beatles' recording schedule. Nor did George find much of an ally in the producer's box. "I'm afraid he didn't get much encouragement from me, either," recalls George Martin. ". . . When you have two who are so enormously talented, like Lennon and McCartney, it's silly to look elsewhere."

Certain members of other well-known groups were even more frustrated than George Harrison (Mick Jagger and Keith Richard condescended only once to allow a Bill Wyman composition onto a Stones record, which was more than Brian Jones ever got for his songwriting efforts). But Harrison's resentment at his little-sibling status in the Beatles contributed to the discord that was beginning to develop behind the colorful sets of what John Lennon, years later, would modestly remember as "the greatest show on earth."

Giving it all away at Apple, July 1968 (UPI)

The Beatles' Hits—June 1967 through August 1968

TITLE AND LABEL	FIRST APPEARANCE	HIGHEST POSITION	WEEKS ON CHART
U.S. Top 100 Singles			
All You Need Is Love (Capitol)*	July 22, 1967	1	11
Baby, You're a Rich Man (Capitol)	July 29, 1967	34	5
Hello Goodbye (Capitol)*	Dec. 2, 1967	1	11
I Am the Walrus (Capitol)	Dec. 9, 1967	56	4
Lady Madonna (Capitol)*	March 23, 1968	4	11
The Inner Light (Capitol)	March 30, 1968	96	1
U.S. Top 200 L.P.'s			
Sgt. Pepper's Lonely Hearts Club Band (Capitol)*	June 23, 1967	1	121
Magical Mystery Tour (Capitol)*	Dec. 23, 1967	1	82
British Top Twenty Singles			
All You Need Is Love (Parlophone)	July 15, 1967	1	10
Hello Goodbye (Parlophone)	Dec. 2, 1967	1	10
Magical Mystery Tour (EP) (Parlophone)	Dec. 16, 1967	2	9
Lady Madonna (Parlophone)	March 23, 1968	1	6

(Chart positions according to *Billboard;* asterisk [*]: Record Industry Association of America certified Gold Record/Million Seller)

L.P., Britain, 1969 (Star Line)

George tweaks a Blue Meanie's nose (UPI)

SHINE ON TILL TOMORROW

A poached egg in the Underground on the Bakerloo line between Trafalgar Square and Charing Cross? Yes, Paul. A sock full of elephant's dung on Otterspool Promenade? Give me ten minutes, Ringo. Two Turkish dwarfs dancing the Charleston on the sideboard? Male or female, John? Pubic hair from Sonny Liston? It's early closing, George (gulp), but give me until noon tomorrow.
—Derek Taylor, the Beatles' Press Officer

On July 17, 1968 the Beatles were besieged by hysterical mobs for the last time. The occasion was the London premiere of *Yellow Submarine,* the last flower of the Beatles' Summer of Love. The film, which received mixed notices in the British press and near-unanimous raves when it surfaced in New York four months later, provided a spectacular climax to the "psychedelic" phase of the Beatles' career, albeit one that the musicians themselves had little hand in orchestrating.

According to producer Al Brodax, the plot was inspired by a three AM phone call from John Lennon, who said: "Wouldn't it be great if Ringo was followed down the street by a yellow submarine?" But that, apart from a brief, awkward appearance at the end, and a soundtrack featuring rejects from the *Magical Mystery Tour* and "Lady Madonna" sessions, was about the extent of the Beatles' contribution to their third feature-length movie. Before the premiere, Paul admitted: "I like what I've seen about it, but . . . it's not us. I won't take the credit even if it's a big smash." *Yellow Submarine* is a classic example of a myth's capacity for self-perpetuation without the participation or even encouragement of the gods themselves.

Though the Beatles had long since assumed total control of their recorded product—by this time including packaging, editing, and promotion—their three major movies all represent outsiders' readings of the Beatle legend. As film stars, the Fab Four had progressed from playing (more or less) themselves in *A Hard Day's Night,* to enacting comic-strip parodies of themselves in *Help!,* to abdicating altogether now in favor of *Yellow Submarine's* 1967-stereotyped animations: Paul as flower-twirling dandy, George as spaced-out mystic, and so on. Even their lines are intoned by actors. But just as *A Hard Day's Night* accurately mirrored people's fantasies of circa-1964 Beatlemania, *Yellow Submarine* succeeds, at least visually, in capturing the mixture of otherworldly naiveté and worldly sophistication that the Beatles seemed to epitomize in 1967.

"We derived a lot from the *Sgt. Pepper* album," said Brodax. "We took the word 'pepper' which is positive, spicy, and created a place called Pepperland which is full of color and music. But in the hills around live Blue Meanies, who hate color, hate everything positive."

Like the records that inspired it, this wonderland was assumed by many to be best explored from an elevated state of consciousness. Only *2001: A Space Odyssey* attracted a comparable cult of glassy-eyed connoisseurs.

Yellow Submarine was assembled, under the supervision of German poster artist Heinz Edelmann, from five million separate sketches (later sold as "one of a kind" souvenirs). The result is if nothing else an extravagant feast for the eyes, aptly described by a review in *The Leader* as a mélange of "Art Nouveau and psychedelic, op and pop, Dada and surrealist, Hieronymus Bosch and just plain bosh."

To this list of ingredients might be added Walt Disney's *Fantasia*—also a favorite with the head set—with which *Yellow Submarine* was often compared. Like *Fantasia, Submarine* works best as a visual complement to music. In its voyage into posterity, however, the yellow sub is in danger of capsizing under the weight of its embarrassingly trite and heavy-handed script (largely contributed by Erich Segal of *Love Story* fame). The soundtrack album, not issued until January 1969, features four new tunes, all trifling baubles in the *Sgt. Pepper/Mystery Tour* tradition. The only one that seems to have taken more than a few hours to write and record is George's "It's All Too Much," whose highlights include some searing Velvet Underground feedback and an unusually witty epigram that just about sums up the Spirit of '67:

Show me that I'm everywhere,
and get me home for tea.

"Only a Northern Song" (also by George) was actually written and recorded within the hour after King Features demanded a new number. According to George Martin, the selection of other songs like John's "Hey Bulldog" (cut from the American prints of the film) was determined by the Beatles deciding: "We don't really need this in the album. Let's just give them that one."

The *Yellow Submarine* L.P. was originally to have contained all the Beatle music in the soundtrack, including the likes of "Eleanor Rigby," "Nowhere Man," and "Baby You're a Rich Man"; but with the exceptions of the title song and "All You Need Is Love" (the moral of the film) these were ditched in favor of Martin instrumentals.

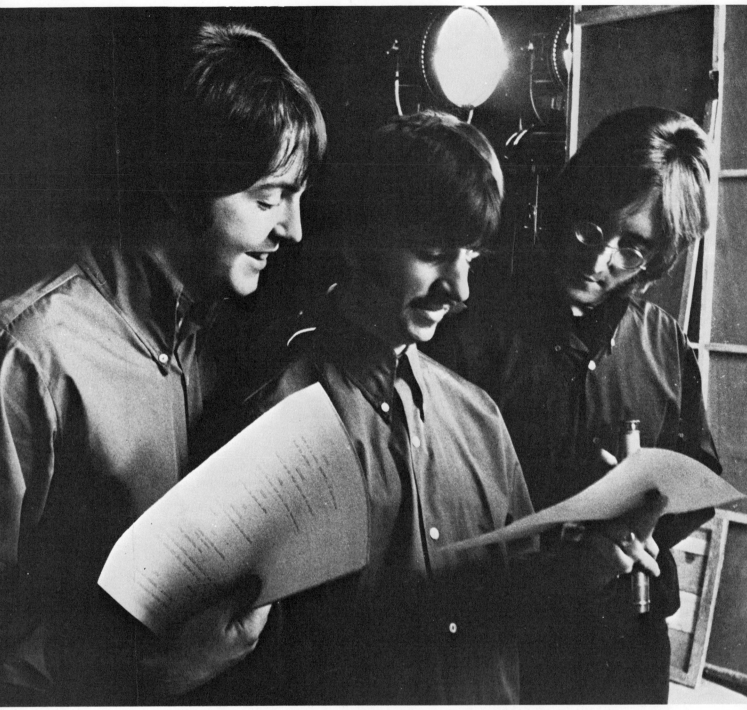

Paul, Ringo and John rehearsing for their appearance in *Yellow Submarine* (Transworld Feature Syndicate)

Yellow Submarine also inspired the second great wave of Beatle novelties—lunchboxes, puzzles, dolls, and keychains that updated the moptop image of the 1964 versions with a dash of the trendy psychedelia as exemplified by the film itself; one of the most charming of these artifacts is the yellow submarine Corgi Toy (complete with revolving periscopes) out of which little plastic Beatles rear their heads at the flick of a switch. As film critic Pauline Kael had the foresight to note: "Attacks on the consumer society become products to be consumed."

By the same process, long hair, marijuana, the alternative press, rock music, and all the other trappings and symbols of the counterculture were rapidly becoming accepted—and coöpted—by the mainstream of society. The Beatles themselves were about to learn how difficult it is to beat the Establishment at its own game.

Yellow Submarine Memorabilia:

The following products were licensed by King Features to appear in conjunction with the film's U.S. release.

Pride Creations (New York):
Papier-mâché banks; key chains; mugs (China, pottery, ceramic); popsies (wooden figures)

Western Publishing Company, Inc. (Racine, Wisconsin):
Punch-out wall decorations; Yellow Submarine Comic Book;
desk calendar

Topps Chewing Gum, Inc. (New York):
Trading cards; pressure sensitive stickers; tattoos; flying things
(styrofoam gliders); posters 10 inches by 18½ inches

A & M Leatherline, Inc. (New York):
Letter desk set: pen; blotter; memo pad; pencil cup; scrap
book; diary; address book; photo album; autograph book;
buttons

Sheffield Watch, Inc. (New York):
Wristwatch; clocks

Henderson-Hoggard, Inc. (New York):
Closet carnival hanger

Mettoy Company, Ltd. (Corgi) (New York):
Die-cast submarine; miniature figures

Thermos Div. of King Seeley (Norwich, Connecticut):
Lunch boxes; vacuum bottles

Unicorn Creations, Inc. (New York):
Boxed writing paper and envelopes; large paper post cards 11
inches by 14 inches; paper book marks; corrugated cardboard
bulletin boards; corrugated cardboard picture frames; paper
posters

Poster Prints (Conshohocken, Pa.):
Posters; post cards; embroidered patches

Ed-u-cards Mfg. Corp. (New York):
Card games of all types; giant trading cards

Collegeville Flag and Mfg. Co. (New York):
Masquerade costumes; flags

Varsity House, Inc. (New York):
Sweatshirts

Ideal Toy Corporation (New York):
Pajama Bags; curler bags; stuffed pillows cloth; shoe bags; felt
wall decorations; stuffed dolls; inflatable swim toys

Model Products Corp. (Mount Clemens, Michigan):
Hobby kits; plastic assembly kits

Hassenfeld Bros. (Pawtucket, Rhode Island):
Pencil-by-number sets; poster-by-number sets; board games

Mass Arts, Inc. (New York):
Inflatable vinyl pillows; three-dimensional inflatable vinyl rep-
licas; inflatable vinyl earrings; inflatable vinyl key chains; vinyl
tote bags; vinyl aprons; plastic and wooden lamps

The Barr Rubber Products Co. (New York):
Vinyl play balls

Craftmaster Corp. (Toledo, Ohio):
Paint-by-numbers sets; mosette sets; dry transfers; paper
sculpture; sandpaper painting sets

Sunshine Art Studios (Springfield, Massachusetts):
Boxed greeting cards and card notes; die-cut mobiles

International Posters (New York):
Posters; laminated book covers; paper bags; paper tiffany
lamps

Golden Press, Inc. (New York):
Yellow Submarine Calendar; four-color Yellow Submarine
comic poster

After John, Paul, George, and Ringo had all trickled home
from Rishikesh, they began to channel their energies into
creating a Pepperland of their own, the first multi-million
dollar, multi-media conglomerate to be operated both by
and for the turned-on generation without any interference
from the "men in suits." The original blueprints of the
Beatles' Apple Corps called for an acid dream come true.

After making arrangements for Capitol and E.M.I. to distribute Apple records in, respectively, North America and the
Rest Of the World—thereby satisfying their contractual obligations to the twin labels—John Lennon and Paul Mc-

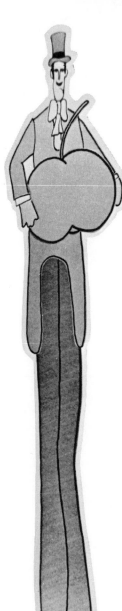

Mobile (© King Features Syndicate Inc. 1968)

Puzzle (© King Features Syndicate Inc. 1968)

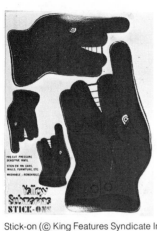

Stick-on (© King Features Syndicate Inc. 1968)

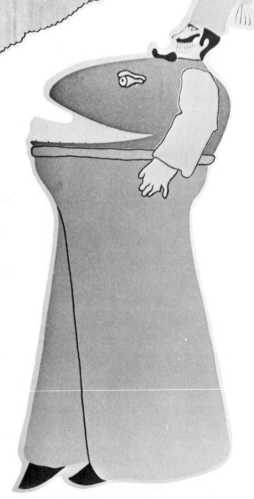

Coin bank (© King Features Syndicate Inc. 1968)

Hanger (© King Features Syndicate Inc. 1968)

Souvenir booklet (© King Features Syndicate Inc. 1968)

Switch plate cover (© King Features Syndicate Inc. 1968)

Notebook (© King Features Syndicate Inc. 1968)

Cartney winged to New York to unveil their plans on a Chinese junk in the Hudson River. Describing the philosophy behind Apple as "Western Communism," Paul told the assembled reporters and businessmen: "We want to set up a system where someone doesn't have to go on his knees in someone's office—probably yours."

As if every struggling would-be superstar on the planet hadn't already heard the word, the Beatles placed ads in the British music papers that coupled a photograph of a young musician with the legend:

THIS MAN HAS TALENT . . . One day he sang his songs to a tape-recorder, and, remembering to enclose a picture of himself, sent the tape . . . to Apple Music, 94 Baker St., London W.1. If you were thinking of doing the same thing yourself—do it now! This man now owns a Bentley!

The Beatles also let it be known that Apple was no less eager to sponsor aspiring writers, film-makers, and even inventors.

The ensuing avalanche of tapes, manuscripts, films, and nutty propositions, many of which were delivered in person, came as no surprise to anyone, except, apparently, the Beatles. George Harrison later told *Melody Maker:* "We were flooded with every person imaginable who could play an instrument or sing a note! . . . Apple just became a lunatic asylum."

Apart from the fact that nobody ever got around to sifting through all this material, Apple managed for about a year to live up to much of its original spirit. Business decisions were often dictated by the I Ching, or by the house astrologer. Liquor flowed freely throughout business hours, and Apple errand boy Richard DiLello—who would title his memoirs *The Longest Cocktail Party*—was in charge of insuring that hashish always be equally available.

Though Apple never managed to unleash any literary or cinematic masterpieces, its electronics division, run by a Greek pal of Lennon's named Magic Alex, busily consumed tens of thousands of dollars producing such inventions as fruit-shaped radios, a transistorized speaker that could pick up sounds from turntables without recourse to wires, and a box guaranteed to do nothing for five years. None of these devices, however, managed to escape to the marketplace before the Blue Meanies were summoned in 1969 to, so to speak, make the trains run on time.

Despite the distractions, a great deal of fine music

Stationery (© King Features Syndicate Inc. 1968)

emanated from Apple. Both Paul and George proved to be remarkably talented both as producers and as A and R men. Through their efforts, Apple gave the music scene its first taste of such stars as Mary Hopkin, Billy Preston, James Taylor, and the group that Paul christened Badfinger (after his original title for "With a Little Help From My Friends"), whose first L.P. *Rolling Stone* would hail as the best early Beatle album since *Beatles '65.*

Apple also sponsored artists who, while hardly destined for superstardom, were no less dear to various Beatles' hearts. George produced an L.P.'s worth of mantras chanted by the London branch of the Radha Krishna Temple, and Ringo signed on his old chum John Tavener to record a classical work called *The Whale.* For a touch of class, the Modern Jazz Quartet was also added to the roster. But all the Beatles would eventually find the anarchic nature of their enterprise a bit less of a turn-on than they had originally envisaged. The building on London's stylish Savile Row, where Apple established permanent residence, proved to be a magnet for every kind of opportunist, Beatlemaniac, and just plain maniac. Hell's Angles, nudists, and Ken Kesey moved in and literally made themselves at home.

Even some of the Beatles' trusted lackeys failed to live up to the Utopian spirit of the venture. In 1970, John would tell *Rolling Stone's* Jann Wenner: "People were robbing us and living on us to the tune of eighteen or twenty thousand pounds a week [that] was rolling out of Apple and nobody was doing anything about it. All our buddies that worked for us for fifty years were all just living and drinking and eating like fuckin' Rome."

The Beatles eventually realized that a hip corporation was something of a contradiction in terms. One day they would all decide to enlist someone ruthless enough to sort out the chaos; only their inability to agree on a candidate would insure the demise of a lot more than the original spirit of Apple Corps. But, in the meantime, the carnival would trip merrily through an eventful first year.

Stationery (© King Features Syndicate Inc. 1968)

Stationery (© King Features Syndicate Inc. 1968)

Apple, like the group itself, quickly became primarily Paul's toy. John was already totally absorbed by his love cloud with Yoko Ono, a liaison that would soon become the most celebrated romance of the Sixties. Over a year before, Lennon had fallen under the spell of the Japanese artist's work at an exhibit at his friend John Dunbar's Indica gallery.

"There was an apple on sale there for 200 quid, I thought that was fantastic," John would recall in his famous *Rolling Stone* interview. "I got the humor in her work immediately . . . 200 quid to watch the apple decompose. . . .

"Dunbar insisted she say hello to the millionaire, you know what I mean. And she came up and handed me a card which said 'Breathe' on it, one of her instructions, so I just went [pant]."

John began keeping Yoko's book *Grapefruit* by his bedside as a constant source of inspiration. After he got back from India, where he had whiled away much of his time corresponding with her, Lennon invited Yoko to his house when the wife was away. They decided to make an album together. "It was midnight when we started *Two Virgins,* it was dawn when we finished, and then we made love. It was very beautiful."

His marriage to Liverpool's self-effacing Cynthia Powell had apparently been growing stale for John—much as was his artistic partnership with McCartney. In Yoko (who was seven years older than John) he seemed to find a single figure to replace them both. By the end of 1968, the Lennons would be divorced; and, while John's involvement with the Beatles would not be officially terminated quite so summarily, it was nonetheless also doomed.

The daughter of a wealthy financier and the veteran of two broken marriages, Yoko had never bothered to listen to the Beatles' music. But this did not bother Lennon. He always knew, he said, that the girl of his dreams "wouldn't be some fan who bought the records." He and Yoko had other things in common. It is easy to see how her work—which was as multi-faceted as his, embracing music, fine arts, writing, and film—might have attracted him. If, as Tom Edison once claimed, "genius is one per cent inspiration and 99 per cent perspiration," John had often seemed to find the second part of the bargain less palatable than the first. Throughout the Beatles' career, it had undoubtedly been Lennon who had most of the inspired brainwaves. Frequently, however, it was Paul's dedication and more mundane talent that had enabled the Beatles to translate this inspiration into

products with mass appeal. Even Lennon's two books (which, incidentally, were adapted for the London stage in 1968 with a little help from Victor Spinetti and Adrienne Kennedy) consisted entirely of vignettes. When John tried to follow *A Spaniard In the Works* with a longer, more coherent work, he soon lost interest in his characters and scrapped the project.

But Yoko Ono apparently convinced Lennon that this was not necessarily a handicap. Her very specialty was "unfinished" art. Instead of troubling to complete pieces herself, she often preferred to invite her audiences to exercise their own imaginations. Many of her works are simply concepts, unencumbered by any tangible presentation. Although occasionally she followed through with her ideas—as, for example, in 1967's *Film No. 4,* a sequence of 310 bare bottoms, or the subsequent *No. 5,* 90 minutes' worth of John's smile—or her famous caterwauling concerts—Yoko was more likely, as in "A Piece For Orchestra," to limit her work to a set of instructions:

Count all the stars of that night by heart.
The piece ends when all the orchestra members finish counting the stars, or when it dawns.
This can be done with windows instead of stars.

This piece, from *Grapefruit,* can be taken either as a poem or a musical score; Yoko was never particularly concerned with such pedantic distinctions. Like John himself, she was more interested in provoking the world's drones with preposterous and outrageous "happenings" calculated to challenge everything they had been conditioned to suppose art—or life—should be like.

As far as John was concerned, Yoko would replace the complements of Paul's more conventional talents and Cynthia's more traditional femininity with the mirror image of himself. The more he immersed himself in her reflection, it seemed to John, the more he found who he really was, and what he wanted to be. Yoko, he marvelled, "is me in drag."

Stationery (© King Features Syndicate Inc. 1968)

Ringo, John, George, Paul watch a preview of *Yellow Submarine* in early 1968 (King Features)

Down the hallway, past piles of parcels, boxes, packages, floppy black hats . . . and a smattering of books such as *The Geography of Witchcraft* and *The Vampire,* was the strangest room I ever entered. And why? It was made up of halves. Half a chair, half a table, half a radio, and even half an ironing board. Half a bookcase carried half-pots, half-pans, and half-kettles. The half-witted ''decorator'' had even cut a single shoe in half. Nearly everything in the room had been painted white. . . . The chessmen on a chess board were white. Both sets.

Dominating the room at one end was a huge picture of John and Yoko in the nude. Beneath it was the slogan: ''John and Yoko forever.''

(From a London *Evening News* story by a reporter who disguised himself as a prospective buyer when Lennon put his $140,000 mansion on the market.)

Having attuned himself to her wavelength, John began collaborating with Yoko on new artistic ventures. The first of these was a "living art" sculpture, consisting of two acorns planted for peace outside the Coventry Cathedral. The project was temporarily aborted when some fans stole the acorns in the dead of night, but two more were soon found to take their place.

Lennon followed this with a London art exhibit of his own. Titled "You Are Here," the display was dedicated to Yoko and showed more than a trace of her influence. Though the exhibit included Lennon-designed collecting boxes for such charities as the National Canine Defense League, the emphasis was on John's White Art. One attraction was an eight-foot circular canvas, its stark whiteness marred only by the minuscule legend "you are here." Another was a helium machine that blew up white balloons all day long. To

Yoko with John and Paul at the *Yellow Submarine* premiere
(Wide World Photo)

these were affixed tags reading "you are here" on one side and "write to John Lennon c/o Robert Fraser Gallery, 69 Duke St., London W.1" on the other. Dressed all in white, the artist released them into the London skies with the words "I declare these balloons high."

John was rather shaken by the tone of some of the responses. To much of the general public, Lennon's shenanigans with his Japanese mistress were even more incomprehensible than the Beatles' Indian junket. Although Ms. Ono's advent had certainly brought a colorful new figure to the Beatle pantheon, she was more often than not characterized as a malignant spirit. Posters appeared cari-caturing Yoko as a monster with a monkey face riding upon poor John's stooped back, her talons digging inextricably into his shoulders. (In light of Lennon's defensive attitude concerning Yoko, however, it is unlikely he had these in mind when he wrote "Everybody's Got Something To Hide Except For Me and My Monkey.")

Even many Beatlemaniacs did not take kindly to Yoko Ono (an aversion that would intensify after she and Linda McCartney were obliged to share the world's blame for the Beatles' split). Nor, for that matter, did Paul and George. Yoko was never far from John's side; she would even follow him into the gents' room, and when she was ill, had a bed in-stalled in the Beatles' recording studios. She thought she could be one of the boys.

"Yoko was very naive," Lennon remembered in *Rolling Stone*. "She came in and would expect to perform with them like you would with any other group." But the others were hardly auditioning a Fifth Beatle, and Paul in particular is said to have felt resentful and jealous of Yoko's monopoly on John's attentions.

Much of this, of course, was not yet apparent to those of us outside the Beatles' close circles, but in a short piece he published at the time John did drop a few hints between the lines of his wordplay:

Wonsapoa time there was two Balloons called Jack and Yono. They were strickly in love-bound to happen in a million years.

. . . But they battled on against overwhelming oddities, includo some of their beast friends.

John's relationship with Yoko also helped point his songwriting in a new direction, as did his abandonment of L.S.D. Instead of building further psychedelic dreamworlds for himself and his listeners to escape into, John was begin-ning to explore more directly his own feelings about himself and about the world around him. Thanks in part to Yoko, John, in both his "image" and his music, was coming out of his shell, no longer hiding from himself or from anyone else.

1968 was the beginning of a new phase in John's work. Several years earlier, he had discarded the mask of the grin-ning moptop in favor of that of the dreamweaver. This time, John Lennon, one of the most famous and idolized figures of his day, was about to do something nobody in his lofty posi-tion had ever dared do. He would attempt to rip away the masks altogether, to use his position as a media hero to ex-pose to millions of eager voyeurs both the man and the ma-chinery that lay behind the glittering facade. In his new work, John began to build a one-way mirror that offered the world a clearer, more intimate picture of a celebrity than it had ever before known on such a scale. In the process, he would also turn his fishbowl existence into more of a theatre of the absurd than ever.

Many found Lennon's exhibitionism extremely distasteful, and even his most loyal followers were frequently embar-rassed by the foolishness, naiveté, and arrogance of some of his exploits. Not everyone relished the brutal honesty with which he attempted to dismantle their fondest illusions, but millions admired him for it and made him more of a hero than ever.

All this would not completely crystallize in his songs until shortly after the Beatles' split, but the jacket of that first album he recorded with Yoko in May 1968—*Two Virgins: Unfinished Music No. 1*—provided as apt a symbol of John's new incarnation as any. Unlike the actual contents it left nothing to the imagination: there were John and Yoko, stark raving naked, not so much as a figleaf in sight.

Two Virgins quickly became the most controversial L.P. of the year, and for reasons that had precious little to do with the record itself (which, by the way, consists of squawks contributed both by birds outside Lennon's window and by Yoko Ono; the sounds of blowing noses; and other drop-

Two Virgins, L.P., 1968 (Apple)

pings of the avant garde). Never had an album been so talked about yet so seldom listened to even by those lucky enough to find a copy.

After a mortified E.M.I. refused to have anything to do with it, smaller, less staid labels—Track in Britain, Tetragammaton in America—had to be persuaded to handle the dread item. Despite the brown-paper wrappers, a number of hapless distributors were arrested on pornography charges. One raid in New Jersey netted the authorities 30,000 copies of the wicked L.P. (Slightly over a year later, Lennon would set in motion the same cycle of denunciations, confiscations, and arrests with a series of original lithographs depicting his sex life with Yoko. He would also produce an equally controversial film, *Self Portrait:* a 42-minute study of his own penis.)

John had not succeeded in offending so many "wholesome" people since his tangle with Jesus two years earlier. For some fans, *Two Virgins* was the final blow; as Rainbo (a.k.a. Sissy Spacek) sang on her first recording "John You Went Too Far This Time":

Everything you asked of me I did John,
from holding hands to living in a sunlight submarine . . .
but since that picture I don't think our love
will be the same.

Many people close to the Beatles, such as Apple press secretary Derek Taylor, are convinced that the *Two Virgins* episode earned John Lennon the enmity of forces considerably more powerful than Rainbo. Heretofore, the British Establishment had always taken a benign attitude toward John, Paul, George, and Ringo, M.B.E.: even if they were clearly no longer happy-go-lucky moptops, they still seemed more harmless than, say, the Rolling Stones, and, most importantly, remained a major source of dollars, marks, and yen. So the powers-that-be had long chosen to turn a blind eye toward the Beatles' self-proclaimed involvement in the drug subculture; and, aside from rubbing a few songs off the airwaves, did not officially hold them accountable for fanning the sweet aroma of cannabis across the Western world. It had often been claimed that George Harrison was at the party at which Mick Jagger and Keith Richard were busted; because he was a Beatle, the story goes, George was quietly ushered from the scene of the crime.

In any case, on October 18, 1968, the "Nude Shock" headlines were replaced by ones reading "Drugs Shock." John and Yoko were awakened by a banging at the door of Ringo's London flat, where they were staying. Their uninvited guests turned out to be Detective-Sergeant Norman Pilcher and the Scotland Yard Drugs Squad, accompanied by enormous police dogs, who promptly sniffed out a lump of hashish. Seven bobbies marched the couple off to the local police station, where John pleaded guilty to possession of cannabis. When the case came to trial, he was fined approximately $500.

John subsequently vowed that the stuff had been planted, and that, because Yoko was pregnant, he had agreed to pay the fine in order to spare her further trauma. (Nonetheless, she suffered a miscarriage a month later.) Little could Lennon know how much that guilty plea would come to haunt him four years later, when he would attempt to make the United States his home.

Although Lennon's bust only served to turn him into something of a martyr, and further alienate his admirers from "the system," Sgt. Pilcher was so pleased with his feat that five months later he resolved to repeat it. On March

John with Yoko before declaring the balloons high (Globe Photos)

12—the evening of Paul's wedding—Pilcher and his "piggies" would invade George Harrison's psychedelic bungalow, and, of course, find exactly what they were looking for.

Harrison would also claim (to David Wigg, on *The Beatles Tapes*) that the bust had been a setup. "To really have a pure state of consciousness and good perception . . . any sort of drugs is out. I haven't taken anything like that personally for a long time. Even before I got busted I never took it, it just happened that they seemed to bring it with them that day."

But he would admit that a few grains found elsewhere on the premises might have been the remnants of a long-forgotten stash, so he and Patti would meekly plead guilty, and cough up the fine. "I hope the police will now leave the Beatles alone," he would say after the sacrifice.

Apple Records got off to a splendid start, both financially and artistically, with its first Beatle single: Paul's "Hey Jude," backed by John's "Revolution." "Jude" clocked in at an unprecedented 7:11, which, for the Beatles, turned out to be a lucky number. Though almost no other artist could have got away with AM airplay for so long-winded a song, "Hey Jude" wound up becoming the Beatles' most successful single ever. By the end of the year, it had chalked up sales of over five million. In 1976, it would place second on *Billboard's* bicentennial chart of the biggest hits of the past two decades, behind only Chubby Checker's "The Twist."

The critics loved it, too; and Elektra Records boss Jac Holtzman, after being treated to the "religious experience" of hearing a stereophonic master recording, went so far as to write an open letter in *Rolling Stone* imploring that this single "one can worship at the feet of" be issued in stereo. (It wasn't, but all subsequent Beatle 45's were.)

The record takes off to the sound of just Paul's piano and vocal, and ends up incorporating fifty instruments and nearly as many voices. As in other pop "epics," instruments and voices are added one by one to build toward the climax. As "Hey Jude" explodes into its frenzied 4-minute-long fade-

Life With the Lions, L.P., 1969 (Zapple)

out (in which Paul, perhaps subconsciously, recalls the mantras the Beatles had been chanting to themselves all spring), we hear not only a forty-piece orchestra but also the overdubbed sound of all its staid members letting their hair down, bellowing along with the Beatles. "We decided to make double use of the forty musicians by asking them if they'd like to do a bit of singing and clap their hands," assistant Mal Evans reported. "They were quite pleased to oblige."

Despite these lavish trappings "Hey Jude"'s bittersweet tune is a miracle of simplicity, with each of its two main sections using only three chords. The arrangement is also quite straightforward: unlike, say, "A Day In the Life," "Jude" deploys its orchestra as just another noisemaker, to underline the mood with unobtrusive sustained notes.

As for the lyrics, a lot of people, Lennon included, assumed Paul was singing to John,* endorsing his liaison with Yoko—

don't be afraid,
you were made to go out and get her,

and cautioning him not to take his troubles so seriously—

anytime you feel the pain
Hey Jude, refrain
don't carry the world upon your shoulder

"When Paul first sang 'Hey Jude' to me . . . I took it very personally," Lennon told Jonathan Cott. "Ah, it's me! I said, it's *me!* He says, no it's *me.* I said, check, we're going through the same bit."

So, as it happens, "Jude," behind the disguise, is Paul McCartney—in a rare self-portrait. Paul talking to himself, consoling himself for his recent breakup with Jane Asher—"waiting for someone to perform with." But he wouldn't have to for very long; the lovely Linda Eastman was in the wings, awaiting her cue.

John's "Revolution," which had been originally eyed for an A-side, proved to be extremely popular—*and* controversial—in its own right. For one thing, a lot of people thought that their copies were defective because the guitars sounded so distorted. But, says George Martin, "that was

---

* The song was originally called "Hey Jules"—after John's son Julian Lennon.

Apple Corps meets the Big Apple (*16* Magazine)

Gene Mahon's label design put a whole apple on a the A-side, a sliced apple on the B-side (Apple)

Patti and George Harrison after paying their fine, with Derek Taylor (Wide World Photos)

done deliberately because John wanted a very dirty sound on guitar and he couldn't get it through his amps. What we did . . . was just overload one of the pre-amps." The record company felt that this just "wasn't done"; but, as always, for the Beatles, that was all the more reason to do it. Lennon also had difficulty getting the right "feel" to his voice, but finally solved the problem by recording his vocal track lying on the floor.

The lyrics, however, inspired far more comment than the distortion. In "Revolution" the Beatles, who had always avoided overt political commentary in their songs, acidly disavow the counterculture's fashionable radicalism.

You say you want a revolution,
well, you know,
we all want to change the world. . . .

But when you talk about destruction,
don't you know that you can count me out.

(In the more subdued rendition that the Beatles would include on their next album, they are more equivocal: John follows the phrase "count me out" with the word "in." "It's a yin-yang thing," said John. "We all have a streak of violence underneath.")

"Revolution" was the first product of the new persona John would later describe as a "singing reporter," chronicling current events and his own personal role in them "in the tradition of minstrels who sang about their times and what was happening." But his counterrevolutionary musical editorial only reinforced the view of those who suspected the Beatles of being irretrievably committed, behind their hip regalia, to the system that had allowed them to become so rich—as opposed to, say, the Rolling Stones, who released their acceptably rabble-rousing "Street Fighting Man" around the same time. (The fact that the Stones were also millionaires didn't seem to enter these analyses.) "Revolution," charged *The Berkeley Barb,* sounded "like the hawk plank adopted this week in the Chicago convention of the Democratic Death Party." The editors were unaccustomed to barbs slung in their direction by fellow long-hairs:

You say you'll change the constitution,
well, you know,
we'd all love to change your head. . . .

The Beatles and friends singing "Hey Jude" for David Frost (UPI)

John gamely agreed to an exchange of open letters with British radical John Hoyland. Richard Neville, editor of a London Underground rag called *Oz*,* succinctly conveys the gist of that debate in his book *Play Power:*

It was a classic New Left/psychedelic Left dialogue, and was syndicated throughout the world's Underground press. Mr. Hoyland explained that the *system* is inhuman and immoral, not people; therefore all relationships within it are poisoned; it must be ruthlessly destroyed; and incidentally, Lennon's music was losing its bite, unlike that of the Stones. In reply, John Lennon asked what system would replace the one currently in use, and argued that what was wrong with the world was people—were they to be ruthlessly destroyed? P.S. Mr. Hoyland could smash it and the Beatle would build around it.

For the next two years, John and Yoko would tirelessly espouse his brand of idealistic nonviolence. Ironically, the unrelenting harassment of authorities on both sides of the Atlantic—who saw in John a symbol of youthful dissent and weren't interested in gradations and nuances in the philosophies of individual "radicals"—would eventually push Lennon all the way into Mr. Hoyland's camp.

The Beatles sang both sides of their new single on television, their first performance before a live audience in two years. For the "Hey Jude" segment, about a hundred starry-eyed fanatics had been plucked from the crowd mobbing the *Yellow Submarine* premiere, to lend some spirited vocals to

the song's finale. (These two film clips, along with one made of the boys rehearsing "Hey Jude," have since become Beatle convention staples.)

Paul got such a buzz out of the shows that he decreed the time was ripe for the Beatles to play some full-length concerts. "I was wanting to go out. . . ." McCartney later recalled. "If you get it on in front of an audience, there's nothing like it. In a recording studio you have to imagine that the audience is thrilled." But John, George, and Ringo had quite different ideas on how to get their thrills.

"Hey Jude"/"Revolution" appeared toward the end of the summer of 1968, along with Apple's three other initial singles. These were all by artists unknown, yet intimately connected with members of the Beatles. "Thingumybob" showed McCartney extending his versatile talents to composing and arranging for the old-timey Black Dyke Mills brass band. "Sour Milk Sea" by Jackie Lomax (formerly of Liverpool's the Undertakers) featured the songwriting, producing, *and* performing talents of George Harrison. (Lomax's subsequent Apple L.P. *Is This What You Want?* would boast a stellar backup band including three Beatles—all but John.)

Neither "Thingumybob" nor "Sour Milk Sea" was destined to make much of a splash, unlike "Those Were the Days" by a 17-year-old Welsh waif named Mary Hopkin. Earlier in the year, Mary had riveted Twiggy's attention at a talent show; the model had passed the word on to Paul McCartney, who was scouting for talent on behalf of Apple. Mc-

*Speaking of *Oz,* it was partly Lennon's generosity that helped keep it afloat. And in 1971, when Neville and Company were busted for obscenity, John responded by forming "The Elastic Oz Band" and wrote and produced an Apple single ("God Save Us"/"Do the Oz") to raise money for the defence.

Cartney was particularly interested in finding the right voice for "Those Were the Days," a song he had been convinced had hit potential since 1964, when he'd first heard it sung by its composer, Gene Raskin, in a London club. When Paul saw and heard Mary, he suspected she too had a feeling for the piece. He was right on both counts: Miss Hopkin's Mc-Cartney-produced Apple single wound up replacing "Hey Jude" at the top of the charts in Britain and throughout Europe.

The new label inaugurated the self-proclaimed National Apple Week—August 11 through 18—by ceremoniously delivering gift presentation boxes containing "Our First Four" to the palaces of Queen Elizabeth II, Princess Margaret, and the Queen Mother, and to the Prime Minister's residence at Ten Downing Street. The Queen Mother promptly sent back a note saying she was "greatly touched by this kind thought from the Beatles" and "much enjoyed listening to these recordings."

While the Queen Mother and the rest of us were kept busy warbling along with "Hey Jude" and tapping our toes to "Revolution," Apple prepared its next release: an album of film music by George Harrison. *Wonderwall Music* represented George's last intense musical fling with India. A peculiar mishmash of Indian sounds and rockabilly instrumentals (the latter reportedly starring Ringo and Eric Clapton under the pseudonyms Roy Dyke and Eddie Clayton), the collection, like many soundtracks, is occasionally engaging but seldom very memorable. George was less than ingenuous in claiming as Harrison compositions a series of improvisations featuring his friend Ashish Khan (Ali Akbar's son and Ravi Shankar's nephew) on the sarod. (But George did give the younger Khan's career a tiny boost around this time by writing liner notes for Ashish's own L.P. *Young Master Of the Sarod.*)

The *Wonderwall Music* artwork offers an intriguing commentary on the "East is East and West is West" theme. A high wall separates skinnydipping maidens, their saris draped upon an overhanging branch, from a dour Englishman in suit and bowler hat. The gap in the wall left by one missing brick provides each side with an extremely limited glimpse of the other.

That's about as much interchange as exists between East and West on George's first solo album; the selections are all on either one side of the Wonderwall or the other, and never do the twain meet. Neither had George ever succeeded in blending the two worlds very smoothly in his Beatle music, which may be why he was about to pretty much kick the raga habit in his own compositions. But he would never tire of proselytizing for the real thing. (*Wonderwall* went out of print in America a few years later—and so joined the ranks of the collectors' items.)

The Beatles toiled in the studios almost non-stop throughout the summer and autumn of 1968, committing to tape a backlog of 34 recent compositions, most of which they had written in India. The first of these to appear was "Hey Jude"—the longest-ever pop single. Then it was announced that 30 of the remaining numbers would be crammed onto a 2-record set titled simply *The Beatles*. (Two cuts, George's "Not Guilty" and John's "What's the News Mary Jane," were dropped at the last minute.) This would be not only their first double L.P. (not counting America's 1964 documentary *Beatles Story*), but also the longest album yet released by a major rock artist. *The Beatles* arrived in late November, continuing a nearly unbroken tradition of Beatles Christmas releases. (Which is why so many old Beatle albums nowadays evoke an intangible sense of Christmas for fans who immersed themselves in them when they first ap-

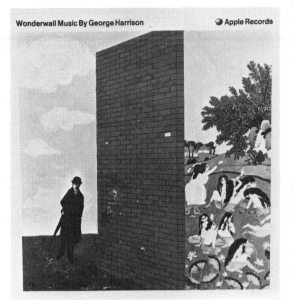

L.P., 1968 (Apple)

Single, Holland, 1968 (Parlophone)

peared. Nothing captures and preserves the mood of the moment like a song.)

As far as most pop music reviewers were concerned, the Beatles could still do no wrong. A typical sample is one by the London *Observer's* Tony Palmer (also director of *All My Loving,* a rock documentary featuring Paul McCartney, and, more recently, author of the pop history *All You Need Is Love*):

If there is still any doubt that Lennon and McCartney are the greatest songwriters since Schubert, then next Friday—with the publication of the new Beatles double L.P.—should surely see the last vestiges of cultural snobbery and bourgeois prejudice swept away in a deluge of joyful music making, which only the ignorant will not hear and only the deaf will not acknowledge.

Even Richard Goldstein hailed *The Beatles* as "a major success . . . far more imaginative than *Sgt. Pepper* or *Magical Mystery Tour.*"

Occasionally, however, a review of *The Beatles* would strike one of two sour notes. The first was that, at 94 minutes, the program occasionally drags. Even George Martin felt uneasy with the concept of an interminable Beatle album, as he would later reveal: "I tried to plead with them to be selective and make it a really good single album, but they wouldn't have it." One reason why is that they were eager to free themselves from the contractual obligations of Epstein's 1967 deal with E.M.I. After *The Beatles'* two L.P.'s, they would have only one left to deliver.

Some of the more egg-head critics also griped that *The Beatles* sounded like a bit of a retreat from the adventurousness of *Sgt. Pepper.* To this McCartney retorted: "We felt it was time to step back because that is what we wanted to do. You can still make good music without going forward. Some people want us to go on until we vanish up our own B-sides."

By late '68 the volatile rock scene did appear to be shifting gears. In February, Bob Dylan, always the trend-setter, had sent much of the *Sgt. Pepper* bandwagon skidding uneasily when he released *John Wesley Harding.*

Instead of trying to compete with 1967's extravaganzas, Dylan—who had reportedly snapped "turn that off" when someone first played him *Sgt. Pepper*—returned from self-

JOE MASSOT

Musique de GEORGE HARRISON

George, Ringo, and the cast of *Wonderwall,* in Cannes for the premiere (Globe Photos)

imposed silence with a low-key collection of 12 short songs, on which he was accompanied only by muted bass and drums. The poetry was still intriguing and, occasionally, unfathomable. But on the subsequent *Nashville Skyline,* Bob would do away even with that, replacing his magic swirling ships and binocular-bedecked mules with precisely the sort of Tin Pan Alley clichés everyone had always imagined him waging guerilla war against.

It may be that, with his new country sounds and celebrations of simple pleasures, Dylan was actually anticipating the back-to-the-earth syndrome that would prove to be the Next Big Thing in countercultural lifestyles. On the other hand, a lot of people thought it was all a manifestation of Bob's surreal sense of humor. Meanwhile, A.J. Weberman consulted his concordance to conclude that it all meant Dylan had become a junkie. In any case, a lot of artists suddenly seemed to notice that their L.S.D.-inspired visions had extended far beyond reach of their music-making talents. Even before the release of *John Wesley Harding,* the Beach Boys had scrapped their cosmic masterwork *Smile* to return to the more familiar West Coast pleasures of *Wild Honey.* (They did release an abortion of *Smile* called *Smiley Smile,*

which included the McCartney-produced "Vegetables.") The Rolling Stones, the Byrds, Eric Burdon, and others quickly followed suit. In addition, Fifties Nostalgia was beginning to brew, bringing the airwaves a fresh dose of vintage rock 'n' roll.

"People just felt that pop was getting out of their hands," The Who's Pete Townshend told *Rolling Stone.* "Groups like Pink Floyd were appearing, scary groups, psychedelic. So they completely freaked out. Nothing like the down-home Rolling Stones who used to have a good old-fashioned piss against a good old-fashioned garage attendant. This Pink Floyd—what were they all about? With their flashing lights and all taking trips and one of them's a psycho. 'What's all this about? That's not my bag.'"

Although many groups—such as Pink Floyd—would relentlessly continue their attempts to propel rock toward the outer limits, it had suddenly become fashionable to "return to the roots." Simpler music was in vogue again. In Britain, the latest rage was home-grown white blues. Instrumental virtuosos began cropping up like last year's magic mushrooms. People for whom the eclectic arrangements and interstellar lyrics seemed pretentious turned instead to 47-

minute improvisations on two-chord blues classics like "Spoonful."

Despite the excesses, the level of rock musicianship had greatly improved. Groups like the Beatles had become good enough to create sophisticated music without needing to rely so heavily on electronic gimmickry and studio musicians. They were ready to do it all themselves again, on their own instruments. As John Lennon told *Rolling Stone's* Jonathan Cott: "Now we're all just coming out, coming out of a shell in a new way, kind of saying: remember what it was like to play?"

The Beatles' cover certainly seemed to represent the ultimate in simplicity. The blank white jacket, discreetly embossed with the equally minimalistic title, would have fit nicely into Lennon's exhibit of White Art, in fact was probably inspired by it. From the day of release, everybody referred to *The Beatles* as "the White Album."

In another nod to conceptual art, the boys directed that the albums all be individually stamped with a number in the order they tumbled off the presses, thus insuring that each copy be a unique work of art. (My own copy, though purchased on the day of publication, is A1481860—the A is for America—which seems to confirm Capitol's claim that the White Album was "the fastest-selling record in the history of the record industry." The proud owner of A0000001 nowadays displays his copy at Beatle convention flea markets; but anyone who can afford the asking price might just as well treat himself to an original Van Gogh.)

If the L.P. jacket appeared to symbolize the opposite extreme from *Sgt. Pepper's* ornate complexities, the music itself proved to be considerably less stark. Although studio effects and mysterious instruments were far less prevalent (George, for instance, had permanently retired his sitar to the closet) *The Beatles* wasn't entirely a step backward.

The White Album inaugurated what could be called the Beatles' "professional" period. Apart from John's impressionistic "drawing of revolution"—which probably owes more to Yoko's influence than to "I Am the Walrus"—the psychedelic collage had apparently gone out with the Beatles' avowed abandonment of L.S.D. On these and subsequent L.P.'s, the Beatles concentrated on producing comparatively straightforward songs in a wide range of styles, relying instrumentally on their own considerably matured expertise on guitars, keyboards, bass, and drums—occasionally supplemented by relatively conventional layers of strings and horns.

Many of the lyrics had as much to say as *Sgt. Pepper's,* but at the same time the music emphasized both unadorned acoustic ballads and the Beatles' most unequivocal rock 'n' roll in years. Yet even "Helter Skelter" sounded nothing like, say, "Dizzy Miss Lizzy" or "I'm Down." Both the riffs and the production were now far more inventive and polished. John, George, Ringo, and, above all, Paul, had become seasoned professionals, exploring their talents within relatively set limitations. The days of unbridled experimentation were over, but the music itself was still as good as ever.

One thing most of the songs, both simple and complex, share, is a sense of satire. The White Album includes pastiches of so many different styles of music that it virtually amounts to an irreverent encyclopedia of pop. *Rolling Stone's* Jann Wenner went so far as to declare: "*The Beatles* is the history and synthesis of Western music." But Lennon and McCartney had developed two very different approaches to satire. Paul's pastiches are clever, affectionate, harmless entertainments; John's lampoons draw blood.

For a superb opener, Paul's B.O.A.C. jet screeches down the runway. . . . "Back In the U.S.S.R.":

Let It Be, E.P., Russia, 1972 (Melodia). The first official Beatles release back in the USSR. Previously, Beatle albums brought $100 on the black market.

Let me hear your balalaikas ringing out,
come and keep your comrade warm,
I'm back in the U.S.S.R.
You don't know how lucky you are, boy,
back in the U.S.S.R.

To folks like the Rev. David Noebel, author of *Communism, Hypnotism, and the Beatles* and *The Beatles: A Study In Sex, Drugs, and Revolution,* this song brought definitive confirmation of all they had been warning Western civilization about for years. "The lyrics have left even the Reds speechless," Noebel declared.

For rock 'n' roll fans, however, "Back In the U.S.S.R." seemed more like a fabulous take-off on all those golden oldies whose hooks revolved around the letters "U.S.A." Especially "Back In the U.S.A.," Chuck Berry's hit of a decade earlier, some of which goes like this:

Just touched ground on an international runway,
jet-propelled back home from overseas to the U.S.A.
*. . . .I'm so glad I'm living in the U.S.A.**

In "Back In the U.S.A.," as in so many of his classic songs, Berry recites like an incantation the names of American cities: "New York . . . Los Angeles . . . Detroit . . . Chicago. . . ." before moving on to skyscrapers, freeways, hamburgers—you know, the simple joys of life in America. In their place, McCartney—belting away in his vintage rock 'n' roll manner—cites Moscow and the Ukraine, balalaikas and bugged telephones.

The Beach Boys, whose early hits included "Surfin' U.S.A." and "Amusement Parks U.S.A.," get the McCartney treatment on the bridge. As John and George parrot those trademark falsetto harmonies, Paul warbles lyrics that transplant the Beach Boys' famous "California Girls" to a Soviet setting. (Harrison later revealed that "Back In the U.S.S.R." actually started out as a patriotic song called "I'm Backing the U.K.")

*"Back in the U.S.A." by Chuck Berry
(copyright © 1959 by Arc Music Corp.)

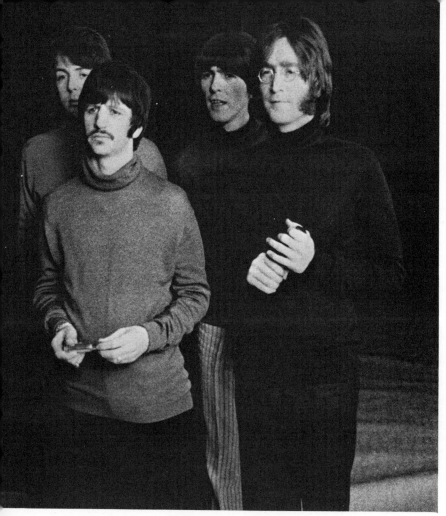

(Transworld Feature Syndicate)

he put it, "three bits strung together." The song drifts from the reptilian sensuality of:

the touch of the velvet hand
like a lizard on a windowpane. . . .

through nonsense imagery reminiscent of Lennon's books:

a soap impression of his wife which he ate
and donated to the National trust. . . .

before settling into a spoof of the sort of C-Am-F-G7 "Duke Of Earl"/"This Boy" schlock rock John had grown up on, complete with "bang-bang-shoot-shoot" choruses.

The title parodies both Charlie Brown's "happiness is a warm blanket" motto and, again, the zeal of gun enthusiasts; the song was originally inspired by a glance at an American gun magazine a few days after Robert Kennedy's assassination. But some Beatleologists, hearing the words "I need a fix" concocted theories to show that the "warm gun" was actually a syringe. While others took lines such as "feel my finger on your trigger" as proof that it was nothing more nor less than a sex organ.

Those songs on the White Album that make no attempt to parody or to puncture are mostly acoustically-oriented ballads, among them "I Will" (a virtual remake, musically, of 1964's "I'll Follow the Sun"), "Mother Nature's Son" (the Beatle song that John Denver would incorporate into his repertoire), and "Martha My Dear" (addressed, as all Paul devotees knew, to his English sheepdog). Like much of McCartney's work, all are remarkably accomplished and tuneful—and tell us absolutely zilch about the writer's own feelings.

The one exception is "Blackbird," which couples one of Paul's most haunting melodies with poignant lyrics:

Blackbird singing in the dead of night,
take these broken wings and learn to fly.
All your life
you were only waiting
for this moment to arise.

This song would prove oddly prophetic when, several years later, McCartney would rise from the ashes of the Beatles' disintegration with a group called Wings, and an album, *Band On the Run,* that would be devoted almost entirely to the "Blackbird" theme of flight, release, and freedom.

Lennon may be less renowned for soft melodies, but the ones he contributed to the White Album do reveal a definite progression in his writing—and a great deal about the man behind them. Much as he was coming to channel his aggression and his anger into his hard rock songs, John was also beginning to bare his most tender and vulnerable side in his ballads.

Some of those on the White Album rank among his most magical. In the whimsical lullaby "Cry Baby Cry," Alice trips gently through Lennonland, for just about the last time. "Like a little child," John radiates more wide-eyed innocence in "Dear Prudence," which he wrote in India for Mia Farrow's sister, who was so dedicated a meditator she would never come out to play. Instead of importing a string ensemble, John, Paul, and George create one of their own by overdubbing six or seven guitar parts, to weave an unusually delicate and intricate tapestry.

"Julia" is Lennon's "song of love" for his mother, to whom he had become very close as a teen-ager though it was her sister Mimi who had brought him up as a child. When John was seventeen, Julia Lennon was fatally struck by a car. This may well be a reason for John's legendary bitterness during the early Sixties; in any case, with his astonishing new determination to unravel and exorcize his most intimate and painful feelings before an audience of millions, he now invokes his mother with heartrending images:

Paul's other pastiches on the White Album—all of which ring equally "authentic"—include a scratchy old 78 ("Honey Pie"); a stab at cock rock ("Why Don't We Do It In the Road?"); and a cowboy melodrama ("Rocky Raccoon"). John in turn deflates the British Blues Boom ("Yer Blues"); machismo as personified by a trigger-happy American tiger hunter he encountered in India ("Bungalow Bill"); and, of course, the fellow who had lured him to that subcontinent in the first place ("Sexy Sadie").

Lennon also slyly deploys a few banana peels for avid Beatleologists to trip on. In "Glass Onion" he sardonically unveils "hidden meanings" to five of the Beatles' more unfathomable songs, e.g.:

Here's another clue for you all,
the Walrus was Paul.

Many sleuths promptly filed the new entries into their concordances, despite the fact that in the same breath John reveals that all he's *really* up to is:

trying to make a dove-tail joint,
looking through a glass onion.

John felt that his contributions to the White Album were the best group of songs he had yet written, and the two he liked most of all were "Happiness Is A Warm Gun" and "I'm So Tired." This last is a harrowing companion piece to 1966's "I'm Only Sleeping"; while in the earlier song Lennon finds it impossible to drag himself out of bed in the morning, now he can't get to sleep at night. The yawning of the lazy dreamer has given way to that of the bleary-eyed insomniac.

"Happiness Is a Warm Gun" is one of Lennon's most inspired collages of free-association non sequiturs—or, as

Julia, seashell eyes,
windy smile, calls me. . . .
Julia, morning moon,
touch me. . . .
sleeping sand, silent cloud,
touch me. . . .

(The song's opening line, incidentally, is pinched from—of all people—Kahlil Gibran.)

Lennon is the only Beatle who appears on "Julia," much as McCartney handles the works on "Blackbird," "Mother Nature's Son," "Why Don't We Do It In the Road," and others. And even when the Beatles *were* playing together, John later said, "it was just me and a backing group, Paul and a backing group. . . ." The sharp differences that had developed in their songwriting styles had become unmistakable, and the joint Lennon-McCartney byline that still adorned both their compositions, a total fiction. *The Beatles* proved to be a somewhat ironic title for an album that can be seen as marking the real beginnings of the individual members' solo careers.

Not only were the Beatles writing separately; they were finding it difficult to muster any interest in each other's work. John made no bones about despising Paul's popular, Jamaican-influenced "Obladi-Oblada" (a song that also alienated the West Indian nightclub singer who had dreamed up the title for his own act) and couldn't even be bothered to participate on George Harrison's compositions.

No doubt McCartney was getting tired of having to weather Lennon's disdain whenever he tried to record one of his more mawkish ditties—although this situation did keep Paul's facile sentimentality within tolerable limits. McCartney, for his part, was less than enthusiastic about including "Revolution 9," the apocalyptic but highly untuneful Lennon collage of tape loops and fragments of dialogue that climaxes with screams and gunfire. (Evidently the fans agreed with Paul, as "Revolution 9" was voted in a *Village Voice* poll the most unpopular Beatle cut ever.) And Harrison was growing restless sitting on an ever-growing backlog of songs for which John and Paul felt there was "no room" on the Beatles' albums.

Nonetheless, the four Harrisongs that did surface on *The Beatles* firmly established him as a contender. George, having finally concluded that his mystical tracts needn't necessarily be accompanied by pseudo-Hindu music, managed to turn in a quartet of more conventionally accessible pop songs that many felt were among the finest on the album. The most popular was "While My Guitar Gently Weeps," with Eric Clapton contributing a characteristically uplifting guitar solo in Lennon's absence (George would soon return the favor by co-writing "Badge" for Cream's *Goodbye*). Harrison had begun to reap the rewards of all those years of subservient apprenticeship to Lennon and McCartney: now he was writing melodies as strong as their own.

"Long Long Long," which retains a vestige of India's yearning drones, is the first of dozens of Harrison love songs that are ambiguous in that he could be singing either to his lady or to his Lord. "I think all love is part of a universal love," he explained to *Rolling Stone* years later. "When you love a woman, it's the God in her that you see. The only complete love is for God."

George's music works best when soft and sweet, when it caresses and envelops his listeners like fine Indian silk. He may not have what it takes to belt out a song like John or Paul, but when he tones his voice down to an ethereal near-whisper, as in "Long Long Long," he can evoke as well as anyone the magic and the mystery of what Jonathan Cott has called "the music of deep silence."

But with "Piggies" Harrison turns from the spirit to the flesh, to sling some caustic barbs at a greedy and materialistic Establishment. 1968—the year of Daley's convention, Nixon's election, and unprecedented numbers of student and anti-Vietnam War demonstrations—was a time when any representative of "the system," particularly a politician or a policeman, was fated to automatically take on the guise of a "pig" in the view of much of the counterculture. Although created before George's drug bust, Harrison's "Piggies" are merciless stereotypes. All dressed up in their starchy finery, they wallow in their "clean dirt" and gorge themselves on bacon (the Beatles themselves had all become vegetarians) to the accompaniment of a drawing-room harpsichord, as the boys oink derisively in the background.

Two sides later, the piggies appear to reap their just karmic deserts by losing all their teeth after stuffing their faces on the "Savoy Truffle." Actually, the song was written for Clapton, who had a sweet tooth. (This selection introduces those beefy horns that would prove to be a trademark of George's post-Beatle work.)

The White Album also showcases the songwriting emergence of an even darker horse: Ringo Starr, who for the first time contributes a tune all his own. Despite some critical condescension, the country-flavored "Don't Pass Me By" made it to Number One in Scandinavia, where it was released as a single.

Ringo also gets to warble the White Album finale, John's "Good Night," in front of a children's choir and 30-piece orchestra. According to Lennon: "I just said to George Martin, 'Arrange it like Hollywood. Yeah, corny.'" Nothing could possibly be more outrageously kitsch—or more outrageously incongruous, coming immediately after eight minutes of "Revolution 9"'s excruciating music concrète.

Which, no doubt, is precisely why John Lennon did it that way.

Since *Revolver,* reading between the lines of Beatle lyrics had become one of America's great national pastimes. To Charlie Manson, leader of a communal "family" in Southern California and self-appointed reincarnation of Jesus Christ, the Beatles were none other than the four long-haired angels cited in the Bible's "Revelation 9"; each of their records was a personal message to the Messiah (i.e., Charlie Manson).

Manson considered the White Album to be both a prophetic description of a racial war that was about to engulf the world, leaving Charlie to preside over the ruins, and a series of instructions on what he and his "family" should do about it. "Blackbird," for instance, was supposedly about black revolutionaries; the next track, "Piggies," described their victims. "Revolution 9" (the similarity of the title to "Revelation 9" struck Charlie as significant) offered an aural picture of the coming holocaust, to which Manson ascribed the name of "Helter Skelter" (a phrase that for Britons designates nothing more apocalyptic than a playground slide).

Their bizarre reading of these and other songs on *The Beatles* led the Manson Family to conclude that it was their mission to help trigger the bloodbath by butchering rich white "piggies" such as Sharon Tate in a manner that would make white people suppose the atrocities were the work of black insurgents and react accordingly. Over the summer of 1969, Manson and his followers embarked on the series of murders that compose one of the most famous and gruesome chapters in criminal history, leaving at the scene of each crime such slogans, scrawled in the blood of the victims, as "Helter Skelter," "Political Piggy," and "Arise" (a word prominent in "Blackbird").

At the Rock 'n Roll Circus: The Stones' Brian Jones (who drowned seven months later); Yoko Ono; Julian and John Lennon; and Eric Clapton (Globe Photos)

In *Helter Skelter,* his best-selling account of the Manson murders and their aftermath, prosecutor Vincent Bugliosi recalls the difficulties he had, not only in unraveling the incredible motives behind the crimes, but in convincing the jurors and his own colleagues that it was not he who had somehow gone round the bend. However, though Charlie Manson was no doubt the most dangerous psychopath ever to come down with Beatlemania, his view of the Fab Four's lyrics as "prophecy" was far from unique in the late Sixties.

In December 1968, John Lennon appeared live on two different stages: at the Royal Albert Hall, where he and Yoko gave the world its first taste of "bagism" by writhing inside a large white sack; and on a Rolling Stones T.V. special called *Rock 'n' Roll Circus,* where John belted "Yer Blues" accompanied by Eric Clapton, the Stones' Keith Richard, and drummer Mitch Mitchell of the Jimi Hendrix Experience. (The show, which also co-starred the Who, was never aired.)

Meanwhile, Paul McCartney had been concocting elaborate plans for the first live Beatle performance in three years. Word of the forthcoming concerts—to be based largely around songs from a brand-new album, and filmed for a T.V. spectacular—seemed almost too good to be true for fans who had long despaired of ever seeing the Fab Four

together again on the same stage. Apple's Derek Taylor, however, was unequivocal: "There will be a show. And that's a promise."

But there wasn't. Almost from the moment the four Beatles filed into the Twickenham Film Studios on the morning of January 2, 1969, for their first rehearsal (they had been obliged to revise their nocturnal recording schedule in order to make use of the facilities) Paul and George began to squabble. Noting his colleagues' unenthusiastic attitude toward the project, McCartney attempted to rouse them with a pep talk, which was preserved for posterity by tape-recorders brought in to capture Beatle dialogue for a book to be packaged with the new L.P.

"We've been very negative since Mr. Epstein passed away. . . . The only way for it not to be a bit of a drag is for the four of us to think, should we make it positive or should we forget it. . . . Mr. Epstein, he said sort of, 'get suits on,' and we did. And so we were always fighting that discipline a bit. But now it's silly to fight that discipline if it's our own. It's self-imposed these days, so we do as little as possible. But I think we need a bit more if we are going to get on with it."

"Well, if that's what doing it is," Harrison snapped back, "I don't want to do anything. . . . I don't want to do any of the songs on the show because they always turn out awful like that. They come out like a compromise whereas in the studio they can work on it until you get it how you want it."

George also attempted to dash cold water on Paul's and director Michael Lindsay-Hogg's newest brain wave, which was to stage the concert either at an ancient coliseum in Tunisia ("You know it's just impractical to try and get all these people and equipment there," said Harrison), or on a ship in the ocean ("Very expensive and insane. . . . I don't think you're going to get a perfect acoustic place by the water out of doors"). Lennon offered his own suggestion: "I'm warming to the idea of an asylum."

On January 10, George finally registered his unequivocal objections to the concert idea by stalking out of the studio and driving home. As sensationalized reports of Beatle fist-fights leaked out in the press, the shows were called off. In place of the promised concert tickets, the 50 winners of a hotly contested *Beatles Monthly* competition were sent L.P.'s.

But the four Beatles would continue rehearsing at Twickenham as subjects of a T.V. film on the making of a Beatle album. The record itself was conceived as something of a documentary on the same subject: the songs were to be interspersed with snippets of studio chatter, plus occasional bits and pieces of the old chestnuts with which the Beatles customarily warmed up between takes. The L.P. also seemed calculated to place the Beatles firmly on the "back-to-the-roots" bandwagon. There would be no overdubs, and, apart from the occasional keyboard tinklings of Billy Preston, no musical contributions from non-Beatles. The record was to be taped "live" and left unedited. "If there's a mistake," said John, "that's hard luck. It's going to be honest." Songs about letting it be, getting back, and going home apparently predominated, and the album was to kick off with a hitherto unused, decade-old relic from Lennon-Mc-Cartney's back drawer called "One After 909." For the cover, the boys returned to the site of their first British L.P. jacket and posed in the same position. Raved *The Beatles Monthly Book:* "It'll prove to those who thought the Beatles' studio ingenuity was getting TOO clever that John, Paul, George, and Ringo are still more than capable of turning out material EVERYONE can UNDERSTAND as well as enjoy."

But some "progressive" fans were distressed at the seemingly reactionary turn of events, among them one S.C. Blake, who wrote *Beatles Monthly:* "Do the fans want to go backwards into the Rock 'n' Roll era? Do we want the simple run-of-the-mill sound of three guitars and a drum kit . . . ? Surely the Beatles shouldn't stop experimenting with new sounds . . . ! Why don't they look to the future instead of 1962?"

Roots or no roots, this particular phase would prove the most dismal of the Beatles' recording career, though as far as the public was concerned, it started splendidly enough with a single, "Get Back" (also said to be the title theme of the L.P.), that arrived in a blaze of ads proclaiming *The Beatles As Nature Intended.* Musically, "Get Back" was indeed stark, high energy rock 'n' roll, nothing more nor less; the lyrics, marginally more cryptic, were filled with coy references to "California grass" and a high-heeled gentleman named Loretta who "gets it while she can." Actually, Paul first wrote "Get Back" as an Enoch Powell-style harangue ("Don't dig no Pakistanis taking all the people's jobs. . . .") but eventually ditched all the trappings of White Power. John Lennon, responsible for the svelte solo guitar work in "Get Back," took over the B-side to deliver his anguished and highly sensuous plea—the first of several written to Yoko—"Don't Let Me Down."

Though the single was a runaway commercial and critical favorite, the *Get Back* album suffered innumerable post-ponements before the Beatles abandoned it altogether. The first official excuse given was that Apple needed time to design the accompanying book, containing photographs by Ethan Russell, commentary by Jonathan Cott and David Dalton, and Beatle dialogue that E.M.I. had insisted be expurgated of unseemly language. But the main reason for the delay was the Beatles' own disenchantment with the whole project. The growing tensions within the group were exacerbated by the conflict between the Beatles' desire for perfection and the audio verité concept behind the album.

In 1976 George Martin recalled in a *Rolling Stone* interview: "It got to the point where we would do a take, and [John] would say, 'How was it George?' . . . I'd say 'it was a little better than take 46 but not quite as good as take 53, and the back drums weren't quite as loud as they were in 69.' It just became ludicrous. You're trying to get *the* perfect one live, it's ridiculous."

Even the songs themselves were mediocre by Beatle standards, with the exceptions of "Get Back" and "Don't Let Me Down"; the *Rubber Soul*-style "Two of Us"; and Mc-Cartney's tuneful, if somewhat melodramatic "The Long and Winding Road" and "Let It Be" (which Paul, thinking he had another "Yesterday" up his sleeve, reportedly secluded himself for a week to compose).

"We couldn't get into it," Lennon later told *Rolling Stone's* Jann Wenner. "And we put down a few tracks and nobody was in it at all. I don't know, it was just a dreadful, dreadful feeling in Twickenham Studio . . . you couldn't make music at eight in the morning or ten or whatever it was, in a strange place with people filming you and colored lights."

The good times—such as the spirited windswept performance on the Apple roof that sent half the neighborhood clambering onto adjacent rooftops, stopped traffic, and finally caused the chief accountant of a nearby bank to summon the police—were apparently few and far between.

"None of us," John went on, "could be bothered going in . . . the tapes were just left there. And we got an acetate each and we called each other and said what do you think, oh, let it out. We were going to let it out with a really shitty condition, disgusted, and I didn't care. I thought it was good to let it out and show people . . . this is what we are like with our trousers off, so would you please end the game now."

It seems ironic that the vast bulk of unreleased Beatle recordings dates from this particularly rocky juncture of the group's career—due, of course, to every stage of *Get Back's* having been filmed and taped. Even so, those out-takes that would find their way into the bootleggers' hands, and many more that remain under guard of private collectors, reveal the dynamic foursome to have been singing encyclopedias of pop.

Over 100 tunes left "in the can" in January 1969 range from "Michael Row Your Boat Ashore" and "The Third Man Theme" to seven selections from the Chuck Berry song-book, five Presley hits, and five Dylan classics—as well as reworkings of "Love Me Do," "You Can't Do That," "Norwe-gian Wood," "She Said She Said," "I'm So Tired" (sung by McCartney) and such future solo entries as George's "All Things Must Pass," Paul's "Teddy Boy," and John's "Gimme Some Truth."

Though the *Get Back* tapes are the only ones to preserve such work-outs for posterity, throughout the Beatles' career their versatility startled anyone eavesdropping on their rehearsals. Their nonchalant impersonations of all the com-petition on the British charts—the latest hits of the Stones, Kinks et al., often rendered while the Fab Four were waiting to plug their own latest offering on such T.V. shows as *Ready Steady Go!* and *Top Of the Pops*—were specially legendary.

Single, Germany, 1969 (Apple)

Single, France, 1969 (Apple)

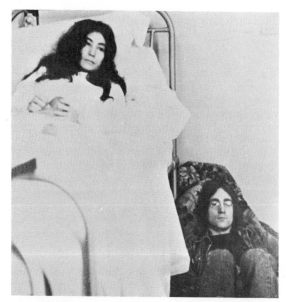

Life With the Lions, L.P., 1969 (Zapple)

To return to *Get Back,* in mid-1969 some radio stations were actually mailed copies of an L.P. containing (on Side One) "One After 909"; a thin wedge of the Drifters hit "Save the Last Dance"; "Don't Let Me Down"; "Dig a Pony"; "I've Got a Feeling"; "Get Back"; and (on Side Two) "For You Blue"; "Teddy Boy"; "Two of Us"; a brief sampling of a smutty Liverpool lay called "Maggie May"; a full five-minute "Dig It"; "Let It Be"; "The Long and Winding Road"; and a short finale of "Get Back."

But it all proved a false alarm, for a certain gentleman from New York, acting on behalf of at least three Beatles, directed that the album get back into the Apple vaults. His reasoning was that the T.V. documentary could make more money for his clients (and, coincidentally, himself) if it were blown up from 16 millimeter to 35, and subsequently marketed as the Fab Four's latest full-length movie—and that the (original motion picture soundtrack) album would also make more money if its release were delayed to coincide with that of the film.

By then, of course (we're getting way ahead of the story) the song "Get Back" would seem slightly out of date to be the theme of a "new" film and L.P., which is why said New York gentleman would eventually rename both the picture and the soundtrack *Let It Be.* In the meantime, execrable recordings of *Get Back* made the rounds as a bootleg.

Despite the ill-starred attempt to get back to where they once belonged, the Beatles' image turned more eccentric than ever. All of them concealed their faces, at one time or another during 1969, behind expansive beards; and George and John let their hair straggle way below the shoulders. Lennon sometimes completed his Hasidic impersonation with a black suit and hat, but more often appeared dressed all in white.

Though the Beatles would regroup in June, sans movie cameras, at the E.M.I. studio on Abbey Road—the birthplace of most of their hits, newly refurbished with 16-track equipment—to tape a magnificent last album, for most of 1969 each would be primarily preoccupied with extra-curricular activities. Many of these would only reinforce the general public's perception of the Beatles as the world's most celebrated group of cranks.

One unorthodox venture was Apple's first and only subsidiary label: Zapple Records. According to the Beatles, this was a "paperback records concept." Zapple releases, to include the spoken word ramblings of such literati as Richard Brautigan, Ken Kesey, Lawrence Ferlinghetti, Allen Ginsberg, and Michael McClure, would be budget-priced specialty items that people were supposed to listen to once or twice and throw away. Typically, however, the Beatles' interest in the project proved to be but momentary. The only two Zapple records that did materialize were John and Yoko's sequel to their less-than-universally-cherished *Two Virgins* affair, and an album's worth of Moog synthesizer doodlings released under George Harrison's byline. Both may indeed have been disposable, but the other part of the "paperback records" bargain had apparently been forgotten by the time the L.P.'s reached the shops: each sported a hardback-sized American list price of six dollars.

With *Unfinished Music No. 2: Life With the Lions,* John and Yoko attempted to chronicle their latest ordeals via the medium of conceptual music. Highlights include 26 minutes of Yoko screeching her heart out at a live "event" at Cambridge University—"like a severely retarded child being tortured," said *Rolling Stone*—backed by free-form feedback from John's guitar; John and Yoko chanting excerpts from news clippings about themselves; the sound of their unborn baby's heartbeat, followed by two minutes' worth of copyrighted silence; and the sound of someone fiddling with a radio dial for 12 minutes. The front cover shows the couple camping out in the hospital room where Yoko subsequently suffered a miscarriage, while the back depicts their marijuana arrest. This L.P. was only the second of a series, threatened Lennon, "that will go on for the rest of our lives. We'd like to be able to produce them as fast as newspapers and television can. It will be a constant autobiography of our life together."

But for most ordinary folk, both John and Yoko's *Unfinished Music* and George's *Electronic Sound* were virtually unlistenable. Harrison seemed to score a further black mark when it was revealed that some of the synthesized burps and farts on his L.P. might not even have been his in the first place.

According to Bernard L. Krause (of Beaver and Krause fame), who had met Harrison when both were working on Jackie Lomax's Apple album, he and George had hung around in the studios one night after the sessions in order for Krause to give the Beatle a Moog synthesizer

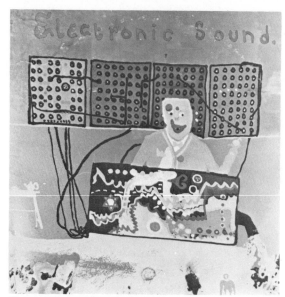

Electronic Sound, L.P., 1969 (Zapple)

Linda, Paul, and Heather after the ceremony (Globe Photos)

demonstration. Krause claims that his performance was taped by Harrison, and subsequently used to fill out a whole side of *Electronic Sound.* In a letter to *Rolling Stone,* Krause stated that on the L.P. cover "under 'produced by Geo. Harrison' you will find my name silvered over. I am frankly hurt and a bit disillusioned by the whole thing."

At least the artwork on the jacket was George's.

Neither Zapple album was destined to remain in print for long. When the two titles dropped out of the Schwann catalogue, they joined the Beatle collectors' list of coveted treasures.

On March 12, 1969, as a weepy crowd kept a rainy vigil outside the Marylebone Register Office, Paul McCartney got married.

One of the international rock whirl's most well-heeled hangers-on, Linda Eastman had been known to enjoy a special relationship with the bachelor Beatle since the previous November, when Paul had stayed with her in New York. Even before that, her intimate photographs of McCartney and the other Beatles had become staples of *Rolling Stone.*

Linda grew up in the rarified upper-class atmosphere of Park Avenue, Scarsdale, and East Hampton. Her father, Lee, after unburdening himself of a Jewish name by substituting Eastman for Epstein, had earned the reputation, and the fortune, of one of America's top show-biz lawyers; an avid art collector, his clients also included such painters as Willem deKooning. But the Picassos on the parlor walls and the country club upbringing didn't prevent his determined daughter from making her camera and her shapely figure virtual fixtures backstage at such legendary New York dives as the Fillmore East. When Paul McCartney came to town to promote his new record company, Linda latched on to one of the brightest stars of them all.

Like Yoko Ono, Linda Eastman had attended Sarah Lawrence College, but despite her cultural background and her knack for photography she came across as a more fun-loving and less intellectual character; yet unlike Maureen Starkey or Patti Harrison, the new Mrs. McCartney would prove one who courted the limelight. Lacking even the more traditional artistic sensibility of Jane Asher, Linda may well have influenced the direction of Paul's long and winding journey from "Penny Lane" to "Bip Bop."

In any case, the McCartneys would soon go out of their way to present the world with a picture of wholesome domestic bliss, of the country squire and his lady leading an upstanding life with the horses, the sheep, and the kids (Linda already had a six-year-old daughter, Heather, whom Paul adopted; Mary McCartney would arrive in August, Stella two years later).

On March 20, John and Yoko took a few hours off from their Paris vacation to fly in a chartered plane to the Crown Colony of Gibraltar for a wedding of their own. "It was perfect," said John upon their triumphant return to Paris later that afternoon. "Quick, quiet, and British."

There were no crowds of fans and photographers milling outside as John—like his bride dressed all in white, right down to the tennis shoes—repeated his vows between puffs on a cigaret. Paul's marriage, which John called "a dry run" for his own, had been a public circus, after which the McCartneys slipped into seclusion for a private honeymoon. With the Lennons, it was the other way around.

"Intellectually, of course, we didn't believe in getting married," said John, explaining that they changed their minds when they saw the potential for a "fantastic happening." Added Yoko: "We're going to stage many happenings and events together and this marriage was one of them. We're planning a big happening in the next seven days or so. You'll know soon enough what it is."

A few days later, John and Yoko moved into the Amsterdam Hilton and let it be known that a happening was about to take place in their bed. Even in permissive Holland, this brought a stern warning from the chief of Amsterdam's vice squad: "If people are invited to such a 'happening,' the police would certainly act."

Some of the 50-odd reporters who rushed over to the Hilton's $70-a-night Presidential Suite would feel cheated. "The only surprise," cabled one, "was that they did nothing at all, except clutch a tulip each."

"I hope it's not a let down," apologized the white-pajamaed Beatle. "We wouldn't make love in public—that's an emotionally personal thing." All he and Yoko planned to do was stay in bed for a week, growing their hair for peace. "This is our protest against all the suffering and violence in the world."

Wedding Album, L.P., 1969 (Apple)

Despite John's explanation that he hoped to put his influence as a youth leader to constructive use, it is unlikely that escapades such as the Bed-in actually won many converts to pacifism. The Lennons betrayed a rather shaky grasp of politics whenever they strayed from their self-appointed role as "the world's clowns" to engage reporters in serious discussions; however, as with most of the Lennons' "events," the main point of interest was not the happening itself, but the way people reacted to it. For the next week or so, the media, particularly the British press, would be the unwitting instrument in a masterpiece of absurd theatre.

Some columnists railed against the Lennons' temerity: "This must rank as the most self-indulgent demonstration of all time. . . . A Biafran mother mourning her child is unlikely to find her heart overflowing with gratitude at the news that this much-publicized couple are sternly applying themselves to seven whole days of connubial comfort on her behalf. The John Lennon peace circus debases the coinage of protest. . . ."

Others expressed sympathy for "a man who found fame and fortune in the evolution of a new sound, a bright image in a dull world, and a not inconsiderable musical talent . . . [who] seems to have come perilously near to having gone off his rocker."

"Letters to the editor" poured in by the thousands, ranging from "How could you permit that disgusting photograph? . . . It is bad enough when valuable space is given to reporting the antics of these creatures!"—and "I see John Lennon considers his idea for a seven day lie-in 'the best idea we've had yet.' So what? I have the same idea every morning—when the alarm clock rings!"—to "Can anyone tell me why the people of Britain are so vicious and vindictive towards anything or anybody that does not fit into their own narrow-minded pattern of living?"

But even publications that denounced the Lennons as the world's biggest bores continued to report faithfully every stage of the happening. "Day Two of the Lennon Lie-in," ran one British headline, "John and Yoko are forced out by Maria, the hotel maid."

After the Bed-in the couple made a lightning trip to Vienna to watch the premiere of their first film collaboration on Austrian T.V. Their Kafkaesque *Rape* shows a girl being pursued by reporters; at first pleased with their attentions, she is eventually hounded to the point of breakdown by the inescapable T.V. cameras.

To the horror of the elegant Sacher's hotel, once the stamping ground of the Hapsburg dynasty, the Lennons summoned reporters to another "happening." This time the pair were concealed inside a bag on top of a table. According to U.P.I.:

Lennon claimed that through "bagism" or "total communication" neither speaker nor listener would prejudge the other according to looks. More "bagism" would mean more peace in the world, he said.
Several times hummed strains of the "Blue Danube" waltz floated out from inside the bag.

On April Fool's Day John and Yoko caught the early plane back to London, clutching 50 acorns tied in a sack. These were to be distributed to world leaders in the name of peace.

"Eventually," said Yoko, "we hope to have had more honeymoons than anyone in the world, maybe even 150."

Lennon lost little time in setting a rhymed account of his latest adventures to music. He was so pleased with "The Ballad Of John and Yoko" that he insisted the Beatles record it immediately, and release it as a single, even though "Get Back" had only just been issued. The fact that George was out of reach and Ringo busy with his second

A portrait of the artist and his bride, by John Lennon (Globe Photos)

Single, Denmark, 1969 (Apple)

film, Peter Sellers' *The Magic Christian,* did not deter the two remaining Beatles from recording "Ballad of John and Yoko" as a duo. McCartney overdubbed drums and Lennon the guitar solos.

John's catchy broadside shares the Fifties Revival sound of "Get Back" and "Don't Let Me Down," but in America it didn't do nearly so well, reaching only number eight. This was because hundreds of Top Forty stations refused to touch a song whose chorus went "Christ, you know it ain't easy . . . ," though some program directors were content merely to blip out the word "Christ," or even snip out the offending segments and splice them backwards into the appropriate places. (Some program directors also detected an unsavory pun in the line about the Lennons going to bed to "get us some peace.")

Calling himself "Christ's biggest fan," John accused the censors of misinterpreting his lyric, adding: "Yes I still think it. Kids are more influenced by us than by Jesus."

The famous honeymoon was also commemorated with Volume Three of John and Yoko's Unfinished Music. A boxed nine-dollar affair, *The Wedding Album* contained a piece of plastic wedding cake, a facsimile of the marriage certificate, and a booklet of press clippings (some of which are quoted a few pages back.) Unfortunately, the elaborate package took so long to prepare that it was not actually released until seven months after the event. On Side One, John and Yoko warble, squawk, and coo each others' names for 22 minutes. Side Two, "Amsterdam," preserves the highlights of their stay in that city, as captured by Lennon's handy cassette machine. These include John ordering toast from room service and Yoko bleating the word "peace" desperately off-key as Lennon's fingers wander aimlessly on his acoustic guitar, occasionally hitting riffs that he would later include on the Beatles' "Because."

The collage also features conversations with earnest Dutch reporters. To one who inquires "What was the biggest success in history in the past 300 years?" Yoko replies: "Maybe it's still yet to happen . . . that's what we're trying to do." She advises those who may wish to join the campaign to "go out on the street now and take off all [their] clothes and say 'Peace.' Of course they would, because they'd think, 'All right, maybe this is a little embarrassing thing to do, but look at John and Yoko, they're doing worser, I can do it.' "

Again, while *The Wedding Album* itself was unlikely to yield very many hours of listening pleasure, some of the critical reactions were priceless. Reviewers were mailed advance test pressings on two separate L.P.'s, each of which contained one side of *The Wedding Album,* backed with a set of empty grooves. *Melody Maker's* Richard Williams, imagining he had a double album on his hands, lavished acclaim on the "blank sides":

Sides Two and Four consist entirely of single tones maintained throughout, presumably produced electronically.

This might sound arid, to say the least, but in fact constant listening reveals a curious point: the pitch of the tones alters frequently, but only by microtones or, at most, a semitone. This oscillation produces an almost subliminal uneven "beat" which maintains interest.

Keeping up with the avant-garde can, evidently, be a hazardous business.

On April 22 Lennon had his middle name officially changed from Winston to Ono. It was unfair, he said, to expect Yoko to take on his last name unless he also adopted hers. He also ventured that nine o's between the two of them would prove a lucky omen.

John had hoped to stage his next Bed-in in the United States, but the authorities, citing his recent drug conviction, refused a visa. Lennon, disappointed at not being able to leave an acorn at the White House, hired a platoon of students to march around New York with peace placards, and personally ventured as close to America as possible.

After finding the Bahamas sticky and unreceptive, the Lennons checked into the Queen Elizabeth Hotel in Montreal for a Bed-in. Just as the Dutch happening had been directed at nearby Britain, this one was calculated to transform the U.S. as well as Canadian media into Radio Free North America, John Lennon style. His antics even caught the attention of Canadian Prime Minister Pierre Trudeau, who responded to John's offer of an acorn by telling reporters: "I don't know about acorns but if he's around I'd like to meet him. He's a good poet."

During his ten days in bed, John composed and recorded his first non-Beatle single—and his most effective contribution to the peace movement. Within hours after writing the "Give Peace a Chance" chorus, Lennon ordered an eight-track recorder installed in his room. As there were no verses to his repetitive new two-chord composition, John made up some harangues against political -ism's and -ation's on the spot, and coaxed his visitors—who included Timothy Leary, Murray the K, Tommy Smothers, Dick Gregory, Petula Clark, a rabbi, and the local chapter of the Radha Krishna Temple—into clapping their hands and singing along with the infectious chorus. This motley crew constituted the first incarnation of the Plastic Ono Band.

Though "Give Peace a Chance" was dutifully credited to "Lennon-McCartney," John took the occasion to launch a new "group," under the byline of which he planned to issue those of his songs that he felt might sound out of place on Beatle records. The Plastic Ono Band—whose line-up encompassed "whoever happens to be in the room at the time"—would also give Lennon a chance to work with the heavy "friends" (as opposed to faceless studio sidemen) that he had long advocated, against McCartney's adamant opposition, be brought into Beatle sessions. But because it provided John with an alternative outlet for his song-writing, the Plastic Ono Band proved to be one more nail in the Beatles' coffin.

To emphasize the conceptual nature of his new combo, John recruited a group of transparent plastic robots and had them assembled on the stage of the Chelsea Town Hall to promote the first Plastic Ono single. Though the record itself failed to crack the Top Ten in America (it did better in Britain), "Give Peace a Chance" was quickly adopted by chanting demonstrators all over the world. John has said that the most stirring experience of his life was hearing his peace jingle over the T.V. news, sung in Washington on Moratorium Day by thousands of anti-war protestors.

Meanwhile, George Harrison kept himself busy recording another hypnotic mantra, which, he claimed, was over a million years older than Lennon's. When John asked members of the London branch of the Radha Krishna Temple whether they thought their Harrison-produced Apple single of "Hare Krishna" would reach Number One, they replied: "higher than that." (In fact, it peaked at #12 in the U.K.) George followed suit with a more rock-oriented Radha Krishna Temple single titled "Govinda," whose combination of opulent, sweeping arrangements and repetitive chanting set the tone for his own solo productions, such as "Isn't It a Pity?"

Not everyone found it easy to tune in to these new tangents. One disillusioned *Disc* correspondent pronounced both "Give Peace a Chance" and "Hare Krishna" "unfit for human ears," and advised the Beatles to "grow up."

"The Young Beatles"

L.P., Japan, 1969 (Polydor)

In January 1969, John Lennon told a reporter for *Disc:* "Apple is losing money. If it carries on like this, we'll be broke in six months." His analysis was given considerable attention by the "mainstream" press, which had not long before recounted that Apple, in its first few months, had sold more records than all but a handful of established labels.

Nobody received the latest news flash with keener interest than Allen Klein. A squat New Yorker with a somewhat shady reputation in the music business, Klein had always wanted to manage the Beatles. He had once tried to strike a deal with Brian Epstein, but the Beatles' normally courtly manager reportedly refused even to shake his hand. Yet despite his acquisition of lucrative consolation prizes such as the Dave Clark Five, Herman's Hermits, and then the Rolling Stones, the President of ABKCO avidly continued to follow the progress of the Beatles' career from his Times Square office, and often boasted that the Fab Four would one day be his.

In his 1971 *Playboy* interview, Klein reveals "the moment I knew for sure I was going to be their manager. I was driving across a bridge out of New York and I heard on the radio that Epstein had died and I said to myself 'I got 'em.'" When Lennon's gloomy prognosis hit the headlines 18 months later, Klein lost no time in flying to London to present his credentials. John was most impressed.

"He not only knew my work, and the lyrics I had written, but he also understood them . . . ," John would remember in *Rolling Stone*. "He told me what was happening with the Beatles, and my relationship with Paul and George and Ringo. He knew every damn thing about us . . . he's a fuckin' sharp man." Lennon also felt an unusual personal affinity with a businessman who took no pains to conceal either his working-class roots or his disdain for the niceties and pretensions of "the faggy elite" ("I don't have the time to be polite," says Klein). Like Lennon, Klein had been abandoned at an early age by his father, a kosher butcher.

But Klein's down-to-earth qualities made a less favorable impression on Paul McCartney, who had in any event set his heart on putting his classy new father-in-law in charge of the Beatles' affairs. Over the next year, the increasingly acrimonious power struggle between Lennon/Klein and McCartney/Eastman would literally blow apart a group that was teetering precariously off balance to begin with.

When Klein arrived on the scene in February, John Eastman—Lee's son and Linda's brother—was already in London to help re-negotiate the Beatles' relationship with NEMS Enterprises, Brian Epstein's company, whose new management continued to take advantage of its legal entitlement to the 25 per cent of the Beatles' earnings that Epstein had charged for his services. Some of the Beatles reportedly felt insulted that Lee Eastman had merely sent his son instead of appearing in person as Klein had.

In any case, John, George, and Ringo all authorized Klein to act on their behalf. Harrison was said to be especially beguiled by Klein's promise to restore to the Beatles the millions of pounds that were being siphoned off by parasites. Part of that promise was that Klein would win control of NEMS for the Beatles, who were substantial shareholders in the company. Despite his confident boasts, however, Klein was unable to wrestle the prize from Triumph Investment. Eventually a compromise was reached whereby NEMS accepted a reduced percentage of the Beatles' income and forfeited all Beatle licensing rights in exchange for assets worth over three million dollars.

Klein was no more successful in his second quest, to capture for the Beatles a majority of shares in their publishing company, Northern Songs. Dick James, the company's managing director and once one of the Beatles' most trusted cohorts, had with no warning sold out his shares to Sir Lew Grade of the ATV entertainment conglomerate. In the ensuing showdown, the Beatles vied with Grade for control of their own copyrights; despite Klein's skillful maneuvering, Sir Lew won out in the end.

In fairness to Klein, he might have been more effective had he been negotiating on behalf of a more united front. Some of his deals were unexpectedly obstructed at the last moment by McCartney and the Eastmans, who had apparently come to view the abrasive little wheeler-dealer and his coarse manners with the utmost distaste. Once Lee Eastman finally arrived in town, he was unable to contain his venom when Klein made some needling comment at an Apple board meeting; according to Lennon, the contemptuous insults that Mr. Eastman hurled back convinced three of the Beatles that they wanted no part of him.

Klein did manage one dazzling coup. Though the Beatles and Apple were still bound to E.M.I. for seven more years, the boys had already delivered nearly the minimum number of new recordings required by their 1967 contract. Klein successfully browbeat E.M.I. into believing that the Beatles wouldn't make another record until the company agreed to an unheard-of royalty scale of up to 69 cents per L.P.; unwilling to risk silencing its number-one asset, E.M.I. caved in to Klein's demands. This would lead to a seven-dollar U.S. list price for subsequent Beatle albums at a time when L.P.'s were still normally pegged at between five and six dollars, which in turn paved the way for across-the-board increases throughout the industry. So much for "Western Communism." (Klein also permanently dissolved the Zapple budget label with the words: "If it's good we'll charge.")

In addition Klein set himself to the task of transforming Apple from a freaks' Utopia to a sensible, ordinary, profit-motivated record company. The likes of Magic Alex and his revolutionary inventions were flushed out onto the street, and the tap was turned off on the liquor and expense accounts that had once flowed so freely at 3 Savile Row. The payroll was purged of anyone who, in the words of one employee, "wasn't indispensable or harmless," and the only nonsense permissible was Beatle nonsense. Fortunately, there was still plenty of that.

The new regime was bitterly blasted by the "alternative" press. In a story titled "Inside Apple Corpse," *Rolling Stone* called Klein the embodiment of "much that's wrong with old-style American business," adding: "We have come to expect innovation, new perspectives, and honesty—above all, honesty—from the Beatles and especially John, and that is what made [Klein's] signing so shocking."

The outvoted McCartney, who had once run the company almost single-handedly, was seldom seen at Apple any more—or anywhere else for that matter, a nuance that some of Paul's more ghoulish observers would find most intriguing.

Yet despite his differences with the rest of the band and his uncustomarily reclusive life style, Paul evidently still considered himself very much a Beatle—if not *the* Beatle. After tapes of the dispiriting *Get Back* episode were temporarily shelved, he managed to pull his group and their act back together on an album that would appear in September 1969, titled after the street where it had been recorded.

The Beatles' producer recalls that both he and McCartney wanted to dispense with Getting Back, and get on with producing another monumental spectacular. The 15-minute suite on Side Two, George Martin told *Rolling Stone,* "was Paul and I getting together because Paul really dug what I wanted to do. I was trying to make a symphony out of pop music. I was trying to get Paul to write stuff that we could then bring in on counterpoint, or sort of a movement that referred back to something else. Bring some form into the thing. John hated that—he liked good old rock 'n' roll. So *Abbey Road* was a compromise too. Side One was a collection of individual songs. John doesn't like tone poems, or whatever you call it."

The album as it stands shows four musicians, all at the height of their powers but each tuned in to very different wavelengths, making one final effort to work together creatively and efficiently (*Abbey Road* was recorded more quickly than any Beatle L.P. since 1965). Lennon, evidently re-energized by his Bed-ins, weighs in with some of his most powerfully idiosyncratic performances; Harrison flowers into full creative and commercial bloom with the two songs that proved to be both his most popular and the most widely covered on the album; and McCartney, who hasn't yet given up on Art, attempts to weld a glittering scrapheap of fragments into an ambitious song cycle. Between them, the sparks fly.

Abbey Road is the most polished of all Beatle productions; yet despite the snappy pace and variety of the 17-tune program, studio embellishments are kept down to White Album levels and the Indian orchestrations and random tape loops seem to have been left permanently behind in Pepperland. Said Ringo: "It's more important that we play good together than to have lots of violins play good together."

Unlike the White Album, *Abbey Road* does indeed feature the entire line-up playing on nearly every track, along with more three-part harmonies than any other Beatle L.P. Certainly there is no better evidence on record of the Beatles' instrumental virtuosity.

Cuts like "Something," "I Want You," and "She Came In Through the Bathroom Window" reverberate with roller coaster runs from Paul's bass—stunningly melodic for that normally rhythm-oriented instrument—though on "Because" and "Golden Slumbers" Paul, with his superb sense of knowing exactly what a song requires, reverts to an almost childlike simplicity. The two guitarists eke out an unusual range of sounds, the newly self-confident Harrison having, with the encouragement of Eric Clapton, re-channeled his devotion to sitar scales into a revived love affair with the guitar. Ringo's fills are consistently inventive—and are rewarded toward "The End" with his first recorded drum solo.

Yet the musicianship is always tasteful, unobtrusive, and supportive of the songs themselves, steering clear of the self-indulgent jamming that dragged so many late Sixties supersessions toward the outer limits of tedium. The Beatles never sounded more together.

Like all their best albums, *Abbey Road* is inhabited by a large cast of whimsical characters—such as Maxwell, who cheerfully bumps off all and sundry with a magic hammer; Mean Mr. Mustard with the 10-shilling note up his nose, who gets his kicks out of screaming obscenities at Her Majesty; and his transvestite sister Pam, resplendent in a polythene bag. The first of these to emerge, in the opening track "Come Together," is a free-associating gumbooted walrus tossing off pithy one-liners like "hold you in his armchair you can feel his disease." Though the song was originally conceived as a theme for Timothy Leary's proposed campaign against Ronald Reagan for Governor of California, the walrus is clearly none other than John Ono Lennon himself.

John's X-rated gobbledegook is delivered to a bumpin'-and-grindin' accompaniment that sounds more like Chuck Berry than any Beatle recording since "Roll Over Beethoven" and "Rock 'n' Roll Music." So distinct was the likeness that the composer found himself on the receiving end of a lawsuit instigated by Berry's publisher, who uncharitably pointed out that the first two lines of lyric and most of the melody were virtually identical to passages of the greasy car classic "You Can't Catch Me." Lennon eventually agreed to make amends by promising to record the original Berry tune on a solo "oldies" L.P.—which would in its turn send yet more multi-million dollar litigation flying in all directions.

With the next number George Harrison at last hit the jackpot. Shortly after authorities ranging from John Lennon to *Time* magazine pronounced "Something" the best song on the album, Allen Klein attempted to curry favor with the composer by releasing it as a single, backed with "Come Together." "They blessed me with a couple of B-sides in the past," George laconically told David Wigg. "But this is the first time I've had an A-side. Big deal!"

That it was. By Mr. Klein's reckoning, "Something" sold more copies in America than any previous 45, save only "Hey Jude" and "I Want To Hold Your Hand."

Though George has since been known to charge Paul with vacuous commercialism, "Something" suggests he

Abbey Road, L.P., 1969 (Apple)

might have learned a trick or two from his authoritarian bassist. Long-haired critics may have shuddered under the onslaught of oozing M.O.R. strings (from which the Beatles' recording is salvaged by their own inventive instrumental work); but Frank Sinatra hailed "Something" as "the greatest love song of the past 50 years." His rendition, along with umpteen others, quickly turned this Harrisong into a standard from the Borscht Belt to the dentist's waiting room, placing it second only to "Yesterday" among the most widely recorded Beatle compositions. (The line "something in the way she moves" was borrowed from the debut L.P. of Apple recording artiste James Taylor, who around this time became the first to bolt from the label's new regime. Klein slapped back with a five-million-dollar lawsuit.)

"Maxwell's Silver Hammer" is one of Paul's kinkiest songs, in that it makes the rampages of a murderer sound as merry and gay as a romp around the mulberry bush. With its Ray Davies-style adaptation of British music hall, it's pretty Kinky as well.

Apparently at least half the group were cringing with embarrassment while this selection was being taped. Shortly after its release, Lennon, never much of a cabaret buff, announced pointedly: "The Beatles can go on appealing to a wide audience as long as they make . . . nice little folk songs like 'Maxwell's Silver Hammer' for the grannies to dig." More recently George carped, in *Crawdaddy:* "Paul would make us do these really fruity songs. I mean, my God, 'Maxwell's Silver Hammer' was so fruity."

Still, Paul has been known to flaunt his candy-ass in a considerably less brilliant light. And George, despite his objections, contributes some tasty synthesizer obbligatos. Already well beyond *Electronic Sound,* he displays here (as on his own "Here Comes the Sun") a far more dextrous touch with the Frankensteinian instrument than most rock stars soon to fumble onto the Moog bandwagon would manage. The lethal hammer itself (an anvil, actually) is clanked by Ringo Starr.

On the next track Paul slips into his butch persona to let rip with his most tonsil-shredding vocal, which he reportedly screamed himself hoarse for days to perfect. "Oh! Darling" is one of the few spots on *Abbey Road* where the Beatles appear to Get Back, but, as with their other freshly minted rock 'n' roll goldies ("Back In the U.S.S.R.," "Ballad Of John and Yoko," "Get Back" itself) that hardly means a Son Of "I Want To Hold Your Hand" or "She Loves You." The Beatles' last three albums present pastiches of the music of their own adolescence in much the same way *Sgt. Pepper* took on more staid styles; in that light "Oh! Darling" doesn't seem so far removed from "When I'm 64" or "She's Leaving Home" as people then tended to assume.

According to Ringo, the fact that "Octopus's Garden" is the last of but two Starkey contributions to the Beatle oeuvre wasn't due to any lack of trying: "I'd write tunes that were already written and just change the lyrics, and the other three would have hysterics just tellin' me what I'd re-written."

But they did let him get away with a remake of one of the Beatles' own greatest splashes; here Ringo refurbishes the old yellow sub with a country beat and an octopus, cheerily blowing bubbles through a straw between chapters of his underwater Utopian bedtime story. George even offered high praise for lines like "warm below the storm": "When you get deep into your consciousness it's very peaceful. So Ringo writes his cosmic songs without knowing."

To John Lennon—as his subsequent "Cold Turkey" and *Plastic Ono Band* L.P. would make plain—Getting Back meant something quite different from spoofing the clichés of the Fifties in ditties like "Oh! Darling." The raw power of rock 'n' roll was the vehicle with which he was coming to express his most primal feelings.

"I Want You (She's So Heavy)"—the weightiest slab of "heavy metal" the Beatles ever quarried—conveys the almost desperate intensity of John's attraction to Yoko. Lennon unleashes some savagely primitive licks with his guitar ("I'm not technically very good, but I can make it howl and move," he told *Rolling Stone's* Jann Wenner) and the words, like those in "Don't Let Me Down," are direct as can be. "When you're drowning," Lennon explained to Wenner, "you don't say 'I would be incredibly pleased if someone would have the foresight to notice me drowning and come and help me,' you just *scream.* And in 'She's So Heavy' I just sang 'I want you, I want you so bad, she's so heavy, I want you,' like that."

During the incessant coda of this longest of all Beatle songs, electronic distortion slowly envelops like a dark mist the menacing riff hammered out in relentless unison by all the instruments. At long last the listener is jolted out of hypnosis when the music is abruptly snapped off mid-bar. A symphonic crescendo could hardly be more startling than this most inspired of the Beatles' many imaginative utilizations of silence.

Side Two opens on a less claustrophobic note with "Here Comes the Sun," arguably George Harrison's most perfect composition. Acoustic guitars coast serenely through tricky time changes as equally understated lyrics present the arrival of sunshine and springtime as symbols of a new beginning. Hardly an original theme, yet "Here Comes the Sun" conveys a sense of the mystic far more eloquently than any turgid rewrite of Hindu scriptures could hope to.

George composed the song in the early spring of 1969 as a reaction to the gloom that had fallen over Apple. His life at that point, he told David Wigg, had been usurped by "bankers and lawyers . . . contracts and shares, and it was really awful because it's not the sort of thing we enjoy. One day I didn't come into the office, it was like slagging off school, and I went to [Eric Clapton's] house in the country and it was . . . a release of the tension that had been building up on me. It was a really nice day and I picked up the guitar which was the first time I'd played in a couple of weeks . . . the first thing that came out was that song."

A sense of wide-eyed wonder lingers through "Because," which both Harrison and McCartney nominated their *Abbey Road* favorite, and which sounds at moments like a Beethoven sonata in a Hawaiian setting. John in fact said he began writing it as a variation on part of *The Moonlight Sonata* (played for him by Yoko). Harpsichord, piano, and muted brass combine with three breathily harmonizing Beatles for some of the most delicate textures on any of their records. Lennon displays the punster's art in an unusually naive light with lines like:

Because the world is round
it turns me on.

McCartney's famous Pop Symphony (which includes three Lennon interludes) begins at the Apple negotiating table with the lament:

You never give me your money,
you only give me your funny paper,

eventually steering out of the Beatles' financial rut with the words:

Step on the gas and wipe that tear away.
One sweet dream
came true
today.

The ensuing sequence resembles a dream not so much in the subject matter of the individual segments (no "Lucy In the Sky" here) but in the almost hallucinatory way one musical/lyrical setting unfolds into another. Despite the occasional recurring motifs, most of these tunes were gathering dust as unfinished fragments before Martin and McCartney were struck with the bright idea of gluing them all together; yet, like "A Day In the Life," they make for an effective collage.

John's "Sun King" (originally called "Los Paranoias") features more "Because" harmonies, and a nice picture in sound devised during the mixing stage—limpid strands of 9th and 11th chords rise like rays of the dawn's early light from one stereo channel, slowly creating the illusion of an arc before dissolving into the other.

In his best outrageous form, Lennon intones passages of a Mediterranean language that turns out to be purely imaginary, then introduces two characters who might have stepped right from the pages of *A Spaniard In the Works*—the unsavory Mr. Mustard and his delectable but unorthodox sister. The story of Polythene Pam is told in the thickest Beatle Liverpudlian on record.

The final stretch of *Abbey Road* is strictly Paul's territory. While Lennon pinched a line or two from Chuck Berry, and Harrison from James Taylor, in "Golden Slumbers" McCartney taps a more venerable source: some 400-year-old lines by the poet Thomas Dekker. The original—which Paul revised slightly—reads:

Golden slumbers kiss your eyes;
smiles awake you when you rise.
Sleep pretty wantons do not cry,
and I will sing a lullaby.
Rock them, rock them, lullaby.

These lyrics had been co-opted long before in a traditional

song that happened to be resting on the piano stand when McCartney was visiting his family. "I can't read music and I couldn't remember the old tune so I started playing my tune to it and I liked the words so I just kept that," Paul told David Wigg.

After the stirring "Carry That Weight" all the Beatles get a chance to show off their chops, which culminates in a ferocious guitar battle. Paul, George, and John alternate, in that order, each taking the lead one bar at a time, after which the song cycle closes with the lilting platitude:

And in the end the love you take
is equal to the love you make.

But just as Side One ended when one least expected, Side Two sounds off again nearly a minute into the run-off grooves. The surprise track (unlisted on the album), a quicky snatch of Paul's irreverent "Her Majesty," effectively punctures what might have been a somewhat pompous finale to an otherwise majestic "The End."

Abbey Road sold over five million copies in the United States alone. That's a million more than *Meet the Beatles*, close to two million over *Sgt. Pepper*.

One reason, no doubt, was *Abbey Road*'s sheer excellence, the way it combines a sense of high adventure (albeit with safety belts firmly strapped in place) and some of the most melodic yet blatantly commercial Beatle music ever, all polished almost beyond perfection (a few sour souls charged that the album was *too* slick).

Also, after *Sgt. Pepper* had established the Beatles as the darlings of countless listeners who normally paid the rock whirl little notice, their next all-new single L.P. was guaranteed the biggest ready-made audience of their career. (At $11.98 a throw, the double White Album was a bit off-putting to casual admirers.)

Yet a third reason for the record-shattering sales was that, as every music biz exec knows, nothing enhances demand for an artist's work more quickly than word of his death.

"What about the movement in Detroit to stamp out the Beatles?"

"We're starting a movement to stamp out Detroit."
—from the Beatles' first U.S. press conference, February 7, 1964

Over five years later, Motor City finally avenged that slight—by spreading a report that, at least in the imaginations of thousands of believers, stamped out Paul McCartney for good.

On October 12, 1969, disk jockey Russ Gibb of WKNR-FM (Detroit's "underground" station) received an eerie phone call, which advised him to listen closely to the fade-outs of certain Beatles numbers, and to play others backward. Following instructions, Gibb and his listeners found (among other "clues") that John mutters "I buried Paul" at the end of "Strawberry Fields Forever," and that "Revolution 9"'s oft-intoned words "number nine, number nine" become "turn me on dead man, turn me on dead man" when one spins the White Album counterclockwise. By the same process, the message "Paul is dead man, miss him, miss him" emerges from the gibberish sandwiched between "I'm So Tired" and "Blackbird." Gibb, smelling a dead, er, Beatle, became the first of many vocal promulgators of Paul's untimely death.

Two days later The Michigan Daily ran a review of Abbey Road by Fred LaBour that took the form of an obituary, illustrated with a gruesome likeness of Paul's severed head. According to LaBour, the L.P. cover shows the Beatles leaving a cemetery dressed as a minister (John), an undertaker (Ringo), and a gravedigger (George). Paul is not only out of step with the others, but barefoot, as British corpses supposedly are prone to be buried. A cigaret in his right hand confirms that this is an imposter for the left-handed McCartney. The license plate of the parked Volkswagen spells out Paul's age: 28 IF he had lived.

One and one and one is three, concluded LaBour, who also cited corroborating "evidence" on earlier L.P. sleeves. Sgt. Pepper shows a grave, with yellow flowers shaped as Paul's four-stringed bass guitar. A hand is extended over McCartney's head—another omen of death. On page three of the Magical Mystery Tour picture book, Paul sits in front of a sign reading "I WAS"; two flags are displayed over his head, in the manner of military funerals. On page 23, Paul sports a black carnation; the other three Beatles' are red.

Soon afterward, Alex Bennett of WMCA-AM (a highly above-ground New York station) turned the controversy into the prime topic of his talk-show (after receiving a call from one Lewis Yager, who claimed to have been awakened in the night by the screams of a Beatlemaniacal girlfriend to whom McCartney's dire fate had been revealed in a dream). Not to be outdone, Bennett's counterpart on WABC quickly did the same. It was only a matter of days before the increasingly complicated tale of Paul's decapitation had swept across the North American airwaves to become the Number One topic of discussion and conjecture on campuses and in the "alternative" press.

A slew of sick novelty records (among them "St. Paul" by Terry Knight, the man who would soon bless the world with Grand Funk) were hurriedly recorded to cash in on the macabre fad. There was even a T.V. special, set in a courtroom presided over by famed defense lawyer F. Lee Bailey. The motley crew of "witnesses" included Allen Klein and Peter Asher, claiming that Paul was alive and well—with Russ Gibb and his fellow ghouls, armed with the paraphernalia of the "evidence," to demonstrate the contrary. Mr. Bailey ruled that it was up to viewers to draw their own conclusions.

Meanwhile, Bennett flew to London to round up more witnesses. Paul's purported undertaker was ambivalent ("I'm not going to say anything because nobody believes me when I do," said Ringo) but photographer Ian Macmillan denied that there was any intentional symbolism on the Abbey Road jacket. Each Beatle was only wearing his usual 1969 finery, and as it was a warm day, McCartney had taken off his shoes. The 28 IF Volkswagen just happened to be parked there.

The Paul-Is-Dead buffs, however, found these explanations unsatisfactory. They ignored Jeanne Dixon, America's best-selling soothsayer, who divined that Paul was still with us. They didn't believe Lennon either, who said that the message at the end of "Strawberry Fields" was actually "cranberry sauce." When it was pointed out that McCartney was only 27 IF still alive, the ghouls countered by citing certain Asian countries where people are given a free extra year to account for time spent in the womb. And when—to all appearances—Paul himself finally emerged from Scottish seclusion ("Reports of my death are greatly exaggerated," he declared. "If I were dead I'd be the last to know."), his statements were scoffed at as the words of an imposter.

Each denial, in fact, was branded another link in the conspiracy; and the clues continued to proliferate. Sleuths all over America, delighted at the chance to put their Beatle-ology to practical use, peered at album covers through mirrors and magnifying glasses, and played the records themselves in every imaginable direction and speed.

Thanks to the demand for clean copies of the evidence, Sgt. Pepper and Magical Mystery Tour, off the charts since February, put in strong re-appearances. Exulted Capitol Records vice-president Rocco Catena: "This is going to be the biggest month in history in terms of Beatle sales." Small wonder both Capitol and Apple reacted to reports of Paul's death with respectful silence.

As is generally the case with rumors, there were as many variations as there were tellers. But most agreed that the accident occurred in November, 1966 (probably on the ninth, a "stupid bloody Tuesday"). Paul had stormed out of the Abbey Road recording studio, upset over a spat with the other Beatles. He took a spin in his Aston Martin (shown sitting in a doll's lap on the Sgt. Pepper jacket) and "blew his mind out in a car/ he didn't notice that the lights had changed."

Single, Japan, 1969 (Apple)

The accident, which "A Day in the Life" chronicles in detail, is also alluded to in "Magical Mystery Tour" (". . . dying to take you away . . .") and "Don't Pass Me By"; and "Revolution 9" features the sounds of an appalling car crash. McCartney's head was severed from its body, and the Beatle was Officially Pronounced Dead (the inside of the Sgt. Pepper sleeve shows him wearing an O.P.D. armpatch) on Wednesday morning at five o'clock (a phrase that George's superimposed likeness clearly points out on the Sgt. Pepper lyric sheet; in the same picture Paul's back is turned).

So then whose dulcet tones are heard on such songs as "She's Leaving Home" and "Magical Mystery Tour"? Well, or so the story goes, the other three Beatles conspired, for a giggle, to "cover up" this information from the general public. To give the impression of business as usual, the winner of a Paul McCartney look-alike contest was assigned plastic surgery and the task of filling a dead man's shoes. Fortunately for John, George, and Ringo, this William Campbell was also a McCartney sound-alike, with a knack for composing such poignant McCartneyesque ballads as "Hey Jude" and "Fool On the Hill."

"Oh Darling," Single, Japan, 1969 (Apple)

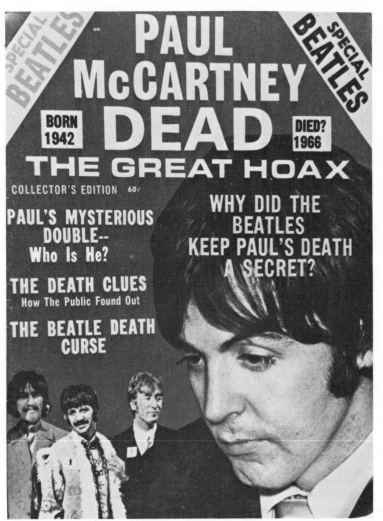

SPECIAL BEATLES

PAUL McCARTNEY DEAD

SPECIAL BEATLES

BORN 1942 **DIED? 1966**

THE GREAT HOAX

COLLECTOR'S EDITION 60¢

PAUL'S MYSTERIOUS DOUBLE-- Who Is He?

THE DEATH CLUES How The Public Found Out

THE BEATLE DEATH CURSE

WHY DID THE BEATLES KEEP PAUL'S DEATH A SECRET?

Meanwhile—and this is the part of the story that people found easiest to swallow—the Beatles began planting a myriad of clues on each subsequent album, to test the fans' perceptiveness. John's "I Am the Walrus" was just one of many songs said to be pregnant with intrigue. Its subtitle— "No You're Not Said Little Nicola"—supposedly established that the Walrus was someone other than Lennon. The later "Glass Onion," of course, confirmed who that someone was: "The Walrus was Paul." In the *Magical Mystery Tour* booklet, the walrus figure appears dressed in black. In Greek, it was claimed, "walrus" means "corpse." The record fades out to a reading of a death scene from Shakespeare's *King Lear.*

Truly, the Paul-Is-Dead saga boasted enough literary references and multilingual puns to do James Joyce proud. As a matter of fact, one erudite Beatlemaniac detected a clue in "I Am the Walrus" 's "goo goo goo joob" chorus; in *Finnegan's Wake* these are Humpty Dumpty's last words before he takes a fall and cracks his head. Someone could base a whole book on the rumor—if no one has already.

Was this all just the collective fantasy of thousands of Beatle-obsessed imaginations? A year later—by which time almost everyone had been persuaded of Paul's continued existence, but not of the Beatles' own innocence in perpetrating the rumor—John Lennon insisted to *Rolling Stone's* Jann Wenner: "The whole thing was made up. We

wouldn't do anything like that. . . . People have nothing better to do than study Bibles and make myths about it, and study rocks and make stories about how people used to live and all that. You know, it's just something to do for them, they live vicariously."

If so, that doesn't necessarily make the saga any less fascinating. That the Beatles cult was capable of spinning an elaborate mythic web without any participation from John, Paul, George, and Ringo indicates how far they had been elevated toward the status of demigods in the imaginations of their disciples. In that sense, the McCartney legend recalls, for example, the film *Yellow Submarine*—but with the difference that the latter was consciously put together by a small, tightly knit group of people. Paul-Is-Dead (whose germ has been traced variously to an Ohio Wesleyan University student's thesis and to a prankish article in an Illinois University student newspaper) was created—or developed—by thousands scattered across America. As such, it can be seen as a genuine folk tale of the mass communications era.

Yet there are many who, despite all the denials, remain convinced that the entire cosmic joke was masterminded by the Beatles themselves. The sheer number of Paul-Is-Dead clues, it is argued, stretches the long arm of coincidence beyond the breaking point. After all, the Beatles were notorious for sly, outrageous stunts—ranging from slipping a falsetto chorus of "tit tit tit" into "Girl" way back in 1965, to the blank L.P. cover and the surprise endings on each side of *Abbey Road.* Why wouldn't they have taken it into their heads to link such pranks into a definite pattern—and in the process perpetrate the most monumental hoax since Orson Welles' *War of the Worlds* broadcast persuaded thousands of panicky New Jerseyites that Martian invaders were in the vicinity?

Eight years on, the Paul-Is-Dead story, like McCartney himself, still seems to be alive and kicking. In a recent essay, sociologist Barbara Suczek presents the rumor as a 20th-century version of the archetypal myth wherein the beautiful youth dies and is resurrected as a god.

A 1976 tome titled *Rumor and Gossip: The Social Psychology of Hearsay,* by Ralph Rosnow and Gary Fine, features an extensive passage on the McCartney hoax, which the authors also explore in the August 1974 issue of *Human Behavior.* The two psychologists conclude that, like most rumors, this one was spread as an unconscious attempt on the part of rumormongers to gain status in exchange for precious information. Yet, "it had markings of a budding legend or literary invention, rather than the news item it supposedly was. . . . The clearest function of this rumor . . . was its entertainment value. It was 'fun' hunting for clues and talking about the mystery with friends. The rumor flourished for many of the same reasons that mystery stories are so popular—suspense without fear and emotional stimulation."

That some people were willing to believe the rumor, according to Drs. Rosnow and Fine, "implies that the world and in particular the mass media are deceptive. This generation had been brought up in the shadow of the Kennedy assassinations and the considerable doubt focused on the Warren Commission report. The credibility gap of Lyndon Johnson's presidency, the widely circulated rumors after the Martin Luther King, Jr. and Robert F. Kennedy assassinations, as well as attacks on the leading media sources by the yippies and Spiro Agnew, no doubt helped to foster an attitude in which a massive conspiracy was not out of the question. A person, one of world renown, could be replaced by another for three years in the eyes of this audience without anyone being the wiser."

Even in 1977, someone like Joel Glazier can electrify audiences at Beatles conventions and free universities with his lectures on the subject, though he is often challenged by earnest young fans who insist that they saw McCartney alive and well on his most recent tour. To which Joel replies: "I've never given any thought to whether Paul really died or not. I've been too busy looking for clues ever since."

Some of his recent unearthings—which he projects onto a screen during the course of his presentation—include skeleton hands reaching out behind Paul toward the lower right of the White Album giveaway poster, a slanted skull following the word BEATLES on the back of the *Abbey Road* jacket, and a large skull on page eight of the *Magical Mystery Tour* booklet. (If you turn the picture 90 degrees to the right and stare from a distance of about 10 feet, the beret of the diner nearest the camera is liable to turn into an eye socket. Joel claims this was deliberately planted, as it is the only photograph not taken from the actual film.)

From his vast dossier of clues, Professor Glazier has concocted two alternative scenarios to account for the whole phenomenon. One revolves around the Devil exacting McCartney's sacrifice as the price of the Beatles' continued success, a theory that drags in not only the Rolling Stones (who offered up Brian Jones by the same arrangement), but also Charlie Manson, who made the Beatles his rationale for murdering the wife of Roman Polanski. The famed director's diabolical *Rosemary's Baby* was filmed in the New York apartment building presently inhabited by John Lennon.

Joel's other scenario blames Paul's assassination on a C.I.A. determined to end the Beatles' baleful influence on the youth of the free world. The three surviving Beatles, however, refused to be thwarted; so they hired William Campbell and proceeded to reveal the truth in as subtle a manner as they could devise.

As Lewis Yager, who hasn't forgotten his own key role in the affair, said recently: "Everyone knows it was a hoax. But people still love hearing the clues. It was the most fascinating stunt in years."

While the rumor snowballed, McCartney remained in Scottish seclusion, going, according to friends, "through heavy changes." During the six months following *Abbey Road* he granted few interviews, and his only audible contribution to the music scene was Badfinger's first hit, "Come and Get It," which he wrote and produced, and which was used as the theme song for the Peter Sellers/Ringo Starr film, *The Magic Christian*.

Starr and Harrison also tended to avoid the public eye, though George did make a low profile return to the concert stage, backing up Delaney and Bonnie. Ringo busied himself with a solo album dedicated to his mother, featuring such "standards" as "Night and Day" and "Love Is a Many-Splendored Thing." ("Get *way* back" went the *Rolling Stone* headline.) Ringo gave Quincy Jones, Richard Perry, Les Reed, Maurice Gibb of the Bee Gees, Paul McCartney, and seven others one song each with which to explore their talents as big band arrangers. But nobody could possibly have brought a more implausible voice to bear on such a project than Mr. Starkey; and when *Sentimental Journey* (originally titled *Ringo Starrdust*) appeared in early 1970, the reaction of critics, fans, and John Lennon was one of embarrassed silence.

Lennon was by far the most visible and prolific Beatle during this period. On September 13 he gave his first major concert in years, at Toronto's huge open-air "rock 'n' roll revival." Only two days beforehand he had received a call from the producers, offering to fly him over at their own expense and reserve him a pair of choice tickets. Lennon's impulsive reply was that he would love to come—but on condition that he and Yoko be allowed to appear on stage with their band, instead of just sitting in the front row "like the King and Queen."

As the Plastic Ono Band was, at that point, still purely conceptual, John persuaded bassist Klaus Voormann, drummer Alan White, and (at the last minute) guitarist Eric Clapton to join forces with him. Then Lennon himself chickened out and missed his plane, before being finally coaxed onto the last possible flight. That, however, ruled out the luxury of a rehearsal; so John kicked off his show with the announcement: "We're just gonna do numbers that we know, y'know, 'cause we've never played together before." The crowd cheered ecstatically at the mere sound of his Liverpool accent, which evidently reassured Lennon, who later said he had been violently ill with a case of nerves just before stepping onto the stage.

The music was certainly raw, yet there has seldom been a rock show so electric with tension and suspense. Driven along by Clapton's quicksilver runs, Lennon stormed through stone-heavy renditions of three rock 'n' roll chestnuts ("Blue Suede Shoes," "Money," and "Dizzy Miss Lizzie"); an exceptionally powerful "Yer Blues"; the previously unheard "Cold Turkey"; and—"this is what we came for"—"Give Peace a Chance." "I was making up the words as we went along," said John. "I didn't have a clue."

Then Yoko emerged from her large white sack to offer a rocked up version of "Don't Worry Kyoko, Mummy's Only Looking for Her Hand in the Snow." Her next showcase—fifteen minutes' worth of blood-curdling shrieks, accompanied by ear-splitting feedback from the amplifiers of the musicians, who had themselves left the stage—ended the show on a note of some confusion.

Lennon himself was delighted with the entire performance, a recording of which was soon released as *Live Peace in Toronto 1969*. Though it contains some fine music, this L.P. (which Capitol inexplicably deleted four years later) is memorable more for its qualities of audio verité. Unlike, say, *The Wedding Album,* it succeeds in communicating all the excitement of the original event.

Upon returning to London, John recorded "Cold Turkey" with Clapton, Voormann, and Ringo. The second Plastic Ono Band single left little doubt about the direction Lennon's rock 'n' roll was taking: no frills, no soft-soap—or, as he himself put it—"no bullshit." In "Cold Turkey" the melody—if it can be called that—seldom strays out of a cramped three-note range. The record is too slow for dancing, too raucous for daydreaming. The words are similarly bleak, both in style and in content:

Temperature's rising, fever is high,
can't see no future, can't see no sky;
my feet are so heavy, so is my head;
I wish I was a baby, I wish I was dead.

After composing "Cold Turkey," Lennon "went to the other three Beatles and said: 'Hey lads, I think I've written a new single.'" Paul, however, wasn't too sold on the idea. "So I thought: 'Bugger you, I'll put it out myself.'"

For good measure, John refused to credit his harrowing piece to "Lennon-McCartney," effectively ending a 13-year tradition.

The singles-buying public, however, also proved unreceptive to a song about a junkie's withdrawal symptoms. That November, when John snatched his M.B.E. off the top of his Aunt Mimi's T.V. set and returned it to the Queen, he listed "Cold Turkey"'s poor showing on the national charts among his grievances against Her Majesty's government, along with British support of the U.S. in Vietnam and of Nigeria in Biafra. Lennon's gesture proved even more controversial

the beatles very together

L.P., Canada, 1969 (Polydor) Paul's "death" was symbolically exploited on this reissue of the Tony Sheridan tapes

than his earning the award in the first place; and many of his sympathizers felt that he cheapened his point by lumping "Cold Turkey" together with such profound issues. John Lennon felt that his critics lacked a sense of humor.

The medal itself was tucked away in a Buckingham Palace drawer for safe-keeping.

John brought his peace campaign to a spectacular climax during the decade's final month. At considerable expense, he aired his new slogan—"WAR IS OVER! IF YOU WANT IT," signed "Happy Xmas from John & Yoko"—via full-page ads in the world's major newspapers, and billboards prominently displayed in New York, Los Angeles, Montreal, Toronto, London, Paris, Amsterdam, Rome, and Athens.

On December 15 the Plastic Ono Band performed a UNICEF benefit at London's Lyceum ballroom, augmented with such superstars as Keith Moon, Billy Preston, and Delaney and Bonnie and Friend George Harrison. The program consisted of extended improvisations on only two songs—"Cold Turkey" and "Don't Worry Kyoko"—which Lennon proclaimed "the most fantastic music I've ever heard." (The recordings that surfaced on 1972's Some Time in New York City suggest he may have been exaggerating.)

The next day the Lennons landed in Canada for the third time in eight months to announce "a big peace and music festival to be held at Mosport Park near Toronto. We aim to make it the biggest music festival in history, and we're going to ask everyone who's anyone to play . . . and then give a percentage of the gross to a new peace fund. . . .

"Everyone who's into peace," John continued, "will regard the New Year as Year One A.P. (for 'After Peace'). All of our letters and calendars from now on will use this method.

"Along with the festival we are going to have an International Peace Vote. We're asking everyone to vote for either peace or war. When we've got about 20 million votes we're going to give them to the United States."

In addition to laying the groundwork for the festival with Toronto "rock 'n' roll revival" producer John Brower, Lennon testified in favor of legalized marijuana before the Canadian Government Commission on Drug Use; met with Marshall McLuhan and Prime Minister Pierre Trudeau (who, the press noted, gave more of his time—about an hour—to Lennon than to recent visiting heads of state); and signed 4200

erotic lithographs, to be sold for $1000 per set of 14 (the originals were impounded a few weeks later under British obscenity laws).

John also announced the imminent release of a reggae-style Plastic Ono Band single titled "Make Love Not War," and a new John and Yoko L.P.: "one side is laughing, the other side is whispering." Neither materialized.

Lennon at this time was also the recipient of the first Rolling Stone Man of the Year award. A lengthy editorial by Jann Wenner began: "Since 1965, the Beatles have been the single dominant force in the new social thought and style for which the Sixties will forever be remembered." Concluded Wenner: "A five hour private meeting between John Lennon and Richard Nixon would be a more significant summit than any Geneva Summit Conference between the U.S.A. and Russia."

Both Lennon's Year One Festival and Wenner's editorial may have been symptoms of the euphoria shared by most of the counterculture in the aftermath of July's Woodstock Music and Art Fair. That event—take it from one who was there—was actually, by normal standards, a monumental catastrophe. The superstar sounds were audible to only a fraction of the 400,000 in attendance (and even then regularly drowned out by helicopters evacuating acid casualties to the nearest hospital); water and food supplies were close to nonexistent; and torrential downpours swiftly transformed Yasgur's Farm into an enormous mudpie.

Out of such humble stuff was the myth of the "Woodstock Nation" created—for the one very good reason that everyone bore up heroically under the disastrous circumstances, sharing weed and supplies with neighbors, taking the opportunity to roll naked in the mud, and doing all the good things that good hippies were supposed to do.

The Woodstock formula, however, proved to be one that could not be consciously duplicated. Subsequent festivals were progressively less idyllic, attracting increasing numbers of thrill-seekers, rip-off artists, and troublemakers. Just as John Lennon was planning "the biggest musical festival in history," a young man was stabbed to death by a Hell's Angel during the Rolling Stones' appearance at a Woodstock-style event in Altamont, California.

In any case, shortly after Year One's organizers passed word that the Beatles, Bob Dylan, and a convoy of U.F.O.'s were all likely to appear, in Toronto the coming July, Lennon

Hey Jude, L.P., USA, 1970 (Apple)

130

called the whole thing quits. The reasons given involved business differences, but after Altamont, the rock festival was on its way out anyway. The counterculture had lost one of its most potent symbols; and it was about to lose another.

The Beatles' few remaining meetings seldom produced anything but further disagreement. Once, when Paul tried to corral the others into going back on the road, John stunned him with the words: "I want a divorce." Both McCartney and Klein persuaded him to reconsider, or at least not to sound off to the press.

On another occasion, preserved on tape (the Beatles having caught Andy Warhol's habit of letting tape recorders eavesdrop on intimate conversations), John and George presented Paul with an ultimatum. Lennon said he was tired of playing a bit part in "pre-packaged productions," conceived by and tailored to the genius of Paul McCartney. Henceforth the three Beatles must each be awarded precisely four songs per album, with Ringo getting to add one or two if he so desired. Paul complained that that kind of arbitrary regimentation was more suited to the military than to the Beatles, but the others insisted it was the only way to insure a fair shake for all.

That proved to be a moot point, however, as the fabulous foursome never made it back into the recording studio. In the absence of fresh Beatles product (the *Get Back/Let It Be* tapes continued to languish on the shelf) Klein patched ten old singles together to create an L.P. for the American market; his title, *The Beatles Again,* was revised by public demand to *Hey Jude.*

Meanwhile, the *Beatles Monthly,* an institution pre-dating "She Loves You," had bit the dust after 77 issues. Its December 1969 swan song consisted primarily of an editorial harangue against the boys in the band—a harsh coda to the gushy tone the publication had sustained throughout the previous six-and-a-half years. The Beatles were denounced for having grown uncooperative about posing for photographs; for having failed to come out against drugs; for having lost their sense of humor ("Everything seems to be very, very serious. Nothing is just plain fun anymore."); and even for their appearance ("The Beatles are certainly tremendously photogenic, or at least they were in the days when you could see all of their faces.").

The main reason for the folding, however, was that rock's greatest partnership was itself on the rocks. But it was not until April 9, 1970 that Paul McCartney—of all people— made that official.

One of dozens of *Get Back* bootlegs

The Lennons' message upstages the government's, Times Square, Christmas, 1969 (Wide World Photos)

The Beatles' Hits—September 1968 through April 1970

TITLE AND LABEL	FIRST APPEARANCE	HIGHEST POSITION	WEEKS ON CHART
U.S. Top 100 Singles			
Hey Jude (Apple)*	Sept. 14, 1968	1	19
Revolution (Apple)	Sept. 14, 1968	12	11
Get Back (Apple)*	May 10, 1969	1	12
Don't Let Me Down (Apple)	May 10, 1969	35	4
The Ballad of John and Yoko (Apple)*	June 14, 1969	8	9
Give Peace a Chance—John—(Apple)	July 24, 1969	14	9
†Something/Come Together (Apple)*	Oct. 18, 1969	1	16
Cold Turkey—John—(Apple)	Nov. 15, 1969	30	12
Instant Karma—John—(Apple)*	Feb. 28, 1970	3	13
Let It Be (Apple)*	March 21, 1970	1	14
U.S. Top 200 L.P.'s			
The Beatles (Apple)*	Dec. 14, 1968	1	101
Wonderwall— George—(Apple)	Jan. 11, 1969	49	16
Yellow Submarine (Apple)*	Feb. 8, 1969	2	24
Two Virgins—John and Yoko— (Tetragammaton/Apple)	Feb. 8, 1969	124	8
Unfinished Music No. 2: Life With the Lions —John and Yoko—(Zapple)	June 28, 1969	174	8
Electronic Sound—George—(Zapple)	July 5, 1969	191	2
Abbey Road (Apple)*	Oct. 18, 1969	1	87
Wedding Album—John and Yoko—(Apple)	Dec. 13, 1969	178	3
Live Peace In Toronto—Plastic Ono Band— (Apple)*	Jan. 10, 1970	10	32
Hey Jude (Apple)*	March 21, 1970	2	33
British Top Twenty Singles			
Hey Jude (Apple)	Sept. 7, 1968	1	11
Get Back (Apple)	April 26, 1969	1	9
The Ballad Of John and Yoko (Apple)	June 4, 1969	1	8
Give Peace a Chance—John—(Apple)	July 12, 1969	2	9
Cold Turkey—John—(Apple)	Nov. 1, 1969	14	6
Something/Come Together (Apple)	Nov. 8, 1969	4	7
Instant Karma—John—(Apple)	Feb. 21, 1970	5	6
Let It Be (Apple)	March 14, 1970	2	6

(Chart positions according to *Billboard;* asterisk [*]: Record Industry Association of America certified Gold Record/Million Seller)
†On Nov. 29, 1969, *Billboard* stopped giving separate listings to both sides of singles.

Harrison and Dylan join forces for Bangla Desh (Wide World Photos)

ALL THINGS MUST PASS AWAY

The boys in their own way gave a great deal of their lives to us by being Beatles, and now they have found their own individual selves. Good luck to them.
—George Martin

Soon after the "McCartney Quits Beatles" headlines were splashed across the world's front pages, John Lennon offered *Rolling Stone* his own epitaph: "The cartoon is this—four guys on a stage with a spotlight on them; second picture, three guys on stage breezing out of the spotlight; third picture, one guy standing there shouting 'I'm leaving.'"

Seven years later, in a syndicated interview with Garth Pierce, Paul would tell a similar tale: "I would never have left the Beatles if everyone else hadn't. . . . There was no question of getting back with them unless I went around with my tail between my legs saying 'please fellas can we get a group once more?' In which case I would have probably got a big fat 'No!' . . . I was not going to sit there sucking my thumbs waiting for everyone to come back."

Over the previous two years, all the Beatles, even Ringo, had privately threatened to walk out on the group, only to be coaxed back by Paul. One didn't have to be an insider to sense that Lennon was more interested in his escapades with Yoko than in the Beatles, and that Harrison now had more to offer than his quota of two songs per L.P. could satisfy.

Since Epstein's death, the Beatles had become pretty much McCartney's show; *Magical Mystery Tour*, Apple, *Abbey Road*, and five out of seven singles had all been his babies. But Paul eventually concluded that this state of affairs couldn't go on indefinitely—especially after the others had outvoted him to install Allen Klein as Apple's business manager and had set conditions for their participation on any new Beatle record. Paul, ever the P.R. man, decided to take the credit for the writing on the wall, and to use it to draw attention to his own solo album. But his tactic apparently backfired.

The sensational news stories were all derived from a self-interview Paul had released to coincide with his *McCartney* L.P. In this interview (inserted in British copies of the album, but deleted by Klein—for understandable reasons—from the American ones) Paul announced a "break with the Beatles" due to "personal differences, musical differences, business differences, but most of all because I have a better time with my family." Not content to leave it at that, McCartney included a few digs at Messrs. Lennon, Starkey, and Klein.

Q: Will Paul and Linda become a John and Yoko?
A: No, they will become a Paul and Linda.

Q: Do you miss the other Beatles and George Martin? Was there a moment, e.g., when you thought "Wish Ringo was here for this break"?
A: No.

Q: Do you foresee a time when Lennon-McCartney becomes an active songwriting partnership again?
A: No.

Q: What do you feel about John's peace effort? The Plastic Ono Band? . . . Yoko?
A: I love John and respect what he does, but it doesn't give *me* any pleasure.

Q: What is your relationship with Klein?
A: It isn't. I am not in contact with him and he doesn't represent me in *any* way.

Because McCartney had dreamed these questions up himself, it wasn't as if he'd merely let slip a few indiscretions to some muckraking reporter; and many observers found the whole thing contrived, tasteless, and rather vicious.

The record itself had, until just weeks before its release date, remained one of the best-kept secrets in rock history. This was largely because Paul had recorded most of it on a Studer 4-track tape recorder at his Scottish retreat, overdubbing all the instruments himself; so only his family and a handful of engineers needed be sworn to secrecy. In that (in)famous self-interview, Paul says he wanted the L.P. to be a surprise "because normally an album is old before it comes out. Witness *Get Back*."

But the music itself was rather sparing on surprises. For those who thought Paul's musical declaration of independence might fulfill all the promise of his *Abbey Road* "pop symphony," *McCartney* was decidedly anticlimactic. True, the fact that Paul handled all the instruments himself (including bass, drums, acoustic and electric guitars, mellotron, organ, piano, toy xylophone, and bow-and-arrow) was impressive. Yet Paul's tour-de-force, though tastefully performed, offered little of the spectacular musicianship he had brought to *Abbey Road*.

With one exception, even the tunes themselves seemed relatively second-rate, and, in many cases, little more than unrealized fragments. "Oo You" and the instrumentals

The Essential Beatles, L.P., Australia, 1970 (Apple)

"Valentine Day" and "Momma Miss America" (which might have made a marvelous soundtrack to a surfing documentary) were, by Paul's own account, "ad-libbed on the spot." The Mexican-sounding instrumental "Hot As Sun" was based on a riff Paul had dreamed up at age 17. Two of the better songs, "Junk" and "Teddy Boy," sounded like obscure Beatle tunes—little wonder, since they were rejects from, respectively, the White Album and *Get Back.* Only "Maybe I'm Amazed," one of Paul's most achingly powerful love songs (and an obvious single, though it wasn't released as such until Wings' live version made the grade in 1977), really stood out from the pack.

Paul himself has since disparaged *McCartney* as "nothing much." Still, *minor* doesn't necessarily mean *bad.* Taken simply as an unassuming evocation of "home, family, love" (as Paul summed it up), the music was certainly pleasant. (The critics' favorite description of the album seemed to be "McCartney's *Nashville Skyline.*")

But Paul, apparently not content to let the music speak for itself, packaged his record with a somewhat cloying collection of snapshots of Linda, the kids, the dog, the cat, and Paul himself: romping in a bathing suit, performing household chores like a real human being—even picking his nose. Together with McCartney's self-interview, all this came across as self-serving propaganda to otherwise sympathetic reviewers such as *Rolling Stone*'s Langdon Winner, who wrote:

McCartney is an album that wants desperately to convince. Its explicit and uniform message is that Paul McCartney, his wife Linda and family have found peace and happiness in a quiet *home* away from the city, and away from the hassles of the music business. This is a beautiful vision and, like most listeners, I wanted very much to believe it was true. On the basis of the music alone I was entirely convinced. . . .

My problem is that all of the publicity surrounding the record makes it difficult for me to believe that *McCartney* is what it appears to be. . . . The overall effect of the *McCartney* literature is to turn the package into an undisguised power play.

. . . What this material is saying is that Beatles fans should recognize that the group is totally defunct and now follow the man who was the real genius of the outfit in the first place.

. . . I cannot help but ask if Paul is really as together as the music indicates, how could he have sunk to such bizarre tactics?

Though *McCartney* sold 2 million copies, Paul's popularity was in for a steep decline. It did not escape the notice of the "alternative" press that the pleasures *McCartney* celebrated were distinctly bourgeois; and, indeed, it would increasingly seem that Paul, in abdicating from the Beatles, had also abdicated from the counterculture.

In addition, much of the general public held Paul personally accountable for the break-up, for the understandable reason that it had been he who had first proclaimed himself an ex-Beatle. This grudge would only deepen upon Paul's instigation, at the end of 1970, of a lawsuit against John, George, and Ringo aimed at dissolving the Beatles partnership to extricate McCartney from his financial ties with the other three, Apple, and by extension, Allen Klein. During the course of these proceedings, some spicy testimony would be aired—such as Ringo's account of his reception *chez* McCartney after the other two had sent him over to persuade Paul to hold back his solo album until after *Let It Be* had been issued:

To my dismay, he went completely out of control, shouting at me, prodding his finger toward my face, saying, "I'll finish you all now" and "you'll pay." . . . He told me to put my coat on and get out. . . . While I thought he had behaved a bit like a spoiled child, I could see that the release date of his record had a gigantic emotional significance for him . . . [and I] felt . . . we should let him have his own way.

Though Paul would win the much-publicized lawsuit, the affair would, for many people, further tarnish his choirboy image.

Let It Be, meanwhile, had been dumped in the lap of Phil Spector—the man who nearly a decade before had revolutionized the recording techniques of pop music to become the genre's first distinctive producer and, indeed, its single towering figure in the Dark Ages of the early Sixties. His trademark, the famous Spector "wall of sound," had transformed otherwise unmemorable songs and groups— the Crystals' "Then He Kissed Me"; the Ronettes' "Be My Baby" and "Walking in the Rain"—into classics, "little symphonies for the kids," as Phil himself called them. Heavenly choirs, extravagant horn and string sections, were but putty in Spector's hands, to be molded with gobs of echo and reverb into one monolithic noise whose individual components were virtually indistinguishable.

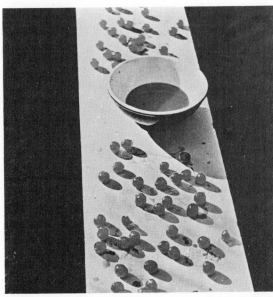

McCartney, L.P., 1970 (Apple) Life is a spilled bowl of cherries?

A freshly shorn Lennon gets "Instant Karma" on TV (Apple Records)

With his omnipresent sunglasses and bodyguards, and hair that inspired ridicule long before 1964, the diminutive Spector cultivated a reputation for being as unusual as his music. But his vision of rock 'n' roll as an art form, to be created by artists and not by hacks, was several years ahead of its time, which may be why Spector was one of the first Americans in the music business to take note of what was then brewing in England. He acted as midwife to the Rolling Stones' debut album, and escorted the Beatles on their first Atlantic crossing. (One of Spector's early 1964 productions was the novelty record "I Love Ringo," by Bonnie Joe Mason, who subsequently changed her name to Cher.) Yet even as the Beatles' promise blossomed so spectacularly, Spector himself, embittered by the industry's rejection of his own recent work, withdrew from the scene to become little more than a golden oldie in the memories of rock fans.

In January 1970, however, he appeared in London at the invitation of Allen Klein, who thought Spector might make an ideal candidate to perform the required surgery on *Let It Be*. John and George had long been outspoken admirers of the Phil Spector sound; in fact, both the Beatles' legendary early 1962 demo and the "Hamburg tapes" feature a rendition of "To Know Him Is To Love Him"—Spector's first hit, which Phil had written, produced, and performed, with his group the Teddy Bears, at age 17.

On January 27, Lennon offered Spector a shot at producing the third Plastic Ono Band single, "Instant Karma," which John had dreamed up that morning and wished to record while the inspiration was hot. They were joined in the Abbey Road studio by George Harrison, Alan White, and Klaus Voormann. After the basic track had been laid down, Spector seated the four musicians at three separate pianos for the first layer of overdubbing; then—as no professional choirs were available at such short notice—Mal Evans was dispatched to the Speakeasy discotheque to collar a dozen unsuspecting background vocalists. Spector tried to persuade Lennon to let him add an orchestra or two, but John wanted his "Karma" released instantly, and so it was.

For *Let It Be,* the Beatles thought of adapting their *Get Back* jacket concept—a parody of their first *Please Please Me*—but scrapped the idea

"Instant Karma" met with far greater commercial success than "Cold Turkey," becoming the first solo Beatle record to "go gold" in America. This was partly because the song itself was so much more joyful and infectious, but Spector deserves a great deal of credit. His contribution is aptly summed up by Richard Williams in *Out Of His Head: The Sound Of Phil Spector:* "No Beatles record had ever possessed such a unique sound; Spector had used echo to make the drums reverberate like someone slapping a wet fish on a marble slab, and the voices sounded hollow and decayed. He'd accentuated the characteristics of Lennon's voice, making it older and more cracked than ever before."

Having passed the audition, Spector proceeded to wreak his grand designs upon *Let It Be.* According to Lennon (*Rolling Stone*): "He worked like a pig on it. I mean he'd always wanted to work with the Beatles, and he was given the shittiest load of badly recorded shit with a lousy feeling to it ever, and he made something of it. . . . When I heard it I didn't puke."

But the critics did, and most blamed Spector for their indisposition. *New Musical Express* called *Let It Be* "a cardboard tombstone," which even *Time* dismissed as "the spectre of the Beatles." According to *Rolling Stone*'s John Mendelsohn, Spector had turned "the rough gems on the best Beatle album in ages into costume jewelry."

Like most of his colleagues, Mendelsohn singled out Spector's "reproduction" of McCartney's "The Long and Winding Road"—which Klein had already singled out as the Beatles' swan song on the U.S. Top Forty—for special abuse: "He's rendered . . . 'The Long and Winding Road' virtually unlistenable with hideously cloying strings and a ridiculous choir. . . . It might have eventually begun to grow on one as unassumingly charming, had not Spector felt compelled to transform [it] . . . into an extravaganza of oppressive mush."

Spector's arrangement was, to be sure, mind-bogglingly kitsch, far more reminiscent of "Good Night" than of the tasteful, understated orchestrations with which George Martin had been wont to embellish other "sincere" Mc-Cartney ballads, such as "Yesterday." Both Martin and McCartney, who had declined to listen to Phil's work in progress, were apparently mortified when they heard the final acetates. "I couldn't believe it," said Paul. "I would *never* have female voices on a Beatles record."

His complaint seems slightly ironic in light of the inescapable prominence of Linda McCartney's voice on all his subsequent albums; just as it appeared odd that Paul personally accepted a Grammy award for *Let It Be* at a time when he was instigating his litigation against the other Beatles, who, Paul insinuated, had deliberately ruined "The Long and Winding Road" out of spite—which he cited in court as one reason why the dissolution of the group was essential to his "artistic freedom."

The most jarring thing about *Let It Be,* however, is not Spector's contribution *per se* (in fact, one should sing his praises for restoring "Across the Universe" to its due magnificence, with orchestral and choral arrangements as dreamy and delicate as the song itself), but the way his extravagant arrangements are juxtaposed against the down-home sounds of the Beatles' tune-ups, false starts, and chit-chat. In its original form, *Get Back* may not have been "the best Beatle album in years," but the audio verité concept at least conveyed a sense of intimacy, informality, and honesty that is effectively destroyed by Spector's lavish overdubbing. The combination of, say, Lennon ad-libbing "Queen says 'no' to pot-smoking F.B.I. members" just as "The Long and Winding Road"'s harps and celestial choirs fade into the west, doesn't exactly gel. Spector should have either just let it be, or else flushed out all the extraneous inanities to really do a number on the music. Either way, the album would at least have been consistent.

As it stands, *Let It Be* is a mess—or, as *The New Musical Express* put it, "a sad and tatty end to a musical fusion which wiped clean and drew again the face of pop music."

In Britain, the first edition of *Let It Be* appeared in a deluxe boxed set, with Jonathan Cott and David Dalton's *Get Back* book, thoroughly expurgated but nonetheless chock full of Ethan Russell's luscious photographs—now a collector's item.

On May 20, 1970, as on three previous occasions, a crowd of Beatlemaniacs congregated outside the London Pavilion. But none of the Fab Four showed up for the premiere of the film *Let It Be.* In fact, the movie turned out to be an unwitting documentary of the quartet's disintegration, complete with inter-Beatle bickering. For that reason it isn't much fun to watch—except at the end, when the Beatles finally get it together on the Apple rooftop. *Let It Be*'s technical shortcomings don't help either; the film is grainy, poorly edited, and frequently inaudible.

On the night of the premiere, George Harrison entered the studio to begin work on his solo album, *All Things Must Pass.* At his side was Phil Spector, apparently destined to play a major role in the Beatles' metamorphosis into ex-Beatles. The album would prove to be the crowning achievement of both their careers.

Ah left Louisian',
Ah had me big plans . . .
—from Ringo Starr's Beaucoups Of Blues

Harrison's album took so long to finish—nearly six months—that it was beaten to the marketplace by a new Ringo album, recorded and mixed in six days.

Beaucoups Of Blues was the brainchild of Pete Drake, the crack Nashville session musician and producer, whose

The Beatles get back on the Apple roof, January 1969 (Apple Records)

Single, France, 1970 (Apple)

Single, France, 1971 (Apple)

chewy horn section. When the single finally materialized in April 1971, however, it gave quite a jolt to those who had supposed Ringo incapable of turning out a memorable—and commercial—record. "It Don't Come Easy" not only scored him a gold single all his own, but easily outshone and outsold John's "Power To the People," Paul's "Another Day," and George's "Bangla Desh," all unleashed at roughly the same time.

For Beatle people, however, the real intrigue lay in the B-side, in which Ringo paints his own picture of the state of the Beatles: "Early 1970." Paul is portrayed as too preoccupied with farm and family to bother playing with Ringo; John is likewise busy with Yoko, yet willing to play when he can spare a moment; while George is "always in town playing for you with me." Ringo then confesses to his own musical shortcomings, concluding that he'd much rather "see all three." As his disarming open letter to McCartney, Lennon, and Harrison made plain, Starr was always the most gung-ho about stitching the Beatles back together.

At Christmas-time, Harrison and Lennon buffs were presented with albums that more than compensated for the absence of the Beatles' customary Yuletide offering. *All Things Must Pass* and *Plastic Ono Band* made it difficult to mourn the group's passing; each appeared not only to be its respective ex-Beatle's definitive artistic statement to date, but one that could never have been made in the context of the group.

George's album has been characterized by *Melody Maker*'s Richard Williams as "the rock equivalent of the shock felt by pre-war moviegoers when Garbo first opened her mouth in a talkie: Garbo talks!—Harrison is free!" It was certainly a thrilling occasion not only for the quiet Beatle, but also for fans who, having long placed their bets on the dark horse of the group, were at last being shown the jackpot.

The very fact that the Beatles had kept George's flowering talents so under wraps proved to be his secret weapon. By mid-1970 he had accumulated enough material to fill no mere double album, but a triple—rock's first elegantly boxed three-record set. The final disc, containing superstar jam sessions revolving around the usual three chords, may have

George Harrison in late 1970
(Apple Records)

steel guitar had lent Bob Dylan's *Nashville Skyline* much of its local color. On Dylan's recommendation, Harrison imported Drake to London to lend a similar ambience to "Behind That Locked Door," "If Not For You," and "Sir Frankie Crisp." During these sessions, Ringo struck up a rapport with Drake, to whom he confided his desire to follow *Sentimental Journey* with an L.P. of country songs. Drake promised to concoct one for Ringo in Nashville in return for only two days of the ex-Beatle's time.

Someone once made a count of a country Top Forty chart to find that half the records listed featured Pete Drake, who by his own estimate played on 600 sessions a year. So Drake had no trouble assembling the cream of Nashville's shitkickers for Ringo's album—including several who had accompanied Dylan, plus the legendary Jordinaires, who had sung back-up on most of Presley's classic hits. A batch of unreleased songs with such titles as "The Fastest Growin' Heartache In the West" and "$15 Draw," also by Nashville's finest, was plucked from the files of Drake's own Window Music Company; and all Ringo had to do was slide into the lead vocalist's slot and act naturally. On each song, a bunch of Nashville cats reportedly wailed along just out of mike range, to keep Ringo on key. He didn't even have to play drums.

Starr's creative input may be slight, but his Liverpool hillbilly voice couldn't have found a cozier setting. *Beaucoups Of Blues,* recorded in June 1970, is a fine, well-crafted country-rock album—and did much to absolve the embarrassment of its predecessor. For Ringo, it was a dream come true, the ultimate sentimental journey. (During the course of those two days, the awesomely efficient Drake managed to capture Ringo's voice on approximately ten more songs, which at one point were promised for a sequel. One of these, Ringo's own two-chord workout "Coochy Coochy," appeared on the flip side of the single "Beaucoups Of Blues.")

Four months prior to his Nashville trip, Ringo had recorded one of his own compositions in London with a little help from bassist Klaus Voormann, guitarist Steve Stills, and George Harrison, who contributed some highly Beatleish guitar hooks and also produced in the best Spector style. But "It Don't Come Easy" rested in the can for thirteen months, during the course of which Harrison overdubbed a

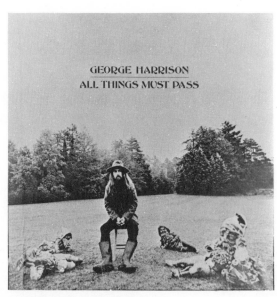

L.P., 1970 (Apple)

been dispensable; but on the two main L.P.'s Harrison generally sustains the high standard set by his compositions on the White Album and *Abbey Road*—even if much of *All Things Must Pass* would have seemed out of place on those Beatle albums. One can hardly picture John and Paul Hare Krishnaing along with "My Sweet Lord."

George painted his masterpiece at a time when both he and his audience still believed music could change the world. If Lennon's studio was his soap-box, then Harrison's was his pulpit. Though increasingly jaded rock critics sometimes found tart words for his sermons, George's music, at least, seemed to indicate that his mystical explorations had unlocked creative resources that only three years earlier few of his fans could have imagined existed.

All Things Must Pass consists primarily of Hindu scriptures set to music, and each of the major tenets of the philosophy get at least a passing mention. "All Things Must Pass" advises a resigned attitude toward external events, and "Beware Of Darkness" warns against *maya*, the material world's wonderwall of illusion. The two most eloquent songs on the album, musically as well as lyrically, have mysterious, seductive melodies, over which faded strings and horns hover like Blue Jay Way fog.

There is an essay on karma, "Run Of the Mill" ("it's you that decides . . . your own made end") and one on reincarnation, "The Art Of Dying." For George, like the adherents of most Hindu sects, the ultimate goal is to break the endless cycle of rebirth by attaining oneness with God. According to the *Bhagavad Gita:* "He . . . who is spurred by desire, being attached to the fruit of action, is firmly bound." In "Awaiting On You All," Harrison seems to agree with his friends in the Krishna movement that the best way to avoid distraction by such fruit is "chanting the names of the Lord." (On "My Sweet Lord" George did just that, and was rewarded with a Number One single all over the world.)

None of this allows for many light or witty moments; according to Ben Gerson, who reviewed *All Things Must Pass* in *Rolling Stone:* "His words sometimes try too hard; he's taking himself or the subject too seriously, or, if the subject is impossible to take seriously, he doesn't always possess the means to convey that impression convincingly." The same critic, however, hailed the sheer sound as "Wagnerian, Brucknerian, the music of mountain tops and vast

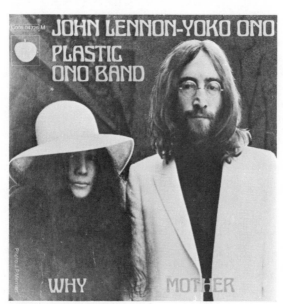

Single, Denmark, 1971 (Apple)

Single, France, 1970 (Apple)

horizons," and summed the album up as an "extravaganza of piety and sacrifice and joy, whose sheer magnitude and ambition may dub it the *War and Peace* of rock 'n' roll."

This miracle would not have been possible without Phil Spector and his sublime walls of sound. Instead of superimposing these on two-minute throwaways such as "Da Doo Run Run," Spector was at last working with a talent comparable with his own. The producer's cosmic sound proved a perfect complement to the artist's cosmic vision.

For *All Things Must Pass,* Harrison and Spector assembled a rock orchestra of almost symphonic proportions, whose credits read like a Who's Who of the music scene: Ringo; Procol Harum's Gary Brooker, Gary Wright, and Billy Preston (all on keyboards); Dave Mason and Eric Clapton (electric guitars); and dozens more. George himself painstakingly overdubbed his voice dozens of times, and credited the result to the "George O'Hara-Smith Singers." Apple house band Badfinger was assigned the task of strumming four acoustic guitars, usually buried deep in the mix in keeping with Spector's credo that some instruments should be "felt but not heard."

"Isn't It a Pity" starts out, like many of the selections, as a plaintive dirge, with a backdrop consisting of brooding strings, the steady clanging of chimes, and the shimmering harmonics of Badfinger's guitars. At the signal of the first cosmic thud of Ringo's foot against the bass drum pedal, however, instruments begin to break out of their metronomic straitjacket to attain an almost ecstatic release. Strings burst into thunderous crescendos; gently weeping guitars start to soar. Like "Hey Jude," which it strongly resembles, "Isn't It a Pity" is a work of towering simplicity with few and basic chord changes and an almost endlessly repetitive fade-out that somehow manages to be hypnotic instead of boring. "Isn't It a Pity" even clocked in one second shy of "Jude"'s seven minutes and eleven seconds.

Besides Spector, another presence is strongly felt on George's album, in spirit if not in person. Harrison had developed a close personal and musical rapport with Bob Dylan over the previous year; in June they even recorded together, though the result has yet to see the light of day. The Dylanesque numbers, if a minority on *All Things Must Pass* and somewhat overshadowed by their Spectorian counterparts, have a distinct character of their own and are far more intimate, both musically and lyrically, than the rest of the album. They include Dylan's own "If Not For You" from *New Morning,* "I'd Have You Any Time," based on a lyric Bob gave George to set to music, and "Sir Frankie Crisp," an olde English ballad dedicated to the man who built Friar Park, George's 17th-century castle. (On the album cover, George is seen in the Friar Park garden with part of Sir Frankie's collection of stone dwarfs.) "Apple Scruffs"—complete with blasts of harmonica, the most Dylanesque of the lot—is George's tribute to those fanatical Beatlemaniacs who literally lived on the steps of Apple. *New York Post* writer Al Aronowitz, who was with George for many of the *All Things Must Pass* sessions, reported: "Outside the studio door, whether it rained or not, there was always a handful of Apple Scruffs, one of them a girl all the way from Texas. Sometimes George would record from 7 P.M. to 7 A.M. and there they would be, waiting through the night, beggars for a sign of recognition on his way in and out. In the morning they'd go off to their jobs and in the evening they'd be back outside the studio door again."

All Things Must Pass was phenomenally successful, quickly reaching Number One on both sides of the Atlantic, staying there for many weeks, and ultimately outselling many of the Beatles' albums—no mean achievement at $13.98. "My Sweet Lord" fared even better in the singles

(Apple Records)

John's album was also co-produced by Phil Spector, but it could hardly have differed more strikingly from George's. In stark contrast to the mystical affirmation of *All Things Must Pass*, *John Lennon/Plastic Ono Band* shows John striving to demolish every icon in sight—be it Krishna, Jesus, sex, dope, or the Beatles. While George had told us that the world of our senses is pure illusion ("beware of *maya*"), John takes exactly the opposite tack, dismissing mysticism as "pie in the sky," another drug to dull the pain of reality. Lennon's music is as raw and claustrophobic as George's was lush, expansive, and uplifting.

Plastic Ono Band sounds more like a demo than a Spector production; surely Phil has never been kept on so tight a rein. Many of the tracks were captured in just one "take," and most feature only two instruments besides John's piano and guitar: Ringo's drums, and the bass of Klaus Voormann, who at the time was cited in numerous "scoops" as McCartney's replacement in a new Beatle line-up.

Plastic Ono Band was nick-named "the Primal Album," as John had composed most of it during the course of four months at Arthur Janov's Primal Institute in Los Angeles. Lennon was initiated into Dr. Janov's radical therapy by the latter's *The Primal Scream,* which had been sent to him at the author's request. After undergoing three weeks of intensive therapy with Dr. Janov in England, the Lennons agreed to come to California in April 1970 for the full treatment.

According to Dr. Janov, Primal Therapy makes patients relive key experiences, mostly dating back to childhood and subsequently repressed from memory, that have forced them to lose their "real" selves behind numerous layers of defenses. This process is so painful that it triggers the blood-curdling Primal Scream with which, the psychologist contends, patients can exorcize the root causes of all their neuroses, and at last feel their "real" needs and emotions.

The therapy's profound impact on Lennon is clearly reflected in his album. A harrowing journey through John's past, *Plastic Ono Band* leaves the bare wires of his ravaged emotions exposed as never before nor since. Songs like John's self-proclaimed revolutionary anthem, "Working Class Hero"—whose melody and solitary droning acoustic guitar recall the angry young Dylan of almost a decade earlier—closely echo Dr. Janov's theories:

As soon as you're born they make you feel small
by giving you no time instead of it all
'till the pain is so big you feel nothing at all. . . .

"Well Well Well" and the "Mama don't go, Daddy come home" segment of "Mother" climax with screams; whether or not these are Primal with a capital P, they are certainly chilling.

"Mother" opens the album with the tolling of funeral bells, as if to symbolize the casting off of John's past (elsewhere he sings "now I'm reborn . . . I was the walrus, but now I'm John"), then introduces a sledgehammer rhythm so slow and so taut that it threatens to snap under the tension. Possibly *Plastic Ono Band*'s most powerful piece, "Mother" stabs directly at the heart of Primal Pain:

Mother you had me, but I never had you.
I wanted you, but you didn't want me.
So I just gotta tell you,
Goodbye, goodbye.

In his book Dr. Janov reveals that he stumbled upon the Primal Scream when, on a whim, he asked one of his patients to call out "Mommy! Daddy!":

Danny refused, saying that he couldn't see the sense in such a childish act, and frankly, neither could I. But I persisted, and finally, he gave in. As he began, he became noticeably upset.

Single, Italy, 1971 (Apple)

Single, Germany, 1971 (Apple)

sweepstakes, and remains not only the best-seller among all the ex-Beatles' solo singles, but also the only one to reach Number One in Britain (where the fragments of the Fab Four have generally been received with less awe than in America). Oddly enough, George originally gave his biggest hit away to Billy Preston, who released "My Sweet Lord" as an Apple single the previous summer, and went nowhere with it.

"My Sweet Lord"'s resemblance to the early Sixties Chiffons hit "He's So Fine" did not escape the notice of the latter's publisher, Bright Tunes, and in late 1976 a judge ruled George guilty of "unconscious plagiarism" and ordered him to fork over a portion of the Harrisong's accumulated royalties. These were doubtless considerable; as John Lennon said in late 1970: "Every time I put the radio on it's 'oh my Lord'—I'm beginning to think there must be a God!"

Suddenly he was writhing on the floor . . . "Mommy! Daddy!" came out of his mouth almost involuntarily in loud screeches . . . finally, he released a piercing deathlike scream that rattled the walls of my office. . . . All he could say afterward was "I made it! I don't know what, but I can *feel*!"

On John's album, the most intimate and scary moment of all is the last: the 48-second "My Mummy's Dead," set to the crushingly banal tune of "Three Blind Mice." This is preceded by *Plastic Ono Band*'s Big Statement, "God," in which Lennon renounces by name all the myths he has ever believed in: magic, Bible, mantra, Gita, Kennedy, Elvis. Like the layers of an onion these are peeled away one by one, and after the climactic "I don't believe in Beatles" all that's left is: "I just believe in me."

Though he might not have produced so unrelentingly intense a work without the therapy, *Plastic Ono Band* was the logical final step in the progression John had begun with his songs on the White Album (where, for instance, he had sung to his mother "Julia"). Lennon had even howled with pain on the pre-Janov "Cold Turkey"; he was, after all, married to the Maria Callas of the torture rack, as *Yoko Ono/Plastic Ono Band,* improvised while the musicians were warming up for John's L.P., eloquently confirmed.

In his *Plastic Ono Band* John takes the honesty of his last Beatle songs as far as it can possibly be taken, wrenching each word and note straight from the gut. At the time, Lennon told Jann Wenner: "The poetry on this album is superior to anything I've done because it's not self-conscious. . . ." Of the equally minimalistic music he said: "I always liked simple rock. . . . I was influenced by acid and got psychedelic like the whole generation . . . but when you just listen, the piano does it all for you, your mind can do the rest. . . . I don't need anything else."

John called the album his "Sgt. Lennon," and many critics seemed to agree with him. Arthur Janov, for his part, declared: "John has made the universal statement. I believe it will transform the world." Yet *Plastic Ono Band*'s impact owed as much, if not more, to non-musical factors as any Beatle record had. Without the myths, the act of puncturing them loses its potency. John may have abdicated as "the dream-weaver," but he had lost none of his self-importance. Many of his new songs were like unpolished entries in the most private of diaries; their meaning, or lack of it, depended upon the nature of the listener's relationship with John Lennon. If only within the context of the man and his previous work, *Plastic Ono Band* was a powerful, fascinating and at times heartbreaking document.

With this music, John attempted not only to shatter the myth he had once helped inspire with his music, but also to re-live and exorcize the traumas from which the music had originally been his most effective escape. In the process Lennon—like Harrison in his own very different way—landed himself at an artistic dead end. Both ex-Beatles would find it difficult either to duplicate their considerable achievements, or to establish a convincing new direction.

John continued the de-mystification process with his two-part *Rolling Stone* interview (December 24, 1970 and January 7, 1971), which must rank as the most revealing and notorious—and at 30,000 words maybe the longest—any rock star has ever given. Lennon responded to Jann Wenner's probing questions as if he were unburdening himself of his past on a psychiatrist's couch, and in the process spilled a lifetime's worth of beans. The world learned for the first time of John's thousand acid trips, and of orgies on the mop-tops' international road shows ("Satyricon on tour," Lennon called them). John minced no words as he ventured his low opinion of not only the

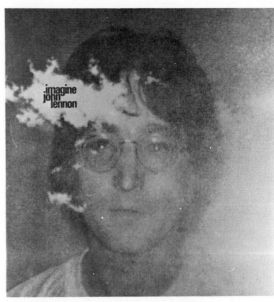

L.P., 1971 (Apple)

Single, Italy, 1970 (Apple)

"Happy Xmas (War Is Over)," Single, Japan, 1971 (Apple)

Eastmans and Paul's recent music, but also such famous Beatles hits as "Hello Goodbye" and nearly all their films; as in *Plastic Ono Band,* anger often spilled over into self-pity:

One has to completely humiliate oneself to be what the Beatles were and that's what I resent. I mean, I did it, I didn't know, I didn't foresee; it just happened bit by bit, gradually, until this complete craziness is surrounding you and you're doing exactly what you don't want to do with people you can't stand, the people you hated when you were ten. . . .

Teachers . . . were trying to beat me into being a fuckin' dentist or a teacher. And then the fuckin' fans tried to beat me into being a fuckin' Beatle or an Engelbert Humperdinck, and the critics tried to beat me into being Paul McCartney.

YOKO: So you were very deprived in a way . . .

JOHN: . . . it's like I've just left school again! I just graduated from the school of show biz.

After the triumphs of *All Things Must Pass* and *Plastic Ono Band,* many observers, including the other Beatles, expected Paul to rise to the challenge with a definitive album of his own. In the *Rolling Stone* interview, Lennon predicted that *Plastic Ono Band* would "probably scare [Paul] into doing something decent. . . . I can't see him doing *[McCartney]* twice."

Such conjecture was reinforced by word that Paul had spent most of the winter ensconced in the recording studios with some of the Big Apple's most prestigious musicians and, on occasion, the New York Philharmonic Orchestra. But visions of Hey Jude Revisited were deflated in late February 1971 with the release of the single, "Another Day"—a pleasant but inconsequential ditty that told the tale of a lonely, frustrated secretary, sort of a pedestrian "Eleanor Rigby":

Alone in her apartment she'd dwell,
till the man of her dreams comes to break the spell . . .
and he comes, and he stays,
but he leaves the next day.
So sad.

Many of the rock critics, out for McCartney's blood, dismissed "Another Day" as more of "Paulie picking his nose." More charitable observers trilled along with the chorus: "It's just another song." But at least the lyrics aimed at making some kind of intelligible point, which was more than could be said for those on the ensuing L.P.

Ram remains something of a puzzle to Beatle people. At the time of its May 1971 release it was roundly and harshly condemned by reviewers such as *Rolling Stone*'s Jon Landau, who called it "the nadir in the decomposition of Sixties rock thus far," "incredibly inconsequential," and "monumentally irrelevant."

Still, to these ears anyway, *Ram* definitely has its moments: the exhilarating "hands across the water/heads across the sky" chorus in "Uncle Albert/Admiral Halsey"; "Eat At Home," a fine McCartney pastiche of his hero Buddy Holly (and about time too); and "Back Seat Of My Car," an elaborate production number almost worthy of Brian Wilson's wet dreams. (These were also the three songs that made it onto singles, though each was released in a different market: respectively, America, Europe, and Britain.) *Ram* is certainly more varied than *McCartney,* and boasts some lovely snatches of melody.

The problem is that these remain snatches, none of which hang together to make for anything terribly memorable. *Ram* brings to mind a hollow chocolate egg: It is tasty, if just this side of sickly sweet, yet crumbles when one tries to sink one's teeth in.

"I tried so very hard and I really hoped people would like it," Paul told *Melody Maker*'s Chris Charlesworth after the critics' verdict was in. "I thought I had done a great album. . . . I don't see how someone can play it and take in all that stuff and turn round and say 'I don't like it.'"

The bum notices came as a particular shock to Paul because he had recorded *Ram* with the critics somewhat in mind. "I thought *McCartney* was quite good," he would recall two years later. "But then it didn't quite do it in every way . . . it was very down-home, funky, just me. . . . After it got knocked I thought . . . do just the opposite next time. So *Ram* was with the top people in the top studio. I thought, this is what they want. But again, it was critically panned."

The production was indeed far more ornate and slick than its predecessor, but the substance—or lack of it—was very similar. The words, when comprehensible, seemed to consist of more celebrations of "home, family, love"; and once again, the package featured a generous selection of family snapshots.

But there was also an obviously symbolic photograph of a beetle fucking another beetle, and, to John Lennon, at least, the more obscure lyrics were no mere random gibberish. "Too Many People Preaching Practices" and "Dear Boy, Betcha Never Knew How Much You Missed" sounded to John like coy, condescending messages from the country squire to the working class hero, and he reacted like the proverbial bull to a red flag. "Give Peace a Chance" notwithstanding, one messed with Lennon at one's own risk.

A pretty face may last a year or two,
but pretty soon they'll see what you can do.
The sound you make is muzak to my ears,
you must have learned something in all those years.
Ah, how do you sleep?

With the appearance of this song (on John's *Imagine,* released October 1971) it could no longer escape the attention of even the casual fan that the battle of the Beatles had turned very nasty indeed. Both Lennon and McCartney had chosen to twist the tools of the superstar's trade—interviews, record jackets, even the music itself—into weapons with which to perpetuate their war of nerves and wits before millions of spectators. Some fans took sides, but for many more John and Paul's abrasive public feud served only to demean both parties—and, in tandem with some increasingly inferior music, contribute to the all-time low to which both Beatles' credibility would plunge by mid-1972.

"How Do You Sleep?" is, nonetheless, a devastatingly powerful piece of music. George Harrison, whose presence makes clear where his own sympathies lie, contributes the most stinging slide guitar work of his career; and John's voice, around which an unusually hard-assed string section weaves nightmarish arabesques, has never sounded more menacing.

The noise of the orchestra tuning up at the beginning of "How Do You Sleep?" is an obvious parody of *Sgt. Pepper*—especially as John charges in the first verse that Paul had let *Sgt. Pepper* go to his head. Lennon's vitriolic open letter goes on to castigate McCartney for living with "straights," for having married a nag, and for being dead after all. The wicked punster sometimes wields a sharp double-edged blade:

The only thing you done was yesterday,
and since you've gone you're just another day.
Ah, how do you sleep?

The performance is highly reminiscent of Bob Dylan's exhilarating character assassinations of six years earlier—songs such as "Like a Rolling Stone" and "Positively Fourth Street," to which Dylan owed much of his celebrity. But while Dylan's characters had been anonymous, enabling us to revel in the catharsis of his anger without feeling sorry for the hapless victim, everyone knew the identity of Lennon's target; and, whatever disappointment some fans may have felt at McCartney's recent work, few enjoyed being witnesses to his execution. Musically, "How Do You Sleep?" is brilliant, in that it forces the listener to share John's anger; for that reason, many of his admirers preferred not to listen. (To drive the point home, *Imagine* was packaged with a postcard depicting Lennon fondling a pig—an unmistakeable lampoon of Paul's L.P. cover, on which McCartney fondles a ram.)

In "Gimme Some Truth" Lennon launches into a similar tirade (again accompanied by Harrison's vicious slide guitar)—this time against nameless hypocrites, bigots, "pig-headed politicians," and "paranoiac prima-donnas" everywhere. A gripping riff and a non-stop torrent of asso-

A poster advertising Yoko Ono's one-woman exhibit with Lennon as guest artist (Courtesy, Everson Museum of Art)

BY YOKO ONO·JOHN LENNON-GUEST ARTIST · AT EVERSON MUSEUM OF ART, SYRACUSE, N.Y. · OCTOBER 9-27

nance and alliteration add up to an electrifying performance; nonetheless, to *Rolling Stone*'s Ben Gerson, "Gimme Some Truth," together with "How Do You Sleep?", raised a disturbing question: "I fear that John sees himself in the role of the truth-teller, and as such can justify any kind of self-indulgent brutality in the name of truth." Lennon's next album would prove Gerson woefully correct.

But the remainder of *Imagine* is far more subdued and benign—and as lush and melodic as anything John has created since the Break-up. Unlike the Spartan, three-piece *Plastic Ono Band, Imagine* gave Phil Spector plenty to work with. The album features over a dozen of rock's top sidemen, and half the tracks are further enhanced with highly commercial strings.

The benign, low-key aura that suffuses *Imagine* (with those one or two curious exceptions) may have been due to more than a fulfillment of Arthur Janov's promise of "a tensionless, defence-free life" for those who complete primal therapy. *Plastic Ono Band,* written during the therapy, had impressed the critics more than it had the public; and sold a relatively modest quarter million copies. Klein's promo man Pete Bennett let slip that "we told John he had to go more commercial if he wanted a big smash."

The general tone of *Imagine* (which, as it turned out, sold well over a million) is set by the title song—easily John's most popular and widely covered solo composition. "Imagine" also sounds very Beatle-ish, with a melody that conveys the poignant innocence (or naiveté) of "Dear Prudence" and "Because." Retrieving the white banner he had waved throughout 1969, Lennon invites us to share his vision of a Utopia devoid of religions ("no hell below us/above us only sky"), possessions, countries, and causes:

You may say I'm a dreamer,
but I'm not the only one.
I hope some day you'll join us,
and the world will live as one.

Single, Italy, 1971 (Apple)

The second most popular song on the album was "Jealous Guy," similar to "Imagine" in its refreshing tunefulness, simplicity, and lush orchestration. To a melody almost identical to the verse of "A Day In the Life" John asks Yoko to forgive his cruelties ("I'm just a jealous guy") in a thin, plaintive voice that often comes close to cracking. Like much of *Imagine,* this touching piece shows Lennon attempting to put across his painful self-discoveries in a more popularly accessible format. (Incidentally, the recording sessions for both *Imagine* and Yoko's companion piece *Fly* were extensively filmed at John's home studio in Ascot. One wonders what happened to the result.)

Two Lennon singles, not included on the L.P., also appeared in 1971. "Power To the People," which opens to the sounds of marching feet, was an ominous omen of worse to come. Heretofore, John had composed a number of songs around slogans of his own device—"All You Need Is Love," "Give Peace a Chance"; here he begins parroting the well-worn clichés of "the movement." Nonetheless, it made sense for Lennon, after his painful attempt at dismantling the myth of superstardom, to cast himself as one of the common people, and to take up their banner. The lyrics begin with a quote from one of John's earlier slogan/songs—"you say you want a revolution"—but instead of "don't you know that you can count me out" Lennon now follows the line up with an emphatic "better get it on right away!" (The original B-side, Yoko's "Open Your Box" ran into trouble with its advice: "Open your trousers . . . skirts . . . legs . . . thighs." Under record company pressure, the Lennons cleaned up their act by substituting "houses . . . church

. . . lakes . . . eyes" on the British version, but by that time the Americans had already released "Touch Me" from Yoko's *Plastic Ono Band* L.P. on the back of the 45.)

John put another of his famous slogans—"Happy Xmas (War Is Over If You Want It)"—to good use at the end of the year. Spector took great pains to turn this into a holiday classic, adding chimes, glockenspiel, sleighbells, a dozen trilling guitars, and 30 kids from the Harlem Community Choir. But the record, released too close to Christmas to catch fire, became the first Beatle single not to even crack America's Hot Hundred.

George Harrison's concerts for Bangla Desh, presented on August 1, 1971, were announced three weeks earlier via a minuscule ad buried in the back pages of the *New York Times.* Sleeping bags in tow, fans immediately descended on Madison Square Garden; fortunately for us, the box office opened in the very wee hours of the morning, well ahead of schedule, to keep the throngs from disrupting Penn Plaza's normal daytime flow of business.

The concerts were devised to raise funds for the victims of the Pakistani civil war, during which the secessionist eastern sector (Bangla Desh) was ravaged by the armies of the less populous but politically and economically dominant West, causing seven million refugees to pour into neighboring India to seek shelter in drainpipes and subsist on the scantiest of supplies. Between famine, disease, the genocidal excesses of the Pakistani troops, and a recent cyclone, the death toll was estimated at well over a million.

The suggestion that Harrison do something to alleviate the refugees' plight originally came from his mentor Ravi Shankar, whose father had been born in Bangla Desh. "I was in a very sad mood, having read all this news," Shankar told *Rolling Stone,* "and I said, 'George, this is the situation. I know it doesn't concern you, I know you can't possibly identify.' But while I talked to George he was very deeply moved . . . and he said, 'Yes, I think I'll be able to do something.'"

Harrison vowed to do a show alone if necessary, but found many of his heavy "friends" eager to donate their services. While assembling his all-star cast, he hastily wrote and recorded the single "(We've Got To Relieve) Bangla Desh" and earmarked the profits for the George Harrison–Ravi Shankar Special Emergency Relief Fund.

By show time, the audience was abuzz with speculation as to exactly who those friends might be, and on the streets outside choice tickets were reportedly changing hands for as much as $1,000 a pair. George himself was extremely nervous about his presentation—"just thinking about it makes me shake"—but the standing ovation he received from 20,000 fans when he first appeared on stage to introduce Shankar and Ali Akbar Khan may have bolstered his confidence, as he seemed remarkably serene from then on. The Indian music, though often lost in the cavernous Garden, set a staid and dignified tone that the rock performers sustained throughout the concert, except during Billy Preston's and Leon Russell's flamboyant showcases.

The big rumor was that the Beatles might come together for the occasion; but most fans were more than content to see just half the Fab Four reunited on stage for the first time in five years. Harrison had indeed invited all his former colleagues, but Paul said he would play only if George agreed to dissolve the Beatles' legal partnership—to which the latter said no deal. John said maybe, but chickened out. Ringo, of course, said sure, and received the show's biggest ovation when he took the spotlight to sing "It Don't Come Easy."

Bob Dylan's appearance was a total astonishment to those of us attending the first concert, as Dylan had virtually

Ringo and George with Bob Dylan at the Concert for Bangla Desh (Keystone Press Agency)

retired from live performance even earlier than had the Beatles. Accompanied by Harrison, Starr, and Russell, Bob, in a magnificent time warp, not only sounded but looked exactly as he had some seven years before. Instead of dishing out the mellow "Blue Moon"'s he had been trafficking in of late, he brought it all back home with five of his most powerfully eloquent Sixties classics—opening with "A Hard Rain's Gonna Fall," which might have been written expressly about the Bangla Desh holocaust.

Most of the rest of the concert featured a full Phil Spector/*All Things Must Pass* rock orchestra, complete to the detail of Badfinger strumming four acoustic guitars that were "felt but not heard." There were two drummers (Ringo and Jim Keltner), four electric guitarists (including Eric Clapton), a horn section, and a 9-voice chorus. Throughout the concert Spector himself worked the dials of a Wally Heider 16-track machine, capturing every note for an Apple three-record set. The performance itself was nearly flawless—an amazing feat, considering that the full band had had only one day's worth of rehearsal time.

The concerts netted $243,418 for UNICEF; as a token of appreciation United Nations Secretary General Kurt Waldheim presented Harrison and Shankar with a special award. The live album and Saul Swimmer's documentary film eventually raised an additional $10 million.

Aside from enhancing George's reputation as the real hero to emerge from the wreckage of the Beatles, his

August 1, 1971: Songs Performed at the Concerts For Bangla Desh In New York
Wah-Wah (George, lead vocal)
Something (George)
Awaiting On You All (George)
That's the Way God Planned It (Billy Preston)
It Don't Come Easy (Ringo)
Beware Of Darkness (George and Leon Russell)
While My Guitar Gently Weeps (George)
Jumpin' Jack Flash (Leon Russell)
Youngblood (Leon Russell)
Here Comes the Sun (George)
A Hard Rain's Gonna Fall (Bob Dylan)
It Takes a Lot To Laugh (Bob Dylan)
Blowin' In the Wind (Bob Dylan)
Love Minus Zero/No Limit (Bob Dylan—first performance only)
Mr. Tambourine Man (Bob Dylan—second performance only)
Just Like a Woman (Bob Dylan)
My Sweet Lord (George)
Hear Me Lord (George—first performance only)
Bangla Desh (George)

A compilation of the Beatles' annual Christmas records, mailed from 1963 to 1969 to members of the fan club, who received this rare Apple L.P. as a farewell present in late 1971

Single, Italy, 1971 (Apple)

Single, France, 1971 (Apple)

magnanimous gesture provided welcome evidence that the Utopian spirit of Sixties rock was still flickering. According to *Rolling Stone:*

The awe of history surrounded the concert and infused all who played and all who saw. Seeing Ringo Starr drumming and singing on stage has a joy in it that is one of the happiest feelings on earth still. It was the first time Dylan and any of the Beatles had ever appeared together.

In a year in which promoters and the press have decried the motives of the musicians and the level of the audiences, and each neo-Woodstock has been more avaricious than the last . . . the Bangla Desh benefit, in the magnificence of its music and the selflessness of its motives, was proof that the art and spirit are still alive.

Unfortunately, the story had a less inspiring epilogue. Contractual hassles delayed the release of *The Concert For Bangla Desh* album until almost the New Year. Then a *New York* magazine article appeared, in which Peter McCabe and Robert Schonfeld charged that some of the receipts had mysteriously found their way into Mr. Klein's bank account. The president of ABKCO struck back with a $100,000,000 libel suit (eventually withdrawn), by which time A. J. Weberman and his Rock Liberation Front commandos had briefly "liberated" Klein's Seventh Avenue office. (One wonders what honorary R.L.F.-er John Lennon thought of the confrontation.)

Six years after the concert, hundreds of thousands of dollars raised by the album and film continued to languish in a New York bank, tied up by Internal Revenue Service red tape, 10,000 miles from a nation still viewed as the worst pocket of misery on earth.

Meanwhile, the other two Beatles continued to slug it out in the press. After Paul granted a rare audience to *Melody Maker* to air his views, John shot back a lengthy open letter to his former colleague, which the publication printed (except for "nine lines omitted in deference to the laws of libel") at Lennon's request for "equal time." Some highlights of the exchange:

Paul [on his lawsuit]: "I just want the four of us to get together somewhere and sign a piece of paper saying it's all over, and we want to divide the money four ways. . . . But

John won't do it. Everybody thinks I am the aggressor but I'm not. I just want out."

John: "For the millionth time . . . I repeat, *what about the TAX?* It's all very well playing 'simple honest ole human Paul' in the Melody Maker, but you know damn well we can't just sign a bit of paper. You say 'John won't do it.' I will if you *indemnify* us against the tax-man! . . . If *you're not* the aggressor (as you claim) who the hell took us to court and shat all over us in public?"

Paul: "John and Yoko are not cool in what they're doing."

John: "If *we're* not cool, WHAT DOES THAT MAKE YOU."

Paul: "I like . . . 'Imagine' [which] is what John is really like, but there was too much political stuff on the other albums."

John: "So you think 'Imagine' ain't political, it's 'Working Class Hero' with sugar on it for conservatives like yourself!! . . . Join the Rock Liberation Front before it gets *you.*"

But it was the music that seemed to suffer most from their falling out. Despite some fine moments, their solo careers were each marked by a lack of artistic direction. Unsure of whether to get back to the basics or be clever, or of what—if anything—they should say, they seemed to drift from one formula to another and then back again. By contrast, nearly every Beatle L.P. had been a direct progression from the previous one, and had defined the directions rock was to move in for the next few months. As individual artists, Lennon and McCartney—and, for that matter, Harrison and Starr—would inspire precious few trends in or out of music.

Part of the reason may be that the Beatles had gone as far as they could go, and accomplished all they could accomplish; that the Sixties, both in fact and in spirit, were slipping away; and that the fabulous foursome had bowed out in the nick of time. But there was more to it than that, which could be summed up with the much-used word, "chemistry."

The Beatles had consisted of four very different elements of roughly comparable importance, and they had complemented one another perfectly. George may have been more crucial to the music than Ringo, but Starr was less dispensable—at least at the beginning—to the Beatles' "image." John may have ignited most of the innovations, but it was Paul's commercial sense (and good looks) that put these across to the multitudes. And so on. For no group, before or since, was so much a *group.* The Who came closest; yet, even so, Pete Townshend dominated the band's music and image as no one Beatle ever did. John's fiery, restless imagination; Paul's airy romanticism; George's quiet, dependable flow; and Ringo's down-to-earth ordinariness— all balanced, enhanced, and inspired the best in one another, while keeping the weaknesses in check. The result was magic.

Minus the inhibitions formerly imposed by his fellow Beatles, each was free to indulge his most maudlin obsessions. The apparent naiveté that had kept them so open to new ideas and experiences only contributed to the lack of artistic perspective that seemed, in varying degrees, to plague each of the Beatles as they struggled to forge individual identities.

John, Paul, George, and Ringo's Hits—May 1970 through November 1971

TITLE AND LABEL	FIRST APPEARANCE	HIGHEST POSITION	WEEKS ON CHART
U.S. Top 100 Singles			
The Long and Winding Road/For You Blue (Apple)	May 23, 1970	1	10
Beaucoups Of Blues—Ringo—(Apple)	Nov. 7, 1970	87	5
My Sweet Lord/Isn't It a Pity—George—(Apple)*	Nov. 28, 1970	1	14
Mother—John—(Apple)	Jan. 19, 1971	43	6
What Is Life—George—(Apple)	Feb. 27, 1971	10	9
Another Day/Oh Woman Oh Why—Paul—(Apple)	March 6, 1971	5	12
Power To the People—John—(Apple)	April 3, 1971	11	9
It Don't Come Easy—Ringo—(Apple)*	May 1, 1971	4	12
Uncle Albert, Admiral Halsey—Paul—(Apple)*	Aug. 14, 1971	1	13
Bangla Desh/Deep Blue—George—(Apple)	Aug. 14, 1971	23	7
Imagine—John—(Apple)	Oct. 23, 1971	3	9
U.S. Top 200 L.P.'s			
McCartney—Paul—(Apple)*	May 9, 1970	1	47
Sentimental Journey—Ringo—(Apple)	May 16, 1970	22	14
In the Beginning (Polydor)	May 16, 1970	117	7
Let It Be (Red Apple)*	May 30, 1970	1	55
Beaucoups Of Blues—Ringo—(Apple)	Oct. 17, 1970	65	15
All Things Must Pass—George—(Apple)*	Dec. 19, 1970	1	38
John Lennon/Plastic Ono Band (Apple)*	Dec. 26, 1970	6	22
Ram—Paul—(Apple)*	June 5, 1971	2	37
Imagine—John—(Apple)*	Sept. 18, 1971	1	30
British Top Twenty Singles			
My Sweet Lord—George—(Apple)	Jan. 23, 1971	1	9
Another Day—Paul—(Apple)	March 6, 1971	2	9
Power To the People—John—(Apple)	March 20, 1971	6	6
It Don't Come Easy—Ringo—(Apple)	April 17, 1971	4	9
Bangla Desh—George—(Apple)	August 14, 1971	10	6

(Chart positions according to *Billboard;* asterisk [*]: Record Industry Association of America certified Gold Record/Million Seller)

L.P., Spain, 1971 (Odeon)

Movie director Ringo Starr succumbs to T-Rextasy (Globe Photos)

TAKE A SAD SONG AND MAKE IT BETTER

Of all the washed-up, moribund, self-pitying, self parodying erstwhile pop giants to survive the Sixties, the four splintered Beatles may well have weathered the pall and decay of the Seventies the worst. . . . McCartney makes lovely boutique tapes, resolute upon being as inconsequential as the Carpenters. . . . Lennon . . . will do *anything*, reach for any cheap trick, jump on any bandwagon, to make himself look like a Significant Artist. . . . Harrison belongs in a day care center for counter-culture casualties. . . . Ringo is beneath contempt . . . marketing that lameness in a slick Richard Perry designed package and getting hits . . . the whole thing reeks.
—Lester Bangs, *Creem*

1972 was a bleak year for Beatle fans. Aside from Ringo's infectious, Harrison-produced "Back Off Boogaloo" single, Messrs. Harrison and Starkey remained musically mute. And when Messrs. Lennon and McCartney weren't saying nasty things about one another, they were turning out records that represented the nadir of both their careers. For a time it seemed as if the dream was indeed over.

Of the two formerly most creative Beatles, one's songs were sounding more and more like the dregs of Tin Pan Alley, while the other's began to mouth the equally banal clichés of a clique of New York "revolutionaries." Letters in the music papers started to imply that both were washed-out has-beens.

In Britain all the headlines were reserved for glitter-rock, especially for David Bowie's theatrical outrages (the blurring of sexual roles that had begun with the Beatles long hair having now reached the point where an avowed bisexual could flaunt his preferences all the way to the top of the charts)—and for "T. Rextasy," which was widely cited, even by ex-Beatles, as a Seventies substitute for Beatlemania. Ringo busied himself directing a film entitled *Born To Boogie,* which documented the elfin cavortings of T. Rex star Marc Bolan. As Ringo wandered around packed auditoriums with his camera crew, none of the glittering, mascaraed teen-agers who screamed for T. Rex seemed to know or care who he was. Starr followed *Born To Boogie* by turning in his best-received non-Beatle film performance for *That'll Be the Day,* which depicted the rock 'n' roll life in late-Fifties Britain. A sequel, *Stardust,* was clearly modeled on Beatlemania—but Ringo's role was played by the Who's Keith Moon.

Despite his sharp differences with John, Paul did appear to have been imitating his ex-colleague in one respect. Just as Lennon had done with Yoko Ono, McCartney propelled *his* wife into the public eye by billing her as his partner in his projects. *Ram* was marketed as a "Paul and Linda Mc-Cartney" album, and Linda was also given a songwriting credit on many of the tracks (a nuance that did not amuse Sir Lew Grade, who had schemed so successfully to gain control of the Beatles' Northern Songs. He took Linda's lack of musical background to court to prove the songwriting "partnership" was a ruse for the McCartneys to keep half the publishing royalties).

Then in late 1971 Paul and Linda decided to form a Plastic Ono Band of their own, which they christened Wings. Linda, to whom Paul was giving elementary music lessons, would sing harmonies and play occasional keyboards. Her unskilled presence, Paul said, would bring to his music a certain "innocence . . . like a child's painting." The lineup was completed by the guitar of Moody Blues co-founder Denny Laine—who had sung lead on "Go Now," the Moodies' first big hit—and the drums of Denny Seiwell, whose skins had graced *Ram*.

Hearing that Dylan cut his albums in three days, McCartney decided to be no less spontaneous and "natural" on his first Wings L.P. "I was inspired by Dylan, the way he just kind of comes in the studio and everyone falls in and makes the track." Unfortunately, what might pass for "rough-hewn" with Dylan translated into "half-assed" in the case of *Wild Life,* released in the last weeks of 1971, and from which McCartney's customary musical craftsmanship was totally missing. The entire record was sloppily performed, musically listless, and lyrically excruciating. The opening track, "Mumbo," was made up on the spot while the tapes rolled—and sounded like it. Another song consisted mainly of the lyric "bip bop bip bom bop bip bop bip bom bam" repeated endlessly to a lobotomized three-note melody. This was the one George said he found hard "to relate to." C'mon Paul, we know ya can do better than *that!* Even the one or two half-decent tunes, like "Tomorrow," were suffocated by Linda's gloppy oohs and aahs unaccountably mixed as high as the lead vocal. And the liner notes were just as obnoxiously cutesy-pie as the music: "Inside this wrapper is the music they made. Can you dig it?"

The rock critics not only couldn't "dig" *Wild Life,* they gored it with a vengeance. Most of them were already inclined to take Lennon's side in the Beatles' civil war; Paul was viewed as a traitor to the counterculture, who had split up the Beatles and sold his soul to bubblegum. In its end-of-1971 awards, *Crawdaddy* wished Wings a "crash landing." Bootleg Beatle albums appeared with covers caricaturing Paul as a bloated pig, while A. J. Weberman staged demonstrations outside the Eastmans' Park Avenue pad. The anti-McCartney hysteria got pretty silly, but *Wild Life* certainly didn't help Paul's case any.

Soon after the album's release, former Grease Band guitarist Henry McCullough was added to the Wings lineup, and immediately found himself in the studio with his new combo, recording a single Paul had hastily composed in reaction to the "Bloody Sunday" killings in Northern Ireland. Some commentators, perhaps unfairly, viewed "Give Ireland Back To the Irish" as a self-conscious ploy to re-ingratiate himself with his country's counterculture, which condemned British military involvement in Ulster almost as strongly as its U.S. counterpart opposed the Vietnam war. "Give Ireland Back To the Irish" *was* a startling reversal from the man who had just railed (on *Wild Life*) about there being too much "political nonsense in the air." The B.B.C. immediately banned it from the British airwaves, but, despite the free publicity thus generated, few people rushed out to buy it. Soon Paul would stop talking about Ireland and, instead, campaign against British entry into the Common Market.

On February 8, Paul unexpectedly popped up at Nottingham University to ask a startled official whether he might play there the following evening. Almost no photographers or reporters were present at Wings' ensuing live debut before a few hundred students. Although the band had only four numbers rehearsed, some old rock 'n' roll "chestnuts" and a lot of jamming helped pad the show to reasonable length.

For the next fortnight or so Wings puttered about England in a van, playing intimate concerts at university dining rooms and ballrooms, often arranged at a few hours' notice. In doing so, Paul succeeded in getting reacquainted with live audiences while avoiding, as much as was possible for an ex-Beatle, any potentially unfavorable publicity (he cancelled an appearance at Leeds University after word of it was leaked to the press). Paul was also fulfilling a pet fantasy; a few years before he had tried to persuade George, John, and Ringo to give surprise performances at pubs. But Lennon had dismissed the idea as "soft."

Meanwhile back in New York City, where they had installed themselves into a Greenwich Village townhouse and a loft in artsy Soho, John and Yoko readied *their* latest joint project, an L.P. of topical songs entitled *Some Time In New York City.* If nothing else, this record was in keeping with Lennon's commitment to making his songs depict the world

L.P., 1972 (Apple)

as he saw it with a brutal honesty untempered by any reassuring gloss of saccharine. *Some Time's* cover layout was based on *The New York Times;* but the lyrics, which protested women's oppression, the killings at Attica State and in Ulster, and the jailings of Angela Davis and John Sinclair, read like a rhymed version of *The Berkeley Barb.* Like any issue of either publication, the album was dated the day after it came out. Which would have been fine had its contents managed in the slightest to illuminate yesterday's news.

Unfortunately, however, the lyrics almost all proved to be heavy-handed, doctrinaire, and simplistic, as embarrassing in their own way as *Wild Life.* As had happened so many times before, John had become so immersed in a new obsession (in this case radical-chic politics) that its influence colored everything he wrote. Only now the political clichés seemed to suffocate his work, to the point where one couldn't find anything uniquely John Lennon in it. For the first time in eight years, John had stopped writing about himself, and instead reduced his art to parroting the views of his new friends in the "Village" radical community: people like Jerry Rubin and A. J. Weberman (Lennon was even spotted about town sporting one of A. J.'s anti-Dylan buttons) who were vastly his inferiors in originality, imagination, and influence. *Some Time* proved to be a somewhat belated reflection of the radical political segment of the counterculture, where the label "fascist" was often tossed about with as much indiscriminate zeal as "Communist" had been by the McCarthyites of the Fifties.

All the well-worn catchwords of "the movement" were now being invoked by the Beatle who had been so famous for his inventiveness with words. Around this time, Lennon said he saw himself as a "reporter" working in the medium of rock music. But the world described on *Some Time in New York City* is a one-dimensional one, populated exclusively by "pigs" and "the people" (whose female contingent consisted of "sisters"), dominated by "the Man," who perpetrates "genocide" at every turn in order to keep "the people" from attaining their "revolution." In *Attica State,* "Rockefeller pulled the trigger/that is what the people feel." Like most such diatribes, the song ignores the unhappy fact that opinion polls all showed well over three quarters of the American people supporting Rocky's heavy handling of the prisoners' uprising. However, it is understandable that John

The Lennons promoting the latest edition of Yoko's collected happenings (Globe Photos)

would choose to focus the anger, evident in much of his recent work, on a political establishment that had caused him and Yoko so much grief in the past—and would do so again in the very near future.

Some Time did contain *some* good music, not to mention John's usual dynamic vocals, but people were too put off by the lyrics to notice. The one excellent track, the Chuck Berry-influenced "New York City," chronicled the Lennons' latest escapades in much the same fashion as "Ballad Of John and Yoko" had once done—and warmly endorsed the Big Apple. ("2,000 years ago we'd all want to live in Rome," says John. "This is Rome now.") "Luck Of the Irish" had a melody reminiscent of folk ballads, enchanting enough to charm a leprechaun, but the lyrics ("the bastards commit genocide," etc.) were fiercely incongruous.

Maybe John was trying to atone for the liberalism of the Beatles' "Revolution," but *nobody* seemed to take to *Some Time in New York City*. The highest it reached on America's L.P. charts was Number 48, a most dismal showing for an ex-Beatle. The single "Woman Is the Nigger Of the World," peaked at a no less unspectacular Number 57. Even John's allies on the countercultural press were aghast; *Rolling*

August 30, 1972:
Songs Performed By John and Yoko Lennon
at the One-to-One Benefits In New York
It's So Hard
Instant Karma
Mother
Well, Well, Well
Woman Is the Nigger Of the World
Sisters O Sisters (Yoko)
Sunday Bloody Sunday
Attica State
Power To the People
Imagine
We're All Water (Yoko)
Now Or Never (Yoko)
Cold Turkey
New York City
Born In a Prison (Yoko)
Come Together
Hound Dog
Give Peace a Chance

John and Yoko dressed for battle (Apple Records)

Stone made ominous noises about "artistic suicide." Now it was John's turn to be exiled to the trendy tastemakers' Siberia for the ex-hip.

In the 30 months since *Abbey Road,* both John and Paul (like Dylan before them) seemed to have made the full transition from the sublime to the ridiculous. In the process they frittered away much of their artistic credibility and clout as "spokesmen" for the counterculture, which was left with precious few (if any) symbols to rally around.

The youth subculture had thrived in large measure upon its pop "prophets" and the direction that the regularly updated gospel of their recordings had provided. The temporary eclipse of its three most respected leaders helped to deflate many of the pretensions of rock music, and the intensity with which people approached it. Meanwhile, interests concerned more with profit than quality were increasingly getting a grip on the "progressive" rock scene, delineating and dictating commercial formulas—and making it correspondingly difficult for less well-known artists to emerge with anything daring or different.

Although Lennon, McCartney, and Dylan would recoup their artistic powers in the mid-1970's, by then most people would buy the albums or the concert tickets more out of nostalgia or curiosity or to take in a good evening's entertainment, than out of any real belief in Dylan or the ex-Beatles as superhuman artistic and social forces.

No longer so relevant, popular music would begin once again to emphasize entertainment over art, body over

mind—and dollars over revolution. The coming resurgence of Beatlemania would in large part be a case of collective nostalgia for a bygone era, one that the disintegration of the Beatles (both as a group and as influential separate artists) had helped bring to a close, much as their emergence had helped bring it about in the first place.

In the autumn of 1972, Lennon, like Rubin and most of the rest of the gang, let his radicalism slide perilously close to liberalism to the extent of urging his fans to register to vote for President—and to vote for the Democratic candidate, George McGovern. Senator McGovern, despite the insinuations of Nixon's cronies, was hardly a wild-eyed leftist, but he did owe his nomination in large part to the dedication of youthful volunteers who shared his adamant opposition to the Vietnam war. McGovern's success in the primaries was a triumph for the counterculture's attempt to wield power via conventional electoral politics, which had begun with the 1968 McCarthy campaign. But this very fact enabled the Republicans to smear McGovern, who quoted the Beatles' "Here Comes the Sun" in his speeches, as the candidate of "acid, amnesty, and abortion," a platform that was still unpalatable to most Americans. Their distaste for "hippies" contributed to the ensuing Nixon landslide, which buried not only McGovern, but also the dream that the "youth vote" might transform Amerika into a Pepperland. After the 1972 disaster, there were no more political crusades, and most of the country's youth drifted back into apathy. The election returns were yet another death knell for the counterculture.

Lennon was also preoccupied throughout 1972 with a pair of more personal campaigns, although one of them proved to be linked to his political convictions after all. On March 6, immigration authorities unexpectedly refused to renew John's visa, allegedly because of a technicality relating to his 1968 marijuana bust. But it seemed strange that around the same time, deportation procedures were instigated against dozens of ranking ex-Nazis only after great pressure was applied by the media—whereas John was singled out for having once kept some pot in the house. In the aftermath of Watergate it came to light that arch-conservative Senator Strom Thurmond had sent a dossier on Lennon's anti-Administration views to Nixon's Attorney General, John "law 'n' order" Mitchell, with the suggestion that Lennon be somehow expelled from the U.S. "Many headaches might be avoided," advised Strom, "if appropriate action be taken in time."

Aware of the ex-Beatle's influence and trouble-making potential with young voters, the Administration mounted a campaign of harassment that included tapping John's telephone. More liberal politicians like New York's Mayor John Lindsay came to Lennon's defense, as did numerous newspaper editorials (including one in *The New York Times*) urging renewal of John's visa. Thousands of fans busied themselves circulating petitions and writing letters to government officials on John's behalf. Among the countless artists, intellectuals, and celebrities who signed were Henry Miller, Kurt Vonnegut, Edmund Wilson, Saul Bellow, Lawrence Ferlinghetti, Leonard Bernstein, Virgil Thomson, Bob Dylan, Fred Astaire, and Jack Lemmon. On behalf of P.E.N. (an international writers' association), Allen Ginsberg weighed in with "a great Roc's voice . . . throbbing to Heav'n that American shores, woods, and lakes not be banned to the great Swain of Liverpool."

On top of all this, the Lennons were also embroiled in a widely publicized search for Kyoko, Yoko's daughter by a previous marriage, who was constantly being spirited away to unknown destinations by her father. This situation dragged the Lennons on a wild goose chase, involving trips to Texas and the Virgin Islands, private detectives and a tangle of lawsuits—and was the official reason Lennon was in America in the first place.

So John certainly had his share of problems at the time—not the least of them being his ongoing legal and personal feud with Paul McCartney—which may help toward explaining away the debacle of *Some Time In New York City.* Aside from a pro-Lennon petition, that album also contained a "free" live L.P., "yours at no extra cost when you purchase *Some Time In New York City.*" Ah, but why then did the package cost $6.98, a dollar more than current list price for pop L.P.'s? Because one of the oldest tricks in the book of "free enterprise" is to raise the price of something and then tack on a "free" bonus, that's why. Capitalist ploys lent themselves just as nicely to the marketing of the Lennons' album of radical diatribes as to the selling of Sugar Pops or President Nixon.

Actually, the "free" L.P., originally intended for separate release under the title *Live Jam,* was barely worth the extra dollar. In keeping with the Lennons' current view that any "happening" they happened to happen onto was worthy of immortalization, it contained yet more recyclings of "Cold Turkey" and Yoko's "Don't Worry Kyoko" (from the 1969 London Lyceum concert with the likes of George Harrison, Eric Clapton, and Keith Moon), a rendition of "Baby Please Don't Go," marred by rather un-apropos screeching from Ms. L., and a tedious jam hosted by Frank Zappa at the Fillmore East in 1971, appropriately entitled "Scumbag."

So when tickets went on sale for John's first "official" American solo concert—a benefit for the retarded children at New York's Willowbrook Hospital—we had no idea what might transpire on the stage of Madison Square Garden. A conceptual "happening"? A self-indulgent jam session? We needn't have worried. John managed to pull himself together for an honest-to-goodness professional show. Backed by New York's gritty Elephant's Memory, he belted his way through all his solo singles, highlights from the post-Beatle albums, and "Come Together," which brought the house down. Yoko didn't exactly bring 'em to their feet, but she did make a sincere effort to *sing* four of her own tunes. Nonchalantly chewing gum throughout, Lennon was in dazzling form; in stronger voice than his audience had ever before heard him, and with his powerful onstage persona vamping perfectly intact. Despite some rancid vinyl, the star gave us reason to predict a speedy recovery on all fronts.

Over the summer, Paul McCartney had also begun to pull his act together. "It became a challenge to me," he later acknowledged. "I thought either I was going to go under or I was going to get something together."

In a colorfully repainted London double-decker bus, Wings careened across nine countries of Europe for seven weeks, playing 26 shows at smallish concert halls. Their magical mystery tour was marred only by Swedish customs officials, who intercepted a stash of the hash that was daily being mailed to Paul from Britain, and fined him $2,000. This left Ringo the only ex-Beatle with a drug-free police record.

Some British fans objected to Paul's neglecting them in favor of out-of-the-way places like Helsinki and Montreux, but there was a definite logic behind Paul's move. His strategy was to follow those surprise appearances before university students—who were, of course, too agog at the presence of Paul McCartney in their campus ballroom to be very critical—with dates in continental Europe, which was still the provinces as far as the rock industry was concerned. Once this was done, his Wings might be sufficiently broken in for him to tackle a major tour of Britain, and, last of all, America.

**Summer 1972: Songs Performed on
Paul McCartney and Wings' European Tour**

Smile Away
The Mess
Hi Hi Hi
Mumbo
Bip Bop
Say You Don't Mind (Denny Laine)
Wild Life
Sea Side Woman (Linda McCartney)
I Would Only Smile
Blue Moon of Kentucky
Give Ireland Back To the Irish
Henry's Blue (Henry McCullough)
1882
I Am Your Singer
Junk
Eat At Home
Maybe I'm Amazed
My Love
Mary Had a Little Lamb
Soily
Best Friend
Momma's Little Girl

(Apple Records)

Single, France, 1972 (Apple)

Single, Germany 1972 (Apple)

Single, Italy, 1973 (Apple)

For McCartney, ever the most cautious Beatle, was not about to get wet without first testing the waters. The rules of the game had changed on the rock concert circuit since Paul had last played in 1966. Audiences weren't screaming any more (except at T. Rex and the likes of David Cassidy) and they had come to expect far lengthier, more sophisticated performances than the Beatles had been wont to give. The mere presence of a star would no longer do, and McCartney planned to learn precisely what *would* do before propelling Wings into the major league.

The European jaunt began with reportedly limp performances in off-the-beaten-track French towns, at one of which Paul exhorted his audience to "chantez a bit if you know les mots." But subsequent shows helped to bolster McCartney's confidence and to tighten up the band. Critics noted that his music sounded much more vital and hard-driving live than on records. He even had some of the later concerts recorded for a proposed album (out of which only a single B-side, "The Mess," materialized). At last Wings looked as though they might be getting off the ground.

Still, the role that McCartney persisted in thrusting upon his wife continued to make Wings the object of widespread ridicule. He was determined to share the spotlight with Linda, as he would make plain in his song "Letting Go" ("I want to put her on the radio . . .").

Much as Lennon had substituted Yoko for Paul as his partner in public life, McCartney seemed intent on proving that Linda could do everything for him John had once done, and more. Linda was encouraged not only to sing along on Paul's songs, but also to write her own. Her "Sea Side Woman" became a Wings concert staple—and the frequent object of unbecoming catcalls.

Even had she been a major musical talent, some of Paul's female admirers would have doubtless resented his sharing the stage with their ultimate rival. But unfortunately, Linda seemed to lack even Yoko's quirky originality, and the way Paul flaunted her struck many fans and most critics as being cloying and tasteless.

Paul's style was even more cramped by his determination to ignore his own remarkable past. He had written some of the greatest songs of the 1960's, yet refused to use any in his show. "It was too much of a trauma," he admitted in 1976. "It was like reliving a sort of weird dream, doing a Beatles tune."

To the inevitable questions about Beatles and reunions, Paul would cooly reply that his present job was singing and playing with Wings, and that anything before that was of no interest to him. (And anyone who pushed the point was likely to meet with a glacial "the Beatles will never get together again.") Unfortunately this limited him to material composed since 1970, a rather meagre repertoire. Even Paul confessed some time later to "a dip for me and my writing—a couple of years when I had a sort of illness. I was a little dry."

The first real sign of recovery was an excellent single late that autumn, the first release from Wings almost worthy of that other group Paul had once worked with, which he now pretended not to remember. The A-side, "Hi Hi Hi," was swiftly banned by the B.B.C., which assumed the "hi"'s celebrated in this chunky rocker were of the chemically-induced variety, and found the taste of those "sweet bananas" equally questionable. Not long after the song's release Paul was busted again, for growing the devil weed up at his Scotland farm. McCartney testified that some fan had sent him a package of seeds, so he planted them to see what they were—an indiscretion that cost him a $250 fine, and, years later, the refusal of a Japanese visa.

A treasure called "C Moon" showed up on the backside of "Hi Hi Hi," which went to show that Paulie could still be cute without being cloying. "C Moon" was also one of the first records made outside Jamaica to feature a touch of reggae. As for the title . . . remember that trashy smash "Wooly Bully," circa 1965, which coined the phrase L7, meaning square, as in un-hip? Well, C☽ , see, is supposed to connote just the opposite of L7. And anyone who could in just one year have two out of three singles banned by the stuffy old B.B.C., get busted for pot twice, *and* release a record as nifty as "C Moon" couldn't be quite as L7 as some people had been insinuating. Maybe Paul McCartney was still pretty C☽ after all. Or so we die-hards hoped.

While other Beatles had long since eased into a more relaxed work schedule, Paul McCartney continued to drive himself relentlessly through 1973, in part because that had always been his nature. Moreover, Paul was determined to re-establish himself as a major force in the music scene—and on his own terms. So he ground out a new album, devised the theme music for the latest James Bond thriller *Live and Let Die,* and starred in his own T.V. special.

The latter, an hour-long extravaganza called *James Paul McCartney* (produced by Sir Lew Grade, who in turn agreed to stop questioning Linda's songwriting abilities in court), was the least successful of these projects. Even those of us who were rooting for Paul found it hard to suppress our groans as Wings nuzzled sheep to the strains of "Mary Had a Little Lamb" and as Paul tried to make passionate faces while crooning "My Love," looking instead as if he'd just sucked a lemon. On the other hand, he tap-danced with some flair through "Gotta Sing, Gotta Dance" (a cabaret-style number he later bequeathed on Twiggy), and, for the first time in a long time, serenaded his fans with such vintage delights as "Michelle," "Yesterday," and "Blackbird." The program attempted to project McCartney as all-round entertainer, an image that would become more convincing in years to come.

The album, the lavishly packaged *Red Rose Speedway,* was originally conceived as a two-record set. But Paul

L.P., 1973 (Apple)

James Paul McCartney, "Gotta Sing, Gotta Dance" (Apple Records)

wisely decided to siphon off extraneous material, such as Linda's and Denny's, and boil the sessions down to one highly commercial disc. The billing was changed to Paul McCartney *and* Wings, as it was supposed that the disappointing sales of those first Wings releases might have been due to people's not knowing exactly who Wings was. (Actually, they didn't sell because they weren't very good.)

Like *Wild Life, Speedway* consisted mainly of silly love songs that sounded as though they could have been composed 15 years earlier, before the Beatles came along to add new dimensions to pop music. But both the tunes and the performances were far better than anything on *Wild Life. Speedway* was pleasingly plump music—charming, harmless, entertaining fluff. All about big barn beds, stolen kisses, chance encounters along Regent's Park canal, and the Miracle of Love. Just right for the brand-new summer, a perfect background to lazy afternoons in the sun.

One of the selections, the smoochy "My Love," caught the public's fancy in a bigger way than anything McCartney had written since the Beatles. The single version, like *Red Rose Speedway* itself, was an almost instantaneous Number One in the U.S.; and of all the Fabs' post-Beatle compositions, only George's "My Sweet Lord" has inspired more renditions by other artists.

**Spring 1973: Songs Performed On
Paul McCartney and Wings' British Tour**

Big Barn Bed
Soily
When the Night
Wild Life
Sea Side Woman (Linda McCartney)
Go Now (Denny Laine)
Little Woman Love/C Moon
Live and Let Die
Maybe I'm Amazed
Say You Don't Mind (Denny Laine)
My Love
The Mess
Hi, Hi, Hi
Long Tall Sally

(Apple Records)

Speedway was the first of several McCartney albums to contain a lyric sheet. Normally these are nice to have, but it didn't help McCartney's dissolving reputation as a Lyricist of Consequence any when people fastened their specs to read lines like "wo wo wo wo, only my love does it good." As far as "meaning" went, Paul was now evidently less interested in the words themselves than in *how* he sang them. And his voice could certainly still convey an impressive range of emotions. (The L.P. jacket also featured a fan message in braille to Paul's blind idol Stevie Wonder.)

"My Love" was followed, rapid-fire, by another chart-topping triumph, a single of "Live and Let Die," whose release coincided with that of the film. Paul enlisted a little help from an old friend on this one; for the first and only time since the breakup George Martin was invited to produce one of his former clients' projects. It was he who devised the record's explosive orchestration.

Some months before, *Rolling Stone* had broken the news of McCartney's commission to write thriller music in tones so snide you would have thought Paul had been caught playing golf with Spiro Agnew. "So it's come to that," groaned the *Stone*. This hipper-than-thou attitude infuriated Paul, who saw nothing criminal in branching out into the "legitimate" world of show-biz. But the counterculture rags still pictured an unbridgeable gulf separating the rock scene and the sort of mere entertainment favored by straights. (Elton John and Alice Cooper had not yet transformed rock back into vaudeville.) For Paul to get involved with a slick thriller was seen as yet another in a long line of sell-outs.

Nonetheless, McCartney performed his secret agent mission well. "Live and Let Die," a deft collage of ominous spy motifs, reggae, and McCartney popcorn, is one of his most inventive tunes. A few months later it earned Paul an Oscar nomination for best movie theme of the year; but "The Way We Were" wound up with the grand prize. (The charmingly laid-back "I Lie Around," which appeared on the flip side, was Paul carrying out his threat to transform Wings from his backup band into a real *group:* Denny Laine sang lead.)

Over the warm months of 1973, Wings embarked on a proper tour of Britain. Now for the first time, they were able to regale their audiences with some smash hits of their own.

For a while there in May and June of 1973, album charts were reminiscent of the golden age of Beatlemania. The top three places on just about all of them were reserved for Paul's *Red Rose Speedway* and two double albums by the Beatles. The compilations *1962–1966* and *1967–1970* were an Allen Klein brainwave, but they were bound to happen eventually, particularly since high-quality bootlegs of the Beatles' greatest hits had begun to flood the market.

The photographs used on the back and front of the album jackets both show the Beatles grouped in identical positions upon a housing project balcony. But they provide a striking study in contrasts, as they were taken six years apart, in 1963 and 1969. With their shoulder-length hair and whiskers, John, George, and Ringo are virtually unrecognizable in the later shot as those apple-cheeked clean-cut lads in matching suits and ties who grace the early one. (And thanks largely to the Beatles, there were millions of other young men in 1969 whose mothers wouldn't have recognized them had they returned to their homes of a few years before.) Only Paul McCartney seemed practically unchanged.

The earlier picture came from their first British L.P. cover, *Please Please Me,* of which the remake, originally intended for the Beatles' abortive 1969 L.P., was a satire. The remake had been intended for 1969's proposed back-to-the-roots album, which was to have been called *Get Back, with Don't Let Me Down and 12 Other Songs,* an L.P. that never materialized, although many of the songs eventually surfaced on *Let It Be.*

The new anthologies' contents were predictable enough—all the big hit singles, interspersed with well-known L.P. tracks. Naturally there were fans and critics who quibbled with Klein's choices, and especially with the absence of three B-sides ("I'm Down," "The Inner Light," and "You Know My Name") that had not yet graced U.S. albums. (*1962–1966* and *1967–1970* also passed up 16 tunes that had never been collected on British L.P.'s.) A less excusable flaw was that seven of the tracks weren't even in stereo, even though all but two of them had previously been issued in stereo on albums in Britain, Germany, or the U.S. The stereo masters, it seems, just didn't happen to be at Klein's fingertips at the time, and he apparently couldn't be bothered with tracking them down before rushing his lucrative brainstorms to the marketplace.

About a month after the release of *Red Rose Speedway* and the Beatle flashbacks, a fourth Apple album arrived to usurp the Number One slot one week after its release: George Harrison's long-awaited and painstakingly crafted *Living In the Material World.*

It was clear by now that each of the Beatles viewed the break-up as a personal and artistic liberation. All were now able single-mindedly to dedicate their careers to pursuits that would have seemed utterly out of context within the framework of the group. At times they seemed defensively determined to disassociate themselves from the past.

Paul was free to shake off all pretentions to consequence. John could devote his life and art to exorcising both his own demons and those of the world at large. And George increasingly viewed his music as a means to transport himself and his listeners into the Holy Kingdom. Harrison, like Lennon, was not one to underestimate the power of rock.

But despite the loftiness of his intentions, the general consensus in 1973 was still that George had his act together more than any of the others. The surprise triumphs of *All Things Must Pass* and the magnanimous Bangla Desh concert, album and film were fresh in the public's mind, and contrasted starkly with such fiascos as *Wild Life* and *Some Time In New York City*—not to mention the petty public bickering of their perpetrators. A receptive audience was guaranteed for *Living In the Material World*.

With this album, whose title was originally announced as *The Magic Is Here Again,* George devised a luxuriant rock devotional designed to transform his fans' stereo equipment into a temple. The record was lavishly packaged with color representations of the Hindu scriptures, decorated with Sanskrit symbols, and —like George's subsequent forays— dedicated "All Glories to Sri Krishna." The lyrics repeatedly hammered home the message that the best way to insure a better deal for yourself in the next life is to keep your mind

focused on God in this one, for "the Lord loves the one that loves the Lord." George had evidently concluded that he had been placed in this vale of tears for a specific reason, that being to reveal the Inner Light to his millions of fans. As he sang on the album's title track, he had "a lot of work to do" getting his "message through," before the Lord Sri Krishna was likely to elevate George from "the material world" to "the spiritual sky." Just about the only secular note on the record was struck by "Sue Me Sue You Blues," a commentary on the Beatles' legal squabbles, complete with the sort of vicious slide guitar work George had provided for John's "How Do You Sleep?"

"Be Here Now," based around a drone played on the tanpura, marked a return to the quasi-Indian mode of George's mid-sixties work; the title and some of the lyrics were borrowed from one of his favorite books, *Be Here Now* by Baba Ram Dass. Indian instruments also made sporadic re-appearances on the title tune. For perhaps the only time, George created an album that showcased all the musical styles with which his name has been associated with the conspicuous exception of good old rock 'n' roll. Whatever one thinks of their solo music, John, Paul, and George had all evolved into surprisingly tasteful and meticulous producers—a job they had always left for George Martin when they were still the Beatles. With one exception, Harrison handled *Material World*'s big production job by himself. As on *All Things Must Pass,* great blocks of strings

The new superStarr gets his gold (*Ringo,* "Photograph," and "You're 16") and platinum (*Ringo*) records from Capitol President Bhaskar Menon (Capitol Records)

(Apple Records)

go to the trouble of erasing Ronnie's voice.)

Thanks in part to the inclusion of his heartfelt Number One single "Give Me Love (Give Me Peace On Earth)," *Material World* chalked up another massive commercial success for George. But some of the critics began to sling a few barbs at his lofty perch, complaining that he had become insufferably preachy and sanctimonious. George had been built up as the surprise winner of the ex-Beatle sweepstakes, but in going out on his limb to embrace the sublime, George was beginning (like Paul and John before him) to risk appearing ridiculous. The Apple Bonkers were starting to rally, and once George would cease to underscore his transcendent dogma with the exquisite musical underpinnings that were still evident on *Living In the Material World,* they would do their best to knock him back down to earth.

The ex-Beatles managed to stay out of the limelight for the next several months, as John, Paul, and Ringo concentrated on completing new albums in time for the Christmas rush. The hottest news flashes in Beatledom were that Allen Klein simultaneously lost his three most famous clients (he subsequently sued Lennon, Harrison, and Starr to the characteristically grandiose tune of $19 million, which in 1977 was whittled down to $5 million, thanks to, in Klein's phrase "Yoko Ono's Kissinger-like negotiating brilliance"; a simultaneous $34 million suit against McCartney was chucked out of court) and that, with one major point of disagreement out of the way, the Fabs were all on speaking terms once more. John found cordial words to say about *Red Rose Speedway* and dubbed Paul "a real pro," and McCartney in turn began intimating that he wouldn't mind playing with his old pals again, should the stars be right.

Reunion rumors were fanned by word that John, George, and Ringo had teamed up in Los Angeles to record "I'm the Greatest," a tune Lennon had written for Starr's forthcoming album. Not wishing to be outdone, Paul also turned up to lend Ringo a helping hand and a new song. Even though all four never showed up in the same studio at the same time, the fact that every one wound up singing, playing, and composing for what Ringo liked to call his "first real album" made the ensuing *Ringo* L.P. just about the next best thing to a reunion.

In the aftermath of the Beatles' breakup, Ringo had wistfully expressed in song the wish that when he went to town he wanted to play with all three of his friends. Not only did he really go to town with his album, which became a runaway commercial and critical success, but all three were there with him. Probably the affable and unpretentious Starr was the only person who both could and would induce his megalomaniacal ex-colleagues to co-operate on a new project. Their collaboration on *Ringo* proved to be just the concoction to wash away the bitter aftertaste that the Beatles' squabbling had left with so many of their fans.

Although the album was an unabashedly lightweight affair, that friendly competitiveness that had spurred the Beatles to such heights resurfaced on this album, bringing out the best in *Ringo's* three most eminent guest stars. "I'm the Greatest" indicated that Lennon had recouped both his wit and his good cheer. His account of being in "the greatest show on earth, for what it was worth," complete with sly references to *Sgt. Pepper,* is as wry and jolly as previous treatises on that theme (such as "Working Class Hero") had been bitter and self-pitying. As they say, time heals all wounds; and John, like the others, was beginning to view his past with affection and justifiable pride.

Similarly, with "Six O'Clock" Paul tapped his most characteristic strengths to produce the strongest, most lyrical pop

and horns and overdubbed guitars were piled onto one another to bring Harrison's somewhat dirge-like hymns to appropriately transcendent heights. Surely Phil Spector never had a more attentive pupil. George furthered his saintly image by donating royalties for nine of the 11 tunes to his "Material World Charitable Foundation." Nonetheless, as with a number of George's other projects, a little dark cloud of disingenuousness was evident on *Material World,* although nobody seemed to notice at the time.

In early 1971, Phil Spector had attempted to pilot a comeback by his wife Ronnie, who as lead chanteuse for the Ronnettes had known fleeting stardom eight years before. George was commissioned to outfit Ronnie with a new tune ("Try Some Buy Some") and Spector outdid himself to transform it into a masterpiece of his patented "wall of sound" production, complete with 40 strings, plus a dozen mandolins trilling in unison. It was one of the crushing disappointments of Spector's career that the resultant Apple single provoked nary a ripple in the music business.

So nearly two years later, George, unwilling to let slip so costly a gem to the waters of oblivion, unceremoniously erased Ronnie's vocal track and substituted his own. Unfortunately his voice did not fit so snugly into Ronnie's key, and went sour on a number of notes; but George stuck the result on *Living In the Material World* all the same. (George also composed and recorded the instrumental tracks for a projected second Ronnie Spector single entitled "You." When her "Try Some Buy Some" bombed, however, the project was shelved—until 1975, when George would add his own voice and release "You" as a single, and as a highlight of the *Extra Texture* L.P. This time he wouldn't have to ballad he had composed since "The Long and Winding Road." George contributed the melody to "Photograph," whose grand, sweeping arrangement recalled his own recent cosmic productions—and contrasted incongruously with Ringo's homespun lyric about a guy who's got nothing to show for his love affair but an old snapshot. Harrison also managed to be amusing for the first time in years in his two other contributions to *Ringo:* the country-flavored "Sunshine Life For Me," about a fellow who'd rather associate with trees than people, and the showbizzy sign-off, "You and Me (Babe)."

As for Ringo himself, he merely turned on that down-to-earth charm the way he had done on his occasional cameos with the Beatles, bumbling through a program of schmaltz and good-time rock custom-made for those trusty five notes that had served him so well in the past.

A galaxy of other "friends" joined the ex-Beatles on *Ringo,* among them Marc Bolan, the Band, Harry Nilsson, and Billy Preston. Their presence helped insure a richly varied and textured album, masterfully if somewhat slickly produced by Richard Perry, who had previously transformed Nilsson, Carly Simon, and others into commercial bonanzas. All *Ringo*'s co-stars turn up in the crowd of faces that adorn the *Sgt. Pepper*-style L.P. cover.

The Starr of the show himself might well have gotten lost in the mix, but the cast of thousands was apparently sympathetic enough to complement, rather than eclipse, the happy-go-lucky personality that glows through all the songs and gives the L.P. some cohesiveness. This, aside from the other Beatles' involvement, was the key to the record's considerable success. Always the Beatles' resident Fool On the Hill, Ringo never needed to do anything more than be himself. The others may have had all the talent and ambition, but their little drummer boy was internationally famous for nothing more—or less—than his loveable personality.

Ringo had nothing to prove; he wasn't trying to save the world, or our souls, or even a dazzling reputation. He only wanted to make us smile, and all he had to do was act naturally. If *Living in the Material World* led the jaded to insinuate that George, in reaching too hard for the sublime, was verging on the ridiculous, *Ringo* saw Mr. Starkey—with a little help from his old friends—turning his inherent ridiculousness into a sublime entertainment.

After the release of his album, Ringo began to seem like a modern incarnation of Aesop's tortoise. Everyone had supposed that the Beatles' breakup signalled the end of his musical career; after all, he had written but two of the over two hundred songs the Beatles had recorded, and could barely even carry a tune. Yet his album proved to be not only a million-seller, but also a seemingly bottomless source of his singles. In rapid succession, "Photograph," Ringo's campy remake of Johnny Burnette's "You're 16," and his own composition (with Vini Poncia) "Oh My My" blanketed the airwaves and topped the charts. John Lennon, who hadn't had a hit for over two years, sent Ringo a telegram reading: "CONGRATULATIONS. HOW DARE YOU? AND PLEASE WRITE ME A HIT SONG."

Ringo Starr, Designer

One facet of Ringo Starr's creativity that may interest the collector of Starr memorabilia is his furniture design partnership, Ringo Or Robin Limited, which has thrived to a minimum of attendant publicity. It was founded in 1970, after designer Robin Cruikshank, who had performed assignments for Apple and assorted Beatles, helped furnish Ringo Starr's home to the drummer's unorthodox specifications. Ringo was so pleased with the results that he bought into Robin Limited with an interest in marketing his own designs, and collaborating with Mr. Cruikshank on others. The pair set up shop in the Apple building on 54 St. James Street in London, rechristening their company Ringo Or Robin Limited, and have since been responsible for a series of dozens of items ranging from ashtrays and mirrors to elaborate furnishings. All are extremely classy—as are their price tags—unusual sometimes to the point of surrealism, and just about as witty as furniture can possibly be.

Although the demands of his recording and acting careers oblige him to leave day-to-day administrative tasks to Robin, Ringo has taken an unflagging personal interest in the designs. One of his favorites (page 162) is a cluster of individually adjustable dining-room tables that was devised so that each member of the Starr household might dine at a level most compatible with his or her own height. Another, installed in Mr. Starr's personal office at Apple Records, proves when unraveled to be not a U.F.O., but the last word in stereo consoles. Also shown are a group of mirrors.

One of Ringo's earliest and most notorious brainstorms for the firm was the Rolls Royce Grille Table, which was recently sold to Elton John's manager for £2,500. Earlier editions went for only £1,500, but the skyrocketing cost of Rolls Royce spare parts is constantly forcing the price upwards. The more niggardly collector, however, can at the time of writing still have an apple paperweight for the relatively paltry sum of £3.

More familiar to the casual Starr-gazer will be the embellished Ringo Or Robin chrome-plated antique telephone that was adopted as the logo for Ring O' Records.

In the United Kingdom, Ringo Or Robin Limited has attracted a motley clientele of pop stars, architects, and businessmen, whose sole common denominator probably is the ability to pay for its merchandise. Attempts to set up a shop in Los Angeles fell through in 1974, but Ringo and Robin have plans for eventual American distribution for their work.

L.P., 1973 (Apple)

Designs by Ringo Starr

(Courtesy, Robin Cruikshank)

Dining tables

Stereo Console

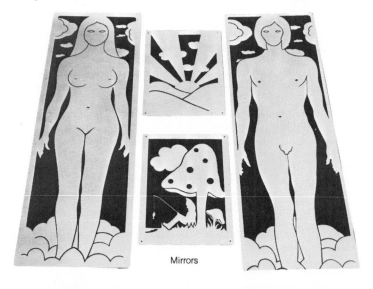

Mirrors

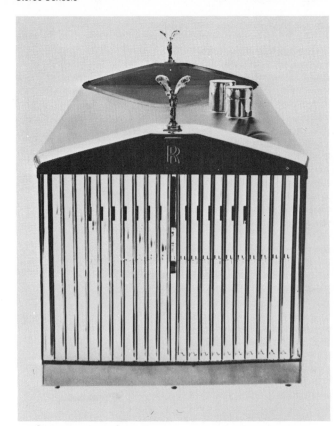

A Rolls-Royce coffee table

They're Going to Put Me in the Movies

Ringo Starr's Solo Film Appearances

CANDY (1968)
Starring Ringo as Emmanuel the Gardener
Screenplay by Buck Henry; Directed by Christian Marquand
Cinerama

THE MAGIC CHRISTIAN (1969)
Starring Ringo as Youngman Grand
Screenplay by Terry Southern, Joseph McGrath, and Peter
Sellers; Directed by Joseph McGrath
Commonwealth United

200 MOTELS (1971)
Starring Ringo as Frank Zappa and The Dwarf
Screenplay by Frank Zappa; Directed by Tony Palmer
United Artists

BLINDMAN (1971)
Starring Ringo as Candy
Screenplay by V. Cerami, Piero Anchisi, Tony Anthony;
Directed by Ferdinando Baldi
20th Century Fox

BORN TO BOOGIE (1972)
Documentary about T Rex; Directed by Ringo, who makes a
brief personal appearance
Apple

THAT'LL BE THE DAY (1973)
Starring Ringo as David Essex's manager
Screenplay by Ray Connolly; Directed by Claude Whatham
Mayfair

SON OF DRACULA (1974)
Starring Ringo as Merlin
Screenplay by Jay Fairbanks; Directed by Freddie Francis
Cinemation Industries

LISZTOMANIA (1975)
Starring Ringo as The Pope
Screenplay by Ken Russell; Directed by Ken Russell
Warner Brothers

Ringo starring as a bandit in *Blindman* (20th Century Fox Film Corporation)

No smashes were forthcoming from John's own new L.P., *Mind Games,* perhaps his most low-key collection ever. The general consensus was that the album had all the fine and familiar ingredients, only some of the fizz had gone out of the pop. Arriving at a time when scores of other superstars (like Ringo and Paul) were dealing out their Yuletide trumps, the unassuming *Mind Games* managed to get rather lost in the shuffle.

Nonetheless, to Lennon devotees, the L.P. came as quite a relief after the strident bad vibes of *Some Time In New York City.* Most importantly, John seemed to have retrieved the sense of humor so lacking in all his deadly-serious earlier post-Beatle work.

While offering nothing spectacularly new or exciting, *Mind Games* did successfully make use of various styles that Lennon had trademarked in more creative times: the zany wordplay ("Tight A$," "Freda Peeple") and the songs of consciousness raising ("Mind Games," "Intuition"). Best of all, *Mind Games* gave us several more of John's poignantly honest and melodic ballads ("I Know" and "You Are Here"—the latter title being, you may recall, a favorite Lennon slogan dating back to his 1968 exhibition of White Art). *Mind Games* could almost have been a collection of out-takes ranging over the past six years of Lennon's career.

The title song flashed back all the way to the John of 1967, with its invocations of "magic, the search for the grail" and its exhortations to "chant the mantra" and "raise the spirit of peace and love." Strange advice, perhaps, from the man who had launched his solo career with the declaration

"I don't believe in magic . . . I don't believe in mantra." But by this time Lennon buffs knew better than to expect their man to be consistent. In "Mind Games," as in the rest of the album and in "I'm the Greatest," John seemed determined above all to think positive for a change. "What I'm back to," said Lennon, "is believing everything until it's disproved." "Yes is the answer," he now sang; and all the new songs were variations on that theme. Yet, despite its appropriately uplifting melody, "Mind Games" fared rather modestly in the 45 rpm sweepstakes.

A possible explanation for *Mind Games'* relative blandness is one that applies equally to so many other recordings released in the 1970's: all that newly fashionable 32- and 64-track machinery, and all those anonymous crack sessionmen who play like machines, often tend to make recordings that are as antiseptic as they are flawless. (Even the most complex recordings *can* do without all those extra tracks; after all, *Sgt. Pepper* didn't fare too badly with a mere four.)

The inner sleeve of *Mind Games* included a fact sheet on the latest brainwave of the man who had sung "imagine no more countries": the "conceptual" nation of Nutopia. Everyone was cordially invited to pledge his allegiance to a state without boundaries or passports, governed only by "cosmic law." "Citizenship of the country can be obtained by declaration of your awareness of Nutopia," the Lennons proclaimed. "All people of Nutopia are ambassadors of the country." In that capacity, John and Yoko requested Nutopia's admission to the United Nations. However, the plain white Nutopian flag has yet to take its place outside the

U.N. building, between the standards of Norway and Oman.

The Nutopian anthem is listed as one of *Mind Games'* twelve selections, but it proved to be even harder to hum than "The Star-spangled Banner," as it consists of nothing but silence. John chose to overlook the fact that he had pulled the same stunt four years earlier with "Two Minutes Silence" on *Unfinished Music Volume Two,* which in turn came two years after the West Coast Pop Art Experimental Band had graced their third album with a band of silence, and decades after John Cage had first treated concertgoers to the splendors of nonexistent music. But as the Nutopian anthem comes at the end of Side One and only lasts three seconds, most listeners remained blissfully unaware of its existence (or lack of it).

Somehow, Nutopia did not grab the public's fancy quite the way long hair, or transcendental meditation, or even the Primal Scream had, and little was heard from Lennon of his conceptual country after 1973—until 1975, when Irving Wallace and his son David Wallechinsky invited Lennon to contribute to a symposium on Utopia for their *People's Almanac.* While other participants like Buckminster Fuller and Benjamin Spock unraveled their earnest Utopian visions, John filled out his questionnaire far more succinctly—and in best "Baby You're a Rich Man" style:

Q: What would the physical environment of your Utopia be like?
A: Typical.

Q: What family structures would exist?
A: Any.

Q: How would government be organized?
A: Toss a coin.

Q: How would work and goods be divided?
A: Color of eyes.

Q: What crimes would there be, and how would they be punished?
A: Plenty. Somehow.

Q: Why isn't life like this?
A: Isn't it?

Around this time John began to enjoy lending his off-beat literary talents to an unlikely assortment of publications, ranging from *The New York Times,* where he reviewed a collection of Goon Show comedy scripts, to a West Coast rag called *Sundance,* which featured a weekly column by the Lennons, to *The Gay Liberation Book,* to which John contributed an illustrated limerick that began "why make it sad to be gay?"

The *Mind Games* jacket is a montage of Lennon's own device, featuring an all-but-hairless John posing before a mountain range that consists of Yoko's profile turned on its side. Lennon had gotten himself scalped in time to startle reporters with his new look when he attended the Watergate hearings as a witness to the downfall of those officials who had so succeeded in disrupting his own life. Once again Lennon captured the headlines with a haircut, as he had when he trimmed his moptop in 1966 to play a soldier in *How I Won the War,* and when he donated his long locks to charity in early 1970.

Yoko may still have loomed large as a mountain range in John's life when he put together *Mind Games,* but shortly after its release Lennon thrilled the gossip columnists by forsaking Yoko and the Big Apple in favor of his secretary, May Pang, and new digs in Los Angeles. This transpired just as that other creative giant of Sixties rock, Bob Dylan, fell out with *his* wife, Sara. That separation jolted Dylan out of his complacent rut enough to inspire *Blood On the Tracks,* his most searing and poetic record in eight years. Similarly, family troubles apparently put some renewed bite into Len-

L.P., 1973 (Apple)

non's songwriting, as the world would discover upon the release of *Walls and Bridges* the following autumn.

Happily, both Lennon and Dylan would eventually manage to patch up their marriages, but the songs they composed in the meantime seem to testify in favor of the axiom: the more restless the artist, the better the art.

Paul McCartney's star also appeared to be crossed in late 1973; only instead of his marriage, it was his band that seemed to be on the rocks. Yet, like Lennon, McCartney sailed through his difficulties, on record anyway, with flying colors.

Having decided it might be far out to cut a new Wings album in Lagos, Nigeria, Paul had already made all necessary arrangements when Henry McCullough and Denny Seiwell announced that he could take that trip without them. Apparently they felt they were being turned into McCartney-programmed robots, and didn't like it any more than George and Ringo had. In their absence, Paul pulled himself together to create an album that picked up where his work on *Abbey Road* had left off. In doing so, he combined a sense of urgency with his renewed self-confidence; as Mrs. McCartney told *Sounds:* "Paul thought, I've got to do it, either I give up and cut my throat or get my magic back."

Supported only by his two unplucked Wings, Linda and faithful rhythm guitarist Denny Laine, Paul painstakingly overdubbed guitars, keyboards, synthesizers, Mellotrons, and some highly competent drumwork, on top of the most lyrical McCartney bass runs in years. (Occasionally Wings were joined by a smattering of local percussion, which led to charges that they had swooped down on Lagos in order to rip off Nigeria's musical heritage.) The process recalled that first do-it-yourself *McCartney* solo L.P., but the results were incomparably more successful on every level. *Band On the Run* more than sufficed to dispel the stigma of all that intervening wimpery. And the aging hippies all said: McCartney Is Back.

Replacing their usual withering disdain with an Album of the Year award, *Rolling Stone* hailed McCartney's "subtle attempts to mythologize his own experience through the creation of a fantasy world of adventure—perhaps remotely inspired by his having written 'Live and Let Die.' He does it

Single, Italy, 1973 (Apple)

Single, Italy, 1974 (Apple)

by uniting the myth of the rock star and the outlaw, the original legendary figure On The Run." Although Paul denied having consciously devised a Concept Album, he admitted to "a thread" loosely tying the songs together. Nearly all of *Band On the Run*'s exceptionally uplifting melodies are coupled with lyrics about escape, flight, and freedom.

Some of the songs seem to use escaping from prison as a metaphor for McCartney's determination (finally realized) to break out of the rut he had landed himself in when the Beatles broke up. He revealed that a key phrase on the song "Band On the Run"—"if we ever get out of here"—was a remark George Harrison had made during one of those interminable Apple board meetings; and in "Helen Wheels"— the punning name he gave his Land Rover—Paul chronicles that first free-wheeling English tour he undertook after the Beatles' split. (This song, in an odd reversal of tradition, was added to the American version of *Band On the Run;* elsewhere it was available only on a single.) The L.P. jacket depicts the remaining three Wings as outlaws, up against the wall in the bad company of James Coburn, Christopher Lee, Michael Parkinson, Clement Freud, Kenny Lynch, and John Conteh.

One of the most talked-about tracks was "Let Me Roll It," in which many critics discerned an affectionate tribute to John Lennon and his Plastic Ono sound—and one more sign that the Beatles were all pals again. Another focus of attention was McCartney's musical interpretation of Cubist painter Picasso's last words, which reportedly were "Drink to me, drink to my health, you know I can't drink any more." When Dustin Hoffman originally brought the quote to Paul's attention with the suggestion that it might make a good lyric, the ex-Beatle responded by whipping out a guitar and setting Picasso's last words to music on the spot, much to the actor's delight. In Lagos, McCartney decided to "cut it up, edit it, mess around with it, like he [Picasso] used to do with his pictures," and wound up weaving other *Band On the Run* melodies and snatches of French dialogue in and out of the recording.

Some of the music may have recalled *Abbey Road* or *Sgt. Pepper;* but when it came time to plug it, Paul regressed all the way back to *Meet the Beatles,* repeating an old stunt that had served the Fab Four so well in promoting their first Capitol album. Radio stations across the U.S. were mailed an L.P.'s worth of McCartney answering questions that only appeared on an accompanying script. This format enabled disk jockeys to conduct the "interview" themselves, thereby fostering the illusion that Paul had journeyed all the way to East Jockstrap, U.S.A., to drop by the local radio station for an intimate chat. The script, which tells the D.J.'s exactly what to do and say, begins:

ANNCR: Hi! This is (YOUR NAME) and guess who's our special guest? Paul McCartney and his wife Linda!!! That's right! and they've got a great new album with their band "Wings" called *Band On the Run.* . . . I understand when you started "Wings" you went around like wandering minstrels and played wherever you could, in various towns and colleges. What was behind that strategy? (Cue Record)

PAUL: *Open Cue:* "Just the idea of I like being in a band. . . ."

Despite the promo gimmicks, *Band On the Run* did not really catch fire until two more of its numbers hit the big time as singles: the supersonic "Jet" and the five-minute, five-part title song (which Capitol hype dubbed "a mini-rock opera"). Finally, four months after its release, the album made itself at home at Number One; three years and five million copies later, it was still on the charts, making *Band On the Run* the most popular of any of the Beatles' solo L.P.'s and one of the Seventies' biggest and most consistent sellers. While Paul would soon abandon some of the sense of adventure that helped turn *Band On the Run* into as much of a smash with the critics as with the public, he would never again forget how to make hit records.

Single, France, 1974 (Apple)

John, Paul, George, and Ringo's Hits—December 1971 through August 1974

TITLE AND LABEL	FIRST APPEARANCE	HIGHEST POSITION	WEEKS ON CHART
U.S. Top 100 Singles			
Give Ireland Back To the Irish—Paul (Apple)	March 11, 1972	21	8
Back Off Boogaloo—Ringo (Apple)	April 1, 1972	9	10
Woman Is the Nigger Of the World—John (Apple)	May 20, 1972	57	5
Mary Had a Little Lamb/Little Woman Love—Paul (Apple)	June 17, 1972	28	8
Hi, Hi, Hi—Paul (Apple)	Dec. 16, 1972	10	11
My Love—Paul (Apple)*	April 14, 1973	1	18
Give Me Love (Give Me Peace On Earth)—George (Apple)	May 19, 1973	1	14
Live and Let Die—Paul (Apple)*	July 7, 1973	2	14
Photograph—Ringo (Apple)*	Oct. 6, 1973	1	16
Mind Games—John (Apple)	Nov. 10, 1973	18	13
Helen Wheels—Paul (Apple)	Nov. 24, 1973	10	13
You're Sixteen—Ringo (Apple)*	Dec. 15, 1973	1	15
Jet—Paul (Apple)	Feb. 9, 1974	7	13
Oh My My—Ringo (Apple)	March 9, 1974	5	14
Band On the Run—Paul (Apple)*	April 20, 1974	1	16
U.S. Top 200 L.P.'s			
Wings Wild Life—Paul (Apple)*	Dec. 25, 1971	10	18
Concert For Bangla Desh—George (Apple)*	Jan. 8, 1972	2	41
Sometime In New York City—John (Apple)	July 1, 1972	48	17
1962–1966 (Apple)*	April 14, 1973	3	105
1967–1970 (Apple)*	April 14, 1973	1	109
Red Rose Speedway—Paul (Apple)*	May 12, 1973	1	31
Living In the Material World—George (Apple)*	June 16, 1973	1	26
Ringo (Apple)*	Nov. 17, 1973	2	37
Mind Games—John (Apple)*	Nov. 24, 1973	9	18
Band On the Run—Paul (Apple)*	Dec. 22, 1973	1	116
British Top Twenty Singles			
Give Ireland Back To the Irish—Paul (Apple)	March 4, 1972	16	4
Back Off Boogaloo—Ringo (Apple)	April 1, 1972	2	8
Mary Had a Little Lamb—Paul (Apple)	June 3, 1972	9	7
Happy Xmas (War Is Over)—John (Apple)	Dec. 9, 1972	4	6
Hi, Hi, Hi/C Moon—Paul (Apple)	Jan. 6, 1973	5	6
My Love—Paul (Apple)	April 7, 1973	9	8
Give Me Love (Give Me Peace On Earth)—George (Apple)	June 2, 1973	8	7
Live and Let Die—Paul (Apple)	June 9, 1973	9	8
Helen Wheels—Paul (Apple)	Nov. 3, 1973	12	7
Photograph—Ringo (Apple)	Nov. 3, 1973	8	6
You're Sixteen—Ringo (Apple)	Feb. 23, 1974	4	7
Jet—Paul (Apple)	March 2, 1974	7	6
Band On the Run—Paul (Apple)	July 6, 1974	3	7

(Chart positions according to *Billboard;* asterisk [*]: Record Industry Association of America certified Gold Record/Million Seller)

Billy, George, Jerry, Jack, and Ravi at the White House (Wide World Photos)

THE ACT YOU'VE KNOWN FOR ALL THESE YEARS

The story of the Golden Temple: A guy fell in love with it and burned it down. He couldn't stand the idea of its falling apart as it got older, and now the Golden Temple exists in perfect form forever. It became a myth. . . .

That's why the Beatles will stay a beautiful myth, because they ended before they deteriorated.
—Yoko Ono

By 1974 there was no getting around it: the Sixties were over. Nixon and Vietnam were out of the picture; the widespread commitment to political change on the part of American and British youth had all but evaporated. Such countercultural trappings as long hair, marijuana, and rock music were increasingly being accepted into the mainstream of society, in the process losing much of their symbolic importance. Meanwhile, we children of the Sixties were growing up: ourselves scrambling for a comfortable spot in the material world, some of us were doing just those things that had seemed anathema only five years earlier—raising families, working 9-to-5, making money.

And for all their occasional solo triumphs, John, Paul, George, and Ringo no longer appeared to mirror the times as they had once done when they were the Beatles.

But this did not mean that interest in the Beatles was about to fade away. Quite the contrary: the Beatles' mystique, filtered through the rosy perspective of nostalgia, seemed to grow increasingly potent with the passing years. The very fact that the group didn't exist any more only made the Beatles' mythical status all the more secure. Unlike so many other Sixties bands, the Beatles hadn't let their fans watch them disintegrate into parodies of their former glory. John, Paul, George, and Ringo might, on their own, stumble, but the last time anyone glimpsed *the Beatles* they were still all under 30, and at the height of their influence and creative powers. And barring a reunion, that's how the Beatles would always be immortalized in the imaginations of their fans.

No doubt there were a few who did grow out of their obsession with the Beatles, but their ranks were amply replenished by newer converts, many of whom were barely old enough to crawl when the Fab Four first appeared on the Ed Sullivan Show. Deprived by the absence of any comparable buzz on the Seventies rock scene, large numbers of teen-agers began to tune into the Beatle legend. Around 1974, yet another wave of Beatlemania started to sweep the world: this one a cult, for the most part, of memories.

The trappings of Sixties nostalgia in general, and retrospective Beatlemania in particular, began to resemble those of science-fiction "fandom." They included conventions, "fanzines" (small amateur publications, usually mimeographed or offset), and—above all—collectors.

Mass nostalgia always seems to be accompanied by a widespread obsession with collecting things, tangible pieces of the past. Beatle memorabilia, which had never before inspired much systematic collecting, was suddenly in tremendous demand.

The merchandise that Paul McCartney had once dismissed as "junk," and which most of us had in the meantime thrown away or inadvertently lost, had almost without warning metamorphosed into coveted collector's items. The Beatle dolls, wigs, and paint-by-numbers kits were finding their way into flea markets—even antique shops—all over the U.S. And selling briskly at five, 10, sometimes 15 times their original retail value. A plastic guitar could be yours for $75, a Flip Your Wig game for $20, a lunchbox for $15, and a yellow submarine Corgi Toy for $25.

The prices of out-of-print Beatle records levitated even more dramatically. These included such rarities as the picture-sleeve singles; those early, and mostly exploitative, non-Capitol releases; conversation pieces like a V-J Records pressing of "Please Please Me" by "the Beattles" *(sic);* and, most prized of all, the notorious *Yesterday and Today* butcher cover. As I write this, "Yesterday" in its original cover is changing hands for $8, "Ticket To Ride" for $15, "Love Me Do" for $30, "Please Please Me" for $60, and "Cold Turkey" for up to $100. *The Beatles Vs. the Four Seasons* brings $45, and *The Beatles Christmas Album, Jolly What!,* and *The Amazing Beatles* in the neighborhood of $25 apiece.

Latter-day Beatle souvenirs—mostly T-shirts, posters, and lapel buttons—also began to glut the market. These were of negligible interest to serious collectors, who were primarily concerned with genuine relics of the past. They faced a tougher challenge discerning the counterfeit record jackets and memorabilia with which shrewd rip-off artists were beginning to infiltrate the rock marketplace.

Beatle fans and collectors were able to keep in touch with each other—and with the latest news and gossip on their heroes—through the grapevine provided by the dozens of fanzines launched in the mid-Seventies by dedicated Beatle people. Many of these adopted the titles of Beatle records: *Strawberry Fields Forever, Across the Universe, Paper-*

Hundreds of fans take in a lecture at a New York Beatle convention (John Jacobson)

Beatles "Fanzines" of the mid-1970's

back *Writer, The Inner Light, With a Little Help From My Friends, Yesterday and Today, Get Back.* Others included *Maclen, The Write Thing, Beatles Digest, Survey* and *The New Beatles Fan Club,* plus fanzines devoted to individual Beatles, such as *The Harrison Alliance, McCartney Ltd.,* and *Our Starr.* Holland had *Beatles Unlimited,* Germany *The Beatles News Book,* and France *The Fab Four Publication.*

Most of the fanzines interspersed original writing with reproductions of Beatle clippings, some current and others dog-eared treasures from old Beatle scrapbooks. In addition, they usually offered Beatle quizzes, crossword puzzles, and several pages of collectors' ads. Fanzines edited by male Beatlemaniacs were likely to focus on facts and figures; *The Inner Light,* for instance, featured, in installments, an alphabetical list of every Beatle and ex-Beatle song ever, complete with running times and the serial numbers of all the records each selection had appeared on.

Female-run fanzines, by contrast, tended to be concerned more with personalities than with arcane trivia: the following sample is from a Wings concert review in *With a Little Help From My Friends:*

Oogling once more thru that huge telephoto at such a short distance from the stage was a killer. Good God, those eyes! A real professional torturer, that McCartney. We were so wrapped up in oogling Paul that again it's hard to recall concert details.

One of the earliest and most authoritative fanzines, *Strawberry Fields Forever,* has pursued a happy medium of these two approaches to Beatlemania. It was founded in late 1972 by Joe Pope, a 25-year-old Bostonian. At loose ends after having graduated from the University of Massachusetts, Joe decided to pass the time "trying to combine the two things I'm good at—writing and the Beatles." At first *S.F.F.* was little more than a hobby: "I figured if I could get the circulation up to 28, I'd break even."

However, like almost everyone else, Joe had little inkling of how many fans still thirsted after every conceivable drop of information on the Fab Four, or of the proportions that the Beatle revival was about to assume. By 1976 his fanzine would boast 3,000 subscribers, and letters would pour in at a rate of 25 or more a day.

In 1974, Joe decided to throw a Beatle party featuring Boston's Tasty Legs, one of the dozens of new groups that specialized in sounding uncannily like John, Paul, George, and Ringo. So many people wanted to attend that the location was shifted to the ballroom of a large downtown hotel, and Beatle films and flea markets were added to the program, which took place over the weekend of July 26, 1974. Almost inadvertently, Joe had launched a new trend: the Beatle convention.

In New York, Mark Lapidos was already preparing an "authorized" celebration for that fall. Both Pope's *Mystery Tour* and Lapidos' *Beatlefest* were so successful that they turned into annual events, with the latter going on the road in 1976, bringing resurgent Beatlemania to half a dozen cities across the U.S. Meanwhile other Beatle conventions had begun to crop up across North America, and in Britain, Holland, and France, In 1976, a mini-convention was held even in Cracow, Poland.

170

The usual ingredients of a Beatle convention included marathon Beatle flea markets; Beatle trivia quizzes, look-a-like contests, and auctions; performances by Beatle sound-alike groups (who were likely to sport grey collarless suits for the early numbers and full *Sgt. Pepper* regalia for the later); lectures by such one-time or would-be Fifth Beatles as promoter Sid Bernstein, disk jockey Murray the K, original manager Allan Williams, and the Beatles' jolly green giant of an assistant Mal Evans, who in late 1975 would become a casualty of trigger-happy Los Angeles cops; and, along with the United Artists movies, seldom-seen flicks like *Around the Beatles, The Beatles At Shea Stadium, Tokyo '66, Magical Mystery Tour,* and the promotional film clips the Beatles made for some of their later singles and solo efforts. Rarely have any movies been shown to such lively audiences as these. The 10-year-old celluloid image of Paul McCartney would often send the girls squealing and screaming as though they were in Shea Stadium all over again; and when Linda or Yoko would appear on the screen, the room was likely to be swept by boos and hisses.

But for many fans the main attraction of the conventions was the opportunity to come in contact with fellow Beatle people. Never before had this been made possible on so large a scale; the closest thing used to be pen-pal ads in publications like *Beatles Monthly* (Beatle concerts themselves hardly offered the ideal ambience for socializing). The conventions created, for the first time, a real sense of community among hard-core Beatlemaniacs. ("No marriages yet," reports Joe Pope. "But people have met roommates, best friends, boyfriends, and girlfriends at the conventions.")

No Beatle convention is complete without rumors trumpeting the impending arrival of John, Paul, George, and/or Ringo. (Joe Pope offered the Beatles a rare "Ticket To Ride" picture sleeve and all the beer they could drink as an inducement to appear at his *Mystery Tour.*) While John Lennon did dispatch his secretary and sometime paramour May Pang to a New York *Beatlefest* to snap up items for his own personal memorabilia collection, such speculation has always proven unfounded.

Even in the Beatles' physical absence, their spirit has sufficed to lure Beatlemaniacs from considerable distances, particularly to Joe Pope's Boston convention, generally recognized as the definitive gathering of the faithful. "Each year you see the same faces from California, Texas, Illinois. . . ." Joe says. "People like Mark from Virginia, he's only thirteen, but he knows every label, serial number, everything."

It was not long before the revival spread beyond the inner circles of Beatle "fandom." Printing presses, as well as mimeograph machines, began rolling again on behalf of the Fab Four. As *Publisher's Weekly* would note: "The Beatles are back. Receding into history as a functioning unit, they are coming to the fore as the subject for reminiscence and research."

For the first time in five years, Beatle fan magazines began popping up on newsstands across the U.S. (In sharp contrast to the fanzines that had preceded them, however, the new magazines betrayed little real familiarity with their subject—other than that the Fab Four were big bucks again.) Beat Publications decided to reprint early issues of the *Beatles Monthly,* complete with addenda on the boys' latest activities. And books about the Beatles started to appear more regularly than at any time since 1968.

Beatle nostalgia also penetrated the world of stage and screen. In London, *John, Paul, George, Ringo . . . and Bert,* a play by Liverpool schoolmaster Willy Russell about the Beatles and an imaginary Merseyside chum, opened on

August 15, 1974. The play scored good reviews and a long, successful run; but Harrison, the only Beatle to see the show, found the experience of seeing his life re-enacted on stage so painfully uncanny that he left during intermission. (George had previously withdrawn permission for Barbara Dickson to sing "Here Comes the Sun" in the show; its place was taken by "Good Day Sunshine".)

In New York, Robert Stigwood (once an Epstein protégé and now a powerful promoter with his own record label) launched a big-production musical titled *Sgt. Pepper's Lonely Hearts Club Band On the Road.* Although we had all been led to believe that John Lennon might be less likely to succumb to sentimentality than Paul McCartney, it was John who gave the extravaganza his blessings. He not only turned up at the November 14, 1974 premiere, but even agreed to attend a press conference promoting the show, and to be photographed holding a placard reading "Sgt. Pepper's Way" over the street sign outside the Beacon Theatre. McCartney, by contrast, unsuccessfully sued to have the show stopped.

Jules Fisher's multi-media musical *Beatlemania,* starring a sound-alike, look-alike quartet, hit Broadway on May 26, 1977. By that time, work on a film version of Stigwood's *Sgt. Pepper* was in full swing, with Peter Frampton in the lead role.

Surely the most bizarre of these efforts was Russ Regan's 1976 film *All This and World War II,* which incongruously juxtaposes Second World War clips, both historical and Hollywood, with 30 Lennon-McCartney classics. Regan at first wanted to use original Beatle recordings, but then it occurred to him that a brand-new soundtrack album might prove even more lucrative an asset than the film itself—as indeed it would.

So he teamed up with Lou Reizner, the perpetrator of 1972's highly successful (commercially, anyway) London Symphony-orchestrated version of the Who's *Tommy,* on which Ringo Starr had sung the part of wicked Uncle Ernie.

Beatles "Fanzines" of the mid-1970's

Beatles "Fanzine" of the mid-1970's

(Courtesy, Mark Lapidos) Artist: Karni Karikoryan

The all-star *Tommy* formula was applied to the *World War II* music; and, while a few imaginative stylists like Bryan Ferry, Keith Moon, and Rod Stewart manage to emerge undamaged from the morass of strings, the rest of the score succeeds in making Lennon-McCartney's greatest songs sound, at best, like the Beatles' rendition of "Good Night."

Many of the couplings on the soundtrack—e.g., Frankie Vallie singing "A Day In the Life"—are every bit as peculiar as the visual dimension *World War II* gives them. Connoisseurs, both of the war and of the Beatles, found *All This* about as tasteful as a mustard and apple jelly sandwich. A reviewer for New York's *Daily News* summed up the general consensus when he wrote that the film's P.G. rating had to have stood for Positively Ghastly.

For many Beatlemaniacs, seeing the Beatles reunited in old filmstrips at nostalgic conventions, or on a West End or Broadway stage, played by look-alike actors, was not enough. A lot of people fondly imagined that the spirit of the Sixties might be resurrected if only John, Paul, George, and Ringo came together again in the flesh.

A number of high-powered entrepreneurs attempted to make names for themselves by offering them fantastic inducements to do just that. The most persistent of these was Bill Sargent, who started off in 1974 with a $15 million dollar bid for just one Beatle concert. By 1976 his offer had swelled to $60 million. Sargent figured on recouping his investment by having the event simultaneously broadcast over closed-circuit T.V. to dozens of arenas around the world. For the privilege of watching their heroes on television at, say, Madison Square Garden, Beatlemaniacs would be charged around $25 apiece. (Sargent also unsuccessfully attempted to stage, on a similar basis, a fight-to-the-death between a man and a killer shark.)

Although Ringo went on record in favor of a reunion ("I'm for it and would join the others in a minute," he revealed in Germany's *Bravo* magazine), both he and Paul expressed distaste for Sargent's schemes. All the Beatles apparently had enough integrity to resist the temptation to rip their fans off in that manner. Any reunion, vowed McCartney, "would only be for the love of it. It would never be for the money. . . . I mean that was never what the Beatles was about and I hope it never would be."

So Alan Amron, a 28-year-old Long Island toy manufacturer, tried a different tactic. Forming Let It Be, a "people's committee to reunite the Beatles," Amron placed newspaper and radio ads requesting that everyone who wanted the Beatles together again mail him a dollar. An impressive grass-roots response, he argued, would provide not only a financial inducement for the Beatles to get back to where they once belonged, but also a conclusive demonstration that "the people" wanted it that way. So many dollar bills wafted into Amron's mailbox that he was able to take on the prestigious public relations services of Solters and Roskin, uncoincidentally the same New York firm patronized by Paul McCartney himself. But the fact that Paul fired Solters and Roskin after hearing about their new client did not appear to augur well for Let It Be.

Over the summer of 1976 Sid Bernstein, the promoter who had first brought the Fab Four to Carnegie Hall and then Shea Stadium, joined the swelling ranks of would-be Beatles matchmakers. In full-page ads in the *New York Times* and other newspapers, Bernstein attempted to combine financial incentives even more astronomical than Sargent's with philanthropic ones. While declining to offer any advance royalties, Bernstein insisted that his blueprint for a single Beatle concert could net the Fab Four no less than $230 million (this startling figure included $100 million for a projected live double album, $75 million for movie and television rights, and $15 million for merchandising tie-ins).

Bernstein suggested that each fan attending the closed-circuit simulcasts be required to bring a can of food or article of clothing in order to change a Third World country of the Beatles' choice "overnight to a nation of hope and light." In addition, he recommended that the Beatles themselves pledge to donate 20 per cent of their $230 million toward "feeding and educating the orphan children of the needy nations." Unlike some of the Beatles' other latter-day pursuers, Sid Bernstein was a genuine fan and meant his plan sincerely. But the tone of his appeal backfired. Complained George Harrison: "It was cute the way the ad in the *Times* tried to put the responsibility for saving the world on our shoulders."

In any case, not everyone was convinced that a reunion would be such a terrific idea. To live up to people's fantastic expectations, any new Beatle album or show would have to be almost unbelievably brilliant. Otherwise, it might only destroy much of the myth that had snowballed in the Beatles' absence. And judging from the extremely disparate nature of the individual Beatles' recent music and lyrics, it might prove difficult for the four even to find any common artistic ground to begin with.

As their former producer George Martin told *Rolling Stone:* "I think it would be a terrible mistake for them ever to go into the studio together. . . . Whenever you try to recapture something that existed before, you're walking on dangerous ground, like when you go back to a place that you loved as a child and you find that it's been rebuilt. It destroys your illusions. . . . If the four men came back together, it wouldn't be the Beatles."

Harrison himself seemed to agree, telling the same publication: "The Beatles were other people a long time

John flanked by Alice Cooper and May Pang at the opening night party for the cast of the *Sgt. Pepper* stage show (Vinnie Zuffante)

ago. They're for the history books, like the year 1492." But McCartney, while hedging his bets on the actual chances for a reunion, insisted that *should* it happen, it would be great. "I don't really think it would be a letdown. You've got to re-member it's only a hypothetical question, but . . . it would only happen because we really wanted to. . . . In that case, if we were really serious about it, I think it would be very good. I don't agree that . . . we could never make it work again."

And, as superfan Joe Pope put it: "They always used to surprise us in the past with each new thing they did. They could do it again." In the meantime, we Beatle addicts were obliged to console ourselves doing one—or both—of two things. We could immerse ourselves further in a nostalgic legend. Or follow the ups and downs of the continuing solo adventures of John, Paul, George, and Ringo.

After John Lennon moved to Los Angeles, he embarked on a six-month spree of partying and dissipation. Though he wrote only one song in that whole period, he inspired a great deal of sensational copy with his drunken escapades. The Walrus, by all accounts, was in sorry shape. The most noto-rious stories appeared in March 1974 after John heckled a Smothers Brothers performance at the Troubadour Club and struck a waitress before being forcibly shown the door. Lennon and drinking companion Harry Nilsson subse-quently sent flowers and apologies and resolved to divert their energies from the bottle to a Lennon-produced Nilsson L.P. called *Pussycats.*

Over the summer John returned to New York, where, in a week's outpouring of creativity, he wrote 10 new songs that synthesized the confused and painful emotions he had experienced on what he would later call his "Sindbad's voyage" to California. An L.P. was recorded as quickly as it had been written; amazingly, considering how Lennon had pretty much conjured it out of thin air in a fortnight, the album proved to be John's most diverse, insightful—and commercial—in years.

Because most of the record's lyrics explore the barriers separating himself from others, while also frequently expressing the hope that these might somehow be overcome, John chose the title *Walls and Bridges*. "Walls," said Lennon, "keep you in either protectively or otherwise, and bridges get you somewhere else." In its searing emotional intensity, *Walls and Bridges* resembles John's first post-Beatle album, while the richly textured arrangements and melodic diversity recall *Imagine*. But *Walls and Bridges* also features an ingredient that those earlier confessionals conspicuously lacked: vintage Lennon humor, which can go a long way toward alleviating the potential heaviness of John's subject matter.

A renewed determination to find a few laughs even in the face of adversity illuminates every aspect of *Walls and Bridges* from the inclusion of a brief, good-natured duet between Lennon and his 11-year-old son—along with a booklet of paintings John himself did when he was that age—to the interchangeable silly faces on the record jacket. The credits include a half dozen playful pseudonyms ranging from Rev. Thumbs Ghurkin (piano) to John's favorite, Dr. Winston O'Boogie (electric guitar); and Lennon's Dylanesque acoustic strumming on "Nobody Loves You When You're Down and Out" is credited to Dwarf McDougal—Dwarf being Dylan's music company and McDougal the name of his Greenwich Village street.

Walls and Bridges' lusher, more languid songs bring to mind similarly reflective Beatle "classics" like "Strawberry Fields Forever." The most popular of these proved to be "Number Nine Dream," easily the most poignant melody Lennon had written since *Imagine*.

John and Yoko once considered nine their lucky number and had often cited it in their work. In "Number Nine Dream" Lennon looks wistfully back at their relationship, which though at the time it "seemed so very real," has now passed into nostalgia as an elusive, magical dream.

On this recording John draws upon the sort of dream-world effects he had used in his late-Sixties Beatle music: gauze-like orchestrations, tapes of voices whispering "John, John" that are reversed toward the end of the song, passages written in an imaginary language (unlike those on "Sun King," however, these reportedly came to Lennon in an actual dream). The words John sings in English are as exquisite as the melody:

On a river of sound,
through the mirror go round, round,
I thought I could feel
music touching my soul,
something warm, sudden cold,
the spirit dance was unfolding. . . .

Another *Walls and Bridges* track, "Bless You," is also dedicated to Yoko:

Bless you,
wherever you are,
windswept child on a shooting star.
Restless spirits depart,
still we're deep in each other's hearts.

On this song, however, the music is most un-Beatle-like, featuring the sort of jazzy diminished-seventh chord progressions Paul had recently dallied with on "Bluebird."

In "Steel and Glass" John paints a considerably less charitable portrait of another "old friend of mine"—a slimy New York wheeler-dealer generally assumed to be Allen

Klein. The melody and the tough, ominous string arrangement are almost identical to those of "How Do You Sleep?" The message of "Steel and Glass" is no less scathing than its predecessor's:

Your phone don't ring, no one answers your call,
how does it feel to be off the wall?
Your mouthpiece squawks as he spreads your lies. . . .
you leave your smell like an alley cat.

Walls and Bridges frequently explores a theme rare in the forever-young world of rock 'n' roll: fear of aging and death. "Nobody loves you when you're old and grey" sings the ravaged ex-Beatle. "Everybody loves you when you're six foot in the ground." A hounded self-portrait called "Scared" is prefaced with an actual recording of howling killer wolves.

Yet the aging process also seems to have brought John a more tolerant and philosophical perspective. Instead of "preaching practices," as had once been his wont, the only advice he doles out now is this:

Whatever gets you thru the night,
'salright, 'salright. . . .
Whatever gets you to the light,
'salright, 'salright.

This good-natured and highly danceable track, which preceded *Walls and Bridges* as a single, features Elton John on piano, organ, and vocal harmonies. Lennon returned the favor by singing and playing guitar on Elton's remake of "Lucy In the Sky With Diamonds." During these sessions, Elton made Lennon promise to put in a guest appearance at his forthcoming New York concert should "Whatever Gets You Thru the Night" reach Number One. "Not thinking in a million years" that it could—none of his earlier solo singles had—John readily agreed.

But "Whatever Gets You Thru the Night" did indeed make it all the way to the top of the charts, as would Elton's "Lucy" shortly thereafter; and John Lennon kept his word. On November 28 he joined Elton on stage at Madison Square Garden to sing both songs. For an encore Lennon announced: "We thought we'd do a number by an old estranged fiancé of mine called Paul," and launched into a rousing version of "I Saw Her Standing There." (The live recording was subsequently released on the B-side of Elton's "Philadelphia Freedom.")

A few weeks later John helped another Seventies superstar record one of his Sixties classics. This time it was David Bowie covering "Across the Universe" for his new *Young Americans* L.P. While working in the studio, Lennon and Bowie whipped off a new collaboration called "Fame," which would eventually earn Bowie *his* first American Number One. Said Bowie of Lennon: "He's the last great original."

Suddenly everything seemed to be coming together again for John Lennon, commercially, artistically, and in his personal life. By early 1975, the only thing John would still lack would be that coveted Green Card assuring him the right to live in America.

He had succeeded in electrifying a live audience for the first time in two and a half years, in the process making the gesture of singing a McCartney song, as if to demonstrate that their spat was now a thing of the past. He had scored his first non-Beatle Number One single (oddly enough, the last of the Fab Four to do so), and produced an L.P. that was a success at every conceivable level (honorary critic Ringo Starr only slightly exaggerated the sentiments of many reviewers when he proclaimed *Walls and Bridges* "the best album of the last five years").

In February, John would quietly move back into the apartment he shared with Yoko in Central Park West's gothic

L.P., 1975 (Apple)

Dakota building. (The second *Walls and Bridges* single, John's nostalgic reminiscence of his love affair with Yoko, "Number Nine Dream," would peak at Number Nine on the *Billboard* charts that very week.) The Lennons' first public reappearance together would be to host the Grammy Awards along with David Bowie and a briefly reunited Simon and Garfunkel (best-engineered L.P.: McCartney's *Band On the Run*). To reporters noting that he and Yoko were back together, John would say merely: "the separation didn't work out."

By the mid-Seventies it had become a common practice for rock stars normally reliant on their own material to indulge their nostalgia with an album of old favorites. Bryan Ferry's *These Foolish Things,* David Bowie's *Pin Ups,* and the Band's *Moondog Matinée* were just three such excursions into musical autobiography. The first ex-Beatle to succumb to this trend was John Lennon, who within weeks after finishing *Mind Games* had begun working with Phil Spector on an album provisionally called *Oldies But Moldies.* (Lennon had come to California, in fact, largely because Spector was living there at the time.) Just as his fans were beginning to pine for the music of the Sixties, John was ready to take a sentimental journey back to the previous decade. In that famous *Rolling Stone* interview, John, when asked about his current listening tastes, had replied: "Wop bop a loo bop. I like rock 'n' roll, man, I don't like much else . . . maybe I'm like our parents, you know, that's my period. . . ."

Lennon had optimistically supposed that an oldies project would merely entail his lying back and having a good time, singing those songs with which he (both with and since the Beatles) had always loosened up before putting down original material; only now, for the first time since 1965, his interpretations of his favorite oldies would be preserved for commercial release. Spector, for his part, would get to produce the album in his own patented style without the usual artistic interference from John, almost as if he were recording one of his early Sixties protégés. However, the affair proved to be far more of a headache than Lennon had imagined.

After the sessions, the mercurial Spector disappeared with the tapes, leaving behind only a trail of false rumors of purported car crashes and terminal illnesses; one of the reasons Lennon stayed on in California was that he was de-

termined to track down both Phil and the tapes. When John, months later, finally succeeded, he found the mad genius alive and relatively well—but the coveted tapes were quite another story. On John's oldie recordings, Phil's genius seemed to have been quite eclipsed by his madness. The famous thirty-piece rock 'n' roll orchestra had been recorded playing woefully out of tune, and the result sounded like a disastrous mess.

Only four of the cuts seemed salvageable, so Lennon rallied the musicians who had just worked on *Walls and Bridges,* and in October 1974 taped self-produced versions of ten more moldy oldies. The L.P.'s title was changed to *Rock 'n' Roll.*

Nearly all the songs had been featured in the Beatles' repertoire at the Cavern and the Star Club, back when they were still wearing greasy hair and leather outfits. For *Rock 'n' Roll's* jacket, John picked one of the legendary Beatle portraits Hamburg photographer Jurgen Vollmer had made in 1961. Depending on which review you read, the L.P. was either a pointless self-indulgence that added little to the originals—or a raw and spirited re-exploration of the music that had ignited the genius of John Lennon in the first place.

Thanks partly to the gritty saxes, *Rock 'n' Roll* undeniably sounded far more authentically "Fifties" than anything the Beatles had attempted with similar material. But while some of the songs stayed scrupulously faithful to the original arrangements, others—particularly the four Spector productions—are extremely idiosyncratic.

One of the former was Buddy Holly's "Peggy Sue," for which the publishing credit read "McCartney Music." On a recent nostalgic binge of his own, Paul had bought up his idol's songwriting catalog—thereby personally owning the tunes that may well have been responsible for the Beatles' greatest original influence.* (In 1976 Paul would arrange the British re-release of several Buddy Holly records; produce an L.P. of Holly songs performed by co-Wing Denny Laine; and kick off "Buddy Holly Month" with a party at which Holly's manager, Norman Petty, would ceremoniously present him with the cuff links Buddy had been wearing at the time of his fatal 1959 plane crash.)

Two *Rock 'n' Roll* songs that bore little resemblance to the originals were Chuck Berry's "You Can't Catch Me" and "Sweet Little Sixteen," the latter of which is drastically slowed down, and dressed up with an eery, most un-Berry-like horn arrangement. John had agreed to record these in 1972, in an out-of-court settlement with Morris Levy, Berry's publisher, who had sued him for plagiarizing "You Can't Catch Me" in the Beatles' "Come Together."

According to Levy, however, his verbal agreement with Lennon had also included permission to release the oldies L.P. on his own Adam VIII label. In February of 1975 Levy conjured an album called *Roots* out of a rough 7½ ips tape Lennon had given him, and hawked it as a mail-order item on T.V.

Capitol/E.M.I. countered by rushing out *Rock 'n' Roll* ahead of schedule, and each side promptly sued the other (with Levy demanding $42 million damages). This time John Lennon surprised almost everyone in the business by refusing to compromise. Despite the prospect of wasting a great deal of time, money, and energy in a tedious legal battle, Lennon decided to take the occasion to stand up to that breed of music industry sharks who thrive on harassing rock artists and tampering with their work, secure in the knowledge that most stars would rather buy them off than fight them off. Writing songs like "Steel and Glass," Lennon felt, wasn't enough.

*More recently McCartney, increasingly the show-biz tycoon, has snapped up publishing rights to such hit musicals as A Chorus Line, Shenandoah, and Annie.

L.P., USA, 1975 (Adam VIII)

Single, Holland, 1974 (Apple)

His gesture paid off: in April 1976, after months of deliberation, Lennon was awarded $45,000 to compensate for the damage *Roots* might have inflicted on his reputation.

Despite the fact that *Roots'* sound quality has all the presence of a cardboard box, the record soon became a collectors' item on account of two Spectorized tunes—"Be My Baby" and "Angel Baby"—that were left off the official version. (*Rock 'n' Roll* also spawned another rarity: after one single from the album, "Stand By Me" [backed by an unreleased Lennon composition called "Move Over Ms. L."] scored a minor hit for John, a few copies of a second, Little Richard's "Slippin' and Slidin'" coupled with Fats Domino's "Ain't That a Shame" [Apple 1883], were issued and sent out to America's disk jockeys. But none made it as far as the record stores.)

Squeezed in between all his other projects, John found the time to write and help record the entertaining, if unremarkable, title song for Ringo Starr's late 1974 album, *Goodnight Vienna* (that's a Liverpool expression meaning, roughly, "let's get out of here"). Partly because he was anxious to prove himself a recording artist in his own right, Ringo made no particular effort to enlist Paul and George on the L.P. Instead he relied on such friends as Elton John and Harry Nilsson.

Unfortunately, the superstar chemistry and Richard Perry's glib production don't jell quite so well this time around. Ringo's own compositions are painfully dull; and, while a remake of the Platters' 20-year-old hit "Only You" and Hoyt Axton's coyly risque "No No Song" did both reach the American Top Ten as singles, neither makes one feel as if he's listening to Ringo Starr. They could have been anyone.

Throughout his solo recording career, Ringo has been pursued by the dilemma of how to entrust his very special persona to competent, commercially-oriented producers without losing himself in the mix. Surrounded by the right people, under the right circumstances, he has shown himself capable of producing an "It Don't Come Easy" or a *Ringo.* Otherwise, oh, well. . . .

The papers had announced over the previous summer that George Harrison was making plans to tour again. Unlike Paul, George was not going to bother with testing his riffs

on Swiss and Finnish audiences. Instead, he had decided to plunge head-first into a full-scale four-million-dollar tour of the United States.

It was initially reported that Ringo and Eric Clapton were planning to help George attempt to recreate the magic of the Bangla Desh concerts in Every City, U.S.A. But—perhaps on account of the three superstars' entangled personal affairs—this was not to be. (Well-placed gossips were leaking word that not only had Patti Harrison moved in with Clapton, but the Liverpool mystic himself had indulged in a fling with Ringo's wife, Maureen, whom Starr subsequently divorced.)

So by the time specific details on George's grueling 27-city, 50-concert tour had coalesced, his band's line-up turned out instead to comprise Billy Preston on keyboards, Tom Scott (the one musician who has played on all four Beatles' solo records) on sax and flute, and a faceless quintet of crack session musicians. Because Harrison wished to take the opportunity to expose an unusually large captive audience to Indian music, Ravi Shankar's orchestra of 15 distinguished musicians received equal billing. The first U.S. tour by an ex-Beatle took place in November and December, and, like Harrison's historic 1971 concerts in New York, many of the shows were benefits for charitable causes.

Immediately prior to the tour, the normally reticent Harrison ("I'm a musician, not a talker," he insisted) presided over a chaotic Los Angeles press conference. He had a number of important announcements to make concerning the tour; the record company he had just founded, Dark Horse; and his own forthcoming album and single, both also to be titled *Dark Horse,* even though George was still contractually obliged to release his own records on the E.M.I.-distributed Apple label. (Starr would follow George's Dark Horse with a custom label of his own called Ring O' Records.) Predictably, most of the reporters were more interested in steering the topic of conversation toward the Beatles.

George offered some unsentimental views on the subject, and on reunion prospects: "I realize the Beatles did fill a space in the Sixties and all the people the Beatles mean anything to have grown up. It's like anything: if you grow up with something you get attached to it. . . . I can understand that the Beatles did nice things, and it's appreciated that people still like them. The problem comes when they want to live in the past. . . .

"It's all a fantasy, the idea of putting the Beatles back together again. If we ever do that, the reason will be that we are all broke. . . . The Beatles was like being in a box, we got to that point. . . . Since I made *All Things Must Pass,* it's just so nice for me to play with other musicians."

A lady from "the women's pages" finally changed the subject, asking George what he liked to have his wife cook for him. Confirming speculation that his marriage—like all the Beatles' save Paul's—was on the rocks, George answered: "I don't have a wife anymore . . . I learned to cook myself. I cook vegetarian Indian food, that's why I'm so pale and thin." He went on to say that he was "very happy about" his wife's liaison with Clapton.

"Seriously? How can you be happy about it?" gaped the lady.

"Because he's great. I'd rather have her with him than with some dope." George himself had a new love, Dark Horse secretary Olivia Arias, whose dusky Mexican features would, in best Paul-and-Linda style, grace the label of George's new album. (As for Clapton, his most popular song, "Layla," turned out to have been an ode to Patti Harrison.)*

* The Harrisons were finally divorced in May 1977; George married Olivia on August 31, 1978, a month after the birth of their son Dhani.

George and guitar gently smile at Madison Square Garden (Michele Garval)

George was also asked if he had "any anxieties as the tour approaches."

"The main one is that I've lost my voice," he revealed nonchalantly. This would prove an ominous omen for a tour and album that afficionados would come to know as *Dark Hoarse.*

It was George's turn anyway, to be inflicted with the poison-pen treatment that the critics had earlier accorded Paul and John. Knocking idols off their pedestals makes for excellent copy.

Like the *Magical Mystery Tour* film, that first Beatle venture to be viciously panned, George's concerts and L.P. were by no means horrendous enough to warrant all the abuse they got. But then again, despite the first-class musicianship of everyone concerned, they were undeniably ill-starred, and something of a letdown even for many of George's most loyal followers.

November, December 1974: Songs Performed on George Harrison's North American Tour

Hari's On Tour Express
The Lord Loves the One
For You Blue
Something
Sue Me, Sue You Blues
Maya Love
Sound Stage of My Mind
Dark Horse
Give Me Love
In My Life
While My Guitar Gently Weeps
What Is Life
My Sweet Lord

(Concerts also included selections featuring Billy Preston, Tom Scott, and Shankar Family and Friends.)

Splinter's Bill Elliott and Bobby Purvis with P. Roducer
(Dark Horse Records)

Single, Italy, 1974 (Apple)

Though George had always been considered more of a guitarist than a singer, the fact that his voice was utterly shot didn't help matters any. Neither did his unwillingness to acknowledge that his having once been a Beatle had something to do with half a million people shelling out up to $10 to see and hear him play. That George was not about to get wrapped up in Sixties nostalgia proved to be a source of considerable friction between the star and his followers.

At first Harrison thought he could get away without performing any Beatle tunes, and it reportedly required a paternal talk from Ravi before George would change his mind. As it turned out, however, Harrison's ventures into the time machine resulted only in his perversely tampering with his—and his listeners'—past. Arrangements were altered almost beyond recognition, and lyrics revised—even John Lennon's. "In my life, I love *God* more," George rasped on one of his rocky rides down memory lane. The number that he was wont to introduce sourly as "a song you hear in every elevator in the world—still have to do it" was inexplicably changed to "something in the way she moves *it*." Another selection was apparently now titled "While My Guitar Gently *Smiles*."

The throngs responded less than ecstatically to the show's mélange of mangled Harrisongs, watered down curry, and supersession jam. Reviewers delighted in reporting—with dubious accuracy—that the cosmically minded star was continually upstaged by Preston's ostentatious song-and-dance routine. *The New York Times* called the show "boring"; and even the "hip" magazines, such as *Fusion,* arrived at the consensus that "the man has totally lost his voice and his feel for rock 'n' roll."

In a *Rolling Stone* cover story (titled "Lumbering in the material world") George attempted to defend his position by saying: "Gandhi says create and preserve the image of your choice. The image of my choice is not Beatle George. If they want that, they can go see Wings. Why live in the past? Be here now, and now, whether you like me or not, this is where I am." And he later told *Melody Maker:* "I like to be successful and popular, but there comes a point where it's unhealthy that people think you're something that you're not—and the next thing is that fans put you out on a trip, and limit what you may be in their eyes."

Though that dig at Paul was unfair (Wings had thus far declined to perform any old Beatle songs at all) some fans did make the effort to get into George's current bag. *Strawberry Fields'* Joe Pope was deluged with letters protesting the nasty reviews. "It was so great to finally see George . . .," wrote one girl. "Simply the most fantastic experience of my life." Nonetheless, George's mood turned increasingly sour as the tour progressed. Kids who floated into the arenas feeling like Lucy In the Sky were startled to hear their hero lecturing them about smoking "dirty reefers" and warning, "you won't find Lord Krishna in a bottle."

The troupe's spirits were further dampened when Ravi Shankar suffered a mild heart attack mid-tour and had to skip some shows. Despite the fact that Shankar had attempted to make his ragas more accessible by offering abbreviated, orchestrated popularizations—on some of which George strummed an acoustic guitar—his sets were often greeted with indifference and, occasionally, jeers. This was a source of great irritation for Harrison, who at one point jabbed a finger at his own cherry Gibson and declared: "I'd die for Indian music, but not for this."

The tour was extensively recorded and filmed. But the album was never released, nor the projected movie projected. Reunion speculation was fanned when all four Beatles were spotted at New York's Hotel Plaza, where George was staying. Despite the rumor-mongers, however, no other Beatle performed at any of George's concerts, though both Lennon and a heavily disguised McCartney did show up in the audience.

One celebrity who did enjoy the concert was Jack Ford, who invited George to drop by his dad's place when the troupe played Washington. George turned up with Ravi and Billy, declared that he sensed "good vibes" in the White House, and wound up swapping pleasantries and lapel buttons with President Ford. In exchange for an anti-inflation "WIN" button, the Beatle presented the President with one bearing the Sanskrit legend "OM."

According to George, having cancelled all his newspaper subscriptions, he rarely saw or cared what they printed about him. This was just as well, because they would only have brought him more grief after his *Dark Horse* L.P. hit the stands. The critics almost unanimously sniped—and with some justification—at what they deemed a shoddy performance and a preachy, humorless message. On *Dark Horse,* the exquisite, painstaking arrangements of George's earlier albums are completely missing.

The L.P.'s nadir is a ghastly rendition of the Everly Brothers' "Bye Bye Love," featuring, of all people, Harrison's estranged wife on back-up vocals and Eric Clapton on guitar. In "Ding Dong" Harrison tries, like Lennon before him, to capture the holiday spirit in a song, but instead serves up a string of greeting-card clichés, with trite music to match.

Occasionally his characteristically tasteful guitar playing does manage to rise above the gutted vocals and relatively weak material (some of which George had previously bestowed on artists like Ron Wood and Alvin Lee). An instrumental called "Hari's On Tour" boasts some mean licks, and the interplay of George's three overdubbed guitars on "So Sad" make for some delectable listening. "Dark Horse" itself might have been one of Harrison's most successful songs had he only waited to recoup his voice before committing it to tape. But, apparently the businessman in George won out over the perfectionist; *Dark Horse* had to be let loose in time to cash in on the tour and the Christmas season.

While waiting in the stands of the sports arena for Harrison's show to begin, some of us took note of the exquisite music wafting from the P.A. It sounded, in fact, like a gorgeous fantasy of what George's new album *should* have sounded like. The opulent production, the jangling guitars, even the silky vocal harmonies, reminded one of the glories of *All Things Must Pass* far more than did George's current *Dark Horse* L.P.

As it turned out, the production and guitars were Harrison's, but the voices belonged to Splinter, a pair of singer/songwriters featuring Bob Purvis and the Bill Elliott who had once supplied the lead vocal for John Lennon's "God Save Us" *Oz* benefit single. Splinter's *The Place I Love* was one of the two initial releases on George's Dark Horse label, the other being *Shankar Family And Friends*. Harrison turned in a characteristically meticulous production on his new protégés' record, of precisely the sort, oddly enough, that seemed so disappointingly lacking on his own L.P. Much of the flawless instrumental work on *The Place I Love* is Harrison's own. Sometimes George is responsible for as many as eight overdubbed parts, as the instrumental credits for one song indicate:

Acoustic bass: Klaus Voormann
Drums: Jim Keltner
Six and twelve string guitars/Dobro: Hari Georgeson
Harmonium/Jew's Harp: P. Roducer
Percussion: Jai Raj Harrisein

(Voormann and Keltner were, of course, the ex-Beatles' favorite Paul-and/or-Ringo stand-ins. But the other three names are all typical Harrison pseudonyms. George, like John and Paul, had by this time accumulated quite a collection.)

At the same time George was pouring his best creative energies into Splinter, Paul McCartney was undertaking a similar labor of love for his brother Mike McGear. Because Mike wished to be judged, as much as possible, on the basis of his own talents and not as "Beatle Paul's brother," he had changed his last name at the height of Beatlemania from McCartney to McGear. He then went on to achieve with his own satirically oriented group, Scaffold, a number of British Top Ten hits—among them "Lily the Pink" and "Thank U Very Much," a musical thank-you-note to Paul for the gift of a camera. In 1974, the two brothers finally decided to stage a musical family reunion with a Warner Brothers album called *McGear*.

Nine of the L.P.'s 10 tunes are Paul originals, with McGear, McCartney, and Roger McGough (a member of Scaffold and Liverpool poet of some renown) sharing the lyrical honors. Vocal and instrumental backing are provided by Wings, including prospective member Jimmy McCulloch. Paul also produces this L.P. It is often difficult to gauge precisely which of the two brothers' similar-sounding voices is singing which part; with Linda's ooh's and aah's also thrown into the mix, *McGear* frequently sounds like nothing so much as a very good Wings album.

To give McGear his due, however, his own unique sense of humor is also very much in evidence. And his album,

more than those released under Paul's name, reflects a keen awareness of what had been happening on the British rock scene since the Beatles' split. "Giving Grease a Ride" spoofs such T. Rex hits as "Jeepster," and the one non-McCartney tune, "Sea Breezes," covers a song off the first album by Roxy Music, then Britain's most inventive up-and-coming band. But inexplicably, despite excellent reviews, *McGear* only sold about 12 copies. (Splinter's L.P. at least managed to reach Number 81 in the U.S.)

Jimmy McCulloch's performance on *McGear* was apparently enough to secure him a steady job as Wings' lead guitarist. Though still only 21, the young Scot was no stranger to the pop scene. Back in 1967, Jimmy's musician-

Signing autographs during the intermission of *Equus*, New York, late 1974 (Vinnie Zuffante)

Single, Italy, 1974 (Apple)

ship had impressed the Who's Pete Townshend enough for Pete to team up his then 14-year-old whiz kid discovery with singer/drummer Speedy Keene and a 250-pound postman-turned-pianist named Andy Newman. The improbable trio went on to score a British Number One with the Townshend-produced "Something In the Air."

When Thunderclap disintegrated, McCulloch drifted through sundry bands and into Stone the Crows, where he caught McCartney's eye and ear as being an ideal candidate for Wings. "We didn't want to ask if he'd join us then, 'cause it's a bit mean, really, splitting up another group if they're doing well," said Paul. "But then that group fell apart when Maggie Bell went solo."

Jimmy's first single with Wings, "Junior's Farm," appeared in October 1974. Reminiscent of the Beatles' "Get Back," it offered some of the most uncompromising rock 'n' roll McCartney had dished out in years. From the heavily metallic riffs McCulloch contributed to the record, it was evident that he would be the ideal person to further bring out this side of McCartney's multi-faceted musical personality in future Wings endeavors.

In an unusual reversal, the follow-up hit to the million-selling "Junior's Farm" turned out to be its own B-side, "Sally G," which began climbing the American charts in early 1975. Both sides of the single were recorded on a working vacation Wings had spent in Nashville the previous June, and in "Sally G" Paul perfectly captures the musical ambience of that city. The song was so convincing it even managed to crack the country-and-western charts, something no long-haired rock artist had ever before accomplished. Trust Paul, with his uncanny ability to master any style of song he might set his mind to, to put one over even on the rednecks.

While in Nashville, Paul also endeavored to boost the musical career of yet another close relative. This time it was his dad, Jim McCartney, who had composed a quaint instrumental called "Walking In the Park With Eloise." Recording under the pseudonym of "the Country Hams," Wings, augmented with a brass band, turned out an E.M.I. single of the elder Mr. McCartney's ditty. The flip side was Paul's own "Bridge Over the River Suite."

Still another McCartney project that summer was writing and producing a schmaltzy tune for Peggy Lee, titled "Let's Love."

Perhaps because he had kept himself so preoccupied with writing and producing other people's records, Paul Mc-

(Vinnie Zuffante)

Cartney didn't manage to complete a Wings album in Nashville. Having fallen into the habit of making each new batch of recordings in a different city, Paul arrived in New Orleans to finish his L.P. during February's Mardi Gras celebrations. (He even wrote and recorded for the occasion an unreleased song called "My Carnival.")

In New Orleans, Paul also found Wings a third drummer, New York-born Joe English. With the personnel of his trans-Atlantic crew in a constant state of flux, Paul's insistence that Wings were an honest-to-goodness *group* had always seemed a wee bit preposterous. But the new line-up—Paul and Linda McCartney, Denny Laine, Jimmy McCulloch, and Joe English—would prove the first to stay intact much longer than a year.

The album, *Venus and Mars,* confirmed, if nothing else, that Paul had totally mastered the craft of turning out hit "product." Many of the songs are the sort that stubbornly stick in the head whether you want them there or not, and the production is McCartney's most polished since the break with the other Beatles and George Martin. And yet there is often something calculated and impersonal in its slickness.

The title track itself, which boasts a typically seductive McCartney melody, proved that Paul *could* still write lyrics when he saw fit to. "Venus and Mars" cleverly makes use of the various connotations of the word "stars." The setting of the version that opens the L.P. is a sports arena, abuzz with anticipation just before a rock show. In the lyric about the "good friend following the stars," the friend could just as easily be a groupie or a rock fanatic as an astrologer; and the stars might even be Venus (Linda) and Mars (Paul) McCartney.

Sure enough, the track segues—or, rather, explodes—into "Rock Show," as spirited a celebration as any on record of the excitement, crowds, noise, and lights at a big rock concert. (Paul admitted that the references to Madison Square Garden and the Hollywood Bowl were a "hint" of Wings' own future plans.)

Yet when "Venus and Mars" resurfaces on Side Two—in the grand old *Sgt. Pepper/ Ram/ Band On the Run* tradition—"following the stars" takes on a different context. The sports arena has metamorphosed into an Isaac Asimov-inspired starship, fueled by Linda McCartney's gurgling synthesizer. Had Paul chosen to extend the "Venus and Mars"/"Rock Show" idea throughout the rest of the L.P., he might have produced an ambitious and fascinating concept album. In any case, he at least now had a great framework for a "Rock Show" of his own, which he would shortly put to use.

If *Venus and Mars'* other selections struck many fans and most critics as being a bit slick and lyrically vacuous, they are nonetheless quite diverse musically, ranging from heavy metal to '30's nostalgia to a musical interpretation ("Magneto and Titanium Man") of the Marvel Comics Paul had taken to reading. Like *Abbey Road* and John's *Walls and Bridges, Venus and Mars* trails off with a joke. The last "real" song, "Lonely Old People," is followed by a brief rendition of "Crossroads," the theme music to a soap opera then in favor with Britain's senior citizens.

Augmented by the jangling guitars and trilling woodwinds of guest artists Dave Mason and Tom Scott, the ultra-catchy "Listen To What the Man Said" quickly scored Wings their eighth consecutive American Top Ten hit (and third Number One). This single, and the album from which it was lifted, were the first McCartney records to sport the familiar Capitol logo since the Beatles' "Lady Madonna." Paul had just signed on again for the record-shattering sum of eight million dollars.

(Capitol Records)

September 1975: Songs Performed on Paul McCartney and Wings' British Tour

Venus and Mars
Rock Show
Jet
Let Me Roll It
Spirits Of Ancient Egypt (Denny Laine)
Little Woman Love/C Moon (medley)
Maybe I'm Amazed
Lady Madonna
Long and Winding Road
Live and Let Die
Picasso's Last Words
Richard Corey (Denny Laine)
Bluebird
I've Just Seen a Face
Blackbird
Yesterday
You Gave Me the Answer
Magneto and Titanium Man
Go Now (Denny Laine)
Call Me Back Again
My Love
Listen To What the Man Said
Letting Go
Junior's Farm
Medicine Jar (Jimmy McCulloch)
Band On the Run
Hi, Hi, Hi
Soily

Single, France, 1974 (Apple)

(Capitol Records)

were almost immeasurably better than those Paul had presented two years earlier.

The runaway international success of *Band On the Run* and then *Venus and Mars* had brought McCartney renewed confidence, as well as a far more impressive reservoir of new material; and the current Wings line-up was considerably more accomplished than the band's previous incarnations. In addition, McCartney, having kept a close eye on performers like Elton John and David Bowie, had put together a dazzling array of visual effects to accompany the music.

Britain, then Australia, then Europe—each in turn succumbed to Wings' onslaught. (Japanese dates had to be cancelled at the last minute when officials heard about McCartney's pot busts and banned him from the land of the rising sun.) It began to look as though Paul might finally work up the nerve to bring his show all the way to America.

Paul McCartney's abandonment of the record label that he, more than anyone, had been responsible for in the first place only emphasized the fact that Apple had all but rotted away. By 1975 all Apple releases, excepting only the Beatles' and most of their solo efforts, had been deleted. The stately building on Savile Row had been abandoned in favor of a modest three-room office across the street. The Apple scruffs had all gone home.

With pointed symbolism, the label of George Harrison's final Apple L.P. reveals an eaten-away core. Yet most people found this logo to be as apt a reflection of the current state of George's music as of the record company itself. George had seemed the mysterious Beatle, not only on account of his mystical beliefs but also because he had always been kept in the shadow of Lennon and McCartney. When his own star emerged with *All Things Must Pass,* Harrison dazzled the world by surprise. Yet every subsequent album seemed slightly inferior to the one before, each diminishing George's magnitude by a few more degrees. Only now that he was his own front man, as he discovered on tour, there were no longer any luminaries for him to hide behind when he wasn't particularly switched on.

Nonetheless, George was apparently determined to make a speedy comeback after the previous winter's fiascos. *Extra Texture* was written and recorded far more quickly than any of his earlier L.P.'s—despite the fact that Harrison is more like McCartney than Lennon in that he seems to work best slowly and methodically. On *Extra Texture,* George's voice still sounds shot, if no longer hoarse, and even his disciples tended to find the music plodding and aimless. Harrison's worldly critics, who had long found his sermons insufferable, responded like bulls to a red flag to *Extra Texture,* which contains a number of treatises on how reviewers always "miss the point." (One of these, "This Guitar Can't Keep From Crying," is also a somewhat limp sequel to "While My Guitar Gently Weeps.")

True, the critics had been unfair, even vicious. But one could only hope George would rise above them, and produce a work good enough to fake them all out. Which is exactly what he would do a year later with *Thirty-Three and a Third.*

In the autumn of 1975, Apple released its two final albums. *Shaved Fish* compiled Lennon's first 11 solo singles, and *Blast From Your Past* Ringo's first eight, augmented by "I'm the Greatest" and "Early 1970," an old B-side. Despite the fact that many of these tunes had never appeared on L.P.'s before, neither collection of greatest-hits-and-flops sold especially well. Apparently the public's craving for recycled Beatles hadn't extended to the solo work.

Shaved Fish is enhanced by its cover's illustrations of

Single, Holland, 1975 (Apple) Paul and Linda with drummer # 2, Geoff Britton (left); Jimmy and Denny

Paul lost little time in rehearsing a new act based around *Venus and Mars.* Soon word was out that Wings were also including not only material from *Band On the Run,* but even a group of songs originally made famous by you-know-who. Sure enough, when Wings hit the road in Britain in September 1975, McCartney electrified his audiences with renditions of "Lady Madonna," "The Long and Winding Road," "I've Just Seen a Face," "Yesterday," and the symbolically appropriate "Blackbird." "They're great tunes. . . ." Paul later allowed. "So I just decided in the end, this isn't such a big deal, I'll do them."

He insisted that the five had been picked pretty much "at random" from the Beatle songbook, saying "I didn't want to get too precious about it." Other numbers Wings tried out for size but dropped included "Let It Be," "The Fool On the Hill," and "Hey Jude," the latter of which was to have closed the show. But, said Paul, "it just didn't feel right."

Paul's faithfully rendered versions of five Beatle songs would in themselves have assured an ecstatic reception for Wings' new shows. Yet at every other level the concerts each selection. Together with the music, these create an evocative document of all the phases John had gone through over the past six years: pacifist, primal screamer, leafleteer, dreamer. "Power To the People" is represented by a scroll bearing the hopeful legend:

We the people of the United States in order to further advance the causes of international artistry and human understanding do ordain one John Lennon with a most prized and coveted "Green Card". . . .

Sure enough, on October 7, 1975, even before *Shaved Fish* had reached the shops, the United States Court of Appeals overturned the order to deport John Lennon, thereby bringing his debilitating three-year-long quest to a happy end. "It's great to be legal again," John beamed as he displayed his Green Card to the reporters and celebrities who filled the courtroom.

Two days later—on Lennon's 35th birthday—Yoko gave him an even longer-awaited present: their first baby, Sean Ono Lennon.

After years of rumors of Paul's imminent arrival, it was officially proclaimed in early 1976 that Wings were indeed touring the U.S. in April and May. Then Paul's beloved father died; on the pretext that Jimmy McCulloch had broken his pinkie, the tour was postponed another month.

An album, *At the Speed of Sound,* preceded Wings' arrival by a few weeks. It was simpler and less varied than the previous two, and for the first time, perhaps to make Wings seem more like a real *group,* Paul delegated nearly half the songs to the other members. Linda got a chance to

George Harrison at New York's Bottom Line, 1975 (Jackie Meyer)

contribute a treatise on the joys of cooking—her place, she wailed, was in the kitchen, though she appeared equally at home on stage with Paul—and Jimmy got to harp on his pet theme: the ups and downs of a "pill freak" (one obviously close to his heart, as "Medicine Jar," his contribution to *Venus and Mars,* had almost identical lyrics). Most fans would have much preferred to hear more of Paul instead, but even most of his numbers sounded like pleasant throwaways.

Nonetheless, *At the Speed of Sound* zoomed to Number One in America, and "went platinum" shortly thereafter, thanks largely to Paul's presence on these shores (which also sent half of his old catalog sailing back up the charts). And to the inclusion of the shamelessly commercial smash hit "Silly Love Songs," with which, warbled Paul, "some people want to fill the world . . . ," and "what's wrong with that?"—a manifesto that many critics assumed was directed at themselves.

Some people also wanted to know why Paul was belatedly trailing after trends—in this case watered-down disco—instead of setting them. An explanation for that, and for why Paul is content to churn out silly love songs, may be that he apparently shed his "I vaguely mind anyone knowing anything I don't know" attitude around the time he shed John, George, and Ringo.

(Jackie Meyer)

John with a heavily pregnant Yoko a few weeks before the birthday (Vinnie Zuffante)

L.P., 1975 (Apple)

Paul had lost none of his musical ability, only his intellectual and artistic ambition. During the *Sgt. Pepper* era, for instance, Paul was wont to curl up with a "great novel"; now he'd much sooner relax with a cheap sci-fi paperback or a comic book. Similarly, he had become a lot less earnest about his work and no longer felt his songs need be particularly "important."

Paul had apparently come to derive more contentment from the cozy family life than he ever had with all the groupies, psychedelics, experiments, and "changes" that had characterized his earlier days. And by 1976 he seemed equally comfortable with the niche he had earned for himself on the music scene—that of manufacturing light-weight pop sufficiently commercial to outsell almost anyone else in the business, including the other ex-Beatles. He alone of the Fab Four appeared to have found a whole new younger audience for his recent work.

Unlike other artists such as John Lennon, Paul seemed to feel little need to say anything new, let alone to exorcize any devils. Maybe he didn't even see himself as an "artist" any more, in the lofty sense of the word. But he had come to do an extremely competent job within the limitations he had chosen for himself.

When tickets went on sale for Paul McCartney's May 24 and 25 concerts at Madison Square Garden—over a month before the shows and to almost no advance word—the scene at the box office was instant, and total, pandemonium. Dozens of fans lost their shoes in the scramble, and within three hours all seats were sold out excepting those available from scalpers for up to $100 or more a pair.

When McCartney and pals took their places on stage, bathed in moody blues and greens, twenty thousand people leapt to their feet, cheering wildly. "Venus and Mars" was all but inaudible in the ecstasy of the moment, as a thousand bubbles tumbled over Wings and smoke engulfed them from behind. "Venus" segued into "Rock Show," and when Paul belted the line "long hair at Madison Square," the crowd roared again. After all the scorn of the early Seventies, it must have been a sweet triumph for Paul, whose face showed up that week in over four million households on a Peter Max-designed *Time* magazine cover. Wings had certainly come a long way from the rinkydink band that had shown up at the University of Nottingham with a repertoire of four songs.

It had been ten years since America's McCartney buffs had last seen their hero on stage. Paul had been holding off on his U.S. "comeback" until he had one of the most stunning extravaganzas in the business under his wings, any kinks ironed out by eight months of intensive touring in Britain, Australia, and Europe. Wings Over America was no Dark Horse, no half-baked super-jam. Yet, unlike Dylan's recent appearance on the same stage, Paul's performance in no way attempted to revive the intensity and import of the Sixties rock scene. If there was a flaw, it was that the presentation seemed just a touch too pre-programmed, too well-oiled, too slick. McCartney was playing the consummate showman, and his show was pure flash entertainment with a touch of class: rock cabaret at its finest.

Paul may have lost interest in writing the Great Works he had shown himself capable of in the past, but his voice was never in finer form than at the Garden those two nights. It is one of the great instruments in rock, certainly among the most versatile. For over two hours it ran the gamut from crooning to belting, always soaring back to notes most rock singers don't know exist, hardly ever faltering, or veering off key. Paul also displayed his all-round talent as an instrumentalist, alternating between his bass, piano, organ, and acoustic guitar, and handling each with great taste and flair.

Paul wows 'em at the Garden (Michele Garval)

(Michele Garval)

Much of the show featured McCartney's brand of hard-rock candy, but many sweets of a gooier sort were offered as well. The variety in the music and theatrical effects kept the pace snappy.

In the Thirties-ish "You Gave Me the Answer" ("dedicated to Gene Kelly and Fred Astaire—and Lenny Bruce") the base of Paul's piano razzle-dazzled with flashing pink and yellow lights; "Live and Let Die" was enlivened by a lethal array of laser beams and blinding mushroom clouds. That, "Maybe I'm Amazed," and, of course, the five Beatle tunes, each brought the entire arena back onto its collective feet.

Indeed, the excitement let up only during the occasional vocal showcases of Denny Laine and Jimmy McCulloch,* who do an admirable job at backing Paul, but as singers and songwriters hopelessly lack the class and distinction of the star of the show. Throughout, Linda hovered behind banks of keyboard as though they were the kitchen sink (to cop a phrase from Richard Goldstein). Content to noodle away at simple embellishments and add her oohs and aahs to the vocal mix, Linda sang no solos, hogged little of the spotlight, and offended almost nobody.

Still, no one was about to coin the word "Wingsmania." The throngs were all here for one reason, to see and hear one individual. In fact, the most moving segment occurred while the rest of Wings were off for a backstage beer, as

---

*This incarnation of Wings finally disintegrated in September 1977, when McCulloch was asked to leave the group on account of "musical differences" with McCartney and, reportedly, excessive personal habits. English's subsequent departure was attributed to homesickness for American T.V. and drive-in movies.

Paul huddled in a chair with his Ovation acoustic, crooning "Blackbird" and "Yesterday," in the latter case augmented by plaintive woodwinds. When McCartney sang "I believe in yesterday," the spell drew almost everyone in the hushed crowd into that nostalgic never-never-land where yesterdays live on as memories that, like vintage wine, only seem to grow increasingly intoxicating with each passing year.

Paul's shows were as much of a success with the critics as with the fans. *Strawberry Fields Forever's* Joe Pope sifted through several hundred reviews mailed in by correspondents from all over North America, and found only two that were downright negative. Others that were a shade less than 100 percent favorable seemed only to suggest that Paul could have been more artistically ambitious, that he had the potential to pull off something even more brilliant. Ironically, one critic to express these sentiments was Richard Goldstein, who nine years before had been the lone voice to denounce *Sgt. Pepper* as pretentious. Wrote Goldstein (the *Village Voice*): "He could have produced daring film scores and astounding musical revues. He could have been a young Kurt Weill, a contender. Instead, he settled for being a star."

Even with America conquered, McCartney was not about to rest his wings. After only a few weeks' break he brought his extravaganza back to Europe, where he staged a magnanimous and unusual gesture: a performance in Venice's St. Mark's Square that raised over $50,000 to help restore that sinking city's crumbling treasures.

Once the tour arrived home in England, McCartney devoted his days to preparing a *Wings Over America* live L.P. in time for Christmas, while in the evenings he'd still sing it with band. Carried away by the ecstatic response he'd received from both audiences and critics, Paul decided to make the album a triple-record set containing every single number in the current Wings repertoire. As recordings had been made of all the American concerts, McCartney had little trouble finding a satisfactory rendition of each song.

Naturally Paul's American tour was attended by much speculation about "guest appearances"; but though John and George were both in New York at the time of the Wings concerts, neither bothered even to watch the show, let alone appear in it. Ringo did join Paul on stage in Los Angeles, but in a strictly non-musical capacity, and only long enough to bestow a floral bouquet and a bearhug on his ex-colleague.

Nonetheless, Paul was throughout the tour plagued more than ever by questions about reunions. In anticipation of this he had prepared a repertoire of demurrals as varied and extensive as the Wings concert program. Favorites included "you can't reheat a soufflé"; "it's about as likely as a divorced couple getting the hots for each other again"; and even a special bit of doggerel drawled Muhammad Ali style:

The Beatles broke up in '69
since then everything's been fine
and if that question doesn't cease
ain't nobody gonna get no peace.

But by this time the folks at E.M.I. had come up with a great idea. Since the Beatles didn't seem too eager to get back together—and if they did, it might well not be for the benefit of E.M.I., which had managed to lure only Paul into renewing his contract—why not put out "new" Beatle records anyway, by re-releasing and repackaging what Capitol Vice President Dan Davis gleefully called "the most valuable catalogue in the history of the recording industry."

Accordingly, all 22 of the Beatles' singles were re-released in Britain in February, complete with snappy new picture sleeves, along with "Yesterday," which had previously only been a *Help!* L.P. track there. The results startled even E.M.I. A million Beatle singles were sold in a

Wings glide in gondola before Venice concert, September 1976 (UPI)

month; "Yesterday" and "Hey Jude" were major hits; and all 23 records made the British top hundred. The label lost little time in adding a 24th title, "Back In the U.S.S.R." (by including "Twist and Shout" on the flip side, E.M.I. broke with a 15-year tradition: never before had a British Beatle single contained anything other than original compositions).

Meanwhile, attractively repackaged Beatle 45's were also resurfacing in countries like Italy and France—and to a similar response.

In the United States, Capitol launched its Beatle revival in May with the relatively obscure, but commercially potent, "Got To Get You Into My Life." Radio stations latched on as though it were an honest-to-goodness-brand-new-Beatle-hit, insuring a place in the Top Ten for a song that had been recorded ten years before. In fact, "Got To . . ." wound up staying on the charts as long as any of the Beatles' original singles had, with the sole exception of "Hey Jude."

Yet it was "Helter Skelter" that had originally been earmarked for the A-side. A few months earlier, renditions of that tune and others from the White Album had been featured in *Helter Skelter,* a T.V. dramatization of the Manson murders, based on the Bugliosi best-seller. The show was so popular that *The Beatles* became a hit all over again, and Capitol rushed radio stations a special new single of the title theme. But then it dawned on someone that exploiting Charlie Manson might not be the classiest way to begin a Beatle revival, so "Helter Skelter" was relegated to the B-side of "Got To Get You Into My Life."

Both tunes popped up on the "new" double album, *Rock 'n' Roll Music,* which scored a gold record on the day of its

release—an unprecedented achievement for a package whose contents were mostly 12 and 13 years old, and were being released for the third, fourth, fifth . . . even eighth time. The Beatles, defunct for over six years, were once again outselling everyone else, a testament both to the durability of their music and to the Seventies' inability to produce a remotely comparable phenomenon.

Sales weren't harmed by the million dollars Capitol injected into its Beatle revival. Beatle albums were hawked on T.V., continuous Beatle filmstrips shown in select record stores, and a hundred miles' worth of clothesline sent out so that dealers might dangle Beatle L.P. covers from the ceiling.

What with all this extravagance and hoopla, one might have expected something a bit more sensitive and less shoddy than *Rock 'n' Roll Music.* One of the few things in its favor is that George Martin remixed the earlier material, boosting the volume of the instruments to give the music a meatier, more powerful sound. And the album did include the elusive "I'm Down."

Otherwise, Capitol blew an opportunity to collect some of the greatest rock 'n' roll ever into one thoughtful compilation of "the fun side of the Beatles." Not only does the package repeat tunes from the two previous anthologies—while passing up such archetypal Beatle rockers as "She's a Woman"—but the information given concerning the original sources of the cuts is often inaccurate or misleading. Worse yet, the tacky silver-foil jacket features such distinctly un-Beatle-ish artifacts as a cheeseburger and a portrait of Marilyn Monroe.

Single, Britain, 1976 (Parlophone)

Single, Britain, 1976 (Apple)

Single, France, 1976 (Apple)

L.P., USA, 1976 (Capitol)

Single, France, 1976 (Odeon)

It was Ringo Starr, of all people, who launched a one-man campaign to let the world know that the Beatles were not amused. "All of us looked at the cover of *Rock 'n' Roll Music* and we could hardly bear to see it," he fumed in *Melody Maker.* "You'd think we'd get a hand in the way we're recycled." And he told *Rolling Stone:* "The cover was disgusting. . . . It made us look cheap and we never were cheap. All that Coca-Cola and cars with big fins was the Fifties."

"John even offered to do a cover," Ringo revealed. "But they refused. I mean, John has more imagination than all those people at Capitol put together." Imagination may not have been one of their top priorities, but had they done it right, the folks at Capitol might have raked in even more millions than they did.

Unsurprisingly, "Got To Get You Into My Life" and *Rock 'n' Roll Music* proved to be only the beginning of something that is likely to continue as long as there are people around to buy Beatle records. In November 1976, Capitol cooked up another Beatle single—"Obladi-Oblada"/"Julia", whose sleeves featured individually stamped numbers à la White Album—and a half-baked anthology of George Harrison favorites.

When control of the Apple catalog passed to Capitol and E.M.I. with the expiration of the Beatles' contract in early 1976, an interesting experiment had become possible: Beatle and post-Beatle music might now be mingled on one record. George Harrison was the obvious guinea pig, the post-breakup work of John and Ringo having already been boiled down into greatest hits L.P.'s. (Paul, the one Beatle to renew his contract, wasn't about to be dissected without his permission.)

For their Harrison anthology Capitol decided to plump for the obvious and take no risks. Perhaps on account of the lackluster commercial fate of Lennon's *Shaved Fish* and Starr's *Blast From Your Past,* a more straightforward title was selected: *The Best Of George Harrison.*

Though its U.S. jacket depicts George's gaunt features superimposed over a cosmic display of novae and galaxies, the record itself neglects Harrison's musical attempts to embrace the cosmic in favor of his more conventional work. The sitar, his trademark for years, is nowhere to be found, nor (aside from the studio version of "Bangla Desh") is there any sop to collectors in the form of uncollected singles. The main criterion for the selections apparently was whether they had previously appeared on two, three, or four Beatle

or Harrison releases.

Harrison promptly disavowed the package, adding that Capitol had ignored his own suggestions as to title and song format. But *The Best Of George Harrison* does confirm that George's big production numbers from *All Things Must Pass* more than hold their own alongside the seven featured Beatle tunes (even if some of his subsequent output doesn't). And the album is undeniably better looking than *Rock 'n' Roll Music.*

For their next Beatle project, Capitol and E.M.I. dusted off old tapes of the Beatles live at the Hollywood Bowl in 1964 and 1965, accompanied by 17,000 shrieking nymphets, which George Martin himself remixed as "a labor of love" and boiled down to one L.P. Each of the two concerts had originally been intended for commercial release, but the Beatles themselves were less than thrilled with their sloppy performances, and refused to let them out.

However, 12, 13 years later, the music itself was no longer the point. *The Beatles At the Hollywood Bowl* was now a slice of history, a fascinating reminder that, among other things, John, Paul, George and Ringo were once the most powerful catalysts for adolescent mass-hysteria the world had ever known. (In any case, the record had, in the intervening years, leaked out to bootleggers; so for Capitol to present it to us in new improved full-dimensional stereo was a nice idea.)

Still more fascinating to Beatle people—if even cruder musically—was another more vintage live album that appeared in April 1977, *The Beatles Live At The Hamburg Star Club 1962,* documenting a time in the Beatles' career that few of us had been a party to, but that millions of fans had fantasized about. The double L.P. materialized out of a recording Liverpool singer King Size Taylor had made in 1962 of John, Paul, George, and Ringo on stage at Hamburg's Star Club. Originally recorded for a lark, the tape was subsequently lost, and not rediscovered until 1972. Original Beatles manager Allan Williams found it, he writes in his memoirs, "by a million-to-one chance" in a deserted Merseyside office "beneath a pile of rubble on the floor."

Williams immediately launched a campaign to have the tape released, but even once legal obstacles had been cleared, a larger one remained: the tape had been recorded with a single microphone at 3¾ ips on a Grundig home tape

L.P., Europe, 1976 (Parlophone)

John Lennon live in Hamburg, 1961 (Apple Records) Photo by Jurgen Vollmer

Single, Italy, 1976 (Parlophone)

recorder; and the verdict of almost everyone who heard it, including the Beatles, was that the sound quality was absolutely hopeless.

But when you're dealing with a property as hot as this one, miracles can be made possible. Lingasong Records, which had obtained rights to the tape, decided to invest some $100,000 (as much as it had cost the Beatles to record *Sgt. Pepper,* their most extravagant work) in the most ambitious "reconstruction" job in the history of the recording industry. The monaural tape was painstakingly converted into a 16-track master recording.

Producer Larry Grossberg, *Billboard* reported,

separated the track-by-track information using Burwen, dbx, and Dolby noise suppressors, UREI compressors and limiters, Orban Farasound and API sibillance controllers, API equalizers, Kepex noise gates, Audio Design spectrum analyzer, and an Orban stereo synthesizer.

A special group of new Ashley parametric equalizers capable of suppressing frequencies of .05 of an octave was extremely valuable in recouping practically all the rhythm tracks and bringing out substantial lead voices and background vocals when they were apparently drowned out by general extraneous sounds. . . .

Despite the performers' own objections, aired in court too late to have any effect, the Beatles' nightclub performance came as a fascinating counterpoint to the sounds of Beatlemania at the Hollywood Bowl.

The two authentic Beatle albums were joined in the charts by a pretender, *Klaatu.* Steve Smith of the *Providence Journal* sparked a minor hoax of the Paul Is Dead variety when he reviewed this album in January; pointing out that no musical credits were given except Klaatu, that there were no photographs of the group, and that the music was unmistakeably Beatlesque, Smith concluded that the mysterious Capitol album might be a secret reunion of

Ever wonder where the Beatles sound-alike group "Klaatu" got its name?

Ringo growing his hair back, 1976 (Atlantic Records)

the Fab Four. He cited various clues, cross-references to Beatle records such as *Magical Mystery Tour,* in support of his thesis.

These may exist, as Klaatu, whoever they were, had obviously set out to imitate the Beatles' late Sixties music; as far as that goes, they did an exemplary job. But it ain't the Beatles, as anyone truly familiar with their voices could tell you after three seconds of close listening. Anyway, lyrically, the Beatles would never have served up such extra-terrestrial pap as "Anus Of Uranus" and "Calling Occupants Of Interplanetary Craft."

Nonetheless, Capitol kept dealers well supplied with copies of Smith's article, while keeping Klaatu's identity a corporate secret.*

Other labels also did what they could to bag a piece of the Beatle vinyl revival. 20th Century Records' all-star symphonic soundtrack to *All This and World War II* arrived for Christmas 1976 in a lavishly boxed two-record set, complete with a garish book of Lennon-McCartney lyrics illustrated with pictures of wounded soldiers, leering dictators, and—in the case of "The End"—an atomic explosion. The heavy promotional campaign that accompanied the album proved to be in as questionable taste as the music and film themselves. One ad depicted Adolf Hitler listening to the album through a pair of headphones.

*It has since been revealed that Klaatu consists of Canadian studio musicians.

In Britain, Polydor issued *The Beatles Tapes,* a double album of interviews *London Evening News* reporter David Wigg had conducted with John, Paul, George, and Ringo between 1968 and 1973. Before the discs had even left the factory, George and Ringo sued to have the package taken off the market, contending that it might be misconstrued as a Beatle album, and that the recordings did not represent their current views on life. The bewigged magistrate, however, ruled these objections "ridiculous," and *The Beatles Tapes* reached the shops intact. That, as it turned out, proved to be most fortunate for the fans: the L.P.'s are a fascinating document, unlike most earlier Beatletalk albums.

All the Beatles are in top form for Wigg's interviews, and hearing them offers a considerably more revealing and intimate picture than just reading them. The transition from "Give Peace a Chance" to "Power To the People" takes on a new dimension when you hear the humorous, soft-spoken, and naive quality of John's 1969 interview switch abruptly to tones of impatience and anger in the segment recorded two years later. Paul turns on the charm as always, and optimistically considers the Beatles' future . . . just days before announcing his resignation from the group. While, in considerably thicker Liverpudlian, George cites Hindu proverbs with a disarming humor and sincerity that don't always survive the transition to the printed page. And the self-effacing Starr comes across as perhaps the most engaging of the lot.

Ringo: "I'm the laziest Beatle. I can enjoy myself just sitting back and playing around with all the toys." (1968)

George: "All I'm doing is acting out the part of Beatle George. We're all acting out our own parts. The world is a stage and the people are the players, Shakespeare said that and he's right. . . . Even if it's being a Beatle for the rest of me life, it's only a temporary thing." (1969)

George (asked whether the Beatles could break up): "To spiritually . . . split is impossible, 'cause if you're listening, I'm the Walrus too." (1969)

John (asked how he would like to be remembered): "As a great peacenik." (1969)

Ringo (asked how he would like to be reincarnated): "As one of our cats. They have a great time." (1973)

At first glance, *Ringo's Rotogravure,* which appeared on Atlantic in America and on Polydor elsewhere, also seemed an attempt to tap past glories. The jacket depicts the ex-door to Apple Records scrawled with the Beatle graffiti of pilgrims from across the universe, and the plastic itself contains original tunes by each of the ex-Beatles. Though John, Paul, and George contributed some inspired work to 1973's *Ringo,* this time around their songs sound more like throwaways. John's bubbly potboiler "Cookin'," and Paul's somewhat gooier "Pure Gold" are forgettably pleasant. However, George's "I'll Still Love You" (originally bequeathed to Cilla Black in 1972, but returned unused) comes across, with its bloated production and trite lyrics, almost as a Harrison parody—right down to ex-Apple artiste Lon von Eaton's fluid imitation of George's guitar style. (Harrison, unlike Lennon and McCartney, couldn't make it to the actual recording sessions.) It is hard to avoid thinking that, if the Beatles all sound this weak on *Rotogravure*—the closest thing to a reunion since 1973—they might be better off letting fond memories be by leaving the creation of new Beatle product to the recycling plant at the Capitol Tower.

(Dark Horse)

Ringo's own writing, at least, seems to have improved. "Cryin' " both recalls, and stands up to, the songs Nashville's seasoned pros had dished up for *Beaucoups of Blues.* "Las Brisas," co-written with Starr's new fiancée Nancy Andrews, uses a Mariachi band (dragged out of a Mexican restaurant) to create a sound still unusual in rock circles. But the surprises end there.

While discussing *Rotogravure* in *Phonograph,* Ringo put his current musical philosophy this way: "I go in to make a record as commercial as I can. I'm not there to tell stories. I want to make as many hit singles as I can, and a hit album. I like being popular."

If Paul were as candid as Ringo, he might have said the same thing. But when McCartney cranks out commercial pap, he at least calls his own shots, while the less self-sufficient Starr casts his fate to the dials of the slick old pros. For *Rotogravure,* Ringo taps the production talents of Arif Mardin, a paunchy veteran who's been producing hits since before your mother was born, almost. (To his credit, Mardin also once named an L.P. of his own after Lennon's "Glass Onion.")

Throughout Ringo's bland album, the alleged Starr winds up sounding more like a mere cog in Mr. Mardin's hit factory. And though one wouldn't have thought a Beatle would need to rely on anonymous hacks for new material, that's just what Ringo does here. One such song, "A Dose of Rock 'n' Roll," was even picked for the single. Artists who sell out like this should at least compensate for their lapse in taste by *selling.* Yet neither "A Dose Of Rock 'n' Roll" nor *Ringo's Rotogravure* so much as dented the Top Twenty.

Ringo made a lot more waves with his new Kojak look. After recording *Rotogravure,* he emerged utterly bald from his hairdresser's in Monte Carlo, his new refuge from England's high taxes and damp weather. Resembling an egg far more than a Beatle, Starr explained: "It was a hot day."

In some ways 1976 was not one of George Harrison's luckier years. It seemed to begin under all the right signs: with a blaze of publicity surrounding his pact with his own A & M-distributed Dark Horse label, accompanied by word of a new L.P., *Thirty-three and a Third,* slated to appear by June 25, George's 33⅓ birthday. Talk of an American tour was in the air.

But these projects had to be scrapped when George was laid low with hepatitis over the spring, and he recovered only to find himself coming down with a severe case of the Sue Me, Sue You Blues. Not only was the "My Sweet Lord" plagiarism case drawing to an unfavorable climax, but George was slapped with a million dollar lawsuit by none other than A & M Records. The official grievance was that George had failed to turn in his album on time; but industry insiders, noting the declining sales of Harrison's own product—along

George at 33⅓ (Dark Horse)

George at 33⅓ (Dark Horse)

with the fact that Dark Horse artists Splinter, Jiva, Attitudes, and Stairsteps had not exactly become household words—say the real reason may be that A & M was having second thoughts about the generous terms by which it had agreed to distribute Dark Horse records in 1974.

In any case, A & M's loss proved to be Warner Brothers' gain. Dark Horse promptly set up shop in the latter's Burbank offices and issued *Thirty-three and a Third* to coincide with George's 33⅔ birthday. The album was trailed with a single, "This Song," a jaunty commentary on Harrison's legal battle with "He's So Fine" publisher Bright Tunes ("This song has nothing bright about it . . ."). *Thirty-three and a Third* was a success on both critical and commercial fronts, though it did not blaze up the charts as most of his earlier records had done. Instead, it sold unspectacularly but steadily for half a year. Perhaps *Dark Horse* and *Extra Texture* had broken the fans' habit of snapping up his albums on the strength of Harrison's name alone. Now the music had to do the selling; but once people heard it the consensus was that George had produced his finest work since *All Things Must Pass.*

Both musically and lyrically, however, *Thirty-three and a Third* is very different from that album. The newer songs have a far more intimate setting, which forces them to rely on pure melody and George's own musicianship instead of dazzling orchestrations and production. The tastefulness of his performance on his two pet instruments, slide guitar and synthesizer, is unmatched in rock, and *Thirty-three and a Third* boasts the most varied and tuneful collection of Harrison melodies to date. "Woman Don't You Cry For Me" borrows the shuffling disco rhythm, yet, unlike, say, "Silly Love Songs," is not souped up with a Philadelphia hit factory arrangement. "Learning How To Love You" (dedicated to A & M president Herb Alpert) has light jazz overtones, while "Pure Smokey" (similar to *Extra Texture's* "Ooh Baby" but better) affectionately pastiches George's long-time idol Smokey Robinson. In "True Love" Harrison makes a Cole Porter song sound like one of his own, and "Beautiful Girl" could just as easily be an A-1 Beatle tune, a great lost *Rubber Soul* classic.

Apparently no longer convinced that his job was to save his listeners' souls, George with *Thirty-three and a Third* showed himself capable of producing excellent commercial music that conveys his deep spiritual convictions with subtlety and taste to those who wish to hear, without belaboring the point for those who don't. In a way he had come full circle: The Beatles had once forced him to keep his more blatant proselytizing under wraps; on *Thirty-three and a Third* he seemed to have finally learned to be his own editor.

"Dear One" may be the album's quintessential song. The liner notes tell us it is dedicated to an Indian holy man, but the lyrics themselves have a universal application. The verses are somber and reverent, awash with the sound of a Radha Krishna-style harmonium; on the chorus the music turns into an ecstatic celebration, complete with uplifting arpeggios from George's cosmic synthesizer. Instead of lecturing us on the joy his inner light has shown him, he lets the music speak for itself—and the music is far more persuasive than any sermon.

Thirty-three and a Third even boasts a rare (for George) flash of surreal wit, in the form of "Crackerbox Palace." The world, he sings, is a mad house, but he takes each indignity with stoic good humor. The song may have been inspired by his association with Monty Python's Eric Idle, who directed a hilarious film-clip to accompany "Crackerbox Palace," starring George as a basket case. Along with Harrison's own courtroom farce illustrating "This Song," Idle's film was aired on "Saturday Night Live" in tandem with George's per-

GEORGE HARRISON'S hates & loves

I HATE having my professional life get mixed up with my private life. It can spoil a night out at a club if there is a constant line of photographers and autograph hunters waiting to get near our table.

I HATE having to hurry past a crowd of fans without stopping for a chat, because we have to rush away for another appointment.

I HATE tea or coffee without sugar.

I HATE days when it never stops raining from dawn to dusk.

I HATE days on tour when every hour is taken up with traveling and there's no chance to relax quietly for a spell.

I HATE the end of any recording session. I'm always ready to go on and on once I'm in a recording studio!

I HATE having my hair cut. To me it is like a major operation and I dread it, so I never plan my visits to the barber until the last minute so that I won't have long to be bad-tempered about the prospect!

I HATE reporters who either turn up without any knowledge about pop music generally or about us, or who twist the things we say to make up whatev

they want to write.

I HATE being closed in a theatre dressing-room for too long. In the end, I can't stand it any longer and have to take a walk around the building or watch the other acts from the wings.

I HATE snatching meals in a hurry. I think eating is a pleasure that should be enjoyed at leisure.

I HATE stupid rumors and the people who delight in making themselves "important" by passing them on when they know very well there's no real evidence for their claims. And I don't just mean rumors about us—I mean guesswork and imagination presented as fact on any subject under the sun.

I HATE getting up in the mornings I'm O.K. once I'm up and washed, but the bad bit is actually coming up from under the sheets!

I LOVE seeing so many new places and meeting so many new people in our travels.

I LOVE spending time with my guitars—just messing about with the strings, polishing the frames or trying out new sounds

I LOVE listening to all the Tamla-Motown artists—live or on records.

I LOVE finding time to be really lazy for a whole day every now and then. I dig just lazing beside a pool or reading a book by a fire in the winter.

I LOVE live concerts. It's great to have the immediate response of an excited audience and know that what the group is doing is providing people with entertainment and enjoyment.

I LOVE being with the rest of the boys. Although we spend so much time in our own company, there are never ANY serious rows between us and we're all right on the same wave length so far as a sense of humor is concerned.

I LOVE fairly small parties with good music and good company.

I LOVE listening to other people telling me about things they do and things they know, especially when these things are nothing at all to do with the life we know. I've always been very, very interested in hearing new opinions and knowing about new subjects which are not part of our own everyday routine.

I LOVE rehearsing new songs. There's a terrific thrill for me in hearing a brand-new number brought to life.

I LOVE making big-headed people look foolish.

I LOVE getting home to England after a long spell abroad and catching up on all the news.

I LOVE being serious now and again—and having a good sensible argument on some subject that a friend disagrees about.

I LOVE trying to put the right name to a familiar face—I always make a point of trying to store up people's names in my mind so that I can remember to say "Hallo, Bill" or "Hi, Joe," even if I haven't met them for about six months.

I LOVE seeing good films or watching interesting plays on television.

22

George Harrison at 21½ (courtesy, *16* Magazine)

George arrives at "Saturday Night Live" with Olivia Arias left, and Harry Nilsson, right (Vinnie Zuffante)

sonal appearance to promote his new album. Having evidently concluded that plugging records was one of the inescapable indignities of his gig in the material world, Harrison barnstormed across the United States upon the release of *Thirty-three and a Third,* chatting up disk jockeys and granting interviews to *Rolling Stone* and *Crawdaddy.* On his Washington stop he took advantage of an invitation to chat with Henry Kissinger, presenting the outgoing secretary of state with his favorite book, *Autobiography Of a Yogi.* Another sign of the times, perhaps. Back in 1964 even the thought of such a meeting would have been preposterous; in 1967 it would have seemed the pinnacle of the surreal.

For vintage Beatle people, it seems hard to believe that more time has lapsed since the Beatles went their separate ways than during the entire period spanning "I Want To Hold Your Hand" and "Let It Be." As Bobby D. once sang, time passes slowly when you're lost in a dream.

The era the Beatles defined was largely one of conflict between two temporarily disconnected facets of our predominantly affluent, white, and Anglo/American culture. As the surface divisions healed, the sparks stopped flying.

Now generals are meditating in the Pentagon; the president has hair over his ears, and can recite the lyrics to "Eleanor Rigby" when occasion demands. His sons, like his predecessor's, have been known to smoke dope. When Carter greets Lennon at his inaugural gala, only four years after Nixon took such pains to give the Beatle the boot, nobody seems particularly astounded.

Whether the changes effected by the Sixties counterculture have been truly profound, or purely cosmetic, has become the subject of debate from *Rolling Stone* to the *New York Times* Sunday magazine (both of which sometimes feature the same writers). Whichever way, the Beatles had a lot to do with it.

Rock music, once the most influential popular art form around, is selling better than ever; but concerning the extent to which it is motivated by art or commerce, opinions differ. Certainly, bands such as Kiss have demonstrated the speed with which "Middle America" could assimilate interstellar

transvestism and supersonic rock 'n' roll; and the only major new style of popular music to come out of the Seventies was disco—Muzak programed to set a mood on the dance floor, rather than in an elevator. Yet the best of rock is as accomplished as ever, even if it lost some of its spirit along with some of its cosmic import.

The four Beatles are now scattered to almost as many corners of the world—with John in New York, Ringo commuting between residences in Monte Carlo and Los Angeles, leaving England with only Paul and George—and their music and careers seem to have gone in equally diverse directions. As a solo contender, Ringo may have faded from the charts somewhat; yet he remains every-

(Vinnie Zuffante)

John and Yoko with James Taylor
and Carly Simon, January 1977
(Vinnie Zuffante)

The Lennons with Muhammad Ali at
President Jimmy Carter's inaugural
gala (Wide World Photos)

body's favorite sideman on records, at social events, and in the movies. George holds the promise of a great deal more fine music; unlikely either to set trends or to follow them, he has always been most interested in perfecting his musicianship, and dedicating that to something larger than himself.

Paul seems to have adapted most readily to post-Beatle fashions—unsurprisingly, as he has always demonstrated an excellent sense of knowing what the times want. Some of his old admirers may complain that he appears less concerned with what the times *need;* yet McCartney seems assured of a long reign as one of the world's most popular entertainers.

The wild card of the pack is, as ever, John Lennon. He was at once the Beatles' most devout rock 'n' roller, the one most committed to the notion that his work was a true art form, and the most inventive manipulator of the power that had been presented to them. It will be fascinating to see what Lennon, closing in on middle age, will attempt to accomplish with a form of music that has always been synonymous with youth—in a medium that may be reverting to its emphasis on entertainment over art, and in an era that seems to be developing a healthy skepticism toward heroes.

Despite their unquestioned charisma and talent, the Beatles were four very human beings who found themselves transformed almost overnight into objects of the world's fascination. Maybe that's why we identified with them so closely. Incredibly, they all seem to have come out of the experience perfectly intact, and since going their separate ways, each appears to have cut himself back down to human proportions by devoting himself to what came most naturally all along. John pursues his artistic vision over commercial and purely musical considerations; Paul has returned to show-biz; George concentrates on being a musician; and Ringo remains "one of history's most charming bit part players."

The world viewed the Beatles at three different levels—as a phenomenon, as personalities, and through their music. The phenomenon has receded into nostalgia and history; the personalities as we knew them have grown apart and middle-aged. But the best of the music they created together is timeless.

John, Paul, George, and Ringo's Hits—September 1974 through April 1977

TITLE AND LABEL	FIRST APPEARANCE	HIGHEST POSITION	WEEKS ON CHART†
U.S. Top 100 Singles			
Whatever Gets You Thru the Night—John—(Apple)*	Sept. 28, 1974	1	11
Junior's Farm/Sally G—Paul—(Apple)*	Nov. 9, 1974	3	17**
Only You (And You Alone)—Ringo—(Apple)	Nov. 16, 1974	6	13
Dark Horse—George—(Apple)	Nov. 23, 1974	15	10
#9 Dream—John—(Apple)	Dec. 21, 1974	9	12
Ding Dong, Ding Dong—George—(Apple)	Jan. 11, 1975	36	6
No No Song/Snookeroo—Ringo (Apple)	Feb. 8, 1975	3	14
Stand By Me—John—(Apple)	March 15, 1975	20	9
Listen To What the Man Said—Paul—(Capitol)*	May 31, 1975	1	13
Goodnight Vienna/Oo-Wee—Ringo—(Apple)	June 14, 1975	31	7
You—George—(Apple)	Sept. 20, 1975	20	10
Letting Go—Paul—(Capitol)	Oct. 4, 1975	39	6
Venus and Mars/Rock Show—Paul—(Capitol)	Nov. 1, 1975	12	9
Silly Love Songs—Paul—(Capitol)*	April 10, 1976	1	19
Got To Get You Into My Life (Capitol)	June 12, 1976	7	16
Let 'Em In—Paul—(Capitol)*	July 4, 1976	3	16
A Dose Of Rock And Roll—Ringo—(Atlantic)	Sept. 25, 1976	26	9
Ob-La-Di, Ob-La-Da (Capitol)	Nov. 20, 1976	49	6
This Song—George—(Dark Horse)	Nov. 20, 1976	25	11
Crackerbox Palace—George—(Dark Horse)	Jan. 29, 1977	17	11
Hey Baby—Ringo—(Atlantic)	Jan. 29, 1977	74	3
Maybe I'm Amazed—Paul—(Capitol)	Feb. 12, 1977	10	12
U.S. Top 200 L.P.'s			
Walls and Bridges—John—(Apple)*	Oct. 12, 1974	1	27
Goodnight Vienna—Ringo—(Apple)*	Nov. 30, 1974	8	24
Dark Horse—George—(Apple)*	Dec. 28, 1974	4	14
Rock 'n' Roll—John (Apple)*	March 8, 1975	6	15
Venus and Mars—Paul—(Capitol)*	June 14, 1975	1	77
Extra Texture—George—(Apple)*	Oct. 11, 1975	8	11
Shaved Fish—John—(Apple)	Nov. 8, 1975	12	13
Blast From Your Past—Ringo—(Apple)	Dec. 6, 1975	30	11
Wings At the Speed Of Sound—Paul—(Capitol)*	April 10, 1976	1	51
Rock 'n' Roll Music (Capitol)*	June 26, 1976	2	29
Ringo's Rotogravure—Ringo—(Atlantic)	Oct. 9, 1976	28	9
The Best Of George Harrison—(Capitol)*	Nov. 27, 1976	31	15
Thirty-Three and a Third—George—(Dark Horse)*	Dec. 11, 1976	11	21
Wings Over America—Paul—(Capitol)*	Dec. 25, 1976	1	19
British Top Twenty Singles			
Junior's Farm/Sally G—Paul—(Apple)	Dec. 7, 1974	16	2
Listen To What the Man Said—Paul—(EMI)	June 7, 1975	6	5
Imagine—John—(Apple)	Nov. 8, 1975	6	7
Yesterday (Parlophone)	March 27, 1976	8	6
Silly Love Songs—Paul—(EMI)	May 29, 1976	3	8
Hey Jude (rerelease) (Apple)	April 17, 1976	12	4
Back In the U.S.S.R. (Apple)	July 31, 1976	19	2
Let 'Em In—Paul—(EMI)	Aug. 21, 1976	2	8

(Chart positions according to *Billboard;* asterisk [*]: Record Industry Association of America certified Gold Record/Million Seller)
**last five weeks listed only under "Sally G"
†as of April 30, 1977

AND IN THE END

In the year following the original publication of this book, the world has heard a great deal *about* the Beatles, but not much at all *from* Lennon, McCartney, Harrison, and Starr themselves. At a rare press conference in Tokyo (October 1977) John confirmed rumors of his extended retirement from the music world by announcing: "We've basically decided, without a great decision, to be with our baby as much as we can until we feel we can take time off to indulge ourselves in creating things outside the family."

Except when the press picked up on his ongoing flirtation with racing cars, little more was heard from George. His tentative plans for a May 1978 California concert benefiting endangered whales foundered when the media started billing it as a likely Beatles reunion.

Paul, feathers unruffled by the loss of Wings' McCulloch and English, scored the biggest selling record in British history (over two million copies) with "Mull Of Kintyre." ("She Loves You" and "I Want To Hold Your Hand" were relegated to Numbers Two and Three on the all-time roll call.) "Kintyre," a McCartney/Laine paean to the misty landscape surrounding Paul's Scottish retreat, featured the Campbelltown Pipe Band and a two-chord three/four melody of inspired simplicity. One of the great mysteries in ex-Beatledom was why the disc managed to reach Number One throughout the rest of Christendom yet barely crack the Top Forty in the United States. In fact, it seems doomed to the status of Wings' all-time *worst* American seller. Those Stateside stations that played the single at all tended to opt for the more conventional rock 'n' roll of the flip side, "Girls' School," whose lyrics consisted of a string of pornographic film titles.

However, Wings' next L.P., *London Town*—largely recorded on a yacht moored off the Virgin Islands with McCulloch and English still in tow—emulated the pleasingly plump sounds, and commercial success, of its antecedents. Paul and Linda also produced their first son, James Louis.

The *Ringo the Fourth* L.P. tapped a trendy disco sound and, once more, the production talents of Arif Mardin—and the result proved even more faceless and mechanical than *Ringo's Rotogravure*. *Ringo the Fourth*'s lamentably dismal sales performance (even the Ono-Lennons' montages of silence and static had stirred up more chart action) caused Atlantic Records to relieve our hero of his contractual obligations.

A follow-up, *Bad Boy,* was hastily thrown together and released by Portrait Records to coincide with April 1978's *Ringo* T.V. special. If neither were precisely inspired events in rock history, at least *Bad Boy* (consisting mostly of oft-recorded chestnuts) shed the phony disco gloss of its predecessors. The show, featuring George Harrison narrating a rewrite of Mark Twain's *The Prince and the Pauper,* and new versions of "Act Naturally" and "With a Little Help From My Friends," demonstrated even more pointedly than *James Paul McCartney* how ill-suited for one another rock music and commercial prime time generally are.

Capitol's recycling operation cranked out *Love Songs,* a two-record compilation of Beatle ballads. But the consumer response to this somewhat pretentious package (pseudo-leather embossed with pseudo-gold) suggested that the novelty of "new" Beatle albums had worn off (highest chart position: #19). Aficionados were intrigued by the careful retouching Capitol had applied to Richard Avedon's famous 1968 poster, which resurfaces on the *Love Songs* sleeve with McCartney's head substantially enlarged and the hapless Starr's correspondingly diminished. (The label clearly remembered where they'd put their money.) Some collectors and audiophiles also griped that Capitol still hadn't bothered to make use of the original stereo masters of such songs as "Yes It Is" and "This Boy."

Despite *Love Songs'* comparative failure, exploitation of the Beatles mystique reached a new high, financially if not artistically, on stage and screen. Broadway's *Beatlemania,* little more than a simulated Fab concert with a fancy light show—and an unconvincing one at that in the eyes and ears of those familiar with the Real Thing—packed in enthusiastic S.R.O. crowds for a year. By that time, additional sets of Beatleoids had been cloned for Los Angeles and the provinces. Withering critical disdain was kept at bay by delaying the official opening for many months, and the emphatic disavowals of real ex-Beatles were offset by a canny media blitz.

Meanwhile, the Sixties' most legendary anthems were being grafted onto a gaudy Seventies-style superstar spectacular, a celluloid *Sgt. Pepper's Lonely Hearts Club Band* that frankly made no attempt to recapture the Spirit of Sixty-Seven. However, an earlier chapter of Beatle lore was indeed evoked to hilarious effect in *I Wanna Hold Your Hand*'s madcap rendition of the siege of the Hotel Plaza.

Then there were the Rutles, conceived by Eric Idle, with a T.V. special and album that rewrote and deflated the entire Beatles saga with brilliant precision. The music, by ex-Bonzo Dog Neil Innes, who played and sang the John Lennon of the "Pre-fab Four," was especially on target. A cameo appearance by Idle's pal George Harrison could be taken as an ex-Beatles' endorsement of the iconoclastic enterprise.

And what does all this suggest to the Long Time Fan? Perhaps that those of us who had devoutly followed the Beatles through an era—the young, impressionable, and idealistic spawn of a consumer society—had reacted against said culture by creating a dream that willy-nilly was fashioned in large part from consumer commodities: records, clothes, posters, rolling papers, and so forth. We tended to overlook the fact that, however anti-show-biz and anti-consumer-society our media heroes, such as the Beatles, may have appeared, they were still putting on a show and helping to sell products to us, the consumers. A decade later that dream itself had been reduced in some circles to yet another commodity: *Beatlemania!* . . . *The Fabulous Sixties!* . . . and the fine line between show-biz and anti-show-biz seemed to have been rubbed away. As for the four pivotal characters in that dream: In 1978 those ex-Beatles still active in the music world appeared to have adjusted quite comfortably to its business-as-usual mood—and John Lennon had yet to suggest an alternative.

But if the attitudes of the Seventies have tended to turn more cynical and less wide-eyed than those of the Sixties, perhaps that is why the undeniable dynamism and excitement of the Sixties could not be approximated in subsequent years. Which in turn may explain the spell the Beatles, their legend, and their music have continued to cast on those for whom there's been little shift in tone between, say, 1974 and 1978. There was a world of difference between 1964 and 1968, and many of the reasons for that are immortalized in the grooves of the Beatles' classic records.

Rare U.S. Singles Collection

The specially printed sleeves that adorned the first editions of many American 45's by the Beatles (collectively and individually) have become prized collector's items. Records not shown here were issued in standard plain sleeves.

1964

1964

1964

1964

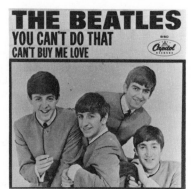

1964

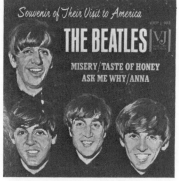

1964

1964

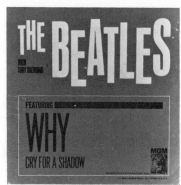

1964

1964

1964

1964

1964

1964

1964

1964

1964

1965

1965

1965

1965

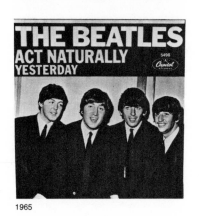

1965

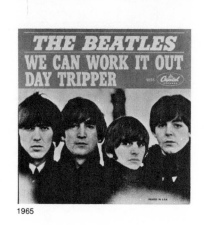

1965

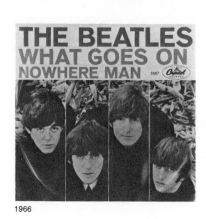

1966

1966

1966

1967 (Front)

1967 (Back)

1967

1967

1968

1969

1969

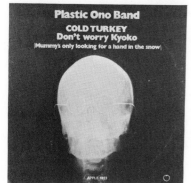

1969

1970

1970

199

1970

1970

1970

1970

1971

1971

1971

1971

1971

1972

1972

1972

200

1972

1973

1973

1973

1974

1974 (Dark Horse/George Harrison)

1974

1975

1975

1975

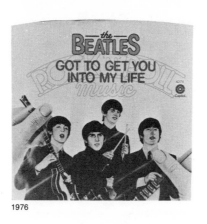

1976

1976

EVERY
LITTLE
THING

THE BUTCHERS

An International Beatle Discography

If you are an American Beatlemaniac, it is possible that you rate albums such as *Beatles '65, Beatles VI,* and *Yesterday and Today* among your favorites. Mention this to a British fan, however, and, unless he is a seasoned collector, he might have little or no idea what you are talking about. None of those albums was ever released in his country.

He, in turn, may cite such unfamiliar titles (to Americans) as *With the Beatles* or *Beatles For Sale;* even should you agree on the respective excellence of, say, the *Hard Day's Night* or *Revolver* albums, you'll actually be talking about quite different compilations. Tell him your favorite tune on *Rubber Soul* is "I've Just Seen A Face" and he may insist it's his favorite on *Help!* You would both be right, for until 1967 and *Sgt. Pepper,* when rock music started to receive serious acclaim as "art" and albums as heterogeneous works (and chopping them up suddenly began to seem somewhat crass, even to hard-headed American record executives), no British rock album could reasonably hope to survive the voyage across the Atlantic intact.

The Beatles recorded 102 songs in the years 1962 to 1966. In Britain these appeared on 8 L.P.'s (including one anthology), 12 E.P.'s, and 13 singles. The very same selections were re-packaged for the American consumer into 11 albums, four E.P.'s, and 20 singles. With the exception of a few of the singles, no two records in the two sets feature the same contents!

Mexico, Japan and Canada boast yet different compilations, while in France there were *no* Beatle singles whatsoever, as that country still stubbornly and exclusively favored the four-song E.P. as the only civilized incarnation of the 45 rpm record, not succumbing to the two-song *simple* until "All You Need is Love" in 1967.

Occasionally discrepancies in the Beatles international discography are due to an album track being so popular in a certain country, sometimes for obvious reasons, that it is released there as a 45. The French, who made "Michelle" a smash E.P. in their country, were no doubt beguiled by the sound of Paul McCartney crooning half the song in their own fair tongue; in India, "Norwegian Wood," the tune that marked George Harrison's recorded debut on the sitar, became a Number One hit. For many of the rest of us, these two songs were made available only as part of the *Rubber Soul* L.P. But, for the most part, discrepancies in various nations' Beatle records were due to lingering differences in music business tradition.

The record industry is a fairly new one, less than a century old, and it's been Big Bucks only since the Second World War. Until this decade it has remained a somewhat provincial business with the relative popularity and function of the single, the E.P., and the album varying from country to country. By the time you read this, though, international conformity to the great American way will have been just about complete, with the E.P. gone the way of the silver sixpence; and most forthcoming releases by major artists will be blessed with identical contents, jackets, and release dates in every country in the Western world. Consequently, international '60's rock record collectors have a far more exciting time with their hobby than prospective connoisseurs of the '70's or '80's can reasonably look forward to.

The three outstanding differences between the United States and most other countries, from the music industry's point of view, is that America's consumers are more affluent, there are more of them, and their taste is governed to a unique degree by countless highly competitive, privately owned commercial radio stations. Nowhere but in America can you find music on almost any point on your radio dial—and switch to your choice of a dozen alternatives should you find yourself dissatisfied with the program you're listening to. In other countries there are seldom more than a mere handful of stations, usually owned and operated by the government. In most parts of the world there is only one station around broadcasting pop music, and then only at selected hours. Occasionally there may be illegal off-shore "pirates" (in the mid-Sixties, Britain had the short-lived Radios Caroline and London), but then again, only one or two.

Somewhat by way of compensation, the Europeans, especially the British, have long kept in touch with the music scene via such sophisticated pop music weeklies as *Melody Maker, The New Musical Express,* and *Disc,* all of which were far more informative and influential than anything America had until *Rolling Stone* came along in 1967. (Unlike their American imitators, the British weeklies have remained exclusively devoted to music and musicians, content to leave be the worlds of drugs, politics, films, and the occult.)

But in the United States, sales were dependent upon radio airplay, and in the early 1960's (this is before the FM rock stations played havoc with all the pat rules) radio stations played "hits." ("Hits" were, by definition, singles that managed to crack the "top forty" singles charts.)

Albums' sales were propelled by the inclusion of hit singles, for it was thought inconceivable that people should buy a pop album that didn't contain hits they had heard over the air. The people who bought albums tended to be a different breed from the singles buyers—they were usually older, richer, and had more elaborate hi-fi equipment—but even American fans who did swing both ways were assumed to be affluent enough not to mind any duplications.

Outside the United States, however, and particularly in Britain, the single was considered a distinct entity from the album; and a new L.P. that did not contain all new material was viewed with suspicious distaste. Not only were European album buyers pretty much the same people who bought 45's, but, because they had less money to spend, they would tend to be more resentful than their American counterparts at the prospect of buying an album that duplicated in part what they already owned on 45's.

Should an album track prove extraordinarily popular, it might *then* be pulled out as a single, or more likely, the dominant selection of an E.P. The E.P., which quickly lost its foothold in the American music-business rat race, was a sort of poor man's album for many fans, often featuring an album's "greatest hits." Some top British groups, such as the Rolling Stones, the Kinks, the Who, and the Beatles themselves, also released E.P.'s containing songs available in no other form. Trade publications used to list British E.P. hit parades alongside their singles and album charts, but the Extended Player in the late Sixties became increasingly unprofitable, and has by now become the quaint relic of a less Americanized age. (Several Beatle E.P.'s were released in America in 1964, but none dented the Top Twenty. All were soon deleted, and have become valuable collectors' items.)

The other major respect in which American albums by artists such as the Beatles differed from British versions, aside from their inclusion of singles, is that they were much shorter. The average mid-Sixties pop album in Britain contained 14 two- to three-minute songs, its American counterpart only 11. Though one side of an L.P. can accommodate as much as a half hour of music, many American Beatle albums contained only 13 minutes per side. The entire contents, then, of *Something New* (25 minutes 49 seconds) or *Beatles '65* (27 minutes 10 seconds) could actually have been squeezed onto one side of a record—with room to spare! It is not difficult to see why there were so many more Beatle albums in America than in Britain.

When the Beatles' fifth British hit, "I Want to Hold Your Hand," netted the boys their first American chart placing in January, 1964, Capitol Records rush-released their debut Beatles L.P. *Meet the Beatles* (which was subtitled "The First Album by England's Phenomenal Pop Combo," even though the Beatles had released an album of earlier material nearly a year before); and naturally "I Want to Hold Your Hand" had to be included—along with its American B-side "I Saw Her Standing There," and its British reverse "This Boy." As none of these were featured on the group's second British album *With the Beatles*, five tunes were siphoned off the British release (later to form the nucleus of the *Beatles' Second Album*), and the remaining nine were thrown together with the three single tracks to create *Meet the Beatles*. So began a tradition of mutilation.

American record companies responsible for marketing the Beatles and other successful mop-topped imports knew that they had enchanted geese on their hands; their job, as they saw it, was to squeeze as many golden eggs out of them as possible before America's fickle adolescents found some other way to dispense with their pocket money. (At the time nobody thought the Beatles' success could last more than a few years; one of the most frequent questions addressed to the Beatles at their madcap press conferences was "When will the bubble burst?" "In about five years," replied John Lennon, optimistically, in 1964.)

The same magic formula was applied to every big-bucks British rock-star's albums: slice it in half, throw in a few singles, and abracadabra . . . the cigar smoke clears to reveal two albums where there had been but one. The first six British Rolling Stones albums translated to 10 in America; the Kinks' two first British L.P.'s were padded out to create four American ones; Donovan's three yielded six, and so on.

Another common maneuver was to deliberately leave the most commercial tune on a British Beatles album off its American counterpart and save it for release as a single (and, of course, a subsequent album). Some of the Beatles' big American singles, like "Nowhere Man" (a British *Rubber Soul* L.P. track) and "Yesterday" (amputated from Britain's *Help!* album), were conjured up in this fashion.

Speaking of *Help!*, it was with this album that Capitol's relentless dismembering of the Beatles' work reached a peak of cynicism. From the British collection of fourteen songs, the firm plucked a mere seven, to which was larded some dreary incidental muzak from the film. On top of which, the album was priced a dollar above current list price on the pretext that this was a "deluxe" movie souvenir package. Like any other Beatles album, *Help!* earned an American gold record within a week.

At least Capitol never stooped to the meanest trick of all: that of duplicating the same song on different albums (although they had no qualms about using material previously released on other labels). This ruse helped fill out such L.P.'s as *Kinks Kinkdom, The Real Donovan,* the Who's *Magic Bus* and the Rolling Stones' *Flowers* when those groups were turning out new material too slowly to suit the record company bureaucrats.

The Beatles themselves couldn't keep up with the various permutations of their recorded work. John, for instance, introduced "Baby's In Black" as a track from *Beatles VI* at their 1965 Shea Stadium concert. (It was, in fact, included on *Beatles '65*, but John was close enough—a single British L.P., *Beatles For Sale,* managed to yield the bulk of both '65 and VI.)

So it is not difficult to guess why the Beatles decided on a photograph depicting them as butchers clutching chopped up babies when they were asked to select a cover for the American release *Yesterday . . . And Today,* an album that consisted of tunes Capitol had amputated from its versions of *Help!, Rubber Soul,* and *Revolver* to create more "product."

* * * * * * *

The basic recordings to be found on all these different Beatles compilations are generally the same, with a few curious exceptions. On the German pressing of *Something New,* for instance, the coda of "And I Love Her" includes six bars of instrumental music instead of the usual four. Germany's *Beatles' Greatest* presents "All My Loving" with a high-hat intro. The British *1962-1966* prefaces "I Feel Fine" with a few seconds of mysterious whispering. In America, *A Hard Day's Night* has an extra verse of "I'll Cry Instead," and the stereo copies of *Rubber Soul* boast a false start to "I'm Looking Through You." None of these nuances are to be found on any other editions, and, though all are exceptionally minor, they nonetheless fascinate collectors.

The audiophile, however, has sound reasons for tracking down imported pressings. In Britain and Germany, records seem to be consistently superior to those made in America, where many of the Beatles' earlier recordings are further mangled by a gratuitous overlay of echo and reverb. A high percentage of the selections on U.S. Beatle albums are also presented in "electronically re-channelled stereo," more accurately known as distorted mono; this is seldom the case on British pressings.

Authentic stereo versions of a handful of songs, however, are hard to find anywhere—but some do exist: "This Boy" on a 1976 Canadian reissue single; "She's a Woman" on the 1965 East Asian/Australian L.P. *Beatles' Greatest Hits Vol. 2;* and "I'm Down" on a 1965 Japanese *Help!* E.P. Only nine Beatle songs have never appeared in true stereo anywhere: "Love Me Do," "P.S. I Love You," "She Loves You," "I'll Get You," "Sie Liebt Dich," "Yes It Is," "The Inner Light," "Only a Northern Song," and "You Know My Name (Look Up the Number)."

An International Beatle Discography

UNITED KINGDOM SINGLES:

Love Me Do/P.S. I Love You
—Parlophone R 4949; (October 1962)

Please Please Me/Ask Me Why—Parlophone R 4983; (January 1963)

From Me To You/Thank You Girl—Parlophone R 5015; (April 1963)

My Bonnie/The Saints—Polydor NH 66-833; (May 1963) OP*

She Loves You/I'll Get You—Parlophone R 5055; (August 1963)

I Want To Hold Your Hand/This Boy
—Parlophone R 5084; (November 1963)

Can't Buy Me Love/You Can't Do That
—Parlophone R 5114; (March 1964)

Ain't She Sweet/If You Love Me, Baby
—Polydor NH 52-317; (May 1964) OP

A Hard Day's Night/Things We Said Today
—Parlophone R 5160; (July 1964)

I Feel Fine/She's a Woman—Parlophone R 5200; (November 1964)

Ticket To Ride/Yes It Is—Parlophone R 5265; (April 1965)

Help!/I'm Down—Parlophone R 5305; (July 1965)

We Can Work It Out/Day Tripper
—Parlophone R 5389; (December 1965)

Paperback Writer/Rain—Parlophone R 5452; (June 1966)

Yellow Submarine/Eleanor Rigby—Parlophone R 5489; (August 1966)

Penny Lane/Strawberry Fields Forever
—Parlophone R 5570; (February 1967)

All You Need Is Love/Baby, You're a Rich Man
—Parlophone R 5620; (July 1967)

Hello Goodbye/I Am the Walrus—Parlophone R 5655; (November 1967)

Lady Madonna/The Inner Light—Parlophone R 5675; (March 1968)

Hey Jude/Revolution—Apple R 5722; (August 1968)

Get Back/Don't Let Me Down—Apple R 5777; (April 1969)

The Ballad Of John And Yoko/Old Brown Shoe
—Apple R 5786; (May 1969)

Something/Come Together—Apple R 5814; (October 1969)

Let It Be/You Know My Name (Look Up the Number)
—Apple R 5833; (March 1970)

Yesterday/I Should Have Known Better
—Parlophone R 6013; (February 1976)

Back In the U.S.S.R./Twist and Shout—Parlophone R 6016; (July 1976)

Falling in Love Again/Twist and Shout—Lingasong NB. 1; (July 1977)

UNITED KINGDOM E.P.'s:

Twist and Shout—Parlophone GEP 8882; (July 1963):
Twist and Shout; A Taste Of Honey; Do You Want To Know a Secret; There's a Place

The Beatles' Hits
—Parlophone GEP 8880; (September 1963):
From Me To You; Thank You Girl; Please Please Me; Love Me Do

The Beatles (No. 1)
—Parlophone GEP 8883; (November 1963):
I Saw Her Standing There; Misery; Anna (Go To Him); Chains

All My Loving
—Parlophone GEP 8891; (February 1964):
All My Loving; Ask Me Why; Money; P.S. I Love You

Extracts from the film A Hard Day's Night
—Parlophone GEP 8920; (November 1964):
I Should Have Known Better; If I Fell; Tell Me Why; And I Love Her

Extracts from the album A Hard Day's Night
—Parlophone GEP 8924; (November 1964):
Anytime At All; I'll Cry Instead; Things We Said Today; When I Get Home

Beatles For Sale—Parlophone GEP 8931; (April 1965):
No Reply; I'm a Loser; Rock and Roll Music; Eight Days a Week

Beatles For Sale (No. 2)
—Parlophone GEP 8938; (June 1965):
I'll Follow the Sun; Baby's In Black; Words of Love; I Don't Want To Spoil the Party

*Out of print.

The Beatles' Million Sellers
—Parlophone GEP 8946; (December 1965):
She Loves You; I Want To Hold Your Hand; Can't Buy Me Love; I Feel Fine

Yesterday—Parlophone GEP 8948; (March 1966):
Yesterday; Act Naturally; You Like Me Too Much; It's Only Love

Nowhere Man—Parlophone GEP 8952; (July 1966):
Nowhere Man; Drive My Car; Michelle; You Won't See Me

Magical Mystery Tour (2 E.P.'s)
—Parlophone SMMT ½; (December 1967):
Magical Mystery Tour; Your Mother Should Know; I Am the Walrus; The Fool on the Hill; Flying; Blue Jay Way

UNITED KINGDOM L.P.'s:

Please Please Me—Parlophone PCS 3042; (March 1963):
I Saw Her Standing There; Misery; Anna (Go To Him): Chains; Boys; Ask Me Why; Please Please Me; Love Me Do; P.S. I Love You; Baby, It's Me; Do You Want To Know a Secret; A Taste Of Honey; There's a Place; Twist and Shout

With The Beatles—Parlophone PCS 3045; November 1963:
It Won't Be Long; All I've Got To Do; All My Loving; Don't Bother Me; Little Child; Till There Was You; Please Mr. Postman; Roll Over Beethoven; Hold Me Tight; You Really Got a Hold on Me; I Wanna Be Your Man; Devil In Her Heart; Not a Second Time; Money (That's What I Want)

The Beatles' First
—Polydor 236-201; (June 1964 — reissued August 1967):
Additional material by Tony Sheridan: Ain't She Sweet?; Cry For a Shadow; My Bonnie; If You Love Me, Baby; Sweet Georgia Brown; The Saints; Why?; Nobody's Child OP

A Hard Day's Night—Parlophone PCS 3058; (July 1964):
A Hard Day's Night; I Should Have Known Better; If I Fell; I'm Happy Just To Dance With You; And I Love Her; Tell Me Why; Can't Buy Me Love; Anytime At All; I'll Cry Instead; Things We Said Today; When I Get Home; You Can't Do That; I'll Be Back

Beatles For Sale
—Parlophone PCS 3062; (December 1964):
No Reply; I'm a Loser; Baby's In Black; Rock and Roll Music; I'll Follow the Sun; Mr. Moonlight; Kansas City; Eight Days a Week; Words of Love; Honey Don't; Every Little Thing; I Don't Want To Spoil the Party; What You're Doing; Everybody's Trying To Be My Baby

Help!—Parlophone PCS 3071; (August 1965):
Help!; The Night Before; You've Got To Hide Your Love Away; I Need You; Another Girl; You're Gonna Lose That Girl; Ticket To Ride; Act Naturally; It's Only Love; You Like Me Too Much; Tell Me What You See; I've Just Seen a Face; Yesterday; Dizzy Miss Lizzie

Rubber Soul—Parlophone PCS 3075; (December 1965):
Drive My Car; Norwegian Wood (This Bird Has Flown); You Won't See Me; Nowhere Man; Think For Yourself; The Word; Michelle; What Goes On?; Girl; I'm Looking Through You; In My Life; Wait; If I Needed Someone; Run For Your Life

Revolver—Parlophone PCS 7009; (August 1966):
Taxman; Eleanor Rigby; I'm Only Sleeping; Love You Too; Here, There and Everywhere; Yellow Submarine; She Said She Said; Good Day Sunshine; And Your Bird Can Sing; For No One; Dr. Robert; I Want To Tell You; Got To Get You Into My Life; Tomorrow Never Knows

A Collection of Beatle Oldies
—Parlophone PCS 7016; (December 1966):
She Loves You; From Me To You; We Can Work It Out; Help!; Michelle; Yesterday; I Feel Fine; Yellow Submarine; Can't Buy Me Love; Bad Boy; Day Tripper; A Hard Day's Night; Ticket To Ride; Paperback Writer; Eleanor Rigby; I Want To Hold Your Hand

Sgt. Pepper's Lonely Hearts Club Band
—Parlophone PCS 7027; (June 1967):
Sgt. Pepper's Lonely Hearts Club Band; With a Little Help From My Friends; Lucy In the Sky With Diamonds; Getting Better; Fixing a Hole; She's Leaving Home; Being For the Benefit Of Mr. Kite; Within You Without You; When I'm Sixty-Four; Lovely Rita; Good Morning Good Morning; Sgt. Pepper's Lonely Hearts Club Band (reprise); A Day In the Life

The Beatles (2 L.P.'s)

—Apple PCS 7067/8; (November 1968):
Back In the U.S.S.R.; Dear Prudence; Glass Onion; Ob-La-Di, Ob-La-Da; Wild Honey Pie; The Continuing Story of Bungalow Bill; While My Guitar Gently Weeps; Happiness Is a Warm Gun; Martha My Dear; I'm So Tired; Blackbird; Piggies; Rocky Racoon; Don't Pass Me By; Why Don't We Do It In the Road; I Will; Julia; Birthday; Yer Blues; Mother Nature's Son; Everybody's Got Something To Hide Except Me and My Monkey; Sexy Sadie; Helter Skelter; Long, Long, Long; Revolution; Honey Pie; Savoy Truffle; Cry Baby Cry; Revolution 9; Good Night

Yellow Submarine

—Apple PCS 7070; (January 1969): Additional material by George Martin and Orchestra:
Yellow Submarine; Only a Northern Song; All Together Now; Hey Bulldog; It's All Too Much; All You Need Is Love

Abbey Road—Apple PCS 7088; (September 1969):
Come Together; Something; Maxwell's Silver Hammer; Oh! Darling; Octopus's Garden; I Want You (She's So Heavy); Here Comes the Sun; Because; You Never Give Me Your Money; Sun King; Mean Mr. Mustard; Polythene Pam; She Came In Through the Bathroom Window; Golden Slumbers; Carry That Weight; The End; Her Majesty

Let It Be

—Apple PXS 1; (May 1970—reissued Apple PCS 7096; November 1970):
Two Of Us; I Dig a Pony; Across the Universe; I Me Mine; Dig It; Let It Be; Maggie Mae; I've Got a Feeling; One After 909; The Long and Winding Road; For You Blue; Get Back (Boxed first edition included *Get Back*, a book of Beatle dialogue and color photographs.)

The Early Years—Contour 287011; (June 1971):
Same songs as **The Beatles' First**

The Beatles 1962—1966

—Apple PCSP 717 (2 L.P.'s); (April 1973):
Love Me Do; Please Please Me; From Me To You; She Loves You; I Want To Hold Your Hand; All My Loving; Can't Buy Me Love; A Hard Day's Night; And I Love Her; Eight Days a Week; I Feel Fine; Ticket To Ride; Yesterday; Help!; You've Got To Hide Your Love Away; We Can Work It Out; Day Tripper; Drive My Car; Norwegian Wood (This Bird Has Flown); Nowhere Man; Michelle; In My Life; Girl; Paperback Writer; Eleanor Rigby; Yellow Submarine

The Beatles 1967—1970

—Apple PSCP 718 (2 L.P.'s); (April 1973):
Strawberry Fields Forever; Penny Lane; Sgt. Pepper's Lonely Hearts Club Band; With a Little Help From My Friends; Lucy In the Sky With Diamonds; A Day In the Life; All You Need Is Love; I Am the Walrus; Hello Goodbye; The Fool On the Hill; Magical Mystery Tour; Lady Madonna; Hey Jude; Revolution; Back In the U.S.S.R.; While My Guitar Gently Weeps; Ob-La-Di, Ob-La-Da; Don't Let Me Down; The Ballad Of John and Yoko; Old Brown Shoe; Here Comes the Sun; Come Together; Something; Octopus's Garden; Let It Be; Across the Universe; The Long and Winding Road

Rock and Roll Music

—Parlophone PCSP 719 (2 L.P.'s); (June 1976):
Twist and Shout; I Saw Her Standing There; You Can't Do That; I Wanna Be Your Man; I Call Your Name; Boys; Long Tall Sally; Rock and Roll Music; Slow Down; Kansas City; Money (That's What I Want); Bad Boy; Matchbox; Roll Over Beethoven; Drive My Car; Dizzy Miss Lizzie; Anytime At All; Everybody's Trying To Be My Baby; The Night Before; I'm Down; Revolution; Back In the U.S.S.R; Helter Skelter; Taxman; Got To Get You Into My Life; Hey Bulldog; Birthday; Get Back

The Beatles Tapes—Polydor 2633 (2 L.P.'s); (July 1976):
Interviews conducted by David Wigg with each Beatle.

Live! at the Star Club in Hamburg, Germany 1962

—Lingasong LNL1 (2 L.P.'s); (April 1977):
I Saw Her Standing There; Roll Over Beethoven; Hippy Hippy Shake; Sweet Little Sixteen; Lend Me Your Comb; Your Feet's Too Big; Twist and Shout; Mr. Moonlight; A Taste Of Honey; Besame Mucho; Reminiscing; Kansas City; Ain't Nothing Shaking Like the Leaves On a Tree; To Know Her Is To Love Her; Little Queenie; Falling In Love Again; Ask Me Why; Be-Bop-A-Lu-La; Halleluja I Love Her So; Red Sails in the Sunset; Everybody's Trying To Be My Baby; Matchbox; Talkin' 'Bout You; Shimmy Shimmy; Long Tall Sally; I Remember You

The Beatles at the Hollywood Bowl—(Parlophone EMTV 4; May 1977):
Twist and Shout; She's a Woman; Dizzy Miss Lizzy; Ticket To Ride; Can't Buy Me Love; Things We Said Today; Roll Over Beethoven; Boys; A Hard Day's Night; Help; All My Loving; She Loves You; Long Tall Sally

Magical Mystery Tour—Parlophone PCTC 255; (December 1976):
The U.S. version, finally issued nine years later (see p. 211)

Love Songs—Parlophone PCSP 721 (2 L.P.'s); (November 1977):
Yesterday; I'll Follow the Sun; I Need You; Girl; In My Life; Words Of Love; Here, There, and Everywhere; Something; And I Love Her; If I Fell; I'll Be Back; Tell Me What You See; Yes It Is; Michelle; It's Only Love; You're Gonna Lose That Girl; Every Little Thing; For No One; She's Leaving Home; The Long and Winding Road; This Boy; Norwegian Wood; You've Got To Hide Your Love Away; I Will; P.S. I Love You

JOHN LENNON'S BRITISH SINGLES:

Give Peace a Chance/Remember Love
—Apple 13; (July 1969) By Plastic Ono Band

Cold Turkey/Don't Worry Kyoko (Mummy's Only Looking For a Hand In the Snow)—Apple 1001; (October 1969) By Plastic Ono Band

Instant Karma (We All Shine On)/Who Has Seen the Wind?
—Apple 1003; (February 1970): By John Ono Lennon with The Plastic Ono Band

Power To the People/Open Your Box (later retitled Hirake)
—Apple R 5892; (March 1971) By John Lennon Plastic Ono Band

Happy Xmas (War Is Over)/Listen, the Snow Is Falling
—Apple R 5970; (November 1972) By John Lennon And Yoko Ono Plastic Ono Band

Mind Games/Meat City
—Apple R 5994; (November 1973) By John Lennon

Whatever Gets You Thru the Night/Beef Jerky
—Apple R 5998; (October 1974) By John Lennon with The Plastic Ono Nuclear Band

No. 9 Dream/What You Got
—Apple R 6003; (January 1975) By John Lennon

Stand By Me/Move Over Ms. L
—Apple R 6005; (April 1975) By John Lennon

Imagine/Working Class Hero
—Apple R 6009; (October 1975) By John Lennon

JOHN LENNON'S BRITISH L.P.'S:

Unfinished Music No. 1—Two Virgins

—Apple SAPCOR 2; (November 1968):
By John Lennon and Yoko Ono:
Two Virgins; Two Virgins No. 1; Together; Two Virgins No. 2; Two Virgins No. 3; Two Virgins No. 4; Two Virgins No. 5; Two Virgins No. 6; Hushaby Hushabye; Two Virgins No. 7; Two Virgins No. 8; Two Virgins No. 9; Two Virgins No. 10

Unfinished Music No. 2—Life With The Lions

—Zapple 01; (May 1969):
By John Lennon And Yoko Ono: "Cambridge 1969": Sing For John; Cambridge 1969; Let's Go On Flying; Snow Is Falling All the Time; Mummy's Only Looking For a Hand In the Snow; No Bed For Beatle John; Baby's Heartbeat; Two Minutes Silence; Radio Play

Wedding Album—Apple SAPCOR 11; (November 1969):
By John Ono Lennon And Yoko Ono Lennon: John And Yoko; Amsterdam

The Plastic Ono Band—Live Peace in Toronto

—Apple CORE 2001; (December 1969):
By The Plastic Ono Band: Blue Suede Shoes; Money (That's What I Want); Dizzy Miss Lizzie; Yer Blues; Cold Turkey; Give Peace a Chance; Don't Worry Kyoko (Mummy's Only Looking For a Hand In the Snow); John, John (Let's Hope For Peace)

John Lennon Plastic Ono Band

—Apple PCS 7124; (December 1970):
By John Lennon Plastic Ono Band: Mother; Hold On (John); I Found Out; Working Class Hero; Isolation; Remember; Love; Well Well Well; Look At Me; God; My Mummy's Dead

Imagine—Apple PAS 10004; (October 1971):
By John Lennon Plastic Ono Band with the Flux Fiddlers: Imagine; Crippled Inside; It's So Hard; I Don't Want To Be a Soldier Mama; I Don't Want To Die; Give Me Some Truth; Oh My Love; How Do You Sleep?; How?; Oh Yoko!

Sometime in New York City
—Apple PCSP 716 (2 L.P.'s); (September 1972):
By John Lennon and Yoko Ono with the Plastic Ono Band, Elephant's Memory, and the Invisible Strings: Woman Is the Nigger Of the World; Sisters O Sisters; Attica State; Born In a Prison; New York City; Sunday Bloody Sunday; The Luck Of the Irish; John Sinclair; Angela; We're All Water; plus LIVE JAM: Cold Turkey; Don't Worry Kyoko; Baby Please Don't Go; Jamrag; Scumbag; Au

Mind Games—Apple PCS 7165; (November 1973):
By John Lennon and the Plastic U.F. Ono Band: Mind Games; Tight A$; Aisumasen (I'm Sorry); One Day At a Time; Bring On the Lucie (Freda Peeple); Nutopian International Anthem; Intuition; Out Of the Blue; Only People; I Know (I Know); You Are Here; Meat City

Walls and Bridges—Apple PCTC 253; (September 1974):
By John Lennon and the Plastic Ono Nuclear Band: Going Down On Love; Whatever Gets You Thru the Night; Old Dirt Road; What You Got; Bless You; Scared; Number Nine Dream; Surprise, Surprise (Sweet Bird Of Paradox); Steel and Glass; Beef Jerky; Nobody Loves You (When You're Down and Out); Ya Ya

Rock 'n' Roll—Apple PCS 7169; (February 1975):
Be Bop a Lula; Stand By Me; Rip It Up/Ready Teddy; You Can't Catch Me; Ain't That a Shame; Do You Want to Dance; Sweet Little 16; Slippin' and Slidin'; Peggie Sue; Bring It On Home To Me/Send Me Some Lovin'; Bony Maronie; Ya Ya; Just Because

Shaved Fish—Apple PCS 7173; (October 1975):
Give Peace a Chance/Cold Turkey; Instant Karma; Power to the People; Mother; Woman Is the Nigger Of the World; Imagine; Whatever Gets You Thru the Night; Mind Games; Number Nine Dream; Happy Xmas (War Is Over)/Give Peace a Chance

PAUL McCARTNEY'S BRITISH SINGLES:

Another Day/Oh Woman, Oh Why
—Apple R 5889; (February 1971) By Paul McCartney

The Back Seat Of My Car/Heart Of the Country
—Apple R 5914; (August 1971) By Paul and Linda McCartney

Give Ireland Back To the Irish/Give Ireland Back To the Irish (version two)—Apple R 5936; (February 1972) By Wings

Mary Had a Little Lamb/Little Woman Love
—Apple R 5949; (May 1972) By Wings

Hi, Hi, Hi/C Moon—Apple R 5973; (December 1972) By Wings

My Love/The Mess
—Apple R 5985; (March 1973) By Paul McCartney and Wings

Live and Let Die/I Lie Around—Apple R 5987; (June 1973) By Wings

Helen Wheels/Country Dreamer
—Apple R 5994; (November 1973) By Paul McCartney and Wings

Jet/Let Me Roll It
—Apple R 5996; (February 1974) By Paul McCartney and Wings

Band On the Run/Zoo Gang
—Apple R 5997; (June 1974) By Paul McCartney and Wings

Walking In the Park With Eloise/Bridge Over the River Suite
—EMI 3977; (October 1974) By The Country Hams

Junior's Farm/Sally G
—Apple R 5999; (October 1974/A and B sides reversed: February 1975) By Paul McCartney and Wings

Listen To What the Man Said/Love In Song
—Parlophone R 6006; (May 1975)

Letting Go/You Gave Me the Answer
—Parlophone R 6008; (September 1975)

Medley: Venus and Mars/Rock Show/Magneto And Titanium Man
—Parlophone R 6010; (November 1975)

Silly Love Songs/Cook Of the House
—Parlophone R 6014; (March 1976)

Let 'Em In/Beware My Love—Parlophone R 6015; (June 1976)

Maybe I'm Amazed/Soily
—Parlophone R 6017; (February 1977) (all by Wings)

Mull Of Kintyre/Girl's School
—Parlophone R 6018; (November 1977)

With a Little Luck/Medley: Backwards Traveller-Cuff Link
—Parlophone R 6019; (March 1978)

PAUL McCARTNEY'S BRITISH L.P.'S:

The Family Way—Decca SKL 4847; (January 1967) Original Soundtrack: Love In the Open Air; Theme From "The Family Way"

McCartney
—Apple PCS 7102; (April 1970) By Paul McCartney:
The Lovely Linda; That Would Be Something; Every Night; Hot As Sun/Glasses; Junk; Man We Was Lonely; Oo You; Momma Miss America; Teddy Boy; Singalong Junk; Maybe I'm Amazed; Kreen-Akrore

Ram—Apple PAS 1000; (May 1971) By Paul and Linda McCartney:
Too Many People; 3 Legs; Ram On; Dear Boy; Uncle Albert/Admiral Halsey; Smile Away; Heart Of the Country; Monkberry Moon Delight; Eat At Home; Long Haired Lady; Ram On (version two); The Back Seat Of My Car

Wild Life—Apple PCS 7142; (December 1971) By Wings:
Mumbo; Bip Bop; Love Is Strange; Wild Life; Some People Never Know; I Am Your Singer; Tomorrow; Dear Friend

Red Rose Speedway—Apple PCTC 251; (May 1973)
By Paul McCartney and Wings:
Big Barn Bed; My Love; Get On the Right Thing; One More Kiss; Little Lamb Dragonfly; Single Pigeon; When the Night; Loup (First Indian On the Moon); Medley: Hold Me Tight/Lazy Dynamite/Hands Of Love/Power Cut

Band On The Run—Apple PAS 10007; (December 1973) By Paul McCartney and Wings:
Band On the Run; Jet; Bluebird; Mrs. Vanderbilt; Let Me Roll It; Mamunia; No Words; Picasso's Last Words (Drink To Me); Nineteen Hundred and Eighty-Five

Venus and Mars—Parlophone PCTC 254; (May 1975) By Wings:
Venus and Mars; Rock Show; Love In Song; You Gave Me the Answer; Magneto And Titanium Man; Letting Go; Venus and Mars (reprise); Spirits of Ancient Egypt; Medicine Jar; Call Me Back Again; Listen to What the Man Said; Medley: Treat Her Gently/Lonely Old People; Crossroads Theme

Wings at the Speed of Sound
—Parlophone PAS 10010; (March 1976) By Wings:
Let 'Em In; The Note You Never Wrote; She's My Baby; Beware My Love; Wino Junko; Silly Love Songs; Cook Of the House; Time To Hide; Must Do Something About It; San Ferry Anne; Warm and Beautiful

Wings Over America
—Parlophone PCSP 720 (3 L.P.'s); (December 1976) By Wings:
Venus and Mars/Rock Show; Jet; Let Me Roll It; Spirits Of Ancient Egypt; Medicine Jar; Maybe I'm Amazed; Call Me Back Again; Lady Madonna; The Long And Winding Road; Live and Let Die; Picasso's Last Words; Richard Cory; Bluebird; I've Just Seen a Face; Blackbird; Yesterday; Let 'Em In; Time To Hide; Silly Love Songs; Beware My Love; Letting Go; You Gave Me the Answer; Magneto And Titanium Man; Go Now; My Love; Listen To What the Man Said; Band On the Run; Hi, Hi, Hi; Soily

London Town—Parlophone PAS 10012; (March 1978):
London Town; Cafe On the Left Bank; I'm Carrying; Backwards Traveller/Cuff Link; Children Children; Girlfriend; I've Had Enough; With a Little Luck; Famous Groupies; Deliver Your Children; Name and Address; Don't Let It Bring You Down; Morse Moose and the Grey Goose

GEORGE HARRISON'S BRITISH SINGLES:

My Sweet Lord/Isn't It a Pity—Apple R 5884; (January 1971)

Bangla Desh/Deep Blue—Apple R 5912; (July 1971)

Give Me Love (Give Me Peace On Earth)/Miss O'Dell
—Apple R 5988; (May 1973)

Ding Dong, Ding Dong/I Don't Care Anymore
—Apple R 6002; (December 1974)

Dark Horse/Hari's On Tour (Express)—Apple R 6001; (March 1975)

You/World of Stone—Apple R 6007; (September 1975)

This Guitar (Can't Keep From Crying)/Maya Love
—Apple R 6012; (February 1976)

This Song/Learning How To Love You
—Dark Horse K16856; (November 1976)

True Love/Pure Smokey—Dark Horse K 16896; (March 1977)

Woman Don't You Cry For Me/It's What You Value—Dark Horse K 16967; (May 1977)

GEORGE HARRISON'S BRITISH L.P.'S:

Wonderwall Music—Apple SAPCOR 1; (November 1968):
Microbes; Red Lady Too; Medley: Table and Pakavaj/In the Park; Medley: Drilling a Home/Guru Vandana; Medley: Greasy Legs/Ski-ing and Gat Kirwani/Dream Scene; Party Seacombe; Medley: Love Scene/Crying; Cowboy Museum; Medley: Fantasy Sequins/Glass Box; On the Bed; Wonderwall To Be There; Singing Om

Electronic Sound—Zapple 02; (May 1969):
Under the Mersey Wall; No Time Or Space

All Things Must Pass
—Apple STCH 639 (3 L.P.'s); (November 1970):
I'd Have You Anytime; My Sweet Lord; Wah-Wah; Isn't It a Pity (version one); What Is Life?; If Not For You; Behind That Locked Door; Let It Down; Run Of the Mill; Beware Of Darkness; Apple Scruffs; Ballad of Sir Frankie Crisp (Let It Roll); Awaiting On You All; All Things Must Pass; I Dig Love; Art Of Dying; Isn't It a Pity (version two): Hear Me Lord; Apple Jam; Out Of the Blue; It's Johnny's Birthday; Plug Me In; I Remember Jeep; Thanks For the Pepperoni

The Concert for Bangla Desh
—Apple STCX 3385 (3 L.P.'s); (January 1972):
Additional material by other artists: Wah-Wah; My Sweet Lord; Awaiting On You All; Beware of Darkness; While My Guitar Gently Weeps; Here Comes the Sun; Something; Bangla Desh

Living in the Material World—Apple PAS 10006; (June 1973):
Give Me Love; Sue Me, Sue You Blues; The Light That Has Lighted the World; Don't Let Me Wait Too Long; Who Can See It; Living In the Material World; The Lord Loves the One (That Loves the Lord); Be Here Now; Try Some, Buy Some; The Day the World Gets 'Round; That Is All

Dark Horse—Apple PAS 10008; (December 1974):
Hari's On Tour (Express); Simply Shady; So Sad; Bye Bye, Love; Maya Love; Ding Dong; Dark Horse; Far East Man; It Is "He" (Jai Sri Krishna)

Extra Texture—Read All About It
—Apple PAS 10009; (October 1975):
You; The Answer's At the End; This Guitar (Can't Keep From Crying); Ooh Baby (You Know That I Love You); World Of Stone; A Bit More Of You; Can't Stop Thinking About You; Tired Of Midnight Blue; Grey Cloudy Lies; His Name Is Legs (Ladies and Gentleman)

The Best of George Harrison
—EMI PAS 10011; (November 1976):
Something; If I Needed Someone; Here Comes The Sun; Taxman; Think For Yourself; For You Blue; While My Guitar Gently Weeps; My Sweet Lord; Give Me Love (Give Me Peace On Earth); You; Bangla Desh; Dark Horse; What Is Life

Thirty-Three and a Third—Dark Horse K56319; (November 1976):
Woman Don't You Cry For Me; Dear One; Beautiful Girl; This Song; See Yourself; It's What You Value; True Love; Pure Smokey; Crackerbox Palace; Learning How To Love You

RINGO STARR'S BRITISH SINGLES:

It Don't Come Easy/Early 1970—Apple R 5898; (April 1971)
Back Off Boogaloo/Blindman—Apple R 5944; (March 1972)
Photograph/Down and Out—Apple R 5992; (October 1973)
You're Sixteen/Devil Woman—Apple R 5995; (February 1974)
Only You (And You Alone)/Call Me—Apple R 6000; (November 1974)
Snookeroo/Oo-Wee—Apple R 6004; (February 1975)
A Dose Of Rock 'N' Roll/Cryin'—Polydor 200194; (September 1976)
Hey Baby/Lady Gaye—Polydor 2001699; (December 1976)
Drowning in a Sea of Love/Just a Dream—Polydor, 2001 734; (September 1977)

RINGO STARR'S BRITISH L.P.'S:

Sentimental Journey—Apple PCS 7101; (March 1970):
Sentimental Journey; Night and Day; Whispering Grass (Don't Tell the Trees); Bye Bye Blackbird; I'm a Fool To Care; Star Dust; Blue, Turning Grey Over You; Love Is a Many Spendoured Thing; Dream; You Always Hurt the One You Love; Have I Told You Lately That I Love You?; Let the Rest Of the World Go By

Beaucoups Of Blues
—Apple PAS 10002; (September 1970):
Beaucoups Of Blues; Love Don't Last Long; Fastest Growing Heartache In the West; Without Her; Woman Of the Night; I'd Be Talking All the Time; $15 Draw; Wine, Women And Loud Happy Songs; I Wouldn't Have You Any Other Way; Loser's Lounge; Waiting; Silent Homecoming

"Ringo"—Apple PCTC 252; (November 1973):
I'm the Greatest; Hold On (Have You Seen My Baby); Photograph; Sunshine Life For Me; You're Sixteen; Oh My My; Step Lightly; Six O'clock; Devil Woman; You And Me (Babe)

Goodnight Vienna—Apple PCS 7168; (November 1974):
(It's All Da-Da Down To) Goodnight Vienna; Occapella; Oo-Wee; Husbands And Wives; Snookeroo; All By Myself; Call Me; No No Song; Only You (And You Alone); Easy For Me; Goodnight Vienna (reprise)

Blast From Your Past
—Apple PCS 7170; (November 1975):
You're Sixteen; No No Song; It Don't Come Easy; Photograph; Back Off Boogaloo; Only You (And You Alone); Beaucoups Of Blues; Oh My My; Early 1970; I'm the Greatest

Ringo's Rotogravure
—Polydor 2382040; (September 1976):
A Dose Of Rock 'n' Roll; Hey Baby; Pure Gold; Cryin'; You Don't Know Me At All; Cookin'; I'll Still Love You; This Be Called A Song; Las Brisas; Lady Gaye; Spooky Weirdness

Ringo the 4th—Polydor 2310 556; (September 1977):
Drowning In a Sea Of Love; Tango All Night; Wings; Gave It All Up; Out On the Streets; Can She Do It Like She Dances; Sneaking Sally Through the Alley; It's No Secret; Gypsies In Flight; Simple Love Song

Bad Boy—Polydor; (April 1978):
Who Needs a Heart; Bad Boy; Lipstick Traces; Heart On My Sleeve; Where Did Our Love Go; Hard Times; Tonight; Monkey See Monkey Do; Old Time Relovin'; A Man Like Me

UNITED STATES SINGLES:

Please Please Me/Ask Me Why
—Vee Jay VJ 498; (February 1963) OP*
From Me To You/Thank You Girl
—Vee Jay VJ 522; (May 1963) OP
She Loves You/I'll Get You
—Swan 4152; (September 1963) OP
I Want To Hold Your Hand/I Saw Her Standing There
—Capitol 5112; (January 1964)
My Bonnie/The Saints—MGM K 13213; (January 1964) OP
Please Please Me/From Me To You
—rereleased: Vee Jay VJ 581; (January 1964) OP
Twist and Shout/There's a Place
—Tollie 9001; (March 1964) OP
Can't Buy Me Love/You Can't Do That
—Capitol 5150; (March 1964)
Do You Want To Know a Secret/Thank You Girl
—Vee Jay VJ 587; (March 1964) OP
Why/Cry For a Shadow—MGM K 13227; (March 1964) OP
Love Me Do/P.S. I Love You—Tollie 9008; (April 1964) OP
Sie Liebt Dich/I'll Get You—Swan 4182; (May 1964) OP
Take Out Some Insurance On Me Baby/Sweet Georgia Brown
—Atco 6302; (June 1964) OP
Ain't She Sweet/Nobody's Child
—Atco 6308; (July 1964) OP
A Hard Day's Night/I Should Have Known Better
—Capitol 5222; (July 1964)
I'll Cry Instead/I'm Happy Just To Dance With You
—Capitol 5234; (July 1964)
And I Love Her/If I Fell—Capitol 5235; (July 1964)
Matchbox/Slow Down—Capitol 5255; (August 1964)
Do You Want To Know a Secret/Thank you Girl
—rereleased: Oldies 45 OL 149; (August 1964)
Please Please Me/From Me To You
—rereleased: Oldies 45 OL 150; (August 1964)

*Out of print.

Love Me Do/P.S. I Love You
—rereleased: Oldies 45 OL 151; (August 1964)

Twist And Shout/There's a Place
—rereleased Oldies 45 OL 152; (August 1964)

I Feel Fine/She's a Woman
—Capitol 5327; (November 1964)

Eight Days a Week/I Don't Want To Spoil the Party
—Capitol 5371; (February 1965)

Ticket To Ride/Yes It Is—Capitol 5407; (April 1965)

Help!/I'm Down—Capitol 5476; (July 1965)

Yesterday/Act Naturally—Capitol 5498; (September 1965)

Twist and Shout/There's a Place
—rereleased: Capitol Starline 6061; (October 1965) OP*

Love Me Do/P.S. I Love You
—rereleased: Capitol Starline 6062; (October 1965) OP

Please Please Me/From Me To You
—rereleased: Capitol Starline 6063; (October 1965) OP

Do You Want To Know a Secret/Thank You Girl
—rereleased: Capitol Starline 6064; (October 1965) OP

Roll Over Beethoven/Misery—Capitol Starline 6065; (October 1965) OP

Boys/Kansas City—Capitol Starline 6066; (October 1965) OP

We Can Work It Out/Day Tripper—Capitol 5555; (December 1965)

Nowhere Man/What Goes On—Capitol 5587; (February 1966)

Paperback Writer/Rain—Capitol 5651; (May 1966)

Yellow Submarine/Eleanor Rigby—Capitol 5715; (August 1966)

Penny Lane/Strawberry Fields Forever—Capitol 5810; (February 1967)

All You Need Is Love/Baby, You're a Rich Man
—Capitol 5964; (July 1967)

Hello Goodbye/I Am the Walrus—Capitol 2056; (November 1967)

Lady Madonna/The Inner Light—Capitol 2138; (March 1968)

Hey Jude/Revolution—Apple 2276; (August 1968)

Get Back/Don't Let Me Down—Apple 2490; (May 1969)

The Ballad Of John and Yoko/Old Brown Shoe
—Apple 2531; (June 1969)

Something/Come Together—Apple 2654; (October 1969)

Let It Be/You Know My Name (Look Up the Number)
—Apple 2764; (March 1970)

The Long and Winding Road/For You Blue—Apple 2832; (May 1970)

Got To Get You Into My Life/Helter Skelter—Capitol 4274; (May 1976)

Ob-La-Di; Ob-La-Da/Julia—Capitol 4347; (November 1976)

UNITED STATES E.P.'S:

The Beatles—Vee Jay VJEP 1-903; (March 1964):
Misery; A Taste Of Honey; Ask Me Why; Anna OP

Four By The Beatles—Capitol EAP 2121; (May 1964):
Roll Over Beethoven; All My Loving; This Boy; Please Mr. Postman
OP

4 By The Beatles—Capitol R 5365; (February 1965):
Honey Don't; I'm a Loser; Mr. Moonlight; Everybody's Trying To Be
My Baby OP

UNITED STATES L.P.'S:

Introducing The Beatles—Vee Jay VJLP 1062; (July 1963):
I Saw Her Standing There; Misery; Anna (Go To Him); Chains; Boys;
Love Me Do †; P.S. I Love You †; Baby, It's You; Do You Want To
Know a Secret; A Taste Of Honey; There's a Place; Twist and Shout OP

Meet The Beatles!—Capitol ST 2047; (January 1964):
I Want To Hold Your Hand; I Saw Her Standing There;
This Boy; It Won't Be Long; All I've Got To Do; Don't
Bother Me; Little Child; Till There Was You; Hold Me
Tight; I Wanna Be Your Man; Not a Second Time

The Beatles With Tony Sheridan and Their Guests
—MGM SE 4215; (February 1964); Additional material by
other artists:
My Bonnie; Cry For A Shadow; The Saints; Why OP

Jolly What! The Beatles and Frank Ifield On Stage
—Vee Jay VJLP 1085; (February 1964) Additional material by Frank Ifield:
Please Please Me; From Me To You; Ask Me Why; Thank
You Girl OP

The Beatles' Second Album
—Capitol ST 2080; (April 1964):
Roll Over Beethoven; Thank You Girl; You Really Got a
Hold On Me; Devil In Her Heart; Money (That's What I
Want); You Can't Do That; Long Tall Sally; I Call Your
Name; Please Mr. Postman; I'll Get You; She Loves You

A Hard Day's Night
—United Artists Uas 6366; (June 1964); Additional material by George Martin and Orchestra:
A Hard Day's Night; Tell Me Why; I'll Cry Instead; I'm
Happy Just To Dance With You; I Should Have Known
Better; If I Fell; And I Love Her; Can't Buy Me Love

Something New—Capitol ST 2108; (July 1964):
I'll Cry Instead; Things We Said Today; Anytime At All;
When I Get Home; Slow Down; Matchbox; Tell Me Why;
And I Love Her; I'm Happy Just To Dance With You; If I
Fell; Komm, Gib Mir Deine Hand

The Beatles Vs. The Four Seasons
—Vee Jay VJDX 30 (2 L.P.'s); (October 1964); Additional
material by The Four Seasons:
I Saw Her Standing There; Misery; Anna (Go To Him);
Chains; Boys; Ask Me Why; Please Please Me; Baby, It's
You; Do You Want To Know a Secret; A Taste Of Honey;
There's a Place; Twist and Shout OP

Ain't She Sweet
—Atco SD 33-169; (October 1964); By Tony Sheridan
and The Beatles; Additional material by The Swallows:
Ain't She Sweet; Sweet Georgia Brown; Take Out Some
Insurance On Me, Baby; Nobody's Child OP

Songs, Pictures and Stories of The Fabulous Beatles
—Vee Jay VJLP 1092; (October 1964): Same songs as
on **The Beatles vs. The Four Seasons** OP

The Beatles' Story
—Capitol STBO 2222 (2 L.P.'s); (November 1964); Includes interviews with the Beatles, narrative, and brief
snatches of songs.

Beatles '65—Capitol ST 2228; (December 1964):
No Reply; I'm a Loser; Baby's In Black; Rock And Roll
Music; I'll Follow the Sun; Mr. Moonlight; Honey Don't; I'll
Be Back; She's a Woman; I Feel Fine; Everybody's Trying
To Be My Baby

The Early Beatles—Capitol ST 2309; (March 1965):
Love Me Do; Twist and Shout; Anna (Go To Him); Chains;
Boys; Ask Me Why; Please Please Me; P.S. I Love You;
Baby, It's You; A Taste Of Honey; Do You Want To Know
a Secret

Beatles VI—Capitol ST 2358; (June 1965):
Kansas City; Eight Days a Week; You Like Me Too Much;
Bad Boy; I Don't Want To Spoil the Party; Words Of Love;
What You're Doing; Yes It Is; Dizzy Miss Lizzie; Tell Me
What You See; Every Little Thing

Help!
—Capitol SMAS 2386; (August 1965); Additional material
by George Martin and Orchestra:
Help!; The Night Before; You've Got To Hide Your Love
Away; I Need You; Another Girl; Ticket To Ride; You're
Gonna Lose That Girl

Rubber Soul—Capitol ST 2442; (December 1965):
I've Just Seen a Face; Norwegian Wood; You Won't See
Me; Think For Yourself; The Word; Michelle; It's Only
Love; Girl; I'm Looking Through You; In My Life; Wait;
Run For Your Life

*Out of print.

† later version of this L.P. contains "Ask Me Why" and "Please Please Me"
instead of these two songs. Released in January 1964.

"Yesterday" . . . And Today—Capitol ST 2553; (June 1966):
Drive My Car; I'm Only Sleeping; Nowhere Man; Dr.
Robert; Yesterday; Act Naturally; And Your Bird Can
Sing; If I Needed Someone; We Can Work It Out; What
Goes On?; Day Tripper

Revolver—Capitol ST 2576; (August 1966):
Taxman; Eleanor Rigby; Love Me Too; Here, There and
Everywhere; Yellow Submarine; She Said She Said;
Good Day Sunshine; For No One; I Want To Tell You; Got
To Get You Into My Life; Tomorrow Never Knows

This Is Where It Started
—Metro MS 563; (August 1966); By Tony Sheridan and
The Beatles; Additional material by Tony Sheridan and
The Beat Brothers and The Titans:
My Bonnie; Cry For a Shadow; The Saints; Why OP*

The Amazing Beatles
—Clarion 601; (October 1966); Additional material by the
Swallows: Ain't She Sweet?; Take Out Some Insurance On Me
Baby; Nobody's Child; Sweet Georgia Brown OP

Sgt. Pepper's Lonely Hearts Club Band
—Capitol SMAS 2653; (June 1967): Same as British release

Magical Mystery Tour—Capitol SMAL 2835; (November 1967):
Magical Mystery Tour; The Fool On the Hill; Flying; Blue
Jay Way; Your Mother Should Know; I Am the Walrus;
Hello Goodbye; Strawberry Fields Forever; Penny Lane;
Baby, You're a Rich Man; All You Need Is Love

The Beatles—Apple SWBO 101 (2 L.P.'s); (November 1968):
Same as British release

Yellow Submarine—Apple SW 153; (January 1969):
Same as British release

Abbey Road—Apple SO 383; (October 1969):
Same as British release

Hey Jude (Also called **The Beatles Again**)
—Apple SW 385/SO 385; (February 1970):
Can't Buy Me Love; I Should Have Known Better; Paper-
back Writer; Rain; Lady Madonna; Revolution; Hey Jude;
Old Brown Shoe; Don't Let Me Down; The Ballad Of John
and Yoko

In the Beginning (circa 1960)
—Polydor 24–4504; (May 1970); Same songs as the
British *Beatles' First*

Let It Be—Red Apple 34001; (May 1970): distributed by
United Artists: Same as British release, but no book

The Beatles 1962—1966
—Apple SKBO 3403 (2 L.P.'s); (April 1973):
Same as British release

The Beatles 1967—1970
—Apple SKBO 3404 (2 L.P.'s); (April 1973):
Same as British release

Rock and Roll Music
—Capitol SKBO 11537 (2 L.P.'s); (June 1976):
Same as British release

The Beatles at the Hollywood Bowl
—Capitol SMAS 11638; (May 1977): Same as the British release

Live! at the Star Club in Hamburg, Germany, 1962
—Lingasong/Atlantic LS-2-7001 (2 L.P.'s); (June 1977):
I'm Gonna Sit Right Down and Cry Over You; Roll Over Beethoven;
Hippy Hippy Shake; Sweet Little 16; Lend Me Your Comb; Your
Feets Too Big; Where Have You Been All My Life; Mr. Moonlight; A
Taste Of Honey; Besame Mucho; Till There Was You; Kansas
City/Hey Hey Hey Hey; Hallelujah I Just Love Her So; Ain't Nothing;
Shaking Like a Leaf On a Tree; To Know Her Is To Love Her; Little
Queenie; Falling in Love Again; Sheila; Be-Bop-a-Lula; Red Sails
In the Sunset; Everybody's Trying To Be My Baby; Matchbox;
Talkin' Bout You; Shimmy Shake; Long Tall Sally; I Remember You

Love Songs—Capitol SKBL 11711 (2.L.P.'s)
(October 1977): Same as the British release

*Out of print.

JOHN LENNON'S AMERICAN SINGLES:

Give Peace a Chance/Remember Love
—Apple 1809; (July 1969) By Plastic Ono Band OP

Cold Turkey/Don't Worry Kyoko (Mummy's Only Looking
For a Hand In the Snow)
—Apple 1813; (October 1969) By Plastic Ono Band OP

Instant Karma (We All Shine On)/Who Has Seen the Wind?
—Apple 1818; (February 1970) By John Ono Lennon with
the Plastic Ono Band OP

Mother/Why?
—Apple 1827; (December 1970) By John Lennon Plastic
Ono Band

Power to the People/Touch Me
Apple 1830; (March 1971) By John Lennon Plastic Ono
Band

Imagine/It's So Hard
—Apple 1840; (October 1971) By John Lennon Plastic Ono Band

Happy Xmas (War Is Over)/Listen, the Snow Is Falling
—Apple 1842; (December 1971) By John Lennon and
Yoko Ono Plastic Ono Band With the Harlem Community
Choir on Side A

Woman Is the Nigger Of the World/Sisters, O Sisters
—Apple 1848; (April 1972) By John Lennon and Yoko
Ono Plastic Ono Band with Elephant's Memory and the
Invisible Strings

Mind Games/Meat City—Apple 1868; (October 1973) By John Lennon

Whatever Gets You Thru the Night/Beef Jerky
—Apple 1874; (September 1974) By John Lennon with
the Plastic Ono Nuclear Band

No. 9 Dream/What You Got
—Apple 1878; (December 1974) By John Lennon

Stand By Me/Move Over Ms. L
—Apple 1881; (March 1975) By John Lennon

JOHN LENNON'S AMERICAN L.P.'S:

Unfinished Music No. 1—Two Virgins
—Apple T 5001; (November 1968) OP

Unfinished Music No. 2—Life With The Lions
—Zapple ST 3357; (May 1969) OP

Wedding Album—Apple SMAX 3361; (October 1969) OP

The Plastic Ono Band—Live Peace in Toronto
—Apple SW 3362; (December 1969) OP

John Lennon/Plastic Ono Band—Apple SW 3372; (December 1970)

Imagine—Apple SW 3379; (September 1971)

Sometime in New York City—Apple SVBB 3392 (2 L.P.'s); (June 1972)

Mind Games—Apple SW 3414; (November 1973)

Walls and Bridges—Apple SW 3416; (September 1974)

Rock 'N' Roll—Apple SK 3419; (February 1975)

Shaved Fish—Apple SW 3421; (October 1975)

All L.P.'s contain same material as British versions.

PAUL McCARTNEY'S AMERICAN SINGLES:

Another Day/Oh Woman, Oh Why
—Apple 1829; (February 1971): By Paul McCartney

Uncle Albert/Admiral Halsey/Too Many People
—Apple 1837; (August 1971): By Paul and Linda McCartney

Give Ireland Back to the Irish (version one and two)
—Apple 1847; (February 1972): By Wings

Mary Had a Little Lamb/Little Woman Love
—Apple 1851; (May 1972): By Wings

Hi, Hi, Hi/C Moon—Apple 1857; (December 1972) By Wings

My Love/The Mess
—Apple 1861; (April 1973) By Paul McCartney and Wings

Live And Let Die/I Lie Around
—Apple 1863; (June 1973) By Wings

Note: Original Capitol releases featured a capitol dome logo on a
"rainbow" label (L.P.'s) or an orange/yellow "swirl" label (all 45's, except
Star Line series, which had a dark green/light green "swirl"). Beatles
records were re-issued in 1968 on a plain green label; in 1971 on the Apple label; and in 1976 on a plain red label.

Helen Wheels/Country Dreamer
—Apple 1869; (November 1973) By Paul McCartney and Wings

Jet/Mamunia
—Apple 1871; (January 1974) By Paul McCartney and Wings

Jet/Let Me Roll It
—Apple 1871; (February 1974) By Paul McCartney and Wings

Band On the Run/Nineteen Hundred and Eighty-Five
—Apple 1873; (April 1974) By Paul McCartney and Wings

Walking In the Park With Eloise/Bridge Over the River Suite
—EMI 3977; (December 1974) By The Country Hams

Junior's Farm/Sally G
—Apple 1875; (November 1974/A and B sides reversed:
January 1975) By Paul McCartney and Wings

Listen To What the Man Said/Love In Song
—Capitol 4091; (May 1975): By Wings

Letting Go/You Gave Me the Answer
—Capitol 4145; (September 1975) By Wings

Medley: Venus And Mars/Rock Show/Magneto and Titanium Man—Capitol 4175; (October 1975) By Wings

Silly Love Songs/Cook Of the House
—Capitol 4256; (March 1976) By Wings

Let 'Em In/Beware My Love —Captiol 4293; (June 1976) By Wings

Maybe I'm Amazed/Soily
—Capitol 4385; (February 1977) By Wings

Seaside Woman/B-Side to Seaside
—Epic 8-50403; June 1977) By Suzy and the Red Stripes (a.k.a.
Linda McCartney and Wings)

Girl's School/Mull Of Kintyre
—Capitol 4504; (November 1977) By Wings

With a Little Luck/Medley: Backwards Traveller-Cuff Link
—Capitol 4559; (March 1978) By Wings

PAUL McCARTNEY'S AMERICAN L.P.'s:

The Family Way—London MS 82007; (June 1967) OP*

McCartney—Apple STAO 3363; (April 1970)

Ram—Apple SMAS 3375; (May 1971)

Wild Life—Apple SW 3386; (December 1971)

Red Rose Speedway—Apple SMAL 3409; (April 1973)

Band On the Run—Apple SO 3415; (December 1974):
Same songs as the British release, plus Helen Wheels

Venus and Mars—Capitol SMAS 11419; (May 1975)

Wings at the Speed of Sound
—Capitol SW 11525; (May 1975)

Wings Over America
—Capitol SWCO 11593; (3 L.P.'s) (December 1976)

London Town—Capitol SW 11777; (March 1978)

All L.P.'s contain same material as British versions.

GEORGE HARRISON'S AMERICAN SINGLES:

My Sweet Lord/Isn't It a Pity (version one)
—Apple 2995; (November 1970)

What Is Life?/Apple Scruffs—Apple 1828; (February 1971)

Bangla Desh/Deep Blue—Apple 1836; July 1971)

Give Me Love/Miss O'Dell—Apple 1862; (May 1973)

Dark Horse/I Don't Care Anymore
—Apple 1877; (November 1974)

Ding Dong, Ding Dong/Hari's On Tour (Express)
—Apple 1879; (December 1974)

You/World Of Stone—Apple 1884; (September 1975)

This Guitar (Can't Keep From Crying)/Maya Love
—Apple 1885; (December 1975)

This Song/Learning How To Love You
—Dark Horse 8294; (November 1976)

Crackerbox Palace/Learning How To Love You
—Dark Horse 8313; (February 1977)

GEORGE HARRISON'S AMERICAN L.P.'S:

Wonderwall Music—Apple ST 3350; (December 1968) OP

Electronic Sound—Zapple ST 3358; (May 1969) OP

All Things Must Pass
—Apple STCH 639 (3 L.P.'s); (November 1970)

The Concert for Bangla Desh
—Apple STCX 3385; (3 L.P.'s) (December 1971)

Living in the Material World
—Apple SMAS 3410; (May 1973)

Dark Horse—Apple SMAS 3418; (December 1974)

Extra Texture—Apple SW 3420; (September 1975)

The Best of George Harrison
—Capitol ST 11578; (November 1976)

Thirty-Three and a Third
—Dark Horse DH 3005; (November 1976)

All L.P.'s include same material as British versions.

RINGO STARR'S AMERICAN SINGLES:

Beaucoups Of Blues/Coochy-Coochy
—Apple 2969; (October 1970)

It Don't Come Easy/Early 1970—Apple 1831; (April 1971)

Back Off Boogaloo/Blindman—Apple 1849; (March 1972)

Photograph/Down and Out—Apple 1865; (September 1973)

You're Sixteen/Devil Woman—Apple 1870; (December 1973)

Oh My My/Step Lightly—Apple 1872; (February 1974)

Only You (And You Alone)/Call Me
—Apple 1876; (November 1974)

No No Song/Snookeroo—Apple 1880; (January 1975)

(It's All Da-Da-Down To) Goodnight Vienna/Oo-Wee
—Apple 1882; (June 1975)

A Dose Of Rock 'n' Roll/Cryin'
—Atlantic 3361; (September 1976)

Hey Baby/Lady Gaye—Atlantic 3371; (November 1976)

Wings/Just a Dream—Atlantic 3429; (August 1977)

Lipstick Traces/Old Time Relovin'
—Portrait 70015; (April 1978)

RINGO STARR'S AMERICAN L.P.'S:

Sentimental Journey—Apple SW 3365; (April 1970)

Beaucoups Of Blues—Apple SMAS 3368; (September 1970)

"Ringo"—Apple SW 3412; (November 1973)

Goodnight Vienna—Apple SW 3417; (November 1974)

Blast From Your Past—Apple SW 3422; (November 1975)

Ringo's Rotogravure—Atlantic SD 18193; (September 1976)

Ringo the Fourth—Atlantic SD 19108; (September 1977)

Bad Boy—Portrait JR 35378; (April 1978)

All L.P.'s include same material as British versions.

BEATLE ALBUMS AROUND THE WORLD

Any attempt at a comprehensive roundup of all the Beatle
singles, E.P.'s, and L.P.'s that were issued in some three
dozen countries would be likely to fill a whole book this size.
The following discography focuses on Beatle albums
released in eight major markets whose contents differ from
any of the American and British L.P.'s

GERMANY:

The Beatles Beat Odeon C-062 04 363, (1964):
She Loves You; Thank You Girl; From Me To You; I'll Get You; I Want
To Hold Your Hand; Hold Me Tight; Can't Buy Me Love; You Can't Do
That; Roll Over Beethoven; Till There Was You; Money; Please Mister
Postman.

*Out of print.

And Now: The Beatles S*R International 73735, (1964): Same songs as **The Beatles Beat** OP*

The Beatles' Greatest—Odeon SMO 83991, (1965): I Want To Hold Your Hand; Twist and Shout; A Hard Day's Night; Eight Days a Week; I Should Have Known Better; Long Tall Sally; She Loves You; Please Mister Postman; I Feel Fine; Rock and Roll Music; Ticket To Ride; Please Please Me; It Won't Be Long; From Me To You; Can't Buy Me Love; All My Loving

The World's Best S*R International 77235, (1967): Good Day Sunshine; All My Loving; Eight Days a Week; No Reply; Rock 'n' Roll Music; A Hard Day's Night; I Should Have Known Better; And I Love Her; Things We Said Today; Michelle; Dr. Robert; Yellow Submarine; If I Fell; And Your Bird Can Sing; Girl; Eleanor Rigby OP

(All the Beatles' British compilations were also issued in Germany, along with America's **Something New, Beatles '65, Beatles VI, Magical Mystery Tour,** and **Hey Jude.**)

ITALY:

The Beatles In Italy Parlophone PMCQ 315006, (1965): Long Tall Sally; She's a Woman; Matchbox; From Me To You; I Want To Hold Your Hand; Ticket To Ride; This Boy; Slow Down; I Call Your Name; Thank You Girl; Yes It Is; I Feel Fine OP

(Contrary to Lennon's 1970 *Rolling Stone* interviews, this is not a live recording. All other Italian L.P.'s corresponded to the British.)

SPAIN:

Por Siempre Beatles Odeon J060-04973, (1971): Day Tripper; Yes It Is; I'm Down; The Fool On the Hill; Strawberry Fields Forever; We Can Work It Out; Your Mother Should Know; Penny Lane; Baby You're a Rich Man; I Call Your Name; The Inner Light; Blue Jay Way

(This is the only album to date to feature "The Inner Light." Other Spanish L.P.'s corresponded to the British.)

FRANCE:

Leurs 14 Plus Grands Succès Odéon OSX 231, (1965): From Me To You; Please Please Me; She Loves You; Twist and Shout; I Saw Her Standing There; I Want To Hold Your Hand; All My Loving; Roll Over Beethoven; Can't Buy Me Love; A Hard Day's Night; I Feel Fine; She's a Woman; Eight Days a Week; Rock 'n' Roll Music

(Other French L.P.'s corresponded to the British.)

CANADA:

Twist and Shout Capitol ST 6054, (1964): Anna; Chains; Boys; Ask Me Why; Please Please Me; Love Me Do; From Me To You; P.S. I Love You; Baby It's You; Do You Want To Know a Secret; A Taste Of Honey; There's a Place; Twist and Shout; She Loves You

Long Tall Sally Capitol ST 6063, (1964): I Want To Hold Your Hand; I Saw Her Standing There; You Really Got a Hold On Me; Devil In Her Heart; Roll Over Beethoven; Misery; Long Tall Sally; I Call Your Name; Please Mister Postman; This Boy; I'll Get You; You Can't Do That

(Capitol's first Canadian L.P., **BEATLEMANIA,** featured the same contents as Britain's **WITH THE BEATLES.** Beginning with July 1964's **SOMETHING NEW,** all subsequent albums corresponded to the American.)

AUSTRALIA:

The Essential Beatles Apple TV 558, (1971): Love Me Do; Boys; Long Tall Sally; Honey Don't; P.S. I Love You; Baby You're a Rich Man; All My Loving; Yesterday; Penny Lane; Magical Mystery Tour; Norwegian Wood; With a Little Help From My Friends; All You Need Is Love; Something; Ob-La-Di, Ob-La-Da; Let It Be

*Out of print.

AUSTRALIA; SINGAPORE-MALAYSIA-HONG KONG:

The Beatles' Greatest Hits, Vol. 1 Parlophone LPEA 1001, (1966): All My Loving; Can't Buy Me Love; From Me To You; Hold Me Tight; I Saw Her Standing There; I Want To Hold Your Hand; I'll Get You; Long Tall Sally; Love Me Do; Please Please Me; Roll Over Beethoven; She Loves You; Twist and Shout; You Can't Do That

The Beatles' Greatest Hits, Vol. 2 Parlophone LPEA 1002, (1966): A Hard Day's Night; Boys; I Should Have Known Better; I Feel Fine; She's a Woman; Till There Was You; Rock and Roll Music; Anna; Ticket To Ride; Eight Days a Week; Help!; Yesterday; We Can Work It Out; Day Tripper

(Other L.P.'s in these countries corresponded to the British.)

MEXICO:

Conozca Beatles Capitol SLEM 007, (1964): I Want To Hold Your Hand; I Saw Her Standing There; This Boy; I'll Get You; Thank You Girl; She Loves You; Don't Bother Me; Little Child; Hold Me Tight; I Wanna Be Your Man; Not a Second Time; From Me To You

The Beatles, Vol. 2 Capitol SLEM 043, (1964): Roll Over Beethoven; Baby It's You; Please Please Me; Boys; Twist and Shout; Ask Me Why; Love Me Do; P.S. I Love You; Taste Of Honey; Do You Want To Know a Secret; All My Loving; It Won't Be Long

The Beatles, Vol. 3 Capitol SLEM 045, (1964): Devil In Her Heart; Money; Anna; Chains; Misery; You Can't Do That; There's a Place; All I've Got To Do; Till There Was You; Please Mister Postman; You Really Got A Hold On Me; Can't Buy Me Love

The Beatles, Vol. 4 Capitol SLEM 008, (1964): A Hard Day's Night; I Should Have Known Better; If I Fell; I'm Happy Just To Dance With You; And I Love Her; Tell Me Why; Anytime At All; I'll Cry Instead; Things We Said Today; When I Get Home; I'll Be Back; Long Tall Sally

(Subsequent Mexican L.P.'s duplicated the American *Help* and *Yesterday and Today,* in other cases the British versions.)

JAPAN:

Meet The Beatles Odeon AR 8026, (1964): I Want To Hold Your Hand; She Loves You; From Me To You; Twist And Shout; Love Me Do; Baby It's You; Don't Bother Me; Please Please Me; I Saw Her Standing There; P.S. I Love You; Little Child; All My Loving; Hold Me Tight

The Beatles' Second Album Odeon AR 8027, (1964): Can't Buy Me Love; Do You Want To Know A Secret; Thank You Girl; A Taste Of Honey; It Won't Be Long; I Wanna Be Your Man; There's a Place; Roll Over Beethoven; Misery; Boys; Devil In Her Heart; Not a Second Time; Money; Till There Was You

Beatles No. 5 Odeon AR 8028, (1965): Long Tall Sally; Sie Lieb Dich; Anna; Matchbox; You Really Got a Hold On Me; She's a Woman; Ask Me Why; I Feel Fine; Komm, Gib Mir Deine Hand; Chains; Slow Down; All I've Gotta Do; I Call Your Name; This Boy

(All the Beatles' British compilations were also issued in Japan, as were the American versions of **Meet the Beatles, Second Album, Something New, Beatles' Story, Beatles VI, The Early Beatles, Help!, Yesterday and Today, Magical Mystery Tour,** and **Hey Jude.** Japan boasts 29 different Beatle albums, more than any other country.)

WITH A LITTLE HELP FROM THEIR FRIENDS

Beatle Interpretations, Tributes, and Cash-Ins

A. **"The Standards"**: Beatle compositions most widely interpreted on recordings available in the U.S.A., 1976. All are Lennon-McCartney, except those marked *, which are by Harrison.

		(NUMBER OF VERSIONS)
1.	Yesterday	76
2.	Something*	65
3.	Hey Jude	39
4.	Eleanor Rigby	34
5.	Let It Be	30
6.	Michelle	23
7.	With a Little Help From My Friends	21
8.	And I Love Her	19
9.	The Long and Winding Road; Fool On the Hill	16
10.	Ob-la-di, Ob-la-da; Norwegian Wood; A Hard Day's Night	14
11.	Get Back; Day Tripper	11
12.	Come Together; Lady Madonna	10
13.	Here Comes the Sun*; Here, There, and Everywhere	9
14.	Ticket To Ride	8
15.	All My Loving; Blackbird; Can't Buy Me Love; Got To Get You Into My Life; She Came In Through the Bathroom Window; She's Leaving Home	7

These figures give some indication of which compositions—as opposed to recordings—may have the most staying power. They represent only a fraction of the total number of "cover versions" the Beatles' work has attracted (since 1965, "Yesterday" alone has inspired over 1,000 renditions), for commercially unsuccessful recordings have lives shorter than· butterflies'. Artists represented in the above tally range from Yusef Lateef to Arthur Fiedler's Boston Pops Orchestra to Joan Baez and Diana Ross, Ray Charles and Herb Alpert's Tijuana Brass, and Chet Atkins and Richie Havens. Note that nearly all the big favorites (except for "Something") are the work of Paul McCartney, whose facile genius for irresistible melodies made him the most widely interpreted songwriter of his day.

Only four post-breakup compositions have received comparable attention from other artists:

		(NUMBER OF VERSIONS)
1.	My Sweet Lord (Harrison)	23
2.	My Love (McCartney)	17
3.	Imagine (Lennon)	11
4.	Live and Let Die (McCartney)	8

B. **Hit Interpretations of Beatle Compositions:** other artists' renditions of songs by Lennon, McCartney, and Harrison that made the *Billboard* Top Ten in Britain and America (titles are followed by release date and peak chart position):

BRITAIN

Do You Want To Know a Secret (Lennon-McCartney)—Billy J. Kramer and the Dakotas (Parlophone)—April 1963 (#2)

Bad To Me (Lennon-McCartney)—Billy J. Kramer and the Dakotas (Parlophone)—July 1963 (#1)

Hello Little Girl (Lennon-McCartney)—The Fourmost (Parlophone)—September 1963 (#9)

I'll Keep You Satisfied (Lennon-McCartney)—Billy J. Kramer and the Dakotas (Parlophone)—November 1963 (#4)

A World Without Love (Lennon-McCartney)—Peter and Gordon (Columbia)—March 1964 (#1)

Nobody I Know (Lennon-McCartney)—Peter and Gordon (Columbia)—May 1964 (#10)

It's For You (Lennon-McCartney)—Cilla Black (Parlophone)—July 1964 (#7)

Yesterday (Lennon-McCartney)—Matt Monro (Parlophone)—October 1965 (#8)

Michelle (Lennon-McCartney)—The Overlanders (Pye)—January 1966 (#1)

Got To Get You Into My Life (Lennon-McCartney)—Cliff Bennett (Parlophone)—August 1966 (#6)

With a Little Help From My Friends (Lennon-McCartney)—The Young Idea (Columbia)—June 1967 (#10)

Step Inside Love (Lennon-McCartney)—Cilla Black (Parlophone)—March 1968 (#7)

With a Little Help From My Friends (Lennon-McCartney)—Joe Cocker (Regal Zonophone)—September 1968 (#1)

Ob-la-di, Ob-la-da (Lennon-McCartney)—The Marmalade (CBS)—November 1968 (#1)

Goodbye (Lennon-McCartney)—Mary Hopkin (Apple)—April 1969 (#2)

Come and Get It (Paul McCartney)—Badfinger (Apple)—December 1969 (#4)

Lucy In the Sky With Diamonds (Lennon-McCartney)—Elton John (DJM)—November 1974 (#10)

Here Comes the Sun (George Harrison)—Steve Harley and Cockney Rebel (EMI)—August 1976 (#10)

AMERICA

Bad To Me (Lennon-McCartney)—Billy J. Kramer and the Dakotas (Imperial)—March 1964 (#9)

A World Without Love (Lennon-McCartney)—Peter and Gordon (Capitol)—April 1964 (#1)

You've Got To Hide Your Love Away (Lennon-McCartney)—The Silkie (Fontana)—September 1965 (#10)

Fool On the Hill (Lennon-McCartney)—Sergio Mendes and Brazil '66 (A & M)—August 1968 (#6)

Come and Get It (Paul McCartney)—Badfinger (Apple)—February 1970 (#7)

You Won't See Me (Lennon-McCartney)—Anne Murray (Capitol)—April 1974 (#8)

Lucy In the Sky With Diamonds (Lennon-McCartney)—Elton John (MCA)—November 1974 (#1)

Fame (John Lennon-David Bowie-Carlos Alomar)—David Bowie (RCA)—June 1975 (#1)

C. Albums of Beatle Interpretations:

Since 1963, at least a hundred artists—ranging from established stars like Chet Atkins, Keely Smith, Mary Wells, Paul Mauriat, and Arthur Fiedler to novelty acts such as the Chipmunks and the Band of the Irish Guards—have paid tribute to the Beatles by recording entire albums of their music. The Fab Four's most prolific interpreters have been the Hollyridge Strings (Capitol) and their own producer, George Martin (United Artists/Parlophone), who issued, respectively, five and four L.P.'s worth of easy-listening Beatle instrumentals. The Martin L.P.'s are especially cherished by collectors, partly because three of them *(Off the Beatle Track, A Hard Day's Night,* and *Help!)* are decorated with Beatle photographs. (Martin's *Help!,* incidentally, presented three Lennon-McCartney tunes titled "Auntie Gin's Theme," "That's a Nice Hat," and "Scrambled Egg"; these turned out to be working titles for the melodies we later came to know and love as "I've Just Seen a Face," "It's Only Love," and "Yesterday.") Santo and Johnny's *The Beatles' Greatest Hits* (Canadian American) and *Sing a Song With the Beatles* (Tower) also sported Beatle pictures, and Ringo Starr contributed liner notes to Count Basie's *Basie On the Beatles* (Happy Tiger).

Most of the Beatles' classic albums were interpreted in their entirety at one time or another; *Abbey Road,* for instance, inspired the critically acclaimed *McLemore Avenue* by Booker T. and the M.G.'s and *The Other Side Of Abbey Road* by George Benson, both of whose sleeves parodied the original. More recently, Ringo Starr and Paul McCartney have played pivotal behind-the-scenes roles in similar readings of their "solo" albums *Ringo* and *Ram:* David Henschel's *Startling Music* was the debut release on Starr's own label, Ring O'Records, and the appearance of *Thrillington* (EMI) was accompanied by speculation that the mysterious Percy Thrillington was none other than P. McCartney.

The most popular and inventive L.P. in the genre may have been *The Baroque Beatles Book* (Elektra), recorded in 1965 under the auspices of Joshua Rifkin, who later turned his talents toward the resurrection of Scott Joplin. In his playful tribute to the music of both the Beatles and the top Baroque composers, Rifkin deftly transformed vintage Lennon-McCartney melodies into convincing pastiches of Handel ("I Want To Hold Your Hand"), Bach ("Please Please Me"), Couperin ("Hold Me Tight"), and Purcell ("I'll Be Back"). (One only regrets the lack of a sequel; surely Joshua could have concocted a Wagnerian "I Am the Walrus," or served up "Strawberry Fields" in best Mahler style.)

Switched On Beatles (Island), recorded a decade later by the New World Electronic Chamber Ensemble, falls into almost the same class. A brisk medley of twenty of the Beatles' more spaced-out offerings, *Switched On Beatles* is far more faithful to the original arrangements than *The Baroque Beatles Book,* yet no less whimsical and irreverent.

Mid-Seventies nostalgia has brought a spate of original scores and soundtracks such as *John, Paul, George, Ringo . . . and Bert* (R.S.O.); *All This and World War II* (repackaged after the film flopped as *The Songs of Lennon-McCartney)* (20th Century); *Beatlemania* (Arista); *Sgt. Pepper's Lonely Hearts Club Band* (R.S.O.); and, of course, the revisionist *Rutles* (Warner Bros.).

D. Beatle "Novelties":

Aside from several thousand interpretations of the Beatles' own music, Beatlemania has spawned an extensive body of original material that attempted to cash in on or (more rarely) illuminate the phenomenon. Again, a comprehensive round-up would be impossible; the bravest attempt so far was made by Ken Barnes' *Who Put The Bomb* in the spring of 1975, which listed 153 titles, albeit missing a few of the better known ones. Most of the Beatles novelties date back to 1964 and range from tributes (ex-Cricket Sonny Curtis' "A Beatle I Want to Be" and Neil Sheppard's "You Can't Go Far Without a Guitar Unless You're Ringo Starr") to parodies (the Bootles' "I'll Let You Hold My Hand"; the Bagels' "I Want To Hold Your Hair") to outright attacks (the Exterminators' "Beatle Stomp"; the Insects' "Let's Bug the Beatles"). In many cases the only tenuous Beatle connection lay in the name of the group (the U.S. Beatlewigs, the Female Beatles, the American Beatles) and even many of the Beatleish titles (Benny and the Bedbugs' "Beatle Beat," for instance) proved on closer inspection to be throwaway instrumentals. Most of the novelties were one-shot affairs, but a few were recorded by past, present, and future hitmakers such as Ella Fitzgerald ("Ringo Beat"), the Four Preps ("Letter To the Beatles"), the Angels ("Little Beatle Boy"), and Bonnie Joe Mason, a.k.a. Cher ("I Love Ringo"). In the early days, Starr, unlike any of the others, was singled out for special eulogy (e.g., "Ringo For President"); this cycle, however, drew to a close shortly after his 1965 marriage with Angie and the Chiclettes' "Treat Him Tender Maureen."

By *Rubber Soul* time, the onslaught of Beatles novelties had slowed to a trickle, though Harry Nilsson won the Fab Four's undying friendship in 1967 with "You Can't Do That," an inventive medley of a dozen Beatle tunes. McCartney's "death" inspired Mystery Tour's "Ballad Of Paul" and Terry Knight's "St. Paul"; and the Ono-Lennons' shenanigans were commemorated with Rainbo's "John You Went Too Far This Time" and Tom Paxton's "Crazy John," and, more recently, the Justice Department's "Let John & Yoko Stay In the U.S.A."

In 1975, Beatle nostalgia gave Barclay James Harvest a minor hit for their collage of Beatle song titles, cogently titled "Titles"; David Peel inspired less enthusiasm for his single and L.P., both called "Bring Back the Beatles."

The only Beatle novelty ever to make the Top Forty, however, was one of the earliest: the Carefrees' reading of "We Love You Beatles, Oh Yes We Do," the lilting anthem that American Beatlemaniacs were apt to chant whenever their heroes were in the vicinity.

POPULARITY CONTESTS

The Beatles' Top Sellers

Sales figures are usually kept a closely guarded secret, partly because an artist's record company prefers to keep the competition in the dark when it comes time to renegotiate his contract. However, after the Beatles broke up, Allen Klein spilled the beans on them, with the self-interested motivation of proving to the critical public and the even more critical Paul McCartney that under his brilliant management the Beatles were selling more records than ever before. So, if Mr. Klein is to be believed, these were the Beatles' all-time American best-selling albums in late 1970, followed by approximate sales figures. (Beatle records continue to sell in quantity, so the picture may have shifted somewhat in the intervening years. Capitol Records refuses to divulge any more information.)

1. Abbey Road (5,000,000)
2. Meet the Beatles (4,300,000)
3. Hey Jude (3,300,000)
4. Let It Be (3,200,000)
5. Sgt. Pepper's Lonely Hearts Club Band (2,700,000)
6. Rubber Soul (2,500,000)
7. A Hard Day's Night (2,500,000)
8. The White Album (2,200,000)
9. Magical Mystery Tour (2,000,000)
10. Revolver and Help (1,500,000 each)

Mr. Klein also revealed that had *McCartney* been a Beatles L.P., it would have come in ninth, with sales topping two million. He listed their top-selling singles as "Hey Jude," "I Want to Hold Your Hand," "Let It Be," and "Something"—in that order.

The Beatles and the All-Time Hit Parade

In its July 4, 1976 bicentennial issue, *Billboard* featured Top 200 charts of the biggest singles and albums of the previous twenty years. These were compiled by giving records points for every week they appeared on the *Billboard* chart, with the number of points for each entry determined by a record's position that week. If the Beatles' showing on the all-time L.P. chart seems less than spectacular, this is because the system is weighted in favor of albums that sell steadily over the years, usually musical scores and film soundtracks.

Singles
- #2: Hey Jude
- #6: I Want To Hold Your Hand
- #39: She Loves You
- #88: Get Back
- #94: Let It Be
- #103: My Sweet Lord/Isn't It a Pity (George Harrison)
- #111: My Love (Paul McCartney & Wings)
- #136: Something/Come Together
- #159: Help
- #164: We Can Work It Out/Day Tripper
- #183: Yesterday

L.P.'s:
- #26: Sgt. Pepper's Lonely Hearts Club Band
- #62: Meet the Beatles
- #70: Band On the Run (Paul McCartney & Wings)
- #100: Magical Mystery Tour
- #101: Beatles '65
- #105: Rubber Soul
- #137: Abbey Road
- #139: Revolver
- #145: The Beatles (White Album)
- #178: Beatles VI

The Beatles' Number Ones

The Beatles netted far more Number One singles and albums than any other artist in recording history. Twenty of their records topped the *Billboard* American singles chart, plus, as of this writing, five post-breakup McCartney tunes, two each by Harrison and Starr, and one of Lennon's. In addition, the Beatles racked up 15 U.S. Number One albums, to which can be added six by Paul and two apiece by John and George.

The Beatles had the Number One single for 59 weeks during the six and a half years spanning "I Want to Hold Your Hand" 's first appearance at the top on February 1, 1964 and the *Let It Be* L.P.'s last Number One week, July 4, 1970. In the same period, they topped the L.P. charts for 116 weeks. In other words, they had the Number One single one out of every six weeks, and the top album one out of three.

The singles that contributed most to these record-shattering totals were "Hey Jude" (#1 for nine weeks), "I Want to Hold Your Hand" (seven weeks), and "Can't Buy Me Love," "Get Back," and Paul McCartney and Wings' "Silly Love Songs" (five weeks apiece). *A Hard Day's Night* and *Sgt. Pepper* topped the L.P. charts for 15 weeks apiece, *Abbey Road* reigned supreme for 12, and *Meet The Beatles* lasted 11.

In Britain, the Beatles had 17 Number One hits; all but five of their original singles hit the jackpot. However, since the split only George and Paul have scored one Number One apiece—with "My Sweet Lord" and "Mull Of Kintyre," respectively. The two songs that were Number One in Britain longest were, surprisingly, "From Me to You" and "Hello Goodbye"—for seven weeks each.

The Beatles' Grammy Awards

1964: Best new artist: The Beatles
      Best vocal performance by a group: "A Hard Day's Night"

1966: Best contemporary pop vocal performance, male: Paul McCartney, "Eleanor Rigby"
      Best album cover: *Revolver*
      Song of the year: "Michelle"

1967: Album of the year; best album cover; best contemporary rock 'n' roll recording; best engineered recording: *Sgt. Pepper's Lonely Hearts Club Band*

1969: Best engineered recording: *Abbey Road*

1970: Best original score for movie or T.V.: *Let It Be*

1971: Best arrangement accompanying vocalists: Paul McCartney, "Uncle Albert/Admiral Halsey"

1972: Album of the year: George Harrison and friends, *The Concert For Bangla Desh*

1973: Best arrangement accompanying vocalists: Paul McCartney and Wings, "Live and Let Die"

1974: Best engineered recording: Paul McCartney and Wings, *Band On the Run*

The Fans' Choice:

In 1976 the U.S. fanzine *Survey* asked Beatlemaniacs to vote for their favorite song. The results:

1. Sgt. Pepper/A Day In the Life
2. Hey Jude
3. Yesterday
4. Let It Be
5. Help
6. All My Loving
7. The Long and Winding Road
8. She Loves You
9. If I Fell
10. And I Love Her
11. Eleanor Rigby
12. Back In the U.S.S.R.
13. Lady Madonna
14. A Hard Day's Night
15. I Am the Walrus

Eleven years earlier, *The Beatles Monthly Book* asked British Beatlemaniacs to do the same thing:

1. Help
2. All My Loving
3. She Loves You
4. I'm Down
5. This Boy
6. A Hard Day's Night
7. Yesterday
8. Twist and Shout
9. If I Fell
10. Ticket To Ride

In 1971, Howard Smith of WPLJ and *The Village Voice* asked people to name their least favorite Beatle song:

1. Revolution 9
2. Mr. Moonlight
3. You Know My Name (Look Up the Number)
4. Helter Skelter
5. Do You Want To Know a Secret

DEAR SIR OR MADAM, WILL YOU READ MY BOOK?

The Complete Beatles Bibliography*

1964

All About the Beatles, Edward De Blasio (McFadden-Bartell)

The Beatle Book, no author credit, photographs by Dezo Hoffman (Lancer)

The Beatles Up To Date, no author credit (Lancer)

The True Story Of the Beatles, Billy Shepherd (Bantam)

Love Me Do: The Beatles' Progress, Michael Braun (U. K.: Penguin)

All the above were published as cheap paperbacks. The first three were each approximately 100 pages slim, and highly symptomatic of early Beatlemania: unpretentious, superficial, and for the most part fictitious. All jelly babies and good clean fun.

Shepherd's book is marginally more comprehensive and authoritative, perhaps because it was originally produced in Britain under the auspices of *The Beatles Monthly Book.*

In contrast to its contemporaries, *Love Me Do,* an account by an American who travelled with the Fab Four on the early tours, is unusually candid and revealing. John Lennon considers it more "real" than Hunter Davies' authorized biography. Yet it was published in the United States only in abridged form, as part of the fan magazine *The Real True Beatles.* All five books contain black and white photographs.

In His Own Write, written and illustrated by John Lennon (Simon & Schuster) and *En Flagrante Delire,* John Lennon (Simon and Schuster)

The "literary Beatle" 's debut, subsequently translated into French.

A Hard Day's Night, John Burke (Dell)

The paperback novelization of the Beatles' first film, based on Alun Owen's screenplay, with eight pages of stills.

Out Of the Mouths Of the Beatles, Adam Blessing (Dell)

64 pages of Beatle pictures, juxtaposed with humorous captions concerning current U.S. politics.

The Beatles Quiz Book, Jack House (U.K.: William Collins)

A 32-page booklet of questions, answers, and pictures

A Cellarful Of Noise, Brian Epstein (Doubleday; Pyramid)

The Beatles' manager's circumspect autobiography, ghost-written by Derek Taylor.

Dear Beatles, edited by Bill Adler (Grosset & Dunlap) and *Love Letters To the Beatles,* edited by Bill Adler (Putnam)

*All editions are American unless otherwise indicated. Publishers are in parentheses; when two are given, the first refers to the hardback edition, the second to a paperback reprint.

217

Mr. Adler, who simultaneously published *Dear President Johnson,* was given the run of a New York warehouse in which were stored 250,000 letters sent to the Beatles by American fans in the early part of 1964. These slim volumes offer choice extracts from the Fabs' unanswered correspondence, by turns touching and hilarious.

1965

A Spaniard In the Works, written and illustrated by John Lennon (Simon and Schuster)

Die Beatles: Fabelwesen Unserer Zeit, Christine Ehrhardt (West Germany: Wolf Frhr. von Tucher)

Communism, Hypnotism, and the Beatles, Rev. David A. Noebel (Christian Crusade)
The Beatles as a Red plot.

Help!, Al Hine (Dell) and *Help! The Beatles,* no author credit (Random House)
The last two books are a paperback and hardback from the Beatles' second film, offering, respectively, the novelization of Marc Behm's script with eight pages of stills, and the deluxe treatment with 30 pages of song lyrics and photographs.

1966

The Penguin John Lennon, John Lennon (Penguin)
John's two books collected in one paperback.

Murray the K Tells It Like It Is, Baby, Murray Kaufman (Holt, Rinehart & Winston)
The revelations of a self-anointed Fifth Beatle, with an introduction by George Harrison.

1968

The Lennon Play: In His Own Write, John Lennon, Adrienne Kennedy, and Victor Spinetti (Simon and Schuster)
A play based on John's two books.

The Beatles: The Authorized Biography, Hunter Davies (McGraw-Hill; Dell)
Lennon has since told us that Davies left a great deal unsaid, but his book remains the most authoritative and comprehensive Beatle biography anyone has yet attempted. Davies was given intimate access to his subjects and their families, sat in on the *Sgt. Pepper* recording sessions, and traveled with the Beatles on their first pilgrimage to the Maharishi. McGraw-Hill outbid eight other major houses to obtain this work for $160,000. Davies' biography subsequently reached #3 on *Time's* best-seller list. Among 32 pages of photographs are four family portraits by "ace photographer Ringo Starr."

The Beatles: The Real Story, Julius Fast (Putnam; Berkley)

The Beatles, Anthony Scaduto (Signet)
This and the preceding book were rushed out to compete with Davies'; both authors have since written best-sellers—in Scaduto's case, controversial biographies of Bob Dylan and Mick Jagger.

The Beatles Book, edited by Edward E. Davis (Cowles)
The Beatles viewed from the perspective of 14 contemporary pundits, including Ned Rorem, William F. Buckley, and Timothy Leary.

Yellow Submarine, Max Wilk (Signet) and *The Yellow Submarine Gift Book,* no author credit (World Publishing)
The former was purportedly the first all-color paperback ever published; along with grainy stills from the film it includes a succinct adaptation of the Lee Minoff-Al Brodax-Jack Mendelsohn-Erich Segal screenplay. The latter is a deluxe hardback.

The Beatles: Words Without Music, edited by Rick Friedman (Grosset & Dunlap)
Famous quotes by and about the Beatles, with several dozen photos.

Beatles and Co., Juan Carlos Kreimer (Argentina: Editorial Galerma)

The Beatles: A Study In Sex, Drugs, and Revolution, Rev. David A. Noebel (Christian Crusade)
The Red Menace updated.

1969

The Beatles' Illustrated Lyrics, edited by Alan Aldridge (Delacorte Press; Dell)
The best of Lennon-McCartney, illustrated by 45 top contemporary artists, including Milton Glaser, Peter Max, and Ronald Searle. The artwork leans heavily toward psychedelia, and, however kitsch some of it may be, is a fitting complement both to the music and to the times. Mr. Aldridge may not have been overstating the case when he wrote in the introduction: "I see [this book] as an illustration of the Sixties."

1970

"The Girl Who Sang With the Beatles," and Other Stories, Robert Hemenway (Alfred A. Knopf)
The prize-winning title story portrays a New York woman who succumbs to Beatlemania in early 1964.

The Beatles Get Back, Jonathan Cott and David Dalton (U.K.: Apple Publishing)
Originally packaged with the British *Let It Be* L.P., this book offers dialogue from the Beatles, rhapsodic commentary from the authors, and 276 photographs from Ethan Russell.

1971

Lennon Remembers, Jann Wenner (Straight Arrow; Pyramid)
The landmark *Rolling Stone* interviews, with historic photographs.

We Love You Beatles, Margaret Sutton (Doubleday)
A 48-page children's picture-book version of the Beatles story.

The Beatles, Aram Saroyan (Barn Dream Press)
Saroyan is a world-renowned minimalist poet; at five cents this was the cheapest (and at eight words and four pages, the briefest) of all Beatle books. The first poem reads "Paul McCartney"; no prizes for guessing the other three.

The Beatles Illustrated Lyrics 2, edited by Alan Aldridge (Delacorte Press)
For this sequel to his 1969 best-seller, Aldridge commissioned Ralph Steadman, Michael McInnerney, Eduardo Paolozzi, and 48 others to illustrate *Abbey Road, Let It Be,* and earlier leftovers.

1972

Apple To the Core: The Unmaking Of the Beatles, Peter McCabe and Robert D. Schonfeld (Pocket Books)
An irreverent but definitive unraveling of the web of financial intrigue that destroyed the Beatles.

The Longest Cocktail Party, Richard DiLello (Playboy Press)
An insider's view of Apple, profusely illustrated with candid shots.

The Lennon Factor, Paul Young (Stein and Day)
A whimsical free-verse retelling of how John and cohorts changed the world.

Body Count, Francie Schwartz (Straight Arrow)
A female Casanova offers intimate details of her conquests, most particularly P. McCartney.

Out Of His Head: The Sound Of Phil Spector, Richard Williams (Outerbridge and Lazard)
Much of this book explores Spector's involvement with assorted Beatles: included is commentary by John Lennon.

1973

As Time Goes By: Living In the Sixties, Derek Taylor (Straight Arrow)

   The "ex-press officer of the ex-Beatles" applies his breezy wit to reminiscences of his days with the Byrds, the Beach Boys, and, of course, . . .

Twilight Of the Gods: The Beatles In Retrospect, Wilfred Mellers (Viking Press; Schirmer)

   A learned and very technical analysis of the Beatles' music by a leading British musicologist and "serious" composer.

1974

The Beatles—Yesterday . . . Today . . . Tomorrow, Rochelle Larkin (Scholastic Book Services)

   An illustrated retrospective paperback.

The Beatles, Patricia Pirmangton (Creative Education)

   The Beatles story, for second graders.

The Paul McCartney Story, George Tremlett (Popular Library)

   One of an extensive series of rock portraits by an author who is also a London politician.

1975

The Beatles: An Illustrated Record, Roy Carr and Tony Tyler (Harmony)

   A lavishly illustrated review of all the Beatles' British releases by two critics from *The New Musical Express.* The book reached #2 on the *New York Times* trade paperback best-seller list, and reported sales of a quarter million make this the most popular book of its type.

The Beatles: The Fabulous Story Of John, Paul, George, and Ringo, Robert Burt and Jeremy Pascall (U.K.: Octopus Press; Phoebus)

   Dominated by photographs, many in color, this book was reprinted as *The Beatles Story.*

The Compleat Beatles Quiz Book, Edwin Goodgold and Dan Carlinsky (Warner)

   Puzzles, games, and trivia tests.

The Man Who Gave the Beatles Away, Allan Williams and William Marshall (Macmillan; Ballantine)

   The Beatles' rough and often seamy origins, as recalled by their first manager. Lennon gave Williams' lurid memoir a rave review and high marks for accuracy; McCartney dismissed it as a work of fiction.

The Beatles, photographs by Dezo Hoffman (Japan: Shinko Music Co) and *The Beatles,* no credit (Japan: Shinko Music Co.)

   Of these two sumptuous picture books, the former features shots from 1964 and the latter spans their entire career.

The John Lennon Story, George Tremlett (U.K.: Futura)

The Beatles Lyrics Illustrated (Dell)

   This mass-market paperback sports the same cover as Alan Aldridge's *Beatles Illustrated Lyrics,* but this time round the words of the Fab Four are accompanied by 100 black and white photographs of themselves, and prefaced with an introduction by Richard Brautigan.

Nothing To Get Hung About, Mike Evans (U.K.: City Of Liverpool Public Relations Office)

   This "short history of the Beatles" was part of a municipal P.R. package containing Beatle postcards, a Liverpool map, and other souvenirs.

1976

All Together Now, Harry Castleman and Wally Podrazik (Pierian Press; Ballantine)

   The most exhaustive Beatle discography ever published in book form, with information about guest appearances, all Apple releases, etc.

John Lennon: One Day At a Time, Anthony Fawcett (Grove Press)

   This abundantly illustrated biography by an ex-assistant focuses primarily on John's post-Beatle career.

Linda's Pictures, Linda McCartney (Alfred A. Knopf; Ballantine)

   A coffee-table edition of Mrs. McCartney's portfolio, with photographs of every major Sixties rock star, including all the Beatles.

Growing Up With the Beatles, Ron Schaumberg (Pyramid)

   A Kansas City fan recalls his Beatle-obsessed adolescence; his "tribute to the Beatles" is illustrated throughout with photographs of John, Paul, George, and Ringo, and himself.

Paul McCartney In His Own Words, Paul Gambaccini (Flash)

   Gambaccini writes for *Rolling Stone,* where much of this was originally printed; unlike Jann Wenner he extracts few controversial revelations from his genial subject. Illustrated throughout.

1977

Paul McCartney: A Biography In Words and Pictures, John Mendelsohn (Sire-Chappell)

   One of a series of brief, illustrated appraisals by top rock critics, this one showcasing Mendelsohn's hyperbolic wit.

Facts About a Rock Group Featuring Wings, David Gelly (Harmony)

   A behind-the-scenes glimpse at Wings' tours and recording sessions, with many photographs by Homer Sykes and an introduction by P. McCartney.

George Harrison Yesterday and Today, Ross Michaels (Flash)

   A slim, illustrated appraisal of George's music and career.

Yesterday Seems So Far Away, John Swenson (Zebra)

   A fast recap of the Beatles Story.

Paul McCartney and Wings, Tony Jasper (U.K.: Chartwell)

Paul McCartney and Wings, Jeremy Pascall (U.K.: Octopus Press)

   In the format of *The Fabulous Story of . . .* (see 1975).

A Hard Day's Night, edited by Philip diFranco (Chelsea House; Penguin)

   The complete screenplay, both as originally written and as actually filmed, with an extended Richard Lester interview and hundreds of stills.

1978

The Beatles Again, Harry Castleman and Wally Podrazik (Pierian Press)

   Addenda and update for *All Together Now* (see 1976)

Paperback Writer: A New History Of the Beatles, Mark Shipper (Grosset and Dunlap)

   An iconoclastic and wildly fictitious rewrite of Beatle history.

Mersey Beat: The Beginnings Of the Beatles (U.K.: Omnibus Press)

   Replica pages from *Mersey Beat,* the early Sixties Liverpool music bible, including otherwise unpublished writings by John Lennon.

The Beatles, Hunter Davies (McGraw-Hill)

   A revised and updated edition of *The Authorized Biography* (see 1968)

The Beatles: An Illustrated Record, Roy Carr and Tony Tyler (Harmony)

   Another best-seller revised and updated (see 1975)

INDEX

Nicholas Schaffner was born—in New York City, where he still lives—around the same time as rock 'n' roll music itself. He grew up with the Beatles after becoming an instant convert at the age of ten when Beatlemania first swept the United States. Twelve years later, inspired by the first emergence of Beatles fandom—the collectors, fanzines, and conventions—he wrote *The Beatles Forever*. Since its initial appearance, the book has been hailed by critics as "the best chronicle of the Beatles legend" and *"the nostal-gia book for those who grew up in the Sixties,"* and has been translated into such languages as Serbo-Croatian and Japanese. Mr. Schaffner has since retold the Beatles saga for "second generation Beatlemaniacs" in *The Boys From Liverpool;* his latest book is *The British Invasion,* forthcoming from McGraw-Hill. He also writes songs, poetry, tales of fantasy, and articles that have appeared in *The Trouser Press, The Village Voice, The Hartford Courant,* and other publications.

* *Strawberry Fields Forever; The San Francisco Sunday Examiner and Chronicle.*

Photo Credit: Peter C. Jones